CW00515260

VALUATION
OF
UNQUOTED
SECURITIES

Christopher G. Glover

Published by
Gee & Co. (Publishers) Ltd
in association with
The Institute of Chartered Accountants
in England and Wales

The Institute of Chartered Accountants in England and Wales considers that this work is a worthwhile contribution to discussion without necessarily sharing the views expressed, which are those of the author. No responsibility for loss occasioned to any person acting or refraining from action as a result of any material in this publication can be accepted by the author or publisher.

While every care has been taken in the preparation of this book, it may contain errors for which the publisher and author cannot be responsible.

© 1986 Gee & Co. (Publishers) Ltd

ISBN 085258 832 1

Gee & Co. (Publishers) Ltd
7 Swallow Place
London W1R 8AB

Typeset by Adlard and Son Ltd, Dorking, Surrey
Printed in England

Contents

CONTENTS

15 Legal or binding valuations

Foreword

I am honoured to have been asked to write a foreword for this useful book, which seems to me to cover all the topics relevant to anyone who is in anyway concerned with the valuation of unquoted securities.

The chapters dealing with the theories of valuation make most interesting reading. Those which cover the various bases of valuation are comprehensive and carefully reasoned. The legal analysis is penetrating.

There are many people who, more or less frequently, find themselves involved with questions of valuation. I believe they will find this book an invaluable aid.

Richard Sykes, QC
Lincoln's Inn, London
March 1986

Acknowledgements

I would not have embarked upon this work, nor would I have completed it, without the encouragement of my wife. My thanks first and foremost are due to her. As to the legal content of the book, I owe a debt of gratitude to the firm of Hopkins and Wood. Roger Hopkins encouraged me to write the book and the advice of himself and his colleagues, in particular Paul Matthews, has been invaluable to me, especially in relation to Chapter 3 (The Legal Framework), Chapter 4 (The Rights of Minorities), Chapter 15 (Legal or Binding Valuations) and Chapter 16 (Fiscal Valuations).

Janette Rutterford and Tony Bird kindly commented on my reviews of the Efficient Market Hypothesis (Chapter 6), Modern Portfolio Theory (Chapter 7) and the Dividend Irrelevance Proposition of Miller and Modigliani (Chapter 12). I am grateful to them both. Any remaining errors or illogicalities are mine alone.

My inability to express myself exactly as I want at the first attempt and my tendency to change my mind has necessitated many drafts. The typing has therefore been a tedious and time consuming job. It has been carried out with patience, cheerfulness and competence and I am grateful to all concerned.

In writing this book I have come to realise that a truly original thought is extremely rare. There is certainly not one in this book. Directly or indirectly, therefore, everything is borrowed. Sometimes it comes from a library shelf in which case I trust I have acknowledged it in the text; at other times it comes from discussions with friends and colleagues, from newspapers, the radio and television or even a chance remark. To all my teachers, sung and unsung, I hereby acknowledge my debt.

Preface

Share valuation has traditionally been the province of the professional accountant but it occupies very little of his time. For the typical accountant, share valuation is no more than an interesting occasional diversion from his main activity and most of his share valuations are for tax purposes. It is not surprising, therefore, that the theory and practice of share valuation have developed little over the years and that many of the techniques lack a sound theoretical basis. This book is an attempt to rectify this state of affairs and to give share valuation a rational basis which can stand up to close scrutiny.

The insistence on a rational approach does not make share valuation any less of an art or more of a science. However, it identifies the different steps in the valuation and exposes each subjective judgement to critical review. It enables the valuer to achieve greater consistency in his valuations and makes the valuation itself more intelligible to the client. As the share valuer's services are increasingly in demand, the need for such an approach is pressing.

Share valuation is an interdisciplinary study; it draws on law, economics, finance, accounting and investment. I have had to delve into all these fields for relevant material. Inevitably with such a wide area to cover I have had to be highly selective, and have confined myself to those theories which seem directly relevant to share valuation or those which conflict with the approach I have evolved. These include modern theories of share price determination on the Stock Exchange, the definition and measurement of risk, the dividend versus earnings argument and the concept of the cost of capital. Although some of these theories contain useful insights, many of them are conceptually unsound. They are in any event too abstract to be of much help to the practitioner. I have set out my reasoning fully so that the reader can make up his own mind about the relevance of these theories.

Although there is an underlying concern with theory the emphasis of this book is entirely practical. All the techniques advocated here are illustrated by practical examples drawn from my experience as a full time share valuer over many years. The book is comprehensive and deals with a host of different valuation problems and circumstances. The aim has been to provide guidance on any valuation problem, no matter how obscure. I have deliberately repeated some of the material so as to emphasise important points and also to make the text as self-contained as possible.

This book is intended primarily for the practitioner — both the occasional share valuer and the specialist. It is also of much interest to the banker, stockbroker, fund manager, venture capitalist and investment analyst — in short, to anyone who is concerned with the financing of unquoted companies. There is also food for thought for the student and the academic.

Christopher Glover
2–3 Cursitor Street
London EC4
March 1986

1
Valuation theory

Introduction

Any definition of the nature of value is fraught with difficulties. The problem has exercised the minds of philosophers and economists for over 150 years and has produced a considerable amount of literature on the subject. Despite this prodigious intellectual effort there still remains much disagreement about what value really is. A more fruitful course is to move the discussions from the nature of value itself, in which value is treated as a thing to be examined, to an enquiry into the nature of valuation. Thus, by examining the process of valuation as it takes place in the individual mind and subsequently in the realm of exchange, the nature of value will itself become clearer. At the same time, the theoretical basis will be laid for the subsequent discussion of the different value concepts. The first part of this chapter is devoted to the valuation process in the individual mind — the creation of 'interior' values.[1] How these interior values interact to produce the 'exterior' values evident in the realm of exchange is discussed in the second part. This analysis is concerned solely with economic values.

The comparative value judgement

It is first necessary to distinguish between the positive value judgement and the comparative value judgement since it is with the latter that economic valuations are concerned. 'I like holidays in the sun' is a positive value judgement. It is a simple positive statement of something which pleases me. Given the almost insatiable appetites of man, the number of positive value judgements for any person must be legion. However, hardly anyone has the means to satisfy all his demands, and a choice has often to be made between the satisfaction of competing demands. 'I like skiing holidays' may be another of my positive value judgements, but if I find that the cost of both a winter holiday and a summer holiday is more than I can afford, I must choose between one or the other. I then make a comparative value judgement and, say,

---

[1] In this first part, the author has drawn heavily on W. D. Lamont, *The Value Judgement* (Edinburgh: The University Press, 1955).

1

choose to go skiing. In so doing I have attributed degrees of satisfaction or 'goodness' to the two types of holiday; both activities are 'good' in the positive sense, but one is 'better' than the other. This is the essence of the comparative value judgement; it is an expression of choice imposed on us by the necessity of forgoing one desirable end if another is to be achieved.

Valuation then in the economic sense is always relative; it is never absolute. A little reflection will also reveal that value is attributed to the non-existent, never to the existent. This becomes clear when the distinction is drawn between the object of demand and the demand itself. My desire to take a skiing holiday is not the same thing as the holiday itself. My demand for a pair of skis is distinguishable from the skis themselves. Even though I may already have seen a pair of skis I wish to buy, my valuation is attributable to a future state of affairs, that is, ownership and use of the skis, and not a present one, the skis themselves. This may seem an unnecessarily fine distinction to draw; but it has a very significant implication, namely, that demand, and hence value, always looks to the future — to the creation, maintenance or destruction of some state of affairs. As will be seen later, this is of fundamental importance when valuing shares.

Opportunity cost

Since valuation is relative, the measure of the value of my winter holiday is the satisfaction I must forgo in not taking a summer holiday. It is not the cost of the winter holiday. In other words, value is measured by opportunity cost not actual cost. This may seem a little strange at first sight. How can it be denied that the skiing holiday is worth anything to me other than the sum of money I am prepared to pay for it? The point being made here will become clearer, however, if it is assumed that the winter holiday is paid for out of the proceeds of sale of my music centre. Removing for a moment the concept of money, the cost of the winter holiday is the music centre. But I no longer like the music centre and intend to replace it with more advanced hi-fi equipment; it has very little value to me at all and in fact once I have bought the new equipment, the music centre will probably never be used. Yet it has an exchange value because others can use it and are prepared to pay for the privilege of so doing. The 'satisfaction' value I place on the music centre does not determine, or even influence, the value I place on the skiing holiday.

If we bring back the conception of money to make the illustration more realistic, the proposition remains valid and, if anything, is reinforced. At first sight it could be argued that I do in fact value the music centre since it can be exchanged for money or for the things, such as the skiing holiday, that money can buy. But assuming I have no use for the music centre and do not value it for itself, any value I place on it must belong to it by virtue of the value placed by me on the skiing holiday or on the other use to which the proceeds of sale may be put. Far from cost, as such, giving value to the skiing holiday, it may even seem that the value placed on the skiing holiday determines, or at least strongly influences, the value placed on the thing constituting its cost, i.e., the music centre. One further point perhaps needs emphasising. In the analogy set out here the alternative to the skiing holiday is the summer holiday. There is no question of choosing between the skiing holiday and the music centre, or between the skiing holiday and the cash needed to pay for it. The opportunity cost therefore is the dissatisfaction from forgoing the summer holiday, not the loss of the music centre.

This somewhat laboured insistence that cost has no necessary relevance to value is justified in view of the great significance of this point to valuation. Despite most people's acceptance of the point in theory, there is often a temptation in practice to impute values on the basis of balance sheet figures, particularly if the company is capital intensive. Furthermore, the widely held belief that high asset backing reduces risk and therefore indicates a higher capitalisation rate needs to be tempered by the acknowledgement that balance sheet amounts have no necessary relevance to values.

Anticipated opportunity cost

If value is measured in terms of opportunity cost and not price or actual cost, and if value is attributed to the non-existent not to the existent, then the value of a thing must be measured in terms of anticipated, not actual, opportunity cost. What does not yet exist cannot have any cost, opportunity or otherwise; we can only forecast what its cost will be. This proposition is so obvious as to need hardly any amplification. It is a corollary of the conclusion that actual cost has no necessary relevance to value and that valuation is always forward-looking. To develop the analogy further, the opportunity cost of acquiring the music centre (it may have been purchased at considerable personal sacrifice) is irrelevant in determining the value placed on the skiing holiday. Admittedly, the contemplation of actual or historical opportunity cost can enhance the enjoyment or satisfaction felt from something, but for this to happen the thing acquired must serve its purpose well. If it turns out to be useless the sacrifice entailed in its acquisition aggravates the sense of dissatisfaction felt. In reality it is not the high cost which is approved of but that which, despite the cost, was done.

As we have seen, things are evaluated relative to one another in terms of estimated opportunity costs. Given that a person will seek to satisfy his demands at the lowest possible cost, the order of value must be the inverse of the order of estimated opportunity cost. A fairly simple example will illustrate this in practice. Let us assume that X wishes to increase his shareholding in XYZ Ltd, a private company. Four other shareholders A, B, C, and D each offer him 50 shares for sale at, respectively, £50, £52, £53 and £60. D's shares have the highest opportunity cost, then C's, B's and finally A's. The order of value to X is, however, the inverse of this. He will first want to buy from A as his is the lowest price: he therefore values A's shares highest. Next, he would buy from B, valuing his shares below those of A but above those of C and D. Third in order of value come C's shares and lastly D's shares, being the most expensive.

Satisfaction of common demand

It will be observed that the items in demand in the above example are qualitatively the same, being shares in XYZ Ltd. However, for the proposition to be true of qualitatively different but competing demands there must exist some point of reference against which the competing demands are assessed; there must be some ultimate goal or common demand. For example, faced with the choice between an apple, a pear and an orange I will evaluate each one against the other. But apples and pears and oranges are qualitatively different and cannot be compared with each other. Thus the comparison I make is the relative capacity of each of these fruits to satisfy my overall objective of, or need for, food. In other words, the demand for apples, pears and oranges are expressions of the common demand for food. In these circumstances, the opportunity cost of a thing is not simply its deprival value but the extent to which satisfaction of the principal or common demand is affected. This can be illustrated by a simple example. Let us assume that the satisfaction derived from food is in direct proportion to its nutritional value, and that the sum available to a purchaser could procure food as follows:

	Units of nutritional value	Satisfaction of food demand forgone
Fish	100	
Meat	75	25
Eggs	70	30

Clearly, the purchaser's preference will be for fish, then meat and lastly eggs.

However, the opportunity cost of the meat, in other words, the measure of its value, is not simply 100 units. In terms of the common demand for food the cost is only 25 units since the meat itself constitutes 75 units of value. Similarly the opportunity cost of the eggs measured in terms of the satisfaction of the common demand forgone is 30 units (i.e., 100 units for fish less 70 units for the eggs). It might be asked, what is the opportunity cost of buying the fish? This is not shown in the above table but it would be measured by the competing demands not satisfied as a consequence of satisfying the common demand for food. Examples of competing common demands would be drink, shelter, clothing and leisure.

To reinforce the point just made, let us take another example. Assume, for instance, that a person has inherited a substantial sum of money which he now requires to invest. His overriding or common demand is the maximisation of his wealth. There are many different forms of investment but this person for various reasons wishes to confine himself to gilts, equities and property. After taking appropriate advice he concludes that gilts offer a rate of return of 11%, equities, 20% and property, 13%. The attractiveness of these competing demands for his funds are then ranged in the inverse order of estimated opportunity costs, that is, equities, property and gilts. But the measure of the opportunity cost of investing in gilts or property is not the loss of 20% on one's capital, i.e., the rate of return forgone on equities, but rather the shortfall in the rate of return resulting from the investment of the funds in gilts or property as opposed to the higher yielding equities. Thus, the opportunity cost of investing in gilts would be nine per cent and in property seven per cent.[2]

Although items in common demand are to some extent substitutes for one another, they are nevertheless qualitatively different demands. A man who has had no food or drink for days may be indifferent as to whether he has white bread or brown bread, or water as opposed to beer. But once the basic quantitative need has been satisfied, his indifference will disappear and he will exhibit marked preferences for one as opposed to the other. In this sense they are like the more comprehensive common demands, such as the demand for sustenance, clothing, accommodation etc., which directly compete with each other for the available scarce resources. Given that man cannot satisfy all these desires with his limited means, some form of rationing or economy must be introduced. He could of course opt to satisfy some desires completely and leave others totally unsatisfied. But in view of the fact that demand for most things is directed to the maintenance of a state of being or standard of living, such a course would be highly unlikely. A person would hardly spend all his income on housing, no matter how avidly he desired a particularly expensive property; he would

[2] To simplify the exposition and illustrate the principle, we ignore risk.

obviously leave some money for food, clothing and other necessities. What therefore determines the degree to which competing demands are satisfied?

'Law' of equilibrium

The rational supposition must be that, in conditions of scarcity, man will endeavour to achieve a balance or equilibrium in the satisfaction of his desires; he will strive for the proportionate satisfaction of competing demands. There is no suggestion here of any correct balance or equilibrium; it is purely a matter of individual choice. For example, a person may, as a matter of fact, spend 30% of his income on food and drink, 35% on accommodation, 20% on transport and the remainder on leisure and other demands. Even though he may never have conceived of allocating his income in these precise proportions, they are nevertheless an indication of the equilibrium or proportionateness he aims for as he spends his income. It is that particular equilibrium which maximises his satisfaction or, more correctly, which minimises the dissatisfaction from unsatisfied demands.

This 'law' of equilibrium, which is no more than a postulate of rational behaviour, means that the demand for one thing is not independent of the desire for another thing. We demand things in certain proportions because our finances are insufficient to satisfy our desires in full. Thus, more of one thing will mean less of another, and the alternatives before us will be not so much the stark choice between A and B but whether, given the allocation of our resources so far, we prefer more of A and less of B or vice versa. Assume, for instance, that a person demands A and B in the proportions 5A and 4B and that so far he has spent his money on 4A and 4B. He now has to choose between another A or another B. In other words, his choice is between 5A and 4B or 4A and 5B. Clearly he will choose another A since this will restore the equilibrium of 5A and 4B which he strives to attain.

The choice between A and B at any one time, i.e., the valuation at the margin, is therefore influenced by:

(a) the proportions in which the demands for A and B have already been satisfied; and
(b) the equilibrium or proportionateness which the person aims to achieve.

How this works in practice can be illustrated by numerous examples. At its simplest, however, it is evident in the observation that a person's preference for, and therefore valuation of, food as opposed to drink will be very different after a substantial meal than before it. On a less obvious level, the principle can be seen to operate in the sphere of investment. Let us assume that the investor mentioned earlier decides to allocate his substantial sum of money between gilts, equities and properties in the proportions of 40:40:20, and to invest any further sums in these proportions. As money becomes available for investment it may not be convenient to invest it in precisely these proportions. For example, a particularly attractive property investment may be on offer and it would be foolish to ignore it. Consequently, the property content of the fund rises to 30% with gilts and equities falling to 35% each. In the jargon of the investment industry, the fund is now overweight in property and underweight in gilts and equities. When investing further sums of money the investor will therefore exhibit a marked preference for gilts and equities over property. But as soon as the correct weightings are re-established the preference will revert to the 40:40:20 ratio. Thus, while this ratio might express the investor's proportionate demand respectively for gilts, equities and property over a period, at any given moment these three forms of investment may be demanded and therefore valued in a very different ratio.

The law of equilibrium therefore governs the valuation of the marginal unit. The economist's concept of diminishing marginal utility may have relevance to economic theory but it is not a law of valuation. At first sight, however, it does appear to be relevant. This law in its simplest form states that the marginal utility of a commodity to anyone diminishes with every increase in the amount he already has. For example, a thirsty soul obtains more satisfaction from the first pint he drinks than from the second one, and more from the second pint than from the third. Logically, therefore, he places a higher value on the first pint than on the second and a higher value on the second than on the third.

This has all the appearances of a significant law of valuation. But here we are dealing with successive satisfactions of the same demand and, as the first pint and the second pint (and any subsequent pints for that matter) are not alternatives for choice, they cannot be valued against each other. The thirsty soul in question does not choose between the first pint and the second one but between the first pint and some other use for his money. Similarly when he comes to buy his second pint the alternatives for choice cannot include the third pint. Thus, while enjoyment may (or may not) diminish as successive pints are consumed, the first pint cannot be valued against the second one or the third one.

Neither is it entirely certain that as satisfaction or enjoyment diminishes with progressive consumption, the strength of the demand is necessarily weakened. In fact the opposite could be argued to be the case. If the first pint produces ten units of pleasure and the second nine units and if the price of a pint remains unchanged, then the thirsty soul, in buying his second pint, was prepared to expend the same resources to secure nine units of pleasure as he was to secure the ten units of pleasure in the first pint. Thus in buying the second pint he could be considered to value each unit of pleasure higher than he did in buying the first pint. Therefore, the value he places on the pleasure of beer drinking could be said to increase with successive pints. The fact that this conclusion does not accord with experience reflects not so much on the logic employed as on the futility of valuing against each other successive satisfactions of the same demand.

It is useful at this stage to summarise the discussion so far. The process of valuation in the individual mind is a function of the comparative value judgement. This was distinguished from the positive value judgement which is merely a statement of one's likes and dislikes. The comparative value judgement is the expression of preference and takes place when a choice is imposed on us by the necessity of forgoing one desirable end if another is to be achieved. Value in the economic sense of the word can only exist — either in the individual mind or in the realm of exchange — in conditions of scarcity of resources. It is with the comparative value judgement, therefore, that any discussion of the nature of economic value must begin.

Because values arise from the comparison of the desirability of one thing with another, valuation is always relative and never absolute. By distinguishing between the object of demand and the demand itself it was seen that value is attributed to the non-existent, never to the existent. This is because demand looks to the future and is concerned with the creation, maintenance or destruction of some state of affairs.

Every choice involves a sacrifice in the sense of an alternative opportunity forgone. This opportunity cost, and not actual cost, is the true measure of value. Historical cost has no necessary relevance to value — an important point discussed at some length. As value is attributed to the non-existent not to the existent it follows that value is measured in terms of anticipated not actual opportunity cost. What does not exist cannot yet have a cost; its cost can only be forecast or estimated. Furthermore, where there are more than two alternatives for choice the order of value is the inverse of the order of estimated opportunity cost. In other words, the lower the opportunity cost the higher the value, people naturally preferring a lower as opposed to a higher cost for something.

The proposition that the order of value is the inverse of the order of estimated opportunity cost implies the existence of some overall objective or common demand in every valuational order. Thus, when qualitatively different demands compete with each other the measure of value is not just the opportunity cost of the demand forgone, but the extent to which satisfaction of the principal or common demand is diminished or increased.

Most of man's demands in the economic sphere are directed towards the maintenance of a state of being or standard of living. In these circumstances he will not choose to satisfy one demand in full (e.g., housing) if this means not satisfying at all a competing demand (e.g., that for food). He will strike a balance between them. As a general rule or law, he will endeavour to satisfy his desires in a certain proportion — that proportion which for him minimises the dissatisfaction from unsatisfied desires. This law of equilibrium is significant for two reasons. Firstly, it underlines the existence of common demand in every valuational order, since if things are demanded in proportions there must be some criterion governing the determination of those proportions. Secondly, it is the key to understanding how the marginal unit of demand is valued.

The economist's law of diminishing marginal utility is not a law governing the valuation of the marginal unit of demand. In fact, it is futile to compare the successive satisfactions of the same desire since these can never be alternatives for choice. The strongest influence on the valuation of the marginal unit of demand is the law or equilibrium, that is, the proportions in which the various competing demands have been met compared with the proportions or equilibrium which a person strives to attain.

Exterior values

The discussion so far has concentrated entirely on the valuational process in the individual mind. We have seen how each person through the comparative value judgement established a veritable constellation of values, ranged in different orders or hierarchies in accordance with the principle of economy — the husbanding of scarce resources to achieve the maximum well-being or to ensure the minimum of dissatisfaction from unfulfilled desires. It is now time to consider how these interior values affect exterior values, that is, those which arise in the realm of exchange. Two obvious assertions can be made in this connection. First, the ratio in which things exchange will be determined by the interior valuations of each party to the transaction. Second, no exchange will take place unless each party perceives some advantage in it for himself. The first assertion follows from the assumption of rational behaviour; it would be highly irrational for someone to conclude a bargain without reference to his own valuations. The second assertion follows from the postulate of personal gainful motive. All persons engaged in the process of exchange seek some advantage thereby. What a person proposes to acquire must be worth more to him than what he proposes to give in exchange.

The crude workings of these two principles can be illustrated quite simply. A sells B a car for £3,000. A's car must, therefore, be worth more to

Figure 1: Illustrative relationship of value to utility.

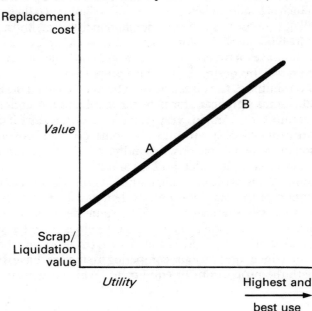

B than £3,000 or, more correctly, the other things that B can buy with £3,000. If this were not so, if B valued an alternative purchase more highly, he would not buy A's car but would spend his £3,000 on the alternative. Similarly, from A's point of view, his car is worth less than £3,000 to him. That is to say, he places a higher value on the alternative goods costing £3,000 than he does on his car. If A were indifferent as to whether he kept his car or whether he switched to other goods or services, no transaction would take place for lack of motive. Similarly with B. This is illustrated in figure 1.

Point A is the value to A of his car and point B is the value which the car has to B. The utility measured along the horizontal axis is not absolute utility or 'desiredness' but utility at the values given along the vertical axis, i.e., utility which the parties are prepared to pay for. Price will be at some point in between A and B. It will depend on the accuracy of each party's perception of the other's interior valuations and their relative negotiating and bargaining skills.

In reality, the interior valuations of A and B will not be conceived as single lump sum amounts but as a range, and the interior valuations themselves may change as the parties negotiate. B, for instance, may be pleasantly surprised by the condition of the car during the test drive, and he may be persuaded that the car is worth more to him than he originally thought. Alternatively, A may change his mind about the new car he intends to buy when he has sold his existing one. Perhaps some extra cost, say a heavy repair bill on his house, has just come to light and he is no longer keen to sell his car at the sort of price which B might have in mind. The bargaining background is therefore fluid and changeable, and if either party errs seriously in his estimate of the other's interior valuations the transaction may fail even though an exchange could have been agreed on mutually beneficial terms.

Interior valuations and price determination

It will be observed that there are at least four interior valuations in the determination of price. A, for example, has his interior valuation of the car and also of the other goods and services he could obtain with the sale proceeds, whilst B has his own interior valuation of A's car and of the goods and services he could acquire if he did not buy the car from A. These are the interior valuations which directly impinge upon the price. As we have seen earlier, the values themselves are influenced in varying degrees by the host of other interior valuations which collectively express that person's allocation of scarce resources in the pursuit of his own concept of well-being.

Although price is a function of the parties' interior valuations, price itself is distinct from value. Price is the ratio in which things exchange. In a barter economy, if one apple exchanges for one orange, the price of an apple is one orange, and vice versa. In a money economy, price is the monetary consideration received for the sale or paid for the purchase of goods and services. The price at which A sells his car to B is unlikely to coincide with any of the interior valuations of A or B with respect to the car itself or the alternative goods and services.

While price is distinguishable from interior value and the significance of an isolated price is limited, prices in general are indicative of exchange or market value. This is an exterior value in the sense that it is independent of the desires, whims and tastes of a given individual. For the individual, market value is an objective reality, and its objective nature is in no way diminished by the difficulties which may sometimes be experienced in ascertaining its amount for a particular property.

In the example of A's car, the effect of exchange value on the transaction was not considered. However, the price that A could obtain for the car from someone else, as well as the price that B would have to pay if he bought a similar car from someone other than A, would normally have a significant influence on the price agreed between A and B. This is illustrated in figure 2. Although A's interior valuation of the car may be very low he will not be prepared to part with it for less than he can sell it for

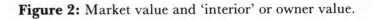

Figure 2: Market value and 'interior' or owner value.

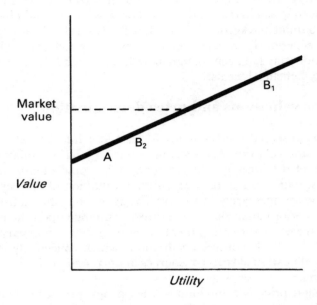

elsewhere. Similarly, B will be reluctant to pay much more for A's car than the price at which similar cars have been trading.

Price and market value

For commodities or properties in frequent demand, prices in general are indicative of market value. Assuming A's car is a popular model and there is a market for it, the extent of the value gap between A and B makes no difference. If any exchange is to take place it will be at or near the market value. If A's car is worth less to B than market value, as at B_2, there will be no exchange.

For many goods and services in a modern economy the price is fixed but it must nevertheless fall within the value range of the transacting parties if any exchange is to take place. If prices thus fixed by suppliers do not fall below the interior valuations of a sufficient number of consumers, there will not be an economic level of sales and the price will have to be fixed at a lower level. Thus, although there is no direct negotiation between supplier and demander for most goods, the prices paid nevertheless reflect the interior valuations of both sides.

Valuation of shares

Whenever property is infrequently or rarely traded, the market value concept — the notion that if comparable property fetches a certain price then the subject property will realise the same price or something near to it — has little relevance. The vast majority of unquoted shares are a prime example of infrequently traded property. The shares in most unquoted companies are closely held and onerous restrictions on their transfer are generally imposed by the articles of association. Most private companies, for instance, give the directors power in their absolute discretion to refuse to register a transfer of shares. Even if willing buyers of the shares could be found, there would be no guarantee that the directors would sanction the sale. In the valuation of unquoted shares, therefore, it is almost invariably necessary to envisage a specific transaction and to assess the interior valuations of both sides. In short, the valuer must always ask the questions 'to whom?' and 'for what purpose?' before valuing unquoted shares.

Consider, for example, a private company with shares held as follows:

	%
A	37
B	33
D	30
	100

D requires a valuation of his shares. A and B are executive directors. D is not a director nor is he employed by the company. He obtained his shares from his father, C, who, until his death a few years ago, was an executive director. A, B and C were the founders of the business. The company is well run, makes reasonable profits and pays a dividend. D, however, feels that he is in an invidious position. He would not of his own choice wish to have such a significant investment in a private company and, although dividends are paid, he resents the high levels of remuneration which A and B enjoy and feels that they are getting more than their fair share out of the company. A and B, on the other hand, see themselves as the wealth creators building up the business through their own endeavours and committed to the business in a way in which D is not. They resent the fact that D has a claim, albeit an indirect one, of 30% of all the value they add to the business. These tensions are at work behind the mask of civilised friendly behaviour which the shareholders show to each other. D, however, wants to realise his investment and seeks a valuation of his shares.

A little reflection will show that it is meaningless to talk purely and simply of the value of D's shares; the word value can only have meaning when related to a particular person or class of person and a specific purpose.

In the first place, the shares have what might be called an investment value. This is the price the shares could reasonably be expected to fetch if sold for investment purposes. Such value would be a function principally of the expected future dividends, the degree of risk and the lack of marketability. Some addition would probably be made for the fact that the shareholding exceeds 25% and can therefore block a special resolution. A valuation on this basis assumes that the directors would sanction the subsequent share transfer. On the face of it, this seems unlikely.

Secondly, D's shares have a special value to A and B considerably in excess of any investment value. If A were to buy D's shares, A would obtain a majority of the votes and management control of the business. This would place A in a dominant position *vis-à-vis* B. If any disagreements were to arise, A would have the final word and *in extremis* could remove B from the board, leaving him in a position similar to that of D at present. If A were to buy D's shares, therefore, it would upset the balance between A and B and almost certainly result in a diminution in the value of B's shareholding. If B and not A were to buy D's shares the positions would be reversed. B would end up with management control and A would be left as the minority shareholder at the mercy of B. There would, therefore, be strong competition between A and B to buy D's shares. A's and B's interior valuations of D's shares would not be based on dividends but on the value of the business for control purposes. Other factors which would influence A and B include the value of having one's own livelihood under one's control and even the possibility of offering one's sons a career.

A third possibility is that a bid for the whole of the issued share capital may be in prospect on terms acceptable to A and B. (In fact a successful bid would be possible even if one and not the other was in favour of it, since the party in favour, together with D, could give majority control of the company.) The value in this case would depend upon the bidder and the value of the company to him. This would be determined not only by the future profits of the company under present arrangements, but also by any benefits (less any extra costs) expected to arise from the integration of the company's operations with those of the bidder.

Yet a fourth possibility exists. D could sell his shares to A and B *pro rata* to their existing shareholdings. The same effect could be achieved by arranging that the company itself buys the shares. This course of action might be appropriate if A and B agree to preserve a united front against D. It means that A would end up with 53% (i.e. 37/70ths) of the equity and B with 47% (i.e. 33/70ths) — not ideal from B's point of view but perhaps

Figure 3: Different 'interior' or owner valuations of D's shareholding.

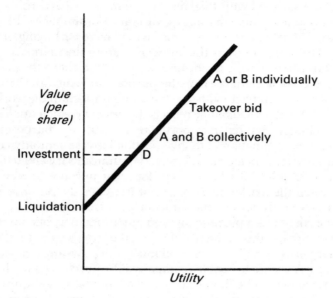

acceptable. In these circumstances the value of D's shares to A and B is probably less than the full control value since A and B collectively exercise management control already. However, their control is not absolute. D with his 33% shareholding is a substantial minority interest. A and B would always have to take into account the effect of their actions on the minority interest. In addition, D's ability to block a special resolution could be both an embarrassment and a nuisance.

Figure 3 illustrates the different values which D's shares could have to different purchasers. The price D could expect to obtain depends therefore on the purchaser and his purpose in acquiring the shares. The general rule, therefore, is as follows:

> The value of something cannot be stated in the abstract; all that can be stated is the value of a thing in a particular place, at a particular time, in particular circumstances. The question 'to whom?' and 'for what purpose?' must always be asked before a valuation can be carried out.

This fundamental rule applies to valuation generally and not just the valuation of unquoted shares. At first sight this may seem to conflict with everyday experience as far as quoted shares are concerned. An investor wishing to buy or sell shares merely enquires of a stockbroker what their value is and, if satisfied with this, instructs him to deal accordingly. The stockbroker is able to value the shares without ascertaining the identity of the purchaser or seller and the reasons he may have for buying or selling the shares. He simply obtains the latest price from the market.

In this case, however, it is not necessary for the client to specify the purchaser or class of purchaser or the purpose for which the shares are required, since it is understood beforehand and implicit in the work of the stockbroker. The Stock Exchange reflects the prices at which small parcels of shares change hands for portfolio investment purposes. The stockbroker's main function is to give portfolio investment advice to his clients and to execute their orders. It would be unnecessary and tedious for the broker to enquire 'to whom?' and 'for what purpose?' every time a client requested the market price of a security, since the purpose and the class of purchaser are always the same for each transaction.

But, if the client has a purpose in mind other than portfolio investment and does not disclose this to the stockbroker, the latter's valuation, i.e., the current share price, will be useless and misleading. Assume, for example, that company A wishes to acquire company B by purchasing its shares on the Stock Exchange. The finance director of company A enquires of its brokers the current market value of company B's shares. This price when mutliplied by the number of shares in issue produces a value for company B of, say, £5 million. But this is not the price at which company A could buy up all company B's shares. In order to acquire company B, company A would have to pay a substantial premium over the current share price. In other words, the value of company B for control purposes is significantly greater than its value for portfolio investment purposes. To obtain the takeover price of company B, the financial director of company A would have to consult his stockbroker or merchant bank, being careful to state the purpose for which the valuation was required.

Some characteristics of value

This characteristic of value, that the value of something cannot be stated in the abstract, is often overlooked or ignored by writers on the theory of finance and investment. In much of modern financial theory generally, particularly in the 'dividend irrelevance' proposition of Miller and Modigliani and in their theory about the optimum level of debt and equity for a company, one finds the careless use of the word 'value'.[3] Phrases such

[3] Some of these theories have startling implications for investment and share valuation — see Chapters 6, 7, 11 and 12.

as, 'the value of the company', are used on numerous occasions in the same discourse meaning at different times the market capitalisation of the company's equity, the equity market capitalisation plus the nominal amount of debt, the value of the company's equity to a bidder, that is, for control purposes, and even the liquidation value. Value is also sometimes used interchangeably with price; notions such as intrinsic value and intrinsic worth also appear. This imprecise use of the word value leads to much confusion of thought and on occasion to serious errors in reasoning.

When a person wants a valuation of something, more often than not he wants to know the most probable buy or sell price, i.e., the likely exchange value. But exchange or market value is not the only form of exterior value. Things may have a value even though no possibility of sale exists. For example, St Paul's Cathedral may be priceless but it could hardly be considered valueless. No doubt if offered for sale a substantial price might be forthcoming from someone who could exploit the building for its tourist potential. But given the reluctance of the authorities to allow this and given the heavy maintenance costs, the profit potential would be limited. Few people would agree that any such price reflected the value of the building. Similar remarks could be made about Stonehenge, the Houses of Parliament and a host of other buildings, sculptures and paintings which form part of the national heritage.

These values are in effect the collective 'interior' valuations of the community. They cannot be measured or expressed in money terms but they have an objective external reality none the less. These manifestations of value are of more interest to philosophy than to economics and need not concern us here. However, one aspect of such values has an interesting counterpart in the realm of economic values. It is a characteristic of such values that they cannot be reduced to the sum of their parts. For example, the visual appeal of St Paul's Cathedral, or any other building for that matter, cannot be accounted for solely by reference to its constituent parts. If the structure were carefully dismantled and the masonry stored in a neat and tidy fashion on the site, what was previously valued would have disappeared despite the presence on the site of all the constituent parts. Although there could be no visual appeal without the masonry, the beauty of the building is more than just the stone and the carving.

In the sphere of economic values a characteristic of the same type is evident. Just as the value of a machine lies not in the value of its individual parts but rather in its functional utility as a whole, so does the value of a business enterprise reside in its own unique combination of land, labour and capital. Its value is not the sum of the values of its constituent parts; still less can it be the sum of its assets, less the liabilities. There is an understandable temptation to think of a company as consisting of its assets less its liabilities. This is, no doubt, because labour, in its wider meaning of management and workforce, is not 'owned' by the business. The human factor, however, is the most important element in a firm's success. Labour is the active ingredient and capital is the passive one. Although the cure for ailing enterprises is often seen in terms of the need to 'make the assets work' it is plain that assets themselves cannot work. Individuals have to make them work. It is the skills, diligence and enterprise of labour in combination with the assets which account for the value of the enterprise. The value of an entire business usually exceeds the aggregate realisable values of the individual assets less the liabilities. This is the economic rationale for that particular combination of assets and labour. If the value of the firm falls below the net realisable asset value for any period of time, liquidation of the business usually ensues, so that the factors of production may regroup elsewhere in more effective combinations.

Finally, has the analysis so far thrown any light on the subjectivity inherent in valuation? What truth is there in Colleye's remark: 'The valuation of an asset is purely subjective. There is no such thing as objective truth in the assessment of value. Value is an infinitely fluid concept changing in time and varying from place to place and individual to individual'?[4]

It is a well known fact that different valuers can produce widely divergent values for the same property, and this is often advanced as evidence of the subjectivity inherent in valuation. But this criticism draws an unjustified generalisation from a handful of celebrated disputes which have come to the public's attention, usually through the courts. It ignores the multitude of successful valuations which are the basis of negotiated bargains in unquoted shares as well as other property. As one valuer has put it: 'Those who . . . spend much of their time in carrying out valuations know that every appraisal proceeds ninety per cent of its distance on well defined principles and that the result can usually be stated in terms of a narrow range of values'.[5]

Value of course is distinct from valuation. The existence of a value requires both a subject, the valuer, and an object, the thing valued. An object cannot have value if no one appreciates or desires it. On the other hand, no object has a value unless it has desirable qualities. It must surely be a mistake, therefore, to conceive of value as being either wholly subjective or wholly objective. It has both subjective and objective elements. The so-called subjectivity in valuation arises not so much because the values themselves are subjective than because the evidence for the values is not easily apprehended. The valuation of unquoted shares entails

---

[4] Joseph Colleye, paper to the Brussels Congress of the U.E.C. 1955, quoted in T. A. Hamilton Baynes, *Share Valuations*, 3rd ed. (London: Heinneman, 1984), p. 234.

[5] D. Y. Timbrell, Foreword to *Business and Securities Valuation*, by George Ovens and Don Beach (Toronto: Methuen, 1972), p. vii.

many judgements about the outlook for the economy, the particular industry and the company itself. These are matters on which not only valuers but other experts, such as economists, may legitimately differ. Compare this with the valuation of an identical quoted company as reflected in its stock market capitalisation. Both companies have an objective value, but the quoted company's valuation can be apprehended with greater speed and certainty.

Because share valuation entails many difficult judgements, there is scope for differences of opinion. In the author's experience, however, these differences of opinion are at their narrowest and often disappear altogether, when the valuation is carried out in contemplation of an actual sale or purchase. The prospect of money or money's worth changing hands brings a reality to the process and concentrates the mind wonderfully. When a valuation is part of the legal process, as it is in share valuations for tax purposes, that vital element of reality is missing and the valuation can become an academic exercise. It ceases to be an objective search for the value and becomes an exercise in the skilful deployment of arguments — not what the value is, but what it can be argued to be. As these are the disputes which usually come before the courts, it is not surprising that an array of different opinions is found.

Because valuation is not a precise art the results of a valuation should usually be stated in terms of a range of values. This does not mean that the value has been estimated (with the connotations of rough approximation which the word implies), rather that value is determined or measured. This implies that the valuer has come to a decision on the value. There is nothing absolute or completely objective about the figure, and others may disagree, but the amount decided upon is still his opinion of the value.

Conclusion

In this chapter the way in which the comparative value judgement arises in the individual mind, and how the resultant 'interior' values determine price, was examined in some detail. As the analysis of the comparative value judgement unfolded, the characteristics of value became apparent: value is a quality and should not be confused with the object of value; value is attributed to the non-existent never to the existent and therefore always looks to the future; value arises because of the need to choose between competing demands in the face of scarce resources; the measure of value is anticipated opportunity cost; where more than two qualitatively different demands compete, the order of value is the increase of the order of opportunity cost, the latter being defined as the extent to which satisfaction of the principal or common demand is diminished or increased.

Man strives to satisfy his competing demands in a certain proportion; he strikes a balance between them. This equilibrium he aims for determines the value of the marginal unit of demand. The economist's law of diminishing marginal utility is not a law of valuation.

The ratio in which things exchange is a function of the interior valuations of the parties to the exchange. Exchange will only take place if there is mutuality of interest, the price, subject to this requirement, being determined by negotiating and bargaining expertise. It was shown that the value of something cannot be stated in the abstract; all that can be stated is the value of a thing in a particular place, at a particular time, in particular circumstances. The questions 'to whom?' and 'for what purpose?' must always be asked beforehand.

An important characteristic of value is that it cannot be reduced to the sum of its parts. The parts separately valued will not equal the value of the whole. Depending on how they are valued they may be greater or less than the value of the whole.

Without an understanding of the valuational process in the individual mind and of the forces which determine price, no one can hope for any success in valuation. It would be rash to attempt a valuation in ignorance or disregard of this fundamental theoretical framework.

2
Concepts of property value

One of the reasons why value theory is so important to the practitioner is that value is a word of many meanings both in popular usage and specialist texts. In the absence of a clear, unambiguous and restricted meaning of value, the valuer cannot appreciate the limitations or indeed the possibilities of his craft; still less can he present a convincing, well reasoned valuation. The analysis in chapter 1 of the comparative value judgement, and of the way in which interior values determine exchange values, provides interesting insights into the nature of value and valuation whilst avoiding contentious definitions. It also lays the groundwork for the detailed examination of those value concepts with which the professional valuer is chiefly concerned. The three main concepts considered here are owner value, market or exchange value and fair value.[1] Various quasi-concepts, notably investment value, liquidation value, going concern value and intrinsic value, are also discussed.

Value to the owner

Owner value is analogous to the notion of interior values introduced in chapter 1, but it is not the same thing. Admittedly, owner value, like interior value, is completely subjective, but, nevertheless, owner value can be assessed by the professional valuer, whereas many interior values are not susceptible to this treatment and often cannot even be measured in money terms. Owner value is a concept which relates only to property rights, and the term is not restricted to the present owner but to any prospective owner or anyone with a beneficial interest in the property.

Property is capable of conferring different advantages on different owners. A combine harvester will be of great value to a farmer but will be of little worth to anyone else, and even amongst the farming community the value to individual farmers will vary with the size of the farm and the use to which the land is put. In the example in Chapter 1,

---

[1] James C. Bonbright's 'magnum opus' *The Valuation of Property: A Treatise on the Appraisal of Property for Different Legal Purposes*, 2 vols. (Charlottesville: The Michie Company, 1937) has been of considerable assistance to the author in writing the sections on owner value and market value.

p. 13, it was seen that D's shareholding had four different values depending on the assumed owner and the use he could make of the shares. The price D's shareholding might fetch would therefore depend on these owner values. In fact, owner values are at the root of all prices whether they be open market prices or prices paid in private treaty transactions. It is for this reason that value to the owner is of such fundamental importance.

How is owner value assessed? Value arises because of the need to choose between competing ends in the face of scarce resources. Value, therefore, is always relative and the value of anything can only be measured by reference to what some other valuable thing is worth. In the valuation of shares that other valuable thing is money. Although money is a standard of value, it is also a commodity or store of wealth and in this latter function its value also varies according to the owner. Thus £1,000 is worth more to a poor man than it is to a millionaire, and by the same token the rich man will outbid the poor man for a given property, not necessarily because he values the property any more than the poor man, but because he values the money less.

The value of a property to its owner is identical in amount to what may be termed its deprival value. This refers to the adverse consequences, both direct and indirect, for the owner if he were deprived of the property. It is important to take into account both direct and indirect consequences. For example, a person may consider that his house is worth, say, £50,000. This is the price he believes it would fetch if sold; it is its market value. However, the sum of £50,000 would not compensate this person adequately for the loss of his property since he would have to pay stamp duty, legal costs and estate agent's fees on the purchase of a replacement property as well as substantial removal costs. In addition, there must be taken into account the inconvenience from the resultant domestic upheaval. Perhaps no other suitable property in that price range exists in the neighbourhood and a less conveniently situated house has to be bought, thereby increasing the time and cost of travelling to work and rendering contact with one's friends more difficult. It may well be that in view of all these hidden costs the true value to the owner is nearer £60,000, if not considerably more.

The fact that market price is not necessarily a measure of value to the owner is tacitly recognised by the courts, sometimes by the use of terms such as 'fair' market value but more commonly by the award of consequential damages. It is also recognised by businesses and firms. For example, business executives frequently have to move to other parts of the country and sometimes abroad. The usual practice in such circumstances is for the employer to pay the executive's full removal costs. This will include: legal costs, stamp duty and estate agent's fees on the purchase of a new house; costs incurred in the disposal of the old house; reasonable removal expenses, hotel bills whilst the executive and his family are temporarily without a home; and often a contribution to expenditure on items such as carpets and curtains which would not have been incurred but for the move. The basis of reimbursement is therefore owner value and not market value, the latter being quite clearly an inadequate measure of the loss.

It should be noted that owner value can fluctuate quite suddenly with changes in circumstances. A firm may be equipped with an emergency electricity generator. When electricity is in normal supply this emergency generator will probably have a value to the business (i.e., owner value) equal to its depreciated replacement cost. However, should a power failure occur, the emergency generator will temporarily have a very high deprival value since its loss might well bring the entire business to a standstill. Similarly, a small minority shareholder may value his shares at their investment value, but the appearance of a bidder for the entire company would cause him to raise this value considerably.

As mentioned earlier, value to the owner must be distinguished from owner's valuation or the notion of interior valuation used in Chapter 1. For example, an owner may value his property at £10,000 but the professional valuer, bearing the owner's needs or interests in mind, may conclude that the property is 'really worth', to him, say, £12,000. In the same way, a person may consider that his house is worth no more nor less to him that its market value, but after reflecting on the costs of moving he would probably agree that its value to him would be somewhat higher than this. In the determination of owner value, therefore, the professional valuer's job is to guide the owner's mind, not to guess it. What is sought is a reasonable or justified value — the amount the owner should value his property at as a wise businessman.

Owner value is sometimes erroneously equated with replacement cost. Thus, under SSAP 16, the inflation accounting standard which has now been withdrawn, the current cost of land and buildings, plant and machinery and stocks were to be stated at their value to the business, this being defined as net current replacement cost or recoverable amount if lower. Recoverable amount was in turn defined as the greater of the net realisable value of an asset and, where applicable, the amount recoverable from its further use. It needs little reflection to see that replacement cost is unlikely to measure value to the business. Consider, for example, a manufacturing business whose fixed assets consist of a factory and its associated plant and machinery. The deprival value of the factory building would in all probability be greatly in excess of its replacement cost. Without the factory, production would cease, orders would be lost and great damage would be done to the business. The business may well have to be wound up, particularly if it is not insured against consequential loss of profits.

Admittedly, if value to the business were defined in this way for each of a firm's assets the total of the asset values would greatly exceed the value of the entire business. But this is precisely the characteristic of value mentioned in the previous chapter; the sum of the parts does not usually equal the value of the whole. Where the parts are valued as separated from the whole, the sum of their values is likely to be far less than the value of the whole. On the other hand, if the parts are valued as parts of the whole, their sum total of values may greatly exceed the value of the whole. The classic, although somewhat extreme, example of this phenomenon is provided by a pair of gloves. Either of the gloves valued on its own is worth next to nothing, but valued as part of the larger whole it is worth almost the price of the pair. It is as meaningless to mutiply either of these figures by two to obtain the value of the pair of gloves as it is to divide the price of the gloves by two to obtain the value of each glove.

Obviously, not all the assets of a business are so indispensable as to give them a deprival value equivalent almost to the value of the firm, and doubtless many assets could be replaced without much loss of earning power. The point made here, however, is that there is no necessary identity between replacement cost and value to the business or owner value. Whilst net replacement cost may well be the appropriate amount at which assets should be stated in a balance sheet drawn up on current cost accounting rules, the identification of such amounts with value to the business is an error of terminology at the very least. Similarly, the sum of the CCA asset 'values' less the liabilities could not be considered as the value of the entire business.

The fact that the sum of the parts valued separately is likely to be less than the value of the whole is often recognised in practice; but the fact that the sum of the parts valued as parts of the whole is likely to exceed the value of the whole is frequently overlooked. This is especially true of the value attributed to intangibles such as goodwill. Goodwill is frequently valued as being the excess of the value of the entire business over the value of the separable net assets. This method of arriving at the value of goodwill can only be justified on the assumption that the sum of the value of the parts must equal the value of the whole.[2] As has been shown, there is no basis for such an assumption. One would not arrive at the value of stock-in-trade by deducting the value of all the other assets, less the liabilities, from the value of the entire business.

[2] The concept of goodwill and how it may be valued is considered in Chapter 8.

Although certain properties are worth more to their owners than market value, there is often a sufficiently close quantitative relationship between the two for one to be taken as an index of the other. Certainly, market value (where it exists) will usually set the lower limit of owner value since, even if the owner has no use for the property, it has a value to him as a means of obtaining money. If an equally desirable replacement for his property is available on the market then market price will also measure the upper limit of owner value. Thus, the owner value of a small parcel of shares quoted on the Stock Exchange would be their current market value. This represents the price at which the owner could both buy and sell his shares (ignoring dealing expenses).

Market value or exchange value

Exchange value is given as a synonym for market value partly because this conforms to the usage in economics, where most of the theory of price and value originates, and partly because for most forms of property there is no difference in practice. However, exchange value is a wider concept than market value, and the reluctance of economics to draw the distinction between the two is probably accounted for by the difficulty of drawing the line between conditions of exchange which constitute a market and those which do not. There are infinite gradations, for example, between the perfectly competitive markets, such as the Stock Exchange and the foreign exchange market, and the conditions of exchange for shares in a closely-held private company. In the case of the former, prices and price-sensitive information are disseminated instantaneously to all participants; there are virtually no restrictions on exchanges or dealings; and the volume of trades is huge. In the case of the latter, information is restricted to the legal minimum; severe share transfer restrictions exist; and transactions in the shares are isolated and infrequent.

In theory, this latter state of affairs could be considered as a rudimentary form of market, and no doubt this is how many economists would view it. Such 'markets' pale into insignificance when set alongside the vast flow of goods and services in a modern economy, and it hardly matters to the economist if his equation of price with market value does not fit neatly into every single exchange, so long as it is a useful working hypothesis. For the share valuer and for shareholders in closely held private companies, however, the distinction between price and exchange value or market value is very important; failure to draw the distinction can mean injustice for one party and bounty for the other.

Although economics is not generally concerned with market value as a concept, it is, nevertheless, vitally interested in the concept of the market. In this connection Lipsey's definition of a market may be noted: 'For our present purposes [price theory], we define a market as an area over which buyers and sellers negotiate the exchange of a well-defined commodity. For a single market to exist, it must be possible for buyers and sellers to communicate with each other and to make meaningful deals over the whole market'.[3] This definition of a market is not without its difficulties. In particular, the use of the word 'commodity' suggests that the author has in mind those commonplace goods and services which are the subject of consumer demand. However, Lipsey's insistence on communications and meaningful deals, both rather vague ideas, merit further examination.

Firstly, no market can exist if actual or prospective participants are unaware of the prices at which others are dealing in similar property. Assume, for example, that A, B, C and D are individual buyers and E, F, G and H are sellers of a particular type of property. A buys from E, B from F, C from G and D from H. Here we have a group of persons engaged in the purchase and sale of a 'well defined' type of property. In appearance this constitutes a market. However, if each of the four sets of buyers and sellers were unaware of the other buyers and sellers, there would be no market. Hence Lipsey's insistence on the possibility of communication between buyers and sellers. However, the possibility of communication between buyers and sellers, although a necessary condition, is not a sufficient one, since if A and E, and likewise B and F, C and G, and D and H, did not in fact communicate with the others, then there would be no market even though the possibility of communication existed. What needs to be added is that prospective buyers and sellers must be informed of prices being achieved in the market. Without this knowledge the parties will merely strike a bargain based solely on respective owner values and bargaining skills.

In addition to information on price, there must also be available to prospective purchasers and sellers sufficient information to enable an intelligent assessment or appraisal of the property. This matters little in certain markets such as produce markets where physical inspection is all that is required. But in securities markets, particularly the market for equities, it is vital. Prices which are based on inadequate information are unreliable guides as to future prices.

The basis of market value, therefore, is the assumption that if comparable property fetches a certain price then the subject property will

[3] Richard G. Lipsey, *An Introduction to Positive Economics*, 5th ed. (London: Weidenfeld and Nicolson, 1979), p. 72.

realise the same price or something near to it. The validity of this assumption depends upon the continuation of the market from which the prices were obtained or, more precisely, the continuation of the trends demonstrated in that market.[4] In this connection there can be a world of difference between a thin market and one which has 'depth'. A market has depth where the property in question is in frequent demand and there are numerous bargains. A thin market is characterised by occasional deals. Prices in a thin market may not be a reliable guide as to the most likely buy and sell price — the central concept in market value. The fewer prospective buyers and sellers there are, the less will be the influence of alternative exchange value on a particular buyer's and seller's own valuation of the property. In such circumstances, prices depend more on the subjective owner values and bargaining skills of the respective parties. This accounts for the volatility of prices in thin markets. Where a market has depth, parties to a transaction generally know with some certainty what price they can buy and sell at, and this will be the dominant influence on the price in a particular transaction.

The definition of market value as the price at which property could be sold needs to be qualified in a number of important respects if it is to be of practical use. For example, is a forced sale price as indicative of market value as one arrived at after reasonable time for negotiations? Is a distinction to be made between a cash offer and a paper-for-paper transaction, or between immediate and deferred payment? What influence does the special purchaser have on market value? Should realisation expenses be taken into account? Different answers to these questions can often have a material bearing on the determination of market value, and the valuer would be well advised, therefore, to state in his valuation what assumptions he has made in this regard.

Most valuers would not regard a forced sale price as indicative of market value and would usually stipulate a reasonable period of time in which to market the property. However, whenever the market is thin — and for shares in the typical private company the market could hardly be much thinner — it may be difficult to distinguish between a forced sale and an 'ordinary' sale. Furthermore, the reasonable period of time necessary to achieve the market value may be inordinately long when applied to unquoted shares.

The time value of money means that £1 received today is worth more than £1 received tomorrow. If the whole or part of the consideration for the sale of property is deferred, a higher price would be required than if the buyer were to pay cash immediately. There also appears to be a

---

[4] Henry A. Babcock, *Appraisal Principles and Procedures* (Homewood, Ill.: Irwin, 1968), p. 117.

distinction between consideration satisfied in cash and consideration satisfied in the bidder's paper. Companies which launch take-over bids on the strength of their own paper often provide a cash alternative. This is usually set at a discount to the value of the paper on offer. A higher price should therefore be achieved if property is sold other than for cash.

The usual practice is to state market value before deducting selling expenses. Although this may seem odd given the idea of cash generation underlying the market value concept, the practice can be justified on practical grounds. First, selling expenses can vary depending on the method of sale and can often be difficult to determine precisely. Second, not all market valuations are commissioned with a view to sale of the property. Quoted property investment companies, for example, often commission periodic market valuations of their portfolios as a guide to their own performance and to assist investors in forming an intelligent assessment of the shares.

The effect of a special purchaser on price can be dramatic. The property developer trying to assemble a site for development may well be prepared to pay considerably more than the normal market price for a property which occupies the only part of the site he does not already own. Similarly, a few isolated acres of agricultural land would have a very different value to the owner of adjoining land than they would to the generality of purchasers.

However, in other circumstances the effect of a special purchaser may be purely marginal. Let us assume, for example, that A Ltd, whose shares are quoted, is a partly owned subsidiary of B Ltd, with the shares held as follows:

	Ordinary shares (000's)	%
B Ltd	3,700	74
Mr C	50	1
Others (4,000 in number)	1,250	25
	5,000	100

Apart from C, no shareholder holds more than 400 shares. The current market price is £10 per share. B Ltd wishes to increase its shareholding to 75% of the total shares in issue, as this will enable it to pass special resolutions and also secure various tax advantages, notably group relief. The value of these benefits to B Ltd is substantial and could easily justify its paying a significant premium over the market price of A Ltd's shares. C perceives this and approaches B Ltd with an offer to sell his entire holding of 50,000 shares at £15 per share — a 50% increase over the market price. B Ltd's brokers advise, however, that they could pick up 50,000 shares in the market over a period of time at an average price within ten per cent of the current one. B Ltd thereupon offers £11 per share for C's shareholding. C accepts.

In this example, C could not hold out for a price much in excess of the market price despite the existence of a special buyer, B Ltd. What distinguishes this example from the one of the property situated in the middle of a development site is the attribute of uniqueness. That property and no other property has a special value to the developer. The developer had no alternative and the property owner knew it. But B Ltd has an alternative to buying from C and competition amongst potential sellers forces down the price to a margin over market value, despite the existence of a special value. In highly developed markets, such as the Stock Exchange, where anonimity is preserved between buyer and seller, the effect of a special purchaser may be virtually imperceptible.

The existence of a special purchaser is not always apparent, and where it is, the assessment of his effect on price may be almost impossible to quantify. No doubt for reasons such as these market value usually excludes the effect of a special purchaser. In the author's view, however, it is unrealistic to exclude the effect of a special purchaser where such is known to exist. If market value is the most probable buy/sell price, and the most probable buyer is the one with the special interest in the property, then it is unrealistic to value that property without taking into account the special buyer. In the example of the property developer, the owner of the sole remaining property on the development site would not be interested in the prices which similar properties might be fetching in the neighbourhood, nor would he contemplate selling to anyone other than the property developer or someone who could pay a similar price. In such a case, the valuer would be doing his client a disservice if he ignored the special purchaser and merely presented an unqualified market value.

Where portfolio investment is not the sole objective — and it rarely is with unquoted shares — there is generally something special about every purchaser and something unique about every shareholding. This, in the author's view, is the fundamental flaw in the market value concept as it is applied to the valuation of unquoted shares. The competitive effect on price of a large body of buyers and sellers is not generally present, and the possibility of buying or selling the shares elsewhere does not exist. Portfolio investment apart, a given percentage shareholding in Company A is not usually a substitute for the same sized shareholding in Company B, assuming both companies are identical in terms of dividends, profits and assets.

If market value is to mean the price at which property can be sold, the effect of the quantity being valued must be taken into account. On the Stock Exchange large blocks of shares typically change hands at a discount to current market price. In North American markets this discount is known as blockage. Thus, it would be incorrect to value such a block of shares simply by multiplying the number of shares by the current price per share. Some discount for blockage would have to be applied. As regards unquoted shares, however, the reverse is usually the case. Large shareholdings generally have a higher unit price than small shareholdings.

In valuing a large block of quoted shares for balance sheet purposes, or even internal management information purposes, blockage would probably be ignored. Similarly, the market values of quoted companies, as stated in investment circulars and other publications, are usually calculated by multiplying the number of shares in issue by the current market price per share. No doubt these conventions serve their purpose, but strictly speaking it is incorrect to apply the term 'market value' to the results of these calculations. Little imagination is needed to see what the effect would be if all the shareholders of a company simultaneously attempted to realise the so-called market value of shares by selling them in the market. The correct term for such calculations is market capitalisation.

Finally, valuations are sometimes stated to be as between a willing buyer and a willing seller in the open market. This phrase has its origins in fiscal valuations and the attempts by the courts to make the concept of market value workable for the statutory valuation of unquoted securities. In so far as it implies that the special buyer or the forced seller is excluded, it is a harmless, though redundant, qualification to the market value concept. But if it is used to assume the existence of a market where no such market exists in reality — this may also be reinforced by the use of the word 'open' as in open market — then it is a dangerous and potentially misleading excursion into the realms of fantasy. In commercial valuations it is better to avoid the use of the willing buyer/willing seller appendage. If no buyer or seller can be envisaged, it makes no commercial sense to invent one.

Fair value

The fair value concept is frequently encountered in the share transfer provisions of private companies' articles of association. These often provide that in specified instances shares shall be transferred at the fair value determined by the company's auditors. Sometimes shareholders enter into side agreements governing the disposal of shares and these, too, may contain pre-emption rights stipulating a fair value to be determined by a nominated expert valuer. The fair values thus determined are generally expressed to be binding on the parties. It is not surprising, therefore, that dissatisfied vendors and purchasers have on occasion resorted to litigation in order to overturn the fair value award. Despite this, there seems to be very little guidance from the legal cases as to what constitutes fair value, the Court's main concern being to define the rights of the parties and the liability of the independent valuer. In these circumstances the valuer himself must judge what is fair, and, provided his judgement is arrived at honestly and not negligently, it must stand.

For the reader who is seeking guidance on this point the author can, therefore, do no more than give his own personal view, based on experience, as to what constitutes fair value. First, fair value is distinct from market value. Were it not, the articles of association or other legal agreement would stipulate market value as this is the more generally recognised value concept. Second, the essence of the fair value concept is the desire to be equitable to both parties. It recognises that the transaction is not in the open market. Buyer and seller have been brought together by the operation of a legally binding agreement in a way which excludes other potential buyers and sellers. Thus, the buyer has not been able to shop around for the lowest price nor has the seller been able to hold out for the highest price. In these circumstances, the fair value must take into account as a minimum requirement what the seller gives up in value and what the buyer acquires in value through the transaction. The valuer must therefore assess the owner value of the shares to both vendor and purchaser.

If vendor and purchaser are both small minority shareholders there will probably be very little difference between the respective owner values, and the determination of fair value will be straightforward. Consider a company whose shares are held as follows:

Shareholder	No of shares	%
A	3,000	60
B	200	4
C	150	3
D	200	4
E	500	10
F	600	12
G	350	7
	5,000	100

B wishes to sell his shares. Under the company's articles of association a member wishing to sell his shares must offer them through the directors to all the other shareholders at the fair value to be determined by the auditors. B's shareholding represents four per cent of the total. It is a small, uninfluential minority interest, and its value to B would be a function of its attractions as an investment. This investment value would be calculated by comparing the return in the form dividends with the return on alternative forms of investment.[5]

Under the articles, B's shares will be offered to the remaining shareholders *pro rata* to their existing shareholdings. If each shareholder took up his entitlement, his percentage shareholding would rise by 4.2% (i.e., 200 as a percentage of 4,800). An increase of this order would make no significant difference to the relative voting strength of the shareholders, or confer a greater advantage on some shareholders than on others. The value of these shares to the remaining shareholders is, therefore, their investment value. In these circumstances the investment value can be taken as the fair value.

But not all shareholding structures are of this type. Consider, for example, a company whose shares are held as follows:

Shareholder	No of shares
A	40
B	40
C	20
	100

None of the shareholders works in the business and all three are happy with the way the directors run the company's affairs. However, for personal reasons C wishes to sell his shares and in compliance with the articles issues a sale notice to the directors. The articles provide that the shares of the selling member shall be offered to the other shareholders *pro rata* to their existing shareholdings and at a fair value to be determined by the auditors.

It is first necessary to assess the value of the 20% shareholding to C, the present owner. Although C's shareholding is substantial, it is not large enough on its own to exert any influence on the management of the company or the payment of dividends. Being less than 25%, it cannot block a special resolution and its nuisance value is therefore small. Any value it has for C over and above its pure investment value is

[5] For companies which do not pay dividends, see Chapter 9.

likely to be slight. Turning now to the value of C's share to A and B, it will be immediately apparent that the acquisition of this shareholding would confer majority voting control of the company on A or B. Assuming they can afford it, both A and B will therefore take up their full ten per cent entitlement since failure to do so on the part of one would vest control of the business in the hands of the other. This means that the company's equity is likely to be held 50/50 by A and B as a result of the sale of C's shares. In practice, the value of a 50% shareholding in such circumstances is usually one half the value of the entire company. As the value of A's and B's 40% shareholding is probably somewhat less than the proportionate part of the value of the entire company, it follows that the value of the ten per cent interest A and B each acquire from C must be somewhat more than ten per cent of the value of the entire company. This can be illustrated by assuming hypothetical values for different percentage shareholdings in the company, as follows:

Equity interest %	Value £
10	1,000
20	2,500
40	8,000
50 (½ of 100%)	15,000
60	16,000

If A acquires one half of C's 20% interest, the value of his stake in the company will rise by £7,000, i.e., from £8,000 to £15,000. Similarly with B. Therefore, the value of these shares to A and B, as measured by the resultant increase in the value of their two shareholdings, is, in total, £14,000. This compares with the pure investment value of £2,500 and the full control value of £6,000 (i.e., 20% of £30,000). In effect, by virtue of the play of changing legal entitlements, this transaction creates value of £11,500, being the difference between the value of these shares to the purchasers, £14,000, and their value to the vendor, £2,500.

Only when the valuer has assessed the likely effect of the transaction in this way is he in a position to determine a fair value. In this hypothetical example there is enormous scope for differences of opinion as to what is fair. In essence, the valuer has to decide how much of this value advantage ought in fairness to go to the vendor and how much to the purchaser. The author's inclination would be to plump for a fair value of £6,000, being the *pro rata* value of the entire company. A fair value of £6,000 confers roughly one third of the value difference on the vendor and two thirds on the purchasers, as set out on the next page:

	Total £
Value of C's shares to A and B (£7,000 each)	14,000
Investment value of C's shares, i.e., their owner value to C	2,500
Value increment	11,500
One third thereof to C	3,833
Add owner value (as above)	2,500
Fair value	6,333
	6,000

This split of the value increment in the ratio 2 to 1 in favour of the purchasers is entirely subjective and another valuer faced with a similar problem might well reach a different conclusion. Nonetheless, the allocation of the value increment in the ratio of 2 to 1 has the merit that it accords with the size of C's shareholding relative to A's and D's individually. There is some crude logic as well as rough justice in such a split.

It is interesting to contrast the determination of fair value with the likely outcome had C been at liberty to sell his shares to A or B at a mutually agreed price. Both A and B stand to gain voting control of the company by acquiring C's shares. The value of the winner's shareholding will rise to £16,000, being the value of a 60% shareholding. The loser in the battle to obtain C's shares will end up as an isolated, although substantial, minority, and as a consequence the value of his shares will have diminished. Competition between A and B could well be intense and either party could justify paying £8,000 for C's shares, i.e. £16,000 less £8,000. If A and B do not get on well together and each has a dread of being placed in an inferior position to the other, the price could well be much higher.

In the two examples given none of the shareholders was employed by the company. No doubt, in theory, the fact that a shareholder is also an employee or director should have no bearing on the value of his shares. There is a quite clear separation of the rights and duties of the employee/director and those of the shareholder. A person offers his services in return for remuneration. Unless his contract of employment specifically provides for it, there is no obvious reason why the value of his shares should be influenced by the fact of his employment with the company.

Although this distinction is certainly true when the market value of shares is being assessed, there is, in the author's opinion, a very good case for going beyond the narrower legalistic approach when applying the fair value concept. Here again, the problems likely to face the valuer can best be illustrated by way of examples. Suppose that some years ago a US manufacturer of specialist hospital equipment decided to enter the UK market. It formed a UK subsidiary and appointed a managing director to whom it ceded a 20% equity stake as an incentive. The managing director succeeded in establishing a profitable business with a significant market share. However, as a result of differences of opinion over the future direction of the business, the managing director resigned from the company. Not wishing to retain his 20% shareholding, he served a sale notice on the company and in accordance with the articles the fair value of the shares has to be determined.

On a narrow view, the managing director's shares have a low value. The company does not pay dividends, and, with the usual private company restrictions on transfer, the shares are virtually unsaleable. Using the approach adopted earlier, the fair value could be pitched somewhere between their value to the managing director and their value to the parent company. This would suggest a substantial discount off the full control value but still a significant premium to any investment value the shares might have. The author's personal inclination, however, would be to set the fair value at or near the full control value in view of the nature of the managing director's connection with the company. He was given his shareholding as an incentive to build up the business. Had it been mentioned at the outset that the shares would be valued for sale purposes as an unmarketable, uninfluential minority interest, the incentive would not have been as great and perhaps a higher remuneration would have been necessary.

In many smaller companies the legal relationship between the proprietors does not mirror the economic reality. Many such companies are *de facto* partnerships. The fair value concept enables the valuer to take into account these *de facto* relationships. Consider another example. Two friends, A and B, formed a company to acquire the engineering business they had built up together. A was given 52% of the equity and B 48%. After some years B died of a heart attack and his widow was left with his shares. The business is fairly small and the company has never paid dividends, the directors preferring to extract the profits by way of remuneration. B's widow is not well off and needs income. Additionally, she has never got on well with A and his family and now wants to realise her investment.

Few individuals would be attracted to such an investment and in the hard world of the marketplace the widow's shares would be valued at a sizeable discount to their full control value. Here again, the approach advocated earlier of pitching the fair value somewhere between the respective owner values may not do adequate justice to the widow, although it would certainly be much fairer than the market value approach. The author feels that in view of the *de facto* partnership arrangement between A and B, B's widow should in fairness receive her *pro rata* share of the value of the entire company, and his inclination would be to determine the fair value at or near that amount.

Generalisations are dangerous and particularly so in the art of valuation. The examples given here of fair value must not be taken as indicative of general rules. Indeed, there are no rules determining fair value. The concept imposes considerable demands on the valuer. Not only is he required to exercise his valuation skills, but he is to employ them in a way which ensures justice between buyer and seller. One valuer's concept of fairness may differ from another's, and no doubt some readers may not agree with the author's concept of fair value as evident in the examples. That does not matter greatly. The purpose of these examples is to illustrate how the concept of fair value can be interpreted so that those who rarely have to determine a fair value may be helped in formulating their own views.

Most fair value determinations fall upon the auditor, although sometimes the parties resort to an independent professional accountant with no connection with the company or with the parties. The auditor, with his detailed knowledge of the business usually acquired over many years, is an obvious choice of valuer. However, the audit approach is different from the valuation approach, and the auditor must ensure that he appraises the business from the correct standpoint. A deep and sympathetic understanding of the business including an appreciation of the industry background is required. A high standard of financial analysis is necessary.

Because the valuation is binding on the parties the auditor must take great care and make all due enquiries. It is a regrettable feature of valuation work that the effort involved does not vary proportionately with the value of the transaction. With small companies, and therefore low values, the work may well prove uneconomic viewed in isolation from the audit or any other professional services rendered to the company. Nevertheless if such assignments are accepted, the work must be done to the proper standard; there can be no question of tailoring the work to suit the likely fee.

Investment value

Investment value is a term which occurs from time to time in this work. It is not a separate value concept like market value or owner value.

Rather it denotes the value for a particular purpose — that of portfolio investment. Share prices on the Stock Exchange reflect the market value of small parcels of shares and are generally representative of investment value. Investors on the Stock Exchange seek their return in the form of dividends and capital appreciation. They are typically minority shareholders taking no part in the management or direction of the companies they invest in.

There are many different forms of investment. These include British Government securities, local authority bonds, money market instruments, bank and building society deposits, as well as real property, commodities, antiques, fine art and the more esoteric investments such as vintage cars and thoroughbred horses. These different forms of investment offer different rates of return. In other words, the price the investor pays for every pound of expected return varies according to the investment. The reason why the investor pays more in some cases and less in others is because of the different degrees of risk and marketability in each form of investment.

This distinction between risk and marketability is not recognised everywhere, and one frequently finds the two concepts confused with each other. When valuing unquoted shares, however, the validity of the distinction becomes obvious. The lack of marketability is a hallmark of the unquoted investment and has no connection with the risk of the underlying business operations. As a general rule, therefore, a discount for lack of marketability is applied in arriving at the investment value of unquoted shares.

However, there could well be exceptions to this general rule when an investment-based owner value is required. Here everything depends on the circumstances of the owner. Consider, for example, Mrs X's substantial holding of 12% preference shares in XYZ Ltd. These shares have unusual, but potentially significant voting rights. The directors would not like these shares to fall into the hands of outsiders and offer to buy them through the company. The independent investment value works out at 72p per preference share as set out below:

	Per share
Gross dividend	12p
Required yield, based on average yield of quoted preference shares	12½%
Notional value as quoted	96p
Less discount for lack of marketability (say 25%)	24p
Market value	72p

However, Mrs X depends on her preference dividend; it is her principal source of income. If she accepted market value for her shares and reinvested the proceeds in quoted preference shares, her income would drop substantially, as set out below:

	Pence per share
Sale proceeds — market value	72
Dividend on reinvestment (assuming 12½% yield)	9
Existing dividend	12
Shortfall	3

Thus Mrs X's dividend income will fall by 25% and in return she will have a much more marketable investment. Investment risk is assumed to be unchanged.

Although Mrs X appreciates the advantages of marketability, it has little value to her since she has no need to switch investments and could not better her income elsewhere. The value of these preference shares to her (their owner value) is therefore no less then 96p per share. In fact, given the expenses of sale and any capital gains tax payable on realisation of the shares, it would probably not be in her interests to sell for less than par. Thus in Mrs X's case there is no justification for deducting the discount for lack of marketability.

Liquidation value

Like investment value, liquidation value is not a fundamental value concept. The term indicates rather that the valuation is to be based on the assumption that the company will be wound up. Where a winding up is in prospect, the need for the valuation to be based on that assumption is obvious, but liquidation value may also be relevant where a company is a going concern. The instances where this is likely to be so are few and far between. Nevertheless, it sometimes happens that a business is worth more on a break-up than it is as a going concern. In such a case the value of the business would be its liquidation value.

Liquidation value is not simple to calculate, and, where the sums are important, it is advisable to obtain the advice of an insolvency practitioner. Many subjective judgements will be required, and specialist valuation advice may be needed for the fixed assets and stock. All the expenses of realisation including legal, estate agent's and liquidator's charges have to be taken into account and the tax position carefully assessed. As a business is wound up, terminal trading losses are frequently incurred, exacerbated by bad debts and stock losses. Redundancy pay and pay in lieu of notice often amount to a significant sum. There are many procedural formalities (e.g., statutory meetings, returns etc.). It is hardly surprising, therefore, that liquidations, even of fairly simple companies, are messy, complicated and protracted affairs.

Any purchaser of shares in a company which is to be wound up would not pay the full amount the shares would be likely to realise on eventual liquidation since this would give him no return on his investment. Furthermore, because of the nature of liquidations, the final outcome is subject to much uncertainty. The estimated amount may or may not be realised in full, and the investor must be compensated for assuming this risk. A discount must therefore be applied to the estimated distributions to reflect both the time value of money and the risk involved. Buying shares in the hope of making a profit on liquidation is not a popular form of investment, and the rate of return expected is accordingly high. As it may be necessary to wait over 12 months, if not considerably longer, for the final distribution, the net present value will usually be much lower than the sum of the eventual distributions.

Liquidation value is often thought of as setting the lower limit to a share's value below which it cannot fall. Whilst this is certainly true of the value of the entire company or of a shareholding with 75% or over of the votes, it is a dangerous assumption to make for any other size of shareholding, particularly a minority interest. Unless a liquidation is actually in prospect or likely to occur in the future, liquidation value does not necessarily set the lower limit to the value of a minority holding. The minority shareholder cannot force a liquidation, and, in the absence of special circumstances, his shares must therefore be worth the present value of any future dividends. It may be desirable to incorporate a premium to recognise the high liquidation value, but this would serve more to recognise the point than to fully reflect it.

The purchaser of a majority shareholding with less than 75% of the votes is in a different position. Although he cannot force a liquidation, he obtains management control and the opportunity to exploit the assets to the full. The fact that liquidation value exceeds going concern value points to under-used assets. In the nature of things these assets are likely to have a value independent of the business, and the controlling shareholder can realise these assets and re-invest the proceeds at a higher return. Freehold and leasehold property are prime examples of such assets. Thus, even though he may not be able to force a winding up, the controlling shareholder can benefit from the higher alternative use values, and the liquidation value may well prove the lowest price he could expect to pay for the shares. Where none of the assets has a significant alternative use value, it is almost inconceivable that liquidation value should exceed going concern value. This is because assets built for a particular purpose, and suitable for no other purpose, usually fetch very low prices when sold piecemeal and second-hand by a liquidator.

Liquidation value features prominantly in Ian Campbell's approach to valuation.[6] According to Campbell, the difference between going concern value and liquidation value is indicative of the absolute risk assumed. As risk influences the capitalisation rate, so liquidation value affects going concern value. A simple example can be used to illustrate the point:

	Company A	Company B
(a) Going concern value	£500,000	£500,000
(b) Liquidation value	£200,000	£350,000
Absolute risk (a)−(b)	£300,000	£150,000

Both companies have the same earnings prospects and face the same degree of business risk. The going concern values represent capitalised earnings and have been arrived at before consideration of liquidation value. The fact that the liquidation values differ so markedly in otherwise identical companies can be explained by factors such as the existence of freehold property in Company B and not in Company A, an aging workforce in Company A entailing higher redundancy costs on closure and so on. The investment risk in Company A is higher than in Company B, because if things went badly wrong, the investor's loss would be lower in the latter than in the former. The investor in Company B would end up with £350,000 compared to £200,000 for the investor in Company A. In view of this Company B should have a higher value than Company A.

This is a persuasive line of reasoning and coming from such an authoritative source it carries great weight. Nevertheless, the author suspects that the example given is an over simplification and that on closer scrutiny no general deductions can be made about the effect of liquidation value on the capitalisation rate. First, if two companies are identical in the ways mentioned, including activity, earnings, tangible asset backing (as distinct from liquidation value), and risk, it would indeed be surprising if their liquidation values were materially different

[6] Ian R. Campbell, *The Principles and Practices of Business Valuations* (Toronto: Richard de Boo, 1975), p. 21.

from each other. According to Campbell, this difference could be accounted for by the fact that Company B owned its premises whereas Company A did not. But if this were so, there must be some difference in the quality of earnings of the two companies. Company A makes the same profit as Company B but the former pays market rent for the use of its premises whereas the latter does not. Ostensibly, Company A is more profitable than Company B and its going concern value should be higher, and therefore the absolute risk lower, than shown in the example. If the difference is accounted for by higher redundancy costs because of an aging workforce, as suggested earlier, this too implies differences in the quality of earnings and hence going concern value.

But it would be churlish to reject the argument purely for these reasons. There is, in the author's view, a more fundamental objection. Nobody invests in a business which has no future and is destined to be wound up. The typical investor looks to the future profits and dividends of a company as a going concern; he would not invest if there was any likelihood of a liquidation.

The investor's evaluation should be based solely on the outlook for the company as a going concern. The capitalisation rate used in such circumstances is normally a function of the perceived degree of business risk facing the company, as in Campbell's example. But business risk by definition covers the possibility of corporate failure. Furthermore, the present liquidation value of a company is no guide to liquidation value in the future. Unless the assessment of a company has been slip-shod or careless, an investment in an apparently healthy business is unlikely to turn sour immediately. When a business encounters difficult trading conditions it does everything in its power to combat them. It may well sustain losses for a number of years in the hope of eventual recovery. Liquidation usually takes place as a last resort and there is generally very little, if anything, left for the ordinary shareholders. It would not be wise therefore to pin one's hopes on today's liquidation value. This unhealthy preoccupation with liquidation value can only distract the investor's attention from what must be his principal concern — the outlook for the company's products and services and the quality of its management and workforce.

Going concern value

Here again, we are concerned not with a fundamental value concept but with value based on a certain assumption — the assumption that the business is a going concern. In a financially stable economy, the vast majority of businesses will be going concerns, and most valuations are carried out on that assumption.

Readers will no doubt be familiar with the concept of a going concern. It implies that there is no threat of liquidation hanging over the business and that the firm can meet its liabilities as they become due. A firm ceases to be a going concern when it is put into liquidation.

Although most businesses in a healthy economy are going concerns, the assumption that a particular business is a going concern should not be made lightly and without proper enquiry. Failure to spot that the business is not a going concern, or that its future as a going concern is in serious doubt, can vitiate the results of a valuation. As has been shown in the previous section, the alternative to going concern value, namely, liquidation value, generally produces a much lower value since it is calculated on the footing that the business ceases to be an entity as such and becomes merely an assortment of assets to be realised piecemeal.

Occasions sometimes arise when a company which is manifestly a going concern has to be valued as though it were not a going concern. In other words, it has to be valued as a break-up. The valuer must be alert to the circumstances in which this applies. The existence of an unusual capital structure is one such circumstance. For example, XYZ Ltd is a private company engaged in the manufacture of soft drinks dispensers. Its share capital consists of 1,000 ordinary shares of £1 each held by Mr and Mrs Smith. It is a profitable, well run business whose value has been assessed for the purposes of a sale of the entire company at £600,000 based on the likely future profits. Its balance sheets shows the following capital structure:

	£000's	£000's
Share capital		1
Reserves		124
		125
Unsecured loan — Mr Smith		400
		525
Fixed assets		350
Current assets	675	
Less current liabilities		
(including bank overdraft of £250,000)	500	
Net current assets		175
		525

Mr Smith's loan dates from the sale of his unincorporated business to the company. No interest is charged on the loan and it is technically payable on demand. The fixed assets consist mainly of specialised plant and equipment. The factory is rented.

If Mr Smith were to call in his loan, the company would probably have to go into liquidation. It would not be in Mr Smith's interests to take this course since he would thereby be jeopardising his own equity investment. From a common sense point of view, therefore, this loan is *de facto* equity. However, once the shares change hands and Mr and Mrs Smith cease to be the owners of the company, there is no reason why they should not demand repayment of the loan. Unless the buyer can find another £400,000 to repay the loan, in which event the cost of his investment will have risen to £1 million, the threat of liquidation must hang over the business. Therefore, the going concern value of £600,000 for 100% of the equity can be put forward only on the assumption that Mr Smith agrees to waive his loan, or that it is first capitalised by the issue to him of more ordinary shares. In the unlikely event that Mr Smith did not appreciate this point and was unwilling to waive the loan, the shares should not be valued on a going concern basis. It must be assumed that the loan is called in, and that the company is forced into liquidation. In the absence of the appropriate undertakings from Mr Smith it would be foolhardy for anyone to buy the shares on any other basis.

Another instance where the going concern basis may not be appropriate despite appearances to the contrary is afforded by the smaller firm whose business depends almost exclusively on one, or perhaps a few, key individuals. Mr Robinson is a controlling shareholder in, and director of, ABC Ltd, a company with 15 employees. The firm operates as a sub-contractor in the building industry. Its customer, which accounts for approximately 85% of turnover, is a well-known construction company. All the employees with the exception of Mrs Robinson, who works as secretary-cum-administrative assistant, work on site. Mr Robinson does all the estimating, surveying, ordering, invoicing and supervision himself. Over the years Mr Robinson has cultivated excellent personal relations with his main customer who is highly satisfied with the service provided. ABC Ltd is a highly profitable company and has a healthy cash flow and a debt-free balance sheet. Mr Robinson, who is aged 50 years, wants to sell up and devote himself exclusively to his hobby of finding and restoring wooden clocks. He intends to spend much of his time abroad and may even emigrate. He asks you for a valuation of his shares.

If Mr Robinson were to leave the company it is unlikely that the business could survive. None of the employees is qualified to replace him, and the personal link with the principal customer would be severed. Because of his versatility, engineering flair and management expertise only a person of high calibre could replace him. Such a person would not be interested in a salaried position in a business with no administrative structure, poor offices and run on a shoe string. The value of the business as a going concern would be relevant only on the assumption that Mr Robinson entered into a service agreement to remain with the company for as long as is necessary for the new owner or his appointee to forge the necessary links with the main customer and the employees. Even this might not be enough in view of the firm's dependence on its major customer. Some undertaking from the customer would probably be required.

Firms with characteristics similar to those of ABC Ltd would usually be valued on the going concern basis but with the appropriate caveat or qualification. It is interesting to note, however, that the statutory valuation hypothesis for fiscal purposes does not require, or indeed permit, the valuer to assume that key individuals or major customers will give the necessary undertakings. This can produce a very different valuation for fiscal purposes. This important point is discussed fully in Chapter 16.

Intrinsic value

This term means different things to different people. Lorie and Hamilton define the intrinsic value of an asset as 'the value that asset *ought* to have as judged by an investor. Discrepancies between current value and intrinsic value are often the basis of decisions to buy or sell the asset.'[7] A more recent definition, also culled from the literature on stockmarket efficiency, has a different emphasis. Keane defines the intrinsic worth of a share as 'the best estimate of a security's value in relation to the total set of information available'.[8] Gole's definition is different again: 'This concept of value is one which is not related to market forces, use value or any of the other considerations of value. It is a value which is justified by the facts which are associated with the thing being valued. It may be described as "true value" inherent in the object of the valuation. This may not be a reflection of current market price or realisable value but is rather an assessment of value computed on true worth irrespective of any other consideration. Intrinsic values change less frequently as a rule than market values.'[9]

[7] James H. Lorie and Mary T. Hamilton, *The Stock Market: Theories and Evidence* (Homewood, Ill.: Irwin, 1973), p. 271.
[8] Simon N. Keane, *Stockmarket Efficiency; Theory, Evidence and Implications* (Oxford: Philip Allan, 1983), p. 170.
[9] V. L. Gole, *Valuation of Businesses, Shares and Property* (Melbourne: Butterworths, 1980), p. 4.

Lorie and Hamilton's definition is quite clear although it appears to be a misuse of the word 'intrinsic'. This word implies something inherent and immutable, but it is difficult to imagine anything less inherent and more variable than the values different investors think a security ought to have. As discrepancies between current value and this so-called intrinsic value are presumed to be the basis of the buy/sell decision, it would be more accurate to call this type of value 'estimated future market value'. It cannot properly be termed intrinsic value.

Keane's definition is imprecise since it begs the question of how we can recognise the best estimate of a security's value when we see it. It clearly is not meant to be the estimate of any one individual, but rather that price of a share which 'fully reflects all the risks associated with the company's future' and whose 'expected return (the average of all possible returns) is commensurate with those risks'.[10] Markets are efficient, he asserts, where the market price of a share represents its intrinsic worth. But how can we know for certain whether a share's price fully reflects all the risks involved? Does not each investor have his own different perception of these risks? And how do we assess whether the expected return, itself almost impossible to quantify precisely, is commensurate with those risks? Keane admits that intrinsic worth is not directly observable but claims that it can be verified retrospectively, 'although, even then, it can never be very specific about individual prices.' It is perhaps a little unfair to criticise Keane's concept of intrinsic worth outside a discussion of the efficient market hypothesis.[11] Whatever the merits of his value concept, however, the use of the word 'intrinsic' to describe it is inaccurate and misleading.

While the definitions given by Lorie and Hamilton and Keane relate to apparently valid concepts — the adjective 'intrinsic' being merely inappropriate to describe them — the same cannot be said of Gole's definition. He uses the word 'intrinsic' in its proper meaning as something 'inherent in the object of the valuation'. But if it 'is not related to market forces, use value or any other considerations of value,' is it real and how may we recognize and measure it? Gole's answer to this is that intrinsic value 'is rather an assessment of value computed on true worth irrespective of any other considerations'. But this is no help at all without a definition of 'true worth'. In fact, as true worth and intrinsic value are virtually synonymous, intrinsic value has merely been defined in terms of itself. Gole's definition, therefore, has no substance; it leaves one with the impression that his 'intrinsic value' is

---

[10] Keane, *Stockmarket Efficiency: Theory, Evidence and Implications*, p. 20.
[11] This can be found in Chapter 6.

merely his own or the valuer's subjective assessment of the value of property in disregard of owner value or market value.

It must be admitted that at times the market valuation of property can appear either too high or too low. For example, the stock market collapse of 1974/75 drove share prices down to levels which, with the benefit of hindsight, reflected almost a loss of faith in the future. The very low earnings multiples, double-digit yields, and savage discounts to net assets had no precedent in post-war stockmarket history. Nevertheless, share prices at that time represented the current market value. At such times it may be tempting to draw a distinction between market value and what the shares are 'really' worth, i.e., what the valuer thinks they ought to be worth. If the valuer yields to this temptation and allows his own personal assessment to override the evidence of the market place, he is in effect usurping the role of the investment analyst/adviser. The latter may quite properly conclude that shares are 'under-valued' at their current prices and accordingly recommend their purchase. But the word 'under-valued' is the jargon of the trade and is merely an elliptical way of stating that, in the analyst's view, the market value of the shares will rise at some time in the future enabling a profit to be made if the shares are bought now.

The analyst may take this view for a variety of reasons. He may have relevant information which he believes is not widely available or has not been fully appreciated, or he may be basing his assessment on a change which he foresees in the mood of the market and the attitude to this type of company. This is properly his function — to seek out investment opportunities. The valuer, however, is not concerned with what market values may be at some indeterminate period in the future; he has generally to give his opinion as to the current market value. He must accept the primacy of the market place and the evidence of current market value. When ascertaining market value his concern with the future is confined to establishing the relationship between perceived prospects and current values; it is not part of his function to pass judgement on the market.

There is no such thing, therefore, as intrinsic value. The notion that property rights could have an intrinsic value is inimical to the very nature of value and valuation. The definitions of intrinsic value cited here show all too clearly that the term is used to invest partial, subjective assessments of value with an objectivity they do not possess.

Conclusion

This chapter examined the three main value concepts encountered in share valuation, namely, owner value, market value and fair value.

Owner value is fundamentally important because it determines price in negotiated private treaty deals such as usually occur when shares in unquoted companies change hands. Owner value must be distinguished from owner's valuation or the notion of interior value used in chapter 1. What is sought is a reasonable or justified value — the amount at which the present or prospective owner as a wise businessman should value the property.

Owner value is equivalent to deprival value and is measured by the adverse consequences, both direct and indirect, which would affect the owner if he were deprived of the property. Owner value is not necessarily measured by market value and commonplace examples of this were given in the text.

The basis of market value is the assumption that if comparable property fetches a certain price, then the subject property will realise the same price or something near to it. It implies that the property can be sold at or near the price without undue delay. This bare definition of market value was then amplified by consideration of various practical points which arise when assessing it. These include the effect of the special purchaser and the forced seller, the distinction between consideration in cash or on deferred terms, and the treatment of expenses of sale.

The fair value concept is more a legal than an economic concept of value although it has no definition in law. It is the value concept usually stipulated in the articles of association of private companies. Its essence is the desire to be equitable to both parties. It recognises that the transaction is not in the open market and that buyer and seller have been brought together by the operation of a legally binding agreement in a way which excludes other potential buyers and sellers. The fair value should, therefore, take into account what the seller gives up in value and what the buyer acquires in value through the transaction. There are no hard-and-fast rules, however, and the valuer has considerable discretion in the matter. Fair value is also discussed in Chapter 15.

The rest of the chapter looked at the meaning and relevance of various quasi-concepts of value, namely, investment value, liquidation value and going concern value. These terms refer to valuations based on a particular assumption and are not value concepts as such. Liquidation value is generally thought to set the lower limit to a share's value, and the difference between going concern value and liquidation value is sometimes seen as a measure of risk. These notions were shown to be incorrect.

Where a company is overly dependent on one or two employees, suppliers or customers, the going concern valuation assumption may not be justified even though the company is financially sound and highly profitable. This is an important point in commercial, legal and fiscal valuation work and the valuer must be aware of the circumstances giving rise to this situation.

The chapter ended with some brief comments on the meaninglessness of the term 'intrinsic value' when applied to share values.

3

The legal framework

Introduction

Valuation procedure is essentially a bringing together of the economic concept of value and the legal concept of property.[1] In the preceding chapters the nature of value and the various value concepts have been examined in some detail. It is now time to consider the legal framework and its relevance to valuation.

When we talk of the value of anything, be it a house, motor car or a piece of furniture, what we really mean is the value of the property rights in that object. Strictly speaking, it is the property right in the motor car, and not the car itself, which has a value. Of course, as that property right is usually absolute we refer elliptically to the value of the car. With most goods and chattels the property rights, consisting of absolute ownership and enjoyment, require little or no attention, and the valuer is concerned primarily with their physical condition and fitness. However, if the ownership interest is not absolute the property rights have to be carefully examined. For example, the existence of a hire purchase agreement would affect the value of a second hand car if the finance company had the right to repossess it for non-payment of instalments. The valuer would have to examine the terms of the agreement, ascertain the extent of the finance company's interest, and gauge its effect on the value.

In the same way, the freehold of an office property would normally have a much higher value on a vacant possession basis than it would if it were subject to a lease with 21 years to run at rentals well below current market levels. This is because with vacant possession the property can be let at current market rentals, whereas with the 21-year lease the freeholder's return over the next 21 years is limited to the rent provided by the lease, and this is less than the current market rent. In all types of property, therefore, the nature and extent of the ownership interest is of fundamental importance. The fact that a share in a limited company is purely a creation of the law renders the legal considerations doubly important.

English company law is contained in the various Companies Acts, now consolidated into the Companies Act 1985. Behind this there is a

[1] Henry A. Babcock, *Appraisal Principles and Procedures* (Homewood, Ill.: Irwin, 1968), p. 25.

vast case law which has formulated most of the basic principles applicable to companies. The topic is beyond the scope of a single book let alone a chapter in this present study. All that can be presented here is a brief discussion of those aspects of company law which are of particular significance to share valuation. These are: the limited company, the memorandum and articles of association, the distinction between public and private companies, the division of powers between the shareholders and the directors, the legal nature of a share, different classes of security, the purchase by a company of its own shares, and the effect of size on a shareholding. The chapter ends with a review of future developments in company law.

The limited company

The joint stock company with limited liability was not suddenly invented but came about through a gradual and sometimes difficult evolution spanning over 150 years. It represents one of the most important contributions by the law to economic progress. By divorcing ownership from management, by investing the company with a separate legal personality and by placing a limit on the liability of the members, the framework has been created within which the factors of production can unite in the ever larger combinations required by industrialisation and the advance of technology.

What then is a company? According to Gower the word implies an association of a number of persons for a common object, that object normally being the economic gain of its members.[2] As he points out, this definition will certainly fit many of the smaller private companies which are quasi-partnerships and which may well have been partnerships prior to incorporation. Such a company could properly be described as an association of a number of persons for a common object of mutual profit. But the description would not fit the sole trader who converts his business into a company. Although he must initially bring in at least one other person, that person need have no beneficial interest in the business and need take no part in running it. The business is, in effect, a one man company and the association of a number of persons is a legal fiction.

The large public company fits this description least of all. The typical shareholder in Unilever, ICI or GEC does not regard himself as associated with his fellow shareholders in running the business. The

[2] L. C. B. Gower, *Gower's Principles of Modern Company Law*, 4th ed. (London: Stevens & Sons, 1979), p. 9. Professor Gower's book has been the source of much of this and the succeeding chapter. Also of considerable help has been A. L. Chapman and R. M. Ballard, eds., *Tolley's Company Law*, (Croydon: Tolley Publishing Co., 1983).

running of the business is left to the directors and professional managers. The shareholder, although in law a member of the company, is at best a supplier of risk capital on which he hopes for a return. Even this degree of involvement overstates the position since most shareholders would have acquired their shares in the secondary market, and apart from the occasional rights issue, will never have supplied any funds to their company. Government statistics show, in fact, that only a very small proportion of companies' cash requirements comes from the shareholder; most of it comes from retained profits and bank and other borrowings. The modern shareholder in the public quoted company is an investor with a clinically detached view of his investment and no particular commitment to the company. More often than not, the money represented by his investment has gone not to the company but to the previous holder of the shares.

Gower divides companies into three functional categories:

(a) Companies formed for purposes other than the profit of their members, i.e., those formed for social, charitable or quasi-charitable purposes. In this case, incorporation is merely a modern and convenient substitute for the trust.
(b) Companies formed to enable a single trader or a small body of partners to carry on a business. In these companies, incorporation is a device for personifying the business and divorcing its liability from that of its members despite the fact that its members retain control and share the profits.
(c) Companies formed in order to enable the investing public to share in the profits of an enterprise without taking any part in its management.

Despite Gower's three categories the Companies Acts provide for only the company limited by shares. Since the passing of the Companies Act 1980, it has no longer been possible to form a company limited by guarantee. Pre-existing companies limited by guarantee are unaffected.

Category (c) includes most quoted companies and a number of large unquoted ones. It is by far the most important economically. Numerically, however, they are dwarfed by the companies in category (b) — these are the type of company the share valuer is most likely to encounter.

The distinction in the Companies Acts between a public and a private company is a recognition that some of the safeguards required to protect the investing public as regards the companies in category (c), would be inappropriate for the smaller business typical of category (b).

Smaller concerns usually wish to restrict membership of the company to preserve its family or partnership characteristics and, until the passing of the Companies Act 1980, the ability to do this was one of the distinguishing features of the private company.

While Gower's three functional categories are very useful, it is important to realise that there is a considerable overlap between categories (b) and (c). Many small- to medium-sized companies have investor shareholders, i.e., members of the company who do not work in the business. Such persons usually obtained their shares by inheritance or gift. It also happens from time to time that a shareholder director falls out with his colleagues, resigns from the board and becomes an investor shareholder. Company law does not draw a distinction between the working shareholder and the investor shareholder, yet the tensions and conflicts of interest which the existence of these two types of shareholder in the one company can create, is probably the greatest single cause of dispute and inequity between shareholders in private companies.

A company registered under the Companies Acts is an incorporated body. The separate legal personality of the company, which was established in the leading case of *Salomon* v. *Salomon & Co Ltd* (1897) AC 22, is its most important attribute and the determinant of most of its characteristics. By virtue of its separate legal personality a company is distinct from its shareholders and exists independently of them: 'the company is at law a different person altogether from the subscribers . . . ; and although it may be that after incorporation the business is precisely the same as it was before, and the same persons are managers, and the same hands receive the profits, the company is not in law the agent of the subscribers or trustees for them.'[3]

As a separate legal personality, a company is liable for its own debts and the members are completely free from any personal liability. The limited liability of the company refers of course not to the company's own liability for its debts — this is absolute and total — but to the fact that the members' liability to contribute to the company is limited to the amount unpaid on their shares. Where the shares are fully paid up, as is almost invariably the case these days, the members have no further liability. The only statutory exception to the rule that a member, as such, is not liable for the debts of the company is provided by s.24 of the Companies Act 1985 (hereinafter 'the 1985 Act'). Under this section, a member may incur unlimited liability if the number of members falls below the legal minimum (now two) for over six months.

[3] Per Lord Macnaghten in *Salomon* v. *Salomon*, supra.

Because of the company's separate legal personality the members have no direct proprietary interest in the company's assets, but have an indirect claim through their shares. 'Shareholders are not, in the eye of the law, part owners of the undertaking. The undertaking is something different from the totality of the shareholding.'[4] As we shall see later, this is one of the most important attributes of the limited company from the valuation viewpoint. Ignorance or disregard of this fundamental legal characteristic of shares in a company is evident in much of the thinking of modern financial and investment theory, and serious misconceptions have arisen as a consequence.

Unlike a partnership, members of the company may come and go but the company continues; it has perpetual succession. This is a great advantage as far as the prosperity and continuity of the company's business is concerned. However, it means that in a quasi-partnership type of company the *de facto* partner, if a minority shareholder, may well have to withdraw on terms much less favourable than if the business were in law a partnership. It should not be forgotten that perpetual succession is a term which applies only to the company; there is nothing perpetual about the company's business!

Perpetual succession is achieved in practice by the creation of transferable shares. These shares constitute a separate form of intangible property which is transferable in such a way that the transferor drops out and the transferee steps into his shoes. Thus, the new member assumes the obligations and duties as well as the rights of the old member. This is in marked contrast to the concept of partnership, where a partner can assign his beneficial interest but not his duties and obligations as a partner. The assignee merely has the right to receive the assigning partner's share; the assignor remains liable for the debts and obligations of the partnership. Transferability of shares is an important attribute of a limited company and, as will be seen later, the different degrees of transferability can have a significant bearing on a share's value.

A limited company may be restricted by its statutes from carrying out certain activities, and any transactions beyond its capacity may be ineffective. This is known as the *ultra vires* rule. The reasons for this rule are rooted in early corporate history in the need to protect creditors and shareholders. To limit, say, a railway company to investment in railway undertakings provided some assurance to interested parties that their money was being used for the purpose they intended. Today, however, the objects clause of the memorandum of association is usually framed in such wide and general terms as to allow the company

[4] Per Sir Raymond Evershed, L. J. in *Short* v. *Treasury Commissioners* [1948] 1 KB 116.

to undertake almost any lawful activity, and it now requires only a special resolution to change the memorandum. Although the *ultra vires* doctrine is still very much a distinguishing mark of the limited company — the *ultra vires* doctrine, for example, does not apply to partnerships — it is most unlikely ever to hold any significance for valuation.

The memorandum and articles of association

As the limited company is an artificial person it must act through human agency, namely, the officers of the company and the shareholders in general meeting. It, therefore, needs a basic constitution plus a set of rules to govern its internal affairs. The former is provided by the memorandum of association and the latter by the articles of association. The memorandum needs only state the company's name, its objects, domicile, authorised share capital, the fact of limited liability, and (where applicable) that it is a public company. Were it not for the need to draft the objects clause so as to include every activity that the modern business enterprise would conceivably engage in, this 'constitution' could take up no more space than a post card. The articles of association have two primary functions: first, they relate the shareholders to the company and determine the rights that exist between themselves; and second, they constitute the basic rules covering the conduct of the directors. As the requirements for changing the memorandum are virtually the same as for changing the articles, the distinction between the two documents is increasingly difficult to justify.

Under s.14 of the 1985 Act the memorandum and articles 'bind the company and the members thereof to the same extent as if they respectively had been signed and sealed by each member, and contained covenants on the part of each member to observe' all their provisions. The implications of this are as follows:

(a) They constitute a contract between the company and each member, subject, however, to the provisions of the Companies Acts. A company is therefore obliged to its members to comply with the terms of its articles of association. Conversely, a company can enforce the articles against the members.
(b) The contract under s.14 is enforceable among the members *inter se*. For example, one member may institute proceedings against another member to enforce pre-emption rights on the sale of shares.
(c) The memorandum and articles operate as a contract only in so far as they confer rights and obligations on the member in his capacity as member. Thus, in *Beattie* v. *Beattie* [1938] Ch 708, the articles

referring a dispute between the company and the member to arbitration was held not to be an agreement to submit a dispute to arbitration, because the dispute involved the company and the member in his capacity as director and not as member.

Although the articles of association are a form of contract, there are important differences between this type of contract and the contract that is commonly encountered. First, the articles can be altered by a special resolution of the company in general meeting. This requires a three-fourths majority. A member of the company, and hence a party to the contract embodied in the articles, may, nevertheless, have to submit to the change in the terms of the contract against his will. Second, there is conflicting judicial authority whether one member may enforce the articles against another member only through the company, or whether he may sue the other member directly. Where personal rights are concerned, such as where the articles confer pre-emption rights on the sale of shares, it appears that the aggrieved member may enforce the articles directly against another member.[5] In other circumstances, however, it appears that a member cannot enforce the articles of association against another member except through the company.[6] In practice, this may be a difficult and costly thing to do.

Third, the normal remedies for breach of contract may not be available. The remedies of a member against the company seem to be restricted to actions for an injunction or declaration or for a liquidated sum due to him as a member (e.g., unpaid dividends); damages for breach of contract are probably not recoverable from the company. Against another member, however, all the normal contractual remedies including damages should be available. Fourth, the contract in the articles is subject to the provisions of the 1985 Act. Articles which provide that a director can be removed only by a special resolution would therefore be invalid.[7]

Table A is a model form of articles of association for a limited company. Under s.8 of the 1985 Act these articles will apply to all companies to the extent that they are not excluded or modified by the articles of the company. Companies registered before the passing of the 1985 Act are subject to the 'Table A' articles of the Act under which they were registered (to the extent, of course, that their own articles do not specifically exclude them).

[5] *Rayfield* v. *Hands* [1960] Ch 1.
[6] *Welton* v. *Saffrey* [1897] AC 299.
[7] Section 303(1) of the 1985 Act.

The distinction between a public and a private company

Section 1 of the 1985 Act defines a public company as one whose memorandum states that it is to be a public company and which has registered itself as such. Any other limited company is a private company. Prior to the 1980 Act, the public company was defined by exclusion; it was any company which did not satisfy the definition of a private company contained in s.28 of the 1948 Act. A public company's name must end with the words 'public limited company', usually abbreviated to 'plc',[8] and its issued share capital must be at least £50,000 — an amount which can be varied by statutory instrument.

The main difference between a public and a private company is that the former may issue securities to the public and the latter may not.[9] In return for this privilege public companies are subject to more stringent controls than private companies, particularly as regards the raising and maintenance of capital and the payment of dividends. In practice, there is usually another important distinction. The private company's articles almost invariably contain restrictions on the transfer of shares. These are designed to ensure that the shares continue to be held by the family, friends and associates or other approved persons. A public company's articles are unlikely to have any share transfer restrictions, and if the company is quoted the Stock Exchange's listing agreement insists that there be no restrictions. It should be remembered, however, that since the passing of the Companies Act 1980 there has not been any legal requirement for private companies to impose restrictions on the transfer of their shares. Similarly, there is nothing in the legal definition of a public company which prevents it from placing restrictions on share transfers.

The choice of public or private company would depend to a large extent on the economic function or purpose of the business undertaking. Private company status would be more appropriate for the sole trader, partnership and smaller business. For the larger undertaking which may wish to raise finance in the capital market public company status would be called for.

Division of power between the shareholders and the directors

The shareholders in general meeting exercise ultimate control over the company and, subject to obvious exceptions, anything resolved upon

---

[8] A company whose registered office is in Wales uses the Welsh equivalent, 'cwmni cyfyngedig cyhoeddus' or c.c.c for short.

[9] Section 81 of the 1985 Act.

by a bare majority of those voting at a meeting binds the company and all the members of it. The ordinary business of the annual general meeting usually consists of the declaration of a dividend, consideration of the annual report and accounts, election of directors in place of those retiring, and the appointment and remuneration of the auditors.

The directors are appointed by the shareholders, to whom they must present an account of their stewardship. If the shareholders so resolve, they can remove the directors. This suggests that the shareholder is all-powerful and the directors are mere appointees to do his bidding. This may well be the reality where there is a controlling shareholder, as he can pass an ordinary resolution and dictate the composition of the board. But where the company's shares are widely held, as they are for most quoted companies, it is rarely so.

In this country most large firms in the private sector are quoted companies and the economic power they represent is firmly in the hands of the directors and senior managers. It rarely filters through to the shareholders. The sovereignty of the shareholder in law is not reflected in economic reality. This probably is of no great concern to the typical shareholder in the quoted company. He is an investor first and foremost, and is unlikely to have any feelings of membership towards his fellow shareholders or the company. His loyalty is fickle and, if the opportunity of a higher rate of return presents itself elsewhere, he would be expected to avail himself of it. Perversely, it is this prospect which often represents the most effective use of the shareholder's position — his ability to 'vote with his feet' and influence the price of the shares in the market.

By contrast, the shareholder in the typical unquoted company is not generally able to dispose of his shares quickly and efficiently. His relationship to the company and to his fellow shareholders is accordingly closer to the legal theory. For him, the division of power between the general meeting and the directors is of direct concern and often is a signficant influence on the value of his shares. The legal position as to the division of powers in the company between the general meeting and the directors is, for him, of great relevance.

The articles of the company invariably vest management of the business in the hands of the directors. Table A gives the directors the right to 'exercise all the powers of the company' subject to the provisions of the Acts, the memorandum and articles and any direction given by special resolution.[10] Under such a formula, the general meeting cannot interfere with a decision of the directors unless the directors are acting contrary to the provision of the Acts or the articles. In *Shaw*

[10] Article 70.

& Sons (Salford) Limited v. *Shaw* [1935] 2 KB 113, the court held to be a nullity a resolution of the general meeting disapproving the commencement of an action by the directors. In the words of Greer L.J.:

> A company is an entity distinct alike from it shareholders and directors. Some of its powers may, according to its articles, be exercised by directors, certain other powers may be reserved for the shareholders in general meeting. If powers of management are vested in the directors, they and they alone can exercise those powers. The only way in which the general body of the shareholders can control the exercise of the powers vested by the articles in the directors is by altering their articles, or, if opportunity arises under the articles, by refusing to re-elect the directors of whose actions they disapprove. They cannot themselves usurp the powers which by the articles are vested in the directors anymore than the directors can use the powers vested by the articles in the general body of shareholders.

A member holding 51% or more of the voting capital can secure the removal of a director by an ordinary resolution,[11] and thereby ensure the appointment of someone more compliant with his wishes. This is an extremely effective sanction and gives the majority shareholder direct access to the powers of the board. But the individual minority shareholder — a category which includes most investors — is very much in the hands of the directors. It is often extremely difficult in practice for the isolated minority shareholder to muster the necessary support to pass an ordinary resolution, and the system of proxy voting gives the directors a powerful advantage. In the vital matter of dividends where the general meeting usually has some control, the directors often have the upper hand in reality. Article 102 of Table A, for example, provides that the company in general meeting may declare dividends, 'but no dividend shall exceed the amount recommended by the directors'. Table A empowers the directors to pay interim dividends. In this commonly adopted regulation the company in general meeting has only negative powers as regards dividends. It can refuse to sanction the amount recommended by the board — an unlikely course in practice — but it cannot increase it. Dividend policy is therefore firmly in the hands of the directors.

The traditional view that the general meeting was the company and the directors were merely the agents of the company, subject to the

---

[11] Section 303 of the 1985 Act.

control of the company in general meeting, has been considerably modified over the years. The modern view seems to be that 'the directors and members in general meeting are primary organs of the company between whom the company's powers are divided. The general meeting retains ultimate control but only through its powers to amend the Articles (so as to take away, for the future, certain powers from the directors) and to remove the directors and to substitute others more to its taste. Until it takes one or other of these steps the directors can, if they are so advised, disregard the wishes and instructions of the members in all matters not specifically reserved (either by the Act or the Articles) to a general meeting. The old idea that the general meeting alone is the company's primary organ and the directors are merely the company's agents or servants, at all times subservient to the general meeting, seems no longer to be the law as it is certainly not the fact.[12]

The legal nature of a share

There is no statutory definition of the nature of a share[13] and it has fallen to the courts in various cases over the years to define this. Perhaps the most recent definition of the term was that given by the House of Lords in *Prudential* v. *Newman Industries (No 2)* [1982] 1 All ER 354: ' . . . shares are merely a right of participation in the company on the terms of the Articles of Association'. The nature of the contract contained in the articles of association has already been discussed. It is a curious, atypical contract in that a member is bound by any subsequent changes in the contract irrespective of whether he voted for the changes and to a great extent regardless of their effect on him. It is true that the law provides certain significant safeguards against the unfair treatment of a minority — a topic discussed in some detail in Chapter 4 — and that it imposes restrictions on the variations of class rights.[14] But this still leaves open the possibility of numerous adverse changes in the articles.

In addition, the shareholder's ability to enforce this 'contract' is circumscribed in that he can only enforce it insofar as it affects his personal rights and obligations as a member. Thus, in the *Prudential* case it was held that a personal claim by a shareholder against a wrongdoer, whose action had diminished the profits of the company, was misconceived because the shareholder's right to participate in the

---

[12] Gower, p.152.
[13] The definition of the term 'share' given in s.744 of the 1985 Act, i.e., 'share means a share in the share capital of a company', says nothing about the nature of a share.
[14] Sections 125 and 127 of the 1985 Act.

company was not directly affected by the wrongdoing. In that case, the court was reluctant to extend further the exceptions to the rule in *Foss* v. *Harbottle* (1843) 2 Hare 461. This rule states that where a duty is owed to the company, as it often is where the directors' conduct is concerned, it is for the company to bring an action, not the individual shareholder. As it normally lies with the directors to bring an action in the name of the company, the remedy for a breach may be in the hands of the persons responsible for it.

For these reasons the contract contained in the articles of association is much weaker than it might appear at first sight. It is, nonetheless, one of the original incidents of a share and no share valuation should ever be carried out without a study of the company's articles and careful consideration of the relevant clauses. But, it may be argued, investors in quoted companies never concern themselves with the articles of association. In fact, many of them would probably be unaware of their very existence let alone their legal significance. Why this preoccupation with a legalism?

There are very good reasons why a stock market investor can afford to ignore the articles. First, quoted companies' articles of association have to conform to Stock Exchange requirements, notably on the removal of restrictions on transfer. Second, the listing agreement itself provides many safeguards for the investor which are not available in company law, and it imposes a greater degree of disclosure. Third, the City Code on Takeovers and Mergers has proved very effective in enforcing a standard of conduct in take-overs and mergers, one of the principal benefits of which is to ensure that the premium for control is available to all the shareholders. Fourth, quoted companies are subject to very close scrutiny, and oddities in the articles, such as unusual voting rights for a particular class of share, are spotted immediately and are reflected in the share price. Finally, the stock market investor is not a valuer of shares. The market value of the quoted share is to all intents and purposes its current market price and it already reflects the rights and obligations of the member under the articles.

The private company shareholder has none of the benefits of greater disclosure, public scrutiny, investment regulation and the ready market for his shares available to the Stock Exchange investor. If dissatisfied with his investment he will not be able to dispose of it quickly and efficiently. He must, therefore, look very closely at the rights and obligations, in particular at the rights attaching to his shares, the restrictions on transfer and the powers of the directors. It would generally be necessary to scan the articles in their entirety and to examine closely those regulations which are relevant to the shares being valued.

It is sometimes as important to appreciate what a share is not as to understand what it is. A share is not in law a proportionate share in the assets and profits of the company. For example, a holder of five per cent of the equity capital does not own, nor is he entitled, except on a winding-up, to five per cent of the assets and profits of the company. He has no beneficial interest in the assets of the company. 'Shareholders are not in the eye of the law, part owners of the undertaking. The undertaking is something different from the totality of the shareholding.'[15] Does this legal principle that shareholders are not part owners of the undertaking accord with the economic reality? The *Short* case throws some interesting light on this.

The whole of the shares in Short Brothers were being acquired by the Treasury under a Defence Regulation and were valued for compensation purposes at their quoted market price. But the shareholders argued that since all the shares were being acquired, compensation should be set at the value per share of the undertaking as a whole or the price per share which a single buyer would pay to acquire all the shares. The court rejected this argument on the grounds that the shareholders were not part owners of the undertaking and because the Defence Regulations implied that each holding was to be valued separately. The court conceded, however, that a controlling shareholder might have been entitled to a higher price than that arrived at by multiplying the number of shares held by the quoted market price per share, since he would then be selling an item of property — control — additional to his shares.

The court did not elaborate on this higher price which a controlling shareholder might receive, and its use of the word 'might' indicates some uncertainty as to whether the controlling shareholder would in fact be entitled to a higher price. But there can be little doubt that such a higher price would be determined by reference to the value of the undertaking as a whole, and even less doubt that the controlling shareholder would be entitled to it. However, if the controlling shareholding is valued as a *pro rata* share of the value of the whole undertaking, is not the controlling shareholder part owner of the undertaking? The court in the *Short* case managed to side-step this highly inconvenient conclusion by claiming that the controlling shareholder was selling not only his shares but an additional item of property — control. But can control be considered as an item of property additional to, and therefore separate from, the shares?

The power of control arises from the voting rights attaching to shares. It is as much an attribute of the shares as the rights to receive

---

[15] Per Sir Raymond Evershed L.J. in *Short* v. *Treasury Commissioners*, supra.

dividends. It can no more be sold separately from the shares than can the dividend entitlement. Whatever the court's view of control as an item of property and something additional to the shares, for valuation purposes at least, it is clear that the nature of a share in this vital respect changes with the size of the shareholding.

The position seems to be as follows. The legal doctrine that the shareholder is not a part owner of the undertaking is certainly consistent with the economic reality as far as a share taken in isolation is concerned. For a small minority shareholding, such as is likely to be held by most stockmarket investors, this legal doctrine is still valid. However, it becomes increasingly difficult to maintain when a shareholding rises above 25% and commands significant negative voting powers. It becomes something of a gamble as the size of the shareholding approaches 50% and it seems futile with regard to a shareholding constituting a bare majority. It breaks down completely with a shareholding commanding 75% or more of the votes and with that the ability to reach the assets.

This analysis is highly significant for the valuer. The legal nature of a share affects the nature of the investment and it is important in determining the appropriate valuation basis. Even for the minority shareholder the share is more than just a right to participate in the company on the terms of the articles. It is an object of property giving a shareholder a proprietary interest in the company as distinct from its assets; he has rights both in and against the company. The majority shareholder has all this and in addition can be considered for practical purposes as a part owner of the undertaking.

Classes of security

The securities of a company can be conveniently classified into three categories, namely, ordinary shares, preference shares and debentures. Within each category there exist different types, such as voting and non-voting ordinary shares, cumulative and non-cumulative preference shares, and secured and unsecured debentures or loan capital. In addition, there may be an overlap between the categories. Participating preference shares, for example, may have certain equity characteristics, and convertible loan stocks are a cross between loan capital and equity. Nevertheless, these three categories are broadly recognisable in law and in practice.

Ordinary shares

If a company's shares are all of one class, then these are necessarily ordinary shares. Ordinary shares constitute the residuary class in which everything is vested after the special rights of other classes, if any, have been satisfied. Ordinary shares bear the highest risk and have the greatest potential for reward. They are generally referred to as the equity. Ordinary shares usually carry votes but not invariably so. It is not voting rights *per se* which are the hallmark of equity, but the entitlement to the residue of profit and any surplus in liquidation.

As mentioned above, the dividing line between the different classes of securities cannot be drawn with precision since it all depends on the terms of issue. Thus, preferred ordinary shares may be created. These usually enjoy some degree of preference over the ordinary shares in the matter of dividends, or return of capital, or both. Conversely, rights to participation may be deferred until some future date or until the other ordinary shares have received a certain return. Such shares are usually terms 'deferred' or 'founders' shares.

Preference shares

The typical preference share carries the right to a fixed preferential dividend and to priority over the ordinary shares as to the return of capital in a winding up. As a general rule, the preference shareholder is not entitled to participate further in the profits of the company or in any surplus in a liquidation. As with ordinary shares, however, the company has complete freedom within the bounds set by the memorandum and articles to create preference shares with whatever rights it wishes.

Preference shares are often expressed to be cumulative so that any arrears of dividend have to be paid before any ordinary dividend can be declared. Some companies issue participating preference shares with rights to participate in profits in addition to their preferential dividend. Not infrequently the articles confer voting rights on the preference shares in limited circumstances as, for example, when the preference dividend falls into arrears. Unfortunately, the rights attaching to preference shares are occasionally drafted imprecisely leaving it unclear as to the nature and extent of the preference enjoyed. Accordingly, the courts have had to formulate rules for the proper construction of the terms of issue when these are unclear. The main rules appear to be as follows:

(a) In the absence of express provision to the contrary, all shares rank equally.
(b) If shares are divided into separate classes, it is a question of construction in each case what the rights of each class are. (Shares may be divided into separate classes but nevertheless have equal rights. Ordinary shares, for example, may be classified as 'A', 'B'

and 'C' to distinguish the person or class of persons permitted to hold them.)

(c) If nothing is expressly said about the rights of one class in respect of either dividend, return of capital or votes, that class has the same rights in that respect as the other shareholders. Hence, a preference as to dividend will not imply a preference as to capital or vice versa. Nor will an exclusion of participation in dividends beyond a fixed preferential rate necessarily imply an exclusion of participation in capital (or vice versa), although it will apparently be some indication of it.

(d) Where the rights as to dividends, return of capital or votes are expressly stated, that statement is presumed to be exhaustive as far as that matter is concerned. Hence, if shares are given a preferential dividend they are presumed to be non-participating as regards further dividends, and if they are given a preferential right to a return of capital they are presumed to be non-participating in surplus assets. If they are given a vote in certain circumstances (e.g., if their dividends are in arrears), it is implied that they have no votes in other circumstances.

(e) A preferential dividend is presumed to be cumulative. This presumption can be rebutted by any words indicating that the preferential dividend for a year is to be payable only out of the profits of that year.

(f) As a preference dividend is only payable if declared, arrears of cumulative dividend are *prima facie* not payable in a winding up unless previously declared. This presumption may be rebutted by the slightest indication to the contrary.[16]

These rules of interpretation can be rendered inapplicable by appropriate drafting of the terms of issue.

Debentures

Although there is no comprehensive legal definition of 'debenture' it is at a minimum a document which creates or acknowledges an indebtedness. It may or may not be accompanied by a charge over the assets of a company. A bank loan secured by a fixed and floating charge over the assets is a common type of debenture, and it seems that a formal loan agreement, with or without security, is also regarded as a debenture.

A single debenture, such as that issued to a bank, is not transferable. For this reason, where loan capital is raised from the investing public

16 Gower, pp. 421–423.

it is usual to issue transferable debenture or loan stock. Debenture stock is normally constituted by a trust deed. This is a convenient arrangement which gives the company a single person, the trustee, with whom it can deal in matters arising out of the debentures. The trustee can take speedy action to protect the debenture holders' interests if so required, since if the debentures are secured, he would be empowered to enforce the security. The trust deed also sets out the procedure for holding meetings and arriving at decisions binding upon all debenture holders. Debenture is a generic term and there can be as many types of debenture stock as there are possible terms of issue. They may be secured or unsecured, they may have equity conversion rights (convertible loan stock); they may even be irredeemable or perpetual.[17]

In law, the debenture holder is a creditor of the company and the remedies available to him are no different from those of any other creditor. He may sue for his money and, on obtaining judgement, levy execution on the company's property. It is open to him, as it is to any other creditor, to present a petition for the winding up of the company. Furthermore, the holder of a secured debenture has the power to appoint a receiver to take possession of the security and sell it. Where the debenture contains a floating charge the receiver may also be a manager with high powers to carry on the business.

The debenture holder is not, in the eyes of the law, a member of the company. Unlike the shareholder, he has no rights in the company but merely rights against it. This is no doubt one of the reasons why the return to debenture holders is termed interest, and is a charge against profits in contrast to the return on share capital which is termed dividends and is treated as an appropriation of profits.

The sharp distinction in law between the shareholder and the debenture holder is not of great import to the share valuer. He is more concerned with the investment characteristics of the different classes of securities. For him, the important distinction will be between those securities having a fixed preferential return and those which bear the brunt of the business risk and which stand to yield a potentially high return — in other words, between prior charges and equity. The former consists of the debenture and preference capital, the latter of the ordinary share capital. The fact that the debenture holder is not in law a member of the company makes little or no practical difference. For a quoted company, the formalities of registration and transfer for debenture stock closely resemble those for shares, and the investment attributes of debenture stock are not fundamentally dissimilar to those of preference shares. To the investor, therefore, the legal distinction

---

[17] Section 193 of the 1985 Act.

between the debenture holder and the preference shareholder is of no great importance.

This is not to say that the distinctions in law between the two classes of security are not relevant to valuation, but merely that they do not point to any fundamental divide. It is highly relevant, for example, that debenture interest is a charge against profits and not an appropriation of it. Debenture interest cannot be passed when profits are insufficient and should a default occur, the debenture holder has powerful and drastic remedies. The preference shareholder depends for his dividend on the availability of profits and has no contractual remedy against the company if no dividend is declared. But these are differences of degree, which in a sound, reputable company where maintenance of the preference dividend was not in doubt, would probably not count for much.

The purchase by a company of its own shares

The protection of creditors through the maintenance of capital has long been a concern of company law. Ever since *Trevor* v. *Whitworth* (1887) 12 App. Cas. 409, it has been an established principle that a company cannot purchase its own shares as this would amount to an unauthorised reduction of capital. This general rule against the company acquiring its own shares is now enshrined in s.143 of the 1985 Act. However, the exceptions allowed by the Act are more important than the rule, and it is now a relatively simple matter for a company to purchase its own shares and to issue redeemable shares.

The provisions governing the purchase by a company of its own shares are contained in ss.162 to 177 of the 1985 Act. A detailed description of the provisions would be out of place here. However, the general features of these powers are as follows:

(a) The power to purchase a company's own shares does not include the power to hold them. The shares must be cancelled on purchase. Strictly speaking, therefore, the Act enables companies to redeem shares not otherwise redeemable.

(b) The terms of purchase must provide for payment on purchase; it is not permissible for the purchase consideration or redemption price to be paid by instalments. Although there may be some point in this stipulation as regards the redemption of shares, it is a needless restriction to impose on a company buying its own shares. It merely serves to limit the efficacy of an otherwise admirable measure.

(c) The articles must contain the authority for the company to purchase its own shares, and the resolution to approve the particular purchase contract must be a special resolution on which the prospective vendors do not vote.

(d) If a private company does not have sufficient distributable reserves, it may nevertheless purchase its own shares out of capital. However, there are stringent requirements to be met and a lengthy and detailed procedure to be observed for any company which seeks to take this course.

The power of the company to purchase its own shares, first introduced in the 1981 Act, is one of the most significant innovations in private company finance for many years. The purchase of the shares of a dissident minority, the provision of short-term equity funding, employee share schemes, the reduction of capital and the buying out of shares of a deceased shareholder — these are some of the principal uses to which the new provisions can be put. Some of the valuation problems which arise when a company purchases its own shares are discussed in chapter 12.

The effect of size on the value of a shareholding

The effect of size on the per share value of a holding can be extremely marked. The most obvious example of this effect is the fact that the value per share of a small minority interest is much lower than that of a controlling interest. Every share enjoys the same rights as any other share in its class. It follows that differences in the value per share of different size shareholdings in the same company must be attributable to particular powers or rights conferred by company law or the articles on the different levels of shareholding.

The shareholders in general meeting are the ultimate controlling body of the company, and their decisions are expressed in the form of resolutions. The power which an individual shareholder exercises depends therefore on the influence he can exert on the resolutions passed by the general meeting. There are three types of resolution, namely, ordinary, extraordinary and special. An ordinary resolution is the usual form in which decisions of the general meeting are expressed unless the Act or the memorandum and articles require a special or extraordinary resolution.

An ordinary resolution, which curiously is not defined in the Act, requires a bare majority of votes. A three-fourths majority is required for extraordinary and special resolutions.[18] The special resolution differs from the extraordinary resolution in that the former requires at least 21 days' notice.

[18] Section 378 of the 1985 Act.

Without doubt the most important provision of company law in this connection is the power to remove a director by ordinary resolution under s.303 of the 1985 Act. As management control of the company is vested in the board of directors, the shareholder who can secure the nomination of himself or his associates to the board can control the company's business. As a bare majority is required to pass an ordinary resolution, a shareholding which carries more than 50% of the votes confers control of the company on the holder. As the directors invariably decide dividend policy, a minority shareholder must accept what dividends the controlling shareholder thinks fit. There is, therefore, a great chasm between a majority shareholding and a minority one.

However, there are degrees of control, and that enjoyed by the bare majority is no more than bare control. Although the degree of control rises to absolute for a 100% shareholding, it does not rise in an even progression but in clearly defined steps. The single greatest disability of the bare majority holder is the lack of voting power sufficient to ensure the passing of an extraordinary or special resolution which, as we have seen, requires a three-fourths majority. The minority shareholding carrying 25% or more of the votes can, therefore, block a number of important measures or steps which require a special or extraordinary resolution.

The precise nature of the limitations which this imposes depends on the circumstances of each case and in particular on the company's memorandum and articles of association. The inability to pass a special resolution may mean that a company cannot buy its own shares, or issue new shares if all its authorised capital has already been issued; it will not be able to change its name or to update is constitution. In general terms, the inability to pass a special resolution is more likely to frustrate the intentions of a strongly managed company with an expansionist policy than one which is just 'ticking over' and happy with the *status quo*.

The biggest step in value per share occurs when a shareholding moves from a minority to a bare majority just exceeding 50% of the votes. A further increase, although usually of much smaller size, takes place when a shareholding reaches the 75% mark. Within the spectrum of minority holdings, the most significant stage is when the shareholding exceeds 25% and can block a special resolution. Depending on the circumstances, this negative power may have a considerable nuisance value.

While the main stages of control are defined by the ability to pass or block resolutions of the company in general meeting, there are various statutory rights conferred on minority shareholdings in certain circumstances and these may (or may not) influence the valuation.

Examples of these statutory minority rights include the right of the holders of 15% of the issued capital to apply to the court for cancellation of alterations made: (a) to the objects of the company;[19] and (b) to conditions in the memorandum which could have been contained in the articles.[20] The holders of 15% of the shares of any class may also apply to the court for cancellation of any variation of their rights.[21] Holders of over ten per cent of the shares in issue can hold out against compulsory acquisition from a take-over;[22] they can apply to the Department of Trade for the appointment of an Inspector to investigate the affairs of the company[23] or to investigate the membership of the company.[24]

In the general run of valuations the effect of these statutory rights will not be very great; they may often be imperceptible. However, the stages at which a shareholding becomes large enough to pass or block resolutions of a company in general meeting are of fundamental significance in share valuation. Indeed, it has been argued above that the nature of a share changes in a fundamental respect when the shareholding commands a majority of votes. Thus, the valuer must be aware of the gradations in powers and rights as the size of shareholding increases and of the effect on value.

Future developments

Almost certainly the most significant event affecting company law in recent times has been the United Kingdom's entry into the Common Market, and the passing of the European Community Act 1972 incorporating Community law into the laws of this country. The drive to harmonise company law throughout the Community has resulted in a number of changes to UK company law[25] and is likely to continue to do so. The areas of the law where EEC inspired changes are in prospect include the content of prospectuses and admission requirements for listing, the content of group accounts, and the structure of companies, two tier boards and worker representation.[26] Proposals also exist to establish a European company to operate alongside nationally registered companies.

[19] Section 5 of the 1985 Act.
[20] Section 17 of the 1985 Act.
[21] Section 127 of the 1985 Act.
[22] Section 428 of the 1985 Act.
[23] Section 431 of the 1985 Act.
[24] Section 442 of the 1985 Act.
[25] Notably in the classification of companies, the payment for share capital, maintenance of capital, restrictions on distributable profits, duties in relation to employees and company accounting and disclosure.
[26] Respectively, the Six, Seventh and Fifth Draft Directives.

The United Kingdom, as well as the other member states, assists in the formulation of Directives and these often represent no more than best procedure within the Community. The consequential changes in company law are, therefore, not nearly as far reaching as may be supposed at first sight. Indeed, many of the changes, such as the introduction of the public limited company and its attendant requirements, are mainly cosmetic and none is of great doctrinal significance. Company law remains shareholder oriented, bowing occasionally in the direction of creditors, and ignoring almost totally the interest of management and labour.

There are, however, pressures for fundamental changes particularly for the implementation of two tier boards and worker participation, although as yet very little progress or agreement seems likely. It is interesting to recall in this connection that s.309 of the 1985 Act specifically imposes on the directors a duty in relation to the company's employees as well as to its members. But this is a duty owed to the company and to the company alone, and it is not clear how the employees could enforce it. Nevertheless, it is official recognition that the limited company is more than an investment medium for shareholders. Indeed in the more socially aware atmosphere prevalent today, not only employees but also consumers, Government and environmentalists are seen as having a legitimate concern in the activities of the corporation. Furthermore, there is greater awareness of the economic power wielded by large international corporations and of the need to curb monopolies and to promote competition. Legislation in these areas could affect companies significantly. None of these changes would strengthen the shareholder's position and not a few of them, particularly those concerning employee participation, would tend to weaken it.

Conclusion

Value arises from things but resides in the right to things. In a civilised society the right to a thing is usually defined by law. Thus, the valuation of anything looks:

(a) to the thing itself; and
(b) to the legal property rights in that thing.

The legal property rights are therefore of cardinal importance in every valuation.

Shares in a limited company evidence a right to participate in the firm's trading surplus and any surplus in a winding up. There are duties too. Obviously the valuer must be thoroughly conversant with the precise nature of these rights and duties if he is to do his job properly. The aim of this chapter and chapter 4 is to describe the basic legal framework and to give an outline of these rights and duties.

A limited company has a separate legal personality. In law, the shareholders own the company but the company owns the business. The shareholders do not own the company's business. This legal doctrine has profound implications for the valuation of shares. For the minority shareholder it makes an enormous difference because it puts him at a considerable remove from the business itself and renders his claim indirect. For valuation purposes, he cannot be considered as a part owner of the company's undertaking. In law, the controlling shareholder, too, is not a part owner of the company's business undertaking. But the law gives him powers to control the destiny of the firm in a way which is analogous to that of a proprietor. For valuation purposes, therefore, the controlling shareholder must be regarded as a part owner of the undertaking.

The rights of shareholders between themselves and the division of powers between the general body of shareholders and the directors was considered. In many companies management is divorced from ownership, and the measure of control the shareholders have over the directors can be of vital importance. Likewise, in many private companies there is an underlying conflict or tension between those shareholders who work in the business and hold the office of director and those who are outsiders. The working shareholders may feel the company is theirs since they create the wealth; the outside shareholder resents being ignored and feels cheated. The rights of shareholders between themselves, as set out in the articles of association, are a key consideration in this context, as are the statutory provisions.

One of the big disadvantages of private company shares is their illiquidity. This arises primarily because of the restrictions on transfer, but also because possible buyers among the existing members may not have sufficient funds. The recent legislation permitting companies to buy their own shares is a major innovation in this respect. It may provide a means of selling the shares where none exists at the moment. It also encourages investment in smaller businesses.

Perhaps the most significant influence on the development of company law in this country is the drive for harmonisation of company law within the EEC. Substantial changes have already been made and more are in prospect. The proposals include the creation of a European company intended to operate alongside nationally registered companies.

4
The rights of minorities

Introduction

Many private companies are run as family businesses or quasi-partnerships. Families are known for their feuds and rifts can occur even in the friendliest of partnerships. When disputes arise in such companies they are often characterised by feelings of deep hostility and even hatred. A man takes infinitely greater offence at an injury or hurt done to him by family or friends than he does by someone he hardly knows. The aggrieved shareholder, who probably had no inkling that in law he stood in contractual relationship with his fellow shareholders and the company, now reads the articles with the avidity of self-interest and acquaints himself with the principles of company law. He is anxious to know what rights he has and what remedies are available to him.

Nothing illustrates more clearly the significance of minority rights. Naturally, a dissident shareholder seeking to exercise what legal muscle the law confers on him will consult a lawyer and not a valuer. Nevertheless, the valuer is often called upon to give valuation advice to one or other of the parties and sometimes in disputes of this nature he is engaged to issue an independent valuation which will often be expressed to be binding on all the parties. It will be recalled from Chapters 1 and 2 that in transactions where both buyer and seller are known, the valuation must be based on an appraisal of each side's owner values. It is essential, therefore, that the valuer is conversant with the general nature of the rights and remedies available to the dissident minority.[1]

The rights available to minorities include those rights available to all shareholders and these have been touched upon in the preceding chapter. These rights derive from the nature of a share and of the contract contained in the memorandum and articles of association. Briefly, a company is obliged to its members to comply with the terms of its articles of association insofar as they affect the rights and obligations of the members as members. Upon the application of a member, a court will grant an injunction to prevent a company infringing its articles.[2] Although the articles also constitute a contract between the

---

[1] For material in this chapter the author is indebted to *Gower's Principles of Modern Company Law*.
[2] *Wood* v. *Odessa Waterworks Co* (1889) 42 Ch D 636.

members themselves, the extent to which a member can enforce them against another member directly is uncertain. The general rule used to be that he could enforce them against another member only through the company,[3] although recent decisions[4] suggest that, on the occasions when the question is likely to arise, such as, the exercise of members' pre-emption rights, a direct action between the shareholders is possible.

The 'Foss v. Harbottle' rule

It is a sad fact, however, that directors bent on lining their pockets at the expense of the company and controlling shareholders with no scruple about using their voting power to the detriment of the minority's interest are, of all people, the most meticulous in the letter of their compliance with the articles and the Companies Acts. Furthermore, the aggrieved minority shareholder in search of a remedy faces a significant legal hurdle, which is the rule in *Foss* v. *Harbottle* (1843) 2 Hare 461, where it was held that in an action over duties owed to the company, the company, and the company alone, is the proper plaintiff. Since directors' duties are owed to the company and not to the members, it is for the company to institute proceedings against the directors for any breach of their duty. As the directors are responsible for the management of the affairs of the company it falls to them in the first place to bring an action, in other words, the miscreants issue proceedings against themselves! If, as might be expected, they show little inclination for this course, it is open to the company in general meeting to institute proceedings. But more often than not, in private companies the directors will themselves be the controlling shareholders and can ensure that any resolution to this effect is successfully blocked. The rigid rule in *Foss* v. *Harbottle*, to which has been added another principle that 'the court will not interfere with the internal management of companies acting within their powers,[5] would therefore leave little or no possibility of redress for those injustices perpetrated by the directors or majority shareholders acting, nevertheless, within the letter of the law. Understandably, the courts have from time to time allowed exceptions to the *Foss* rule, and these are of considerable importance in the context of minority rights.

A discussion of the remedies available to an aggrieved minority must start therefore with those exceptions which judges have made to the

---

[3] *Welton* v.*Saffrey* [1897] AC 299.
[4] E.g., *Rayfield* v. *Hands* [1960] Ch 1.
[5] Per Lord Davey in *Burland* v. *Earle* [1902] AC 83.

rule in *Foss* v. *Harbottle*. These amount to the common law remedies. These in turn are supplemented by the statutory remedies contained in ss.459–461 and s.517(g) of the Companies Act 1985 (hereinafter the 1985 Act). Section 517(g) empowers the court to order a winding up of the company on just and equitable grounds, and ss.459–461 allows the court to grant what relief it thinks fit where the affairs of the company are being conducted in a way unfairly prejudicial to a member. Last, but by no means least, there are the Department of Trade investigations under various sections of the 1985 Act. The use of these powers can provide speedy and effective relief at little or no cost.

The exceptions to the rule in *Foss* v. *Harbottle*

The *Foss* rule has no doubt survived so long because of its great practical advantages and because it buttresses that other pillar of company law, the doctrine of the company as a separate legal entity. The practical advantages of the rule stem from the fact that it prevents similar suits from being brought by a large number of plaintiffs, and it avoids the futility of a successful action being brought only to be subsequently overturned by an ordinary resolution ratifying the act complained of. The rule consciously preserves the rights of the majority with the intention of ensuring that the conduct of the company's business is not fettered by a fractious or stubborn minority.

Unfortunately judges and jurists have not been entirely successful in extracting from the various judgements the guiding principle determining the exceptions to the basic rule, and no two authorities seem to be entirely agreed on the matter. It seems, nonetheless, that the minority shareholder is able to bring an action in the following circumstances:

(a) where the act complained of is illegal or *ultra vires;*
(b) where the act complained of required an extraordinary or special resolution, and this has not been passed;
(c) where the act complained of infringes a personal right of the shareholder bringing the action;
(d) where what has been done amounts to a fraud on the minority; and
(e) where s.461(2)(c) of the 1985 Act applies.

Additionally, it has been suggested that there is a residual exception 'whenever the justice of the case requires'.

Exception (a) is clear and needs no further explanation. To the layman, however, exceptions (b) and (c) seem no more than the exercise of the member's general right to enforce the articles against the company as described earlier: he would not consider these as true exceptions. In any event, exception (c), it seems, would not include the right to bring an action for an internal irregularity which could be put right by an ordinary resolution. But the difficulty here lies in judging what type of wrong is ratifiable. A mere irregularity, such as the refusal of the chairman of a meeting to take a poll on a question of an adjournment, is ratifiable and therefore subject to the *Foss* rule.[6] The attempted removal of the right to vote, on the other hand, would be considered of fundamental importance and not ratifiable. The individual shareholder could therefore bring an action in such a case.[7] Unfortunately, there are no generally agreed criteria for determining whether or not a particular act is ratifiable.

Under s.461(2)(c) of the 1985 Act the court may authorise civil proceedings to be brought in the name and on behalf of the company by such person or persons as the court may direct. The circumstances in which the court may make such an order are discussed later under the general heading of the minority protection afforded by ss.459–461 of the 1985 Act.

The remaining exception is where the act or conduct complained of amounts to a fraud on the minority and the wrongdoers are in control. This is a highly significant exception to the *Foss* rule and one which requires a fairly lengthy exposition.

Fraud on the minority

The expression 'fraud on the minority' has no precise judicial definition, although it is clear that fraud in this context is wider than the narrow common law concept of deliberate deceit. It connotes an abuse of power of which 'familiar examples are when the majority are endeavouring directly or indirectly to appropriate to themselves money, property or advantages which belong to the company or in which the other shareholders are entitled to participate'.[8] Fraud in this sense, however, does not include negligence, no matter how gross.[9] Furthermore, the wrongdoers must be in control of the company for an action to be permissible under this heading.[10] Whether control for this purpose has a meaning wider than pure voting control has not been established. In *Prudential Assurance Co Ltd* v. *Newman Industries Ltd* (No 2) [1980] 2 All ER 841, Vinelott J. held that the fraud on the minority

---

[6] *McDougall* v. *Gardiner* (1875) 1 Ch D 13.
[7] *Pender* v. *Lushington* (1877) 6 Ch D 70.
[8] Per Lord Davey, in *Burland* v. *Earle*, supra.
[9] *Pavlides* v. *Jensen* [1956] 1 Ch 565.
[10] *Russell* v. *Wakefield Waterworks & Co* (1875) LR 20 Eq 474.

exception applied where there was no voting control but the wrongdoer, by manipulating his position in the company, could ensure that the majority would not allow a claim to be brought for the alleged wrong. However, this reasoning was subsequently rejected by the Court of Appeal in the same case, without offering their own interpretation of the meaning of control. This still awaits judicial clarification. On the above general principles it is instructive to consider the type of action which the courts have in the past considered to be a fraud on the minority. Professor Gower has managed to classify most of the relevant cases under four headings, which we shall now discuss.

(a) *Expropriation of the company's property*

In *Menier* v. *Hooper's Telegraph Works* (1874) LR 9 Ch App.350, the court held that a minority shareholder could bring an action where the majority shareholder voted for the voluntary liquidation of the company in order to compromise an action being brought in the name of the company, the compromise being to the advantage of the majority shareholder. This principle was upheld in *Cooks* v. *G. S. Deeks and Others* [1916] 1 AC 554, where the directors were required to account to the company for the profit on a contract which they appropriated to themselves. They were adjudged to be in breach of duty to the company, and this could not be ratified by resolution of the company in general meeting secured by their controlling interest, since, in the words of Lord Buckmaster L.C.: 'It appears quite certain that directors holding a majority of votes would not be permitted to make a present to themselves'.

(b) *Expropriation of members' property*

Just as those in control of a company cannot exercise their voting power so as to deprive the company of its property, so, it seems, they are not entitled to use it so as to deprive the other members of their shares in the company. However, this is not an absolute rule, and expropriation may be allowed if it can be shown that in the honest opinion of the majority the transaction was *bona fide* for the benefit of the company as a whole.

Two cases provide the authority for this prohibition on the majority's expropriation of the minority's shares. In *Brown* v. *British Abrasive Wheel Co* [1919] 1 Ch 290, a public company was in urgent need of further capital which the majority, holding 98% of the shares, were willing to supply if they could buy out the minority. Having failed to persuade the minority to sell, they proposed to pass a special resolution adding to the articles a clause whereby any shareholder was bound to transfer his shares on a request in writing of the holders of nine-tenths of the issued capital. Although such a clause could have been validly inserted in the original articles and although the good faith of the majority was not challenged, the court held that an attempt to add the clause in order to acquire compulsorily the shares of the minority, who had bought when there was no such power, would not be for the benefit of the company as a whole but was solely for the benefit of the majority. It accordingly granted an injunction restraining the company from passing the resolution.

The principle laid down in the *Brown* case was subsequently upheld in *Dafen Tinplate Co* v. *Llanelly Steel Co* [1920] 2 Ch 124. In that case Peterson J. found that a new article conferring on the majority an unrestricted and unlimited power to buy out any shareholder they might think proper, went much further than was necessary for the protection of the company from conduct detrimental to its interest. The judge conceded, however, that the alteration would have been valid if it had been for the benefit of the company as a whole. Nonetheless, in *Shuttleworth* v. *Cox Brothers & Co* [1927] 2 KB 9, a case which was not concerned with the expropriation of shares, the Court of Appeal laid down that it was for the members, and not the court, to decide what was beneficial to the company, and that the court could only interfere if they had not acted in good faith. If the resolution was such that no reasonable man could consider it for the benefit of the company as a whole, this might be grounds for finding lack of good faith. Bearing in mind that the phrase 'the company as a whole' means the corporators as a general body and not the company as a commercial entity,[11] one may legitimately question whether the decisions in the *Brown* case and the *Dafen Tinplate* case would be effective in preventing expropriations. If the members are the arbiters of what is in the interests of the company as a whole, and the company for this purpose is defined as the corporators as a general body, is not the interest of the majority synonymous with the interests of the general body of shareholders?

The decision of the Court of Appeal in *Sidebottom* v. *Kershaw Leese & Co* [1920] 1 Ch 154, of the same period as the *Brown* case, is relevant in this connection. There, a director-controlled private company had a minority shareholder who was interested in a competing business. The majority passed a special resolution empowering the directors to require any shareholder who competed with the company to transfer his shares, at their fair value, to nominees of the directors. The Court of Appeal, reversing the trial judge, held that the alteration was valid, being made *bona fide* for the benefit of the company as a whole.

---

[11] Per Evershed MR in *Greenhalgh* v. *Arderne Cinemas Ltd* [1951] Ch 286.

Despite the somewhat conflicting decisions and 'dicta' of subsequent cases, it is generally believed that the *Brown* and *Dafen Tinplate* cases are still good law. As Professor Gower points out, they are in any event consistent with s.428 of the 1985 Act which empowers a nine-tenths majority to compulsorily acquire the minority in certain limited circumstances and subject to certain safeguards. If the *Brown* case and the *Dafen Tinplate* case were not good law, there would be no need for s.428 since a three-fourths majority could always compulsorily acquire the minority.

(c) Certain breaches of directors' duties

Any breaches of directors' duties are ratifiable by the company in general meeting. Thus, the general meeting can ratify an act by the directors in excess of the powers conferred on them, or resolve not to sue in respect of a breach of their duties of skill and care as, for instance, where it was alleged the directors had negligently sold an asset of the company at a gross under-valuation.[12]

But it has been definitely established that the company in general meeting cannot authorise the directors to act in fraud of the company, fraud here being used in a wider sense than deceit or dishonesty. If the directors have acted in their own interests or those of a third party rather than in the interests of the company, a resolution of a general meeting will not protect them. In *Atwool* v. *Merryweather* (1867) LR 5 Eq 464n, an individual shareholder was allowed to institute proceedings where directors sold a mine to the company for an excessive price, part of which was satisfied by the issue of shares, giving the wrongdoers voting control. This was a fraud on the minority and could not therefore be ratified by the general meeting.

However, not every wrongful issue of shares by the directors is non-ratifiable. In *Hogg* v. *Cramphorn Ltd* [1967] 2 Ch 254, shares were issued by the directors, acting *bona fide*, which gave them voting control. It was held that an individual shareholder could bring an action in respect of this breach because otherwise the wrongdoers would have had control by virtue of the very transaction complained of. In fact, the court adjourned the proceedings to enable the directors to convene a shareholders' meeting to ratify the issue. Solely for the purposes of this meeting the shares issued by the directors were deemd to have no voting rights. It was accepted in this case that the directors had acted in good faith, but the ratification itself could have amounted to a fraud on the minority had it been achieved by reliance on wrongly issued shares.

---

[12] *Pavlides* v. *Jensen*, supra.

(d) Cases where the majority do not exercise their powers 'bona fide' for the benefit of the company as a whole

Although a director must act, and therefore vote at all meetings, in the best interests of the company, the shareholder has no such duty to the company when voting at general meetings. He may vote as he wishes even though he has an interest in the subject matter of the vote.[13] However, as the discussion under headings (a) to (c) shows, there appears to be a general principle that where the majority have not exercised their power *bona fide* for the benefit of the company as a whole, there may be an action for fraud against the minority. If this principle has any application outside categories (a) to (c) above, it seems that the onus of proving that the majority's powers have not been exercised in the interests of the company as a whole lies with the minority, not the majority.

It would appear that without an extension of this general principle beyond the categories (a) to (c) above, alterations to members' rights which fall short of an attempted expropriation of shares may still be permissible. In *Shuttleworth* v. *Cox Brothers & Co supra*, for example, the majority were permitted to get rid of an unsatisfactory life director by adding to the articles a clause providing that a director should be disqualified if called upon to resign by the other directors.[14] And in *Greenhalgh* v. *Arderne Cinemas* [1951] Ch 286, the majority were held entitled to abridge the pre-emption rights in the articles. The articles stipulated that shares should be offered to existing members at a fair value before any sale to a non-member. The majority secured the passing of a special resolution altering the articles so as to allow shares to be transferred to any named person if sanctioned by an ordinary resolution. This allowed the majority to dispose of their shares without offering them to the minority.

It is an open question whether this principle does, in fact, extend beyond circumstances other than those in categories (a) to (c). The recent case of *Clemens* v. *Clemens Bros Ltd* [1976] 2 All ER 268 would suggest that it does. In this case, ordinary resolutions were passed issuing shares to directors and trustees of an employees' share ownership scheme, the effect being to reduce the plaintiff's holding from 45% to under 25%. Foster J. set aside the resolutions saying:

> They are specifically and carefully designed to ensure not only that the plaintiff can never get control of the company

---

[13] *Burland* v. *Earle*, supra.
[14] Since the passing of the Companies Act 1948 it has been possible to remove any director by an ordinary resolution.

but to deprive her of what has been called her negative control. Whether I say that these proposals are oppressive to the plaintiff or that no one could reasonably believe that they are for her benefit matters not.

The court, in judging whether the resolutions were in the interests of the company as a whole, substituted for the hypothetical neutral member an actual minority member. The decision in the *Clemens* case, which has apparently been criticised, was strongly influenced by recent developments relating to other remedies of an oppressed minority under what is now ss.459–461 of the 1985 Act.

The form a shareholder's action takes under the various exceptions to the *Foss* rule depends on whether he seeks to enforce the company's rights (e.g., to ensure that controlling directors do not 'make a present' to themselves), or his own rights as a member (e.g. where wrong is being done or threatened by the company). Although the distinction between the company's rights and the members' rights is not always clear in practice, it seems that a derivative action is appropriate for the former and a personal action for the latter. In a derivative action the member is allowed as a matter of grace to bring an action in the name of the company (this it will be recalled is normally the prerogative of the directors or the company in general meeting), but the member will be disqualified from doing this if he has participated in the wrong himself.[15]

Obviously, the wrongdoers must be in control. As the minority member sues on behalf of the company, he stands to gain nothing directly apart from any appreciation in the value of his shares reflecting the amount recovered from the wrongdoers. Any sums recovered go to the company in which, of course, the majority are also interested. If unsuccessful, he will be liable not only for his own costs but the taxed costs of all the defendants, including the company. Even if successful, he will recover only his taxed costs. In practice, therefore, an action to enforce the company's rights exposes the aggrieved minority to considerable financial risks. However, the Court of Appeal's recent decision in *Wallersteiner* v. *Moir* (No 2) [1975] QB 373 has mitigated this situation by finding that it is open to the court to order that the company should indemnify the plaintiff shareholder against the costs incurred in the action, whether or not the action succeeds. The plaintiff can apply at the beginning of the action to proceed on this basis.

In a personal action based on the contract in the memorandum and articles the appropriate remedy will be an injunction or a declaration

[15] *Towers* v. *African Tug* [1904] 1 Ch 558 and more recently *Nurcombe* v. *Nurcombe* [1984] BCLC 557.

and not a money judgment against the company. Whereas with a derivative action the mere fact that the plaintiff was not a member at the time of the wrong will not bar him from bringing the action, with a personal action it will bar him.

Statutory remedies available to individual shareholders

The restrictive remedies available to the shareholder at common law as a result of the rule in *Foss* v. *Harbottle* have led to two main statutory remedies. These are s.517(g) and ss.459–461 of the 1985 Act.[16] These extend the foregoing remedies for a particular wrongful act or acts to a remedy where there has been a course of oppressive or unfairly prejudicial conduct, whether or not this has involved any particular wrongful action.

Section 517(g) of the 1985 Act

Under this sub-section the court may order a company to be wound up if it is of the opinion that is it 'just and equitable' to do so. Although the remedy is generally regarded as being available to minority shareholders a petition may be presented by the company or a creditor. A member must have a 'tangible interest' in the liquidation. This normally means that there must be a surplus for distribution amongst the shareholders. The size of his shareholding is irrelevant.

The leading case on section 517(g) is *In re Westbourne Galleries Ltd* [1973] AC 360, which considerably widened the ambit of the section. The facts of the case were as follows: Ebrahimi and Nazar formed a company in 1958 to acquire the business of carpet dealers in which they had both been equal partners since about 1945, 'a fact of cardinal importance'. Ebrahimi held 500 shares and so did Nazar. Soon after the formation of the company Nazar's son became a shareholder by acquiring 100 shares each from his father and Ebrahimi. Thus the Nazars, father and son, had a majority of votes in the general meeting.

The company made good profits all of which were distributed as directors' remuneration. No dividends were paid. Around 1965 the business relationship between Ebrahimi and Nazar began to deteriorate. It was alleged that Nazar, who spent large parts of each year in Persia buying carpets, which were bought in his own name and subsequently were invoiced to the company, had begun to invoice the carpets at arbitrary prices which yielded substantial profits for himself and little or no profit for the company. In addition, the premises occupied

---

[16] Formerly s.222(f) of the 1948 Act and s.75 of the 1980 Act.

by the company, and for which it paid the rent, were also being used for an antique business carried on personally by Nazar. Ebrahimi's protests were of no avail as he was invariably outvoted by the Nazars. Finally, in August 1969 an ordinary resolution was passed removing Ebrahimi from the office of director. Thereafter, he ceased to have any part in the management of the company, and, as no dividends were paid, he ceased to participate in the profits.

Ebrahimi presented a petition under s.210 of the 1948 Act (the predecessor of ss.459–461 of the 1985 Act), the relief sought being an order that Nazar and his son be ordered to purchase his shares. In the alternative he sought an order for the winding up of the company under what is now s.517(g) of the 1985 Act. The trial judge found that some of the allegations of oppression and misconduct were unfounded and others unproved, and that the case made out did not amount to such a course of action as would justify an order under s.210 of the 1948 Act. However, Plowman J. found that there was a case for a winding up on the 'just and equitable' grounds of s.222(f) of the 1948 Act:

> . . . while no doubt the Petitioner was lawfully removed, in the sense that he ceased in law to be a director, it does not follow that in removing him the respondents did not do him a wrong. In my judgment, they did do him a wrong, in the sense that it was an abuse of power and a breach of the good faith which partners owe to each other to exclude one of them from all participation in the business upon which they have embarked on the basis that all should participate in its management. The main justification put forward for removing him was that he was perpetually complaining, but the faults were not all on one side and, in my judgment this is not sufficient justification. For these reasons, in my judgment, the petitioner . . . has made out a case for a winding up order.

On appeal this order was reversed by the Court of Appeal but restored unanimously by the House of Lords.[17] The Court of Appeal had placed much reliance on the fact that the resolution removing Ebrahimi was *bona fide* in the interests of the company. Lord Wilberforce's remarks on this are particularly illuminating:

> This formula 'bona fide in the interests of the company' is one that is relevant in certain contexts of company law and I

[17] Ebrahimi did not appeal against the refusal of the trial judge to make an order under s.210.

do not doubt in many cases decisions have to be left to majorities or directors to take which the courts must assume had this basis. It may, on the other hand, become little more than an alibi for a refusal to consider the merits of the case, and in a situation such as this it seems to have little meaning other than 'in the interests of the majority'. Mr Nazar may well have persuaded himself . . . that the company would be better off without Mr Ebrahimi but if Mr Ebrahimi disputed this, or thought the same with reference to Mr Nazar, what prevails is simply the majority view. To confine the application of the just and equitable clause to proved cases of 'mala fides' would be to negative the generality of the words.

There need therefore be no fraud or wrongdoing on the part of those in control.

There are many interesting developments in the *Westbourne Galleries* case, not least the fact that the wrong of which a member complains need not necessarily affect him in his capacity as a member. Ebrahimi's rights as a shareholder were in no way affected by his expulsion from office, yet he was entitled to a remedy. It is also clear from the judgment that the words 'just and equitable' enable the courts to look beyond the exercise of legal rights to the substance of the underlying relationship, obligations or understandings between the parties. The words are general in character and in order to remain so must be free from the fetters of any judicial definition. The section is not restricted to small companies or to 'quasi-partnerships' and such a term may in fact be misleading. Lord Wilberforce indicated, however, that 'one or probably more' of the following elements would have to be present:

(a) an association formed or continued on the basis of a personal relationship, involving mutual confidence — this element will often be found where a pre-existing partnership has been converted into a limited company;
(b) an agreement or understanding, that all, or some (for there may be 'sleeping' members), of the shareholders shall participate in the conduct of the business;
(c) restrictions upon the transfer of the member's interest in the company, so that if confidence is lost, or one member is removed from management, he cannot take out his stake and go elsewhere.

In the light of the above it is revealing to list the circumstances in which the courts have in the past made an order for winding up under s.517(g). In view of Lord Wilberforce's strictures on the dangers of rigid classifications, the list must be considered as no more than illustrative.

(a) Expulsion from office as in the *Westbourne Galleries* case.
(b) Justifiable loss of confidence.

The petitioner's lack of confidence in the ability or determination of the management to conduct the company's affairs in a proper manner must be based on actual conduct and must normally rest upon some lack of probity or some impropriety.[18] Typical examples are where the management persist in withholding from the shareholders information which they are entitled to or where those in control treat the business as if it were entirely their own without regard to minority interests. Mere disagreement with management policy or annoyance at being outvoted is not enough.

(c) Deadlock.

This might arise where shares are held equally by opposing factions. Total technical deadlock such as the inability to secure a quorum or to pass any resolution is not necessary, and the existence of the casting vote would not prevent a winding up order being made.[19]

(d) Failure of substratum.

Where the principal object for which a company was formed has been achieved or is no longer achievable, a member may petition for a winding up order on the 'just and equitable' ground. Where, for example, a company has sold its business or divested itself of its major asset, a dissenting shareholder may be entitled to a winding up order.

A winding up order under s.517(g) is a drastic remedy, and the courts will not give an order if some other remedy is available and a petitioner acted unreasonably in not pursuing that remedy.[20] As explained in Chapter 2, liquidation value is very much lower than going concern value for most businesses and it is not difficult to imagine circumstances in which a successful petition under s.517(g) would be no more than a pyrrhic victory. Nevertheless, the section has been used to considerable effect, and under the more liberal interpretation of it by the courts in the *Westbourne Galleries* case, it represents a potent threat.

---

[18] *Lock* v. *John Blackwood Ltd* [1924] AC 783.
[19] *Re Davis and Collett Ltd* [1935] Ch 693 and *Re National Drive-in Theatres Ltd* [1954] 2 DLR 55 BC Sup Ct.
[20] Section 520 of the 1985 Act.

Sections 459 to 461 of the 1985 Act

Under s.461 the court may make such order as it thinks fit where any member petitions and shows, under s.459, that 'the affairs of the company are being or have been conducted in a manner which is unfairly prejudicial to the interests of some part of the members (including at least himself), or that any actual or proposed act or omission of the company (including an act or omission on its behalf) is or would be so prejudicial'. This form of relief was first introduced by s.75 of the 1980 Act. This in turn replaced s.210 of the 1948 Act which was the alternative remedy to a winding up in cases of oppression. There were only two successful cases brought under s.210, namely, *Scottish Cooperative Wholesale Society Ltd* v. *Meyer* [1959] AC 324 and *In re H. R. Harmer Ltd* [1959] 1 WLR 62. The section was restrictively construed and its greatest limitation was that it was available only if the circumstances were such as to justify a winding up order under s.222(f) of the 1948 Act (now s.517(g) of the 1985 Act).

In contrast to s.210 of the 1948 Act, the relief is available without proof that the court would order a winding up under s.517(g), and the test is no longer one of oppression but of conduct unfairly prejudicial to some part of the members. The full meaning of the words 'unfairly prejudicial' will no doubt be clarified in due course as cases come before the courts. The phrase was intended to be of wider import than oppression, which was defined by Viscount Simonds in the *Scottish Cooperative* case as 'burdensome, harsh and wrongful'.

The Jenkins report recommended that relief should be available to a petitioner in respect of conduct falling short of illegality but 'involving a visible departure from the standards of fair dealing'. The report mentions as possible examples the payment by the directors of excessive remuneration to themselves, the refusal to register shares in the name of deceased members' personal representatives, the issue of shares to directors and others on advantageous terms, and the passing of non-cumulative preference dividends on shares held by the minority. Whether the courts adopt this interpretation remains to be seen.

Whereas s.210 of the 1948 Act was construed as referring to a course of conduct over a period of time, s.459 applies not only to this but also to an isolated prejudicial act or omission. As such, a petition under this section may be an alternative to a minority shareholder's suite (derivative or personal), where the action taken or proposed is unfairly prejudicial to some part of the members. There must be some doubt as to whether s.459 covers conduct unfairly prejudicial to all the members, as distinct from 'some part of the members'. If it does not, it is difficult to see how s.459 will help in circumstances similar to those in the

Pavlides case, where the directors allegedly sold the company's property at a wholly inadequate price and all the shareholders were prejudiced.

Like s.210 of the 1948 Act, however, the conduct complained of has to affect the member in his capacity as member. In practice, this is a severe restriction on the efficacy of s.459 as a safeguard of minority rights. As the *Westbourne Galleries* case clearly illustrates, in the smaller, informal private company the members often participate in the profits of the company through directors' remuneration, and it is unfortunate that the wider interpretation adopted for a winding up on the just and equitable ground has not been applied to s.459.

Any member of a company is entitled to present a petition under s.459, including trustees and personal representatives to whom shares have been transmitted by operation of law. This means that where directors refuse to register shares in the name of a trustee or personal representative, thereby applying pressure on them to sell their shares either to the directors or other members, the trustee or personal representative can petition under this section even though he is not registered as a member. It appears also that a transferee whose transfer the company refuses to register will be able to petition.[21]

If satisfied that the petition is well founded, the court may make such order as it thinks fit. Without limit to this wide discretionary power, an order under s.461 may:

(a) regulate the conduct of the company's affairs in the future;
(b) require the company to refrain from doing or continuing an act complained of by the petitioner or to do an act the petitioner has complained it has omitted to do;
(c) authorise civil proceedings to be brought in the name and on behalf of the company by such person or persons and on such terms as the court may direct;
(d) provide for the purchase of the shares of any members of the company by other members or by the company itself and in the case of a purchase by the company itself, the reduction of the company's capital accordingly.

Even when the petition is well founded, there is no guarantee that the court will grant relief in the form requested. In *Re H. R. Harmer Ltd*, supra, two sons successfully petitioned the court under s.210 of the 1948 Act in respect of the oppressive conduct of the company's affairs at the hands of their father who, through a special class of voting shares,

---

[21] This is the inference of the word 'transferred', as distinct from transmitted, in sub-section 459(2). For further discussion see *Gower*, p. 667, Note 90.

had voting control of the company although owning only ten per cent of the equity. The sons requested the following relief:

(a) that the articles be altered giving all the ordinary shareholders one vote each;
(b) that the father should be ordered to sell to them all his ordinary shares, or alternatively, all his 'B' ordinary shares at named figures or such price as the court should think proper;
(c) that the father should be relieved from his office as a director;
(d) that such other order might be made as might be just.

In the event, Roxburgh J. ordered *inter alia* that the company should contract for the services of the father as consultant at a named salary, that the father should not interfere in the affairs of the company otherwise than in accordance with the valid decisions of the board of directors, and that he should be appointed president of the company for life but that this office should not impose any duties, rights or power.

Finally it is noteworthy that s.461(2)(c), under which the court may authorise civil proceedings to be brought on behalf of the company, was specifically introduced in order to enable an aggrieved shareholder wishing to bring a derivative suit to by-pass the rule in *Foss* v. *Harbottle*. This subsection enables the member to petition initially for an order authorising him to institute proceedings in the name and on behalf of the company.

If the court were to order that the minority's shares be bought by the majority or by the company, much would hinge on the matter of valuation. Should the shares be valued on the discounted minority basis or should they be valued *pro rata* to the value of the entire company? Nourse J. gave some guidance on this point in *Re Bird Precision Bellows Ltd* [1984] Ch 419. From this it would appear that in a quasi-partnership type of company characterised by the typical elements referred to by Lord Wilberforce in the *Westbourne Galleries* case, the minority, if a quasi-partner, would be entitled to the full control value of the shares. Where the minority shareholder was an investor pure and simple and did not participate in the company's affairs, or where the company was not a quasi-partnership, it may well be appropriate for the minority to be bought out on the discounted basis, particularly where he had acquired his shares on the same basis. But no general rule could be laid down in such circumstances.

Department of Trade investigations

The Department of Trade's powers to appoint inspectors to investigate the affairs of a company have in the past been used sparingly and often spectacularly, with the inspector's report being issued in a blaze of publicity. The formal appointment of an inspector can itself have a damaging effect on the company's image and on its affairs. Doubtless this accounts for the Department's reluctance to make an appointment unless a strong *prima facie* case has been established. The Department's powers have, therefore, not been used frequently. However, these powers have been considerably strengthened by recent legislation so that they are now of great significance as a remedy against unfair treatment, and as a preliminary to civil or criminal proceedings against miscreants. The outcome of litigation in the courts is still highly uncertain despite the improvements in statutory and common law remedies, and the litigant assumes a considerable financial risk. An approach to the Department of Trade therefore has its advantages, particularly where insufficient evidence is available to found an action in the courts.

The Department of Trade now has two distinct, but inter-related, sets of powers; namely, the power to insist on the production of books and papers from the company and the power to appoint inspectors. The former enables the Department to obtain the information needed to form a preliminary view on the merits of the case without the formal appointment of an inspector and its attendant publicity and may in itself be sufficient to ensure that the wrong complained of is put right. The latter concerns the appointment of inspectors, the conduct of the inquiry and the action, if any, which may follow it. The general nature of these powers is described below.

Under s.447 of the 1985 Act the Department of Trade may at any time, if they think there is a good reason to do so, direct a company to produce any specified books or papers. No warning is necessary, and ss.448–451 provide the Department with the necessary supplementary powers to obtain any books or papers from third parties, to take copies, to require explanations of past or present officers or employees, and to obtain search warrants. It is a criminal offence to destroy or falsify relevant documents and to intentionally give false explanations or statements to the Department. These enquiries may, if necessary, be followed by the appointment of an inspector or by the institution of civil or criminal proceedings without more ado.

The main power to appoint inspectors is contained in ss.431 and 432(2) of the 1985 Act.[22] Under s.431, members holding at least ten per cent of the shares in issue or constituting 200 in number may apply to the Department of Trade as may the company itself. The applicants

---

[22] Under ss.442–446, the Department also has powers to investigate the ownership and control of companies and to investigate share dealings. As these powers are of more concern to shareholders in quoted companies they are not considered further here.

must satisfy the Department that they have good reasons for their application, and the Department may require them to give up to £5,000 security for costs. It has absolute discretion whether to appoint inspectors or not.

Section 431 is little used in practice, the Department almost invariably proceeding under its other discretionary powers in s.432(2). Under this section anyone — shareholder, creditor, director or member of the public — may draw the Department's attention to circumstances which may justify an investigation by inspectors. The Department may appoint inspectors if there are circumstances suggesting:

(a) that the company's affairs are being or have been conducted with intent to defraud its creditors or the creditors of any other person or otherwise for a fraudulent or unlawful purpose or in a manner which is unfairly prejudicial to some part of its members; or
(b) that any actual or proposed act or omission of the company (including an act or omission on its behalf) is or would be so prejudicial, or that it was formed for any fraudulent or unlawful purpose; or
(c) that persons concerned with the company's formation or the management of its affairs have in connection therewith been guilty of fraud, misfeasance or other misconduct towards it or towards its members; or
(d) that its members have not been given all the information with respect to its affairs which they might reasonably expect.

As with s.431, the minority shareholder has no rights under s.432(2) beyond reporting the matter. The Department has no obligation to take action. Nevertheless, s.432(2) is of considerable importance to the enforcement of corporate duties and to the protection of the minority shareholder. Although (a), (b) and (c) above would suggest conduct which, if proved, would justify the bringing of civil or criminal proceedings, under (d) above, the Department is empowered to investigate into circumstances where there has been no legal wrong, since the information shareholders 'might reasonably expect' is more than they are legally entitled to.

An important advantage of an appointment under s.432(2) is that the person who draws the matter to the Department's attention cannot in any circumstances be liable for costs. The Department has considerable follow-up powers. Under s.440 it may petition the court to wind up the company on the 'just and equitable' ground. It may also petition the court for the alternative remedies stipulated under s.461.

The Department may also bring civil proceedings in the name and on behalf of the company.[23]

Thus, the Department of Trade's powers may help a shareholder in a number of ways. Firstly, it may enable him to obtain information to support his suspicions. One of the minority's greatest disadvantages in this respect is the lack of access to the company's records and any means of countering arguments or justifications advanced by the controlling faction. Secondly, like a petition under s.517(g) or one under s.459, an application to the Department can be made by a single member without regard to the rule in *Foss* v. *Harbottle*, but unlike those remedies, it may lead to a successful conclusion entirely without expense or trouble to the complainant. Thirdly, prompt exercise of the Department's powers, especially those concerning the production of books and papers and the power to demand explanations, may nip oppression in the bud.

Conclusion

If this chapter has shown anything, it is that the rights of an oppressed minority, certainly as regards the common law rights enshrined in the exceptions to the *Foss* v. *Harbottle* rule, are obscured by a plethora of sometimes conflicting cases from which the layman, if not the lawyer, has great difficulty in discerning the threads of guiding principle. The circumstances of each case vary so much that judges have considerable scope for their personal whims. Precedents can be effectively ignored by distinguishing an earlier case on some quirk of circumstance. The result may be a bold innovative judgment or it may just as easily be a precedent-determined victory of form over substance.

Despite the uncertainties, however, one thing is clear. There is a definite trend in the law favouring greater protection for the minority shareholder. The *Westbourne Galleries* case, with its recognition of rights arising from economic as opposed to merely legal relationships, has injected new life into the 'just and equitable' remedy under s.517(g), and ss.459 to 461 adopt the concept of unfairly prejudicial conduct which is wider than the restrictive meaning of oppression under s.210 of the 1948 Act. Section 461 also provides a means in certain circumstances of by-passing the rule in *Foss* v. *Harbottle*. The minority protection under ss.459 to 461 was first introduced as s.75 of the 1980 Act. This statutory protection is, therefore, of fairly recent date and no conclusive view has yet emerged of its judicial interpretation. As petitions under this section are frequently compromised, cases are in any event likely to be few and far between.

---

[23] Under s.438 of the 1985 Act.

Finally, the Department of Trade's powers under ss.431 and 432 are significantly greater than they were under the 1948 Act. It is no longer necessary for the Department to appoint an inspector prior to obtaining information. The Department's extensive powers to procure information and explanations from a company can be exercised discreetly without harmful publicity. Anyone may apply to the Department although the Department is under no obligation to act. The powers of follow-up are considerable, including the bringing of civil proceedings. An application to the Department of Trade could well be a more effective approach for the minority shareholder, almost certainly where he lacks sufficient information and cannot countenance the financial risks of litigation. On the other hand, the Department's powers are largely discretionary and, on past showing it has been conservative, if not timid, in making use of them.

5

The Stock Exchange and other security markets

Introduction

In highly developed capital markets such as those of the UK and the US, where the structural impediments are few, the many different investment opportunities are seen as alternatives and are priced in terms of each other. Although the link between investments at both ends of the risk spectrum may be somewhat tenuous — a building society deposit would hardly be considered as an investment alternative by someone who habitually invests in thoroughbred horses, antiques or objets d'art — the bond between those forms of investment which lie contiguous to each other on the chain of investment opportunities is strong and direct. Thus, building society deposit rates are fixed in the light of the various immediate alternatives, such as bank deposits, national savings bonds, local authority deposits and even money market instruments. Just where investment in equities fits into the picture is a matter of debate, but it seems hardly in doubt that an individual contemplating the purchase of unquoted shares for portfolio investment purposes would regard the purchase of shares quoted on the Stock Exchange as the nearest alternative. It is for this reason that the stockmarket exerts such a powerful influence on the value of unquoted shares.

This chapter does not aim to provide a detailed analysis of the workings of the Stock Exchange, but rather to consider in what circumstances the investment ratings of quoted stocks can be used in the valuation of unquoted shares, and what tools are available to this end. This entails a discussion of the role and legitimacy of comparisons in the valuation process, since not everyone would agree that unquoted shares can be valued by reference to quoted equivalents. This is followed by a brief overview of security markets in the UK. The criteria for selection of comparable companies, the significance of Stock Exchange prices and the nature of the various share price indices are then considered. The chapter ends with an introduction to the Efficient Market Hypothesis and Modern Portfolio Theory. These theories, which have radical implications for investment analysts, portfolio managers and financial reporting, have, as yet, unexamined implications for the valuation of unquoted shares. The theories themselves are reviewed in detail in Chapter 6 (The Efficient Market Hypothesis) and Chapter 7 (Risk and the Rate of Return). First, however, we consider the validity of comparisons based on quoted stocks and shares.

The extent and nature of comparability

Those who object to deriving capitalisation rates from quoted companies usually argue that most private companies have little in common with the typical Stock Exchange company and any comparisons are therefore invalid. However, this objection ignores the fact that within the quoted sector itself, and even within a particular industry, there is often a great diversity of business undertakings. Yet the comparison of such dissimilar companies with one another is at the very heart of investment analysis and portfolio management, and it is accepted everywhere that investment ratings, such as the P/E ratio or the yield, express the preferences of investors for one security in regard to another. This practice accords with valuation theory which holds that for properties to be comparable they do not have to be identical or equivalent; they are comparable if the elements of their value are of a like kind.[1] Quoted and unquoted shares are not generically different. They are the same type of legal property (choses in action), they are both claims on wealth (i.e., profits), and their value derives from the expected return. Since the object of portfolio investment is, put crudely, to make money, the essence of an investment is not the physical characteristics of the particular business but rather the perceived level of risk and the expected return. These two critical elements enable the investment merits, and therefore the values, of different companies to be compared.

If quoted and unquoted shares are the same type of legal property, there is, nevertheless, one important difference in their investment attributes: marketability. Quoted shares can be sold in the marketplace without much more ado, whereas it may be difficult, almost impossible, for the shareholder in an unquoted company to realise his investment. Is this disability not of the essence, completely changing the nature of the investment? The answer to this question must depend on the circumstances. Perhaps for very small, family-owned companies with a handful of shareholders and severe share transfer restrictions, the lack of marketability may completely alter the nature of the investment and render comparisons with quoted companies inappropriate. But for many unquoted companies, the lack of marketability can be regarded

---

[1] Henry A. Babcock, *Appraisal Principles and Procedures* (Homewood, Ill.; Richard D. Irwin, 1968), p. 340.

not so much as a fundamental flaw, but rather as a depreciatory attribute of the shares to be taken into account when deriving an appropriate capitalisation rate from comparable quoted stocks. The question of marketability is discussed in more detail in Chapter 9.

The existence of these common elements of risk and return in all securities does not imply, however, that all securities are equally comparable. The degree of risk in an investment stems, in large part, from the nature of the company's activities, and for this reason a comparison, say, of two mechanical engineering firms with each other would have more force than would a comparison of one of those companies with, say, an electrical engineering firm. Size, too, is another indicator of risk. Other things being equal, the larger organisations are more secure and better placed to withstand bad times than are the smaller ones. Therefore, it is more credible to compare firms of the same size than it is to compare firms of very different sizes. This analysis could, of course, be extended to every aspect of the business such as products, markets, plant, labour, management, financial structure and so on. The better the fit in all these aspects, the more force has the comparison.

No two firms are identical and one should not be surprised if, even in the best of comparisons, the particular companies exhibit some markedly different characteristics. Indeed, in the author's experience one is fortunate to find companies closely comparable by reference to both activity and size — perhaps the two most significant determinants of risk.

Where portfolio investment is the objective, therefore, it is entirely permissible to value unquoted shares by reference to comparable quoted companies. This is, in fact, the practice of that growing band of professionals drawn from a wide cross section of financial institutions who invest in unquoted securities. But appropriate and sometimes severe adjustment must be made for the different risk characteristics and poor marketability of the unquoted company.

Financial and investment institutions, however, are only one segment of the demand for unquoted shares. Most commercial valuations of unquoted companies are not for portfolio investment purposes. Considerations of employment, control, family and sentiment often predominate in such valuations, and in the appraisal of the respective owner values of purchaser and vendor the prices at which shares in comparable quoted companies have traded will, in all probability, have no direct bearing. It is in the realm of fiscal share valuations, where an imputed market value is required, that the professional valuer will have most occasion to value by analogy with comparable quoted companies. The fiscal valuation hypothesis is discussed in Chapter 16.

UK security markets

The Stock Exchange

The Stock Exchange is by far the largest trading market in securities in the UK and dwarfs the tiny but growing OTC market. The Stock Exchange has two roles: its primary one of raising new money from investors, and its secondary one of providing a market in which existing securities can be traded. Although the stock market may be a significant source of funds for individual companies, new capital issues comprise probably less than five per cent of companies' total requirements for new funds. The vast bulk of new money raised on the Stock Exchange is represented by Government borrowing through the issue of gilt-edged securities. In the secondary market, too, most Stock Exchange trading in value terms occurs in gilts. Table 1 shows the breakdown of Stock Exchange turnover in a typical month. Gilts, it will be noted, accounted for 75% of turnover by value. However, in terms of numbers the major proportion of transactions — 79% — was in company securities, and it is this aspect of the market which is of most interest to the share valuer.

Table 1: Analysis of Stock Exchange Turnover

| Category | September 1984 | | | |
	Value £m	%	No. of bargains	%
British funds	20,071.7	74.6	55,819	14.2
Irish funds	843.8	3.1	3,025	0.8
UK local authority	298.8	1.1	2,430	0.6
Overseas government	206.9	0.8	1,889	0.5
Other fixed interest	273.7	1.0	17,612	4.5
	21,694.9	80.6	80,775	20.0
Ordinary shares	5,199.1	19.4	310,486	79.4
	26,894.0	100.0	391,261	100.0

Source: Financial Times.

Since November 1980 the Stock Exchange has operated a two-tier market in company securities. The main market comprises securities in those companies admitted to the Official List. There are over 2,700 such companies. To obtain a Stock Exchange Official Listing a company has to satisfy stringent conditions including those as to size, percentage of securities available to the market and disclosure of information. A full listing is expensive to obtain and maintain, and, because the standard expected of a quoted company is so high and its affairs are subject to public scrutiny, a Stock Exchange Listing is evidence of a certain status or rank.

The second tier market is known as the Unlisted Securities Market (USM), which is something of a misnomer in that the USM is a fully-fledged market operating alongside the official market. USM shares are traded on the floor of the Stock Exchange in the same way as officially listed stocks, and jobbers make markets in both types of share. The distinction between the official market and the USM is essentially one of standing. The USM was established to provide a market for the securities of companies who could not satisfy the stringent conditions for admission to the Official List. It is considerably easier and less expensive to obtain a USM listing than it is a full listing. There are no limitations as regards size, only ten per cent of the shares need be in general circulation, and a three-year trading record (as opposed to five years) is acceptable.

In the five years of its existence, the USM has proved a notable success and the number of companies has risen from 11 at the inception of the market to well over 200 currently. In addition, there has been an encouraging number of USM companies graduating to the Official List. The market in many USM stocks is thin because, generally speaking, only a small percentage of the shares is in the hands of the public. This tends to create volatile prices and buttresses the view of the USM as a risky market. Because of its junior status, the USM company does not have the same scope for issuing its paper as does the officially listed company, and its standing in the market is not as high. Nevertheless, a glance at the share price columns of any newspaper will show that the investment ratings of many USM stocks are anything but modest.

Under Rule 535.2 of the Stock Exchange, brokers are permitted to do occasional deals in unquoted shares on a matched bargain basis. The broker must obtain permission to transact each bargain and before any transactions are allowed, the latest accounts of the company must be submitted to the Quotations Department of the Stock Exchange. One broker will often specialise in a particular company and another broker, asked to find a buyer or seller for shares in that company, will usually approach the specialist. The price is negotiated between buyer and seller, the broker merely acting as intermediary. He does not fix the price or necessarily make any recommendations. Several weeks, if not months, may elapse between bargains, and the fact that a transaction has taken place is no guarantee that it will be possible to deal near that price in the future.

The Stock Exchange's decision to abolish minimum commissions by 1987 (a move it agreed to in order to secure the withdrawal of the Restrictive Practices Court's investigation into its Rule Book) has set in train forces which will entirely re-shape the securities industry. The present single capacity system which separates the jobbing or market-making function from the broking one is to end, and the restrictions which limit the interest which outsiders may take in member firms to 29.9% will be completely lifted.

After discussions and consultations, the Council of the Stock Exchange has chosen the competing market maker system for equities. Under this system, prices can be actively negotiated between dealers and members can continue to act in single capacity if they so wish. The market will be able to accommodate both market makers and broker/dealers, who would continue to act as agents. The attractions of this system are that it is the nearest in kind to the present jobbing system; it places all members on an equal basis; it could be readily expanded; and it does not confine activity to a market floor or to particular trading hours. It would, therefore, be possible to take advantage of London's central time zone position in the security markets of the world.

The system being proposed for gilts is broadly similar to that used in the US for the Treasury bond market. The market makers in gilts, who, like their US counterparts, will probably be known as primary dealers, will have direct access to the Bank of England and will be expected to make two-way prices in Government securities on demand. The institutions, which dominate the gilts market, will probably deal directly with the market makers by telephone rather than on the trading floor. The small investor will continue to transact business with broker/dealers who will be able to deal both as principal and agent but may choose to act only in one capacity. Many of these deals will take place on the trading floor. In addition there will be a group of dealers called 'inter-dealer brokers' who will act as arbitrageurs dealing between market makers. A casualty of these new arrangements is the Government Broker whose role will cease when the new dealing system starts.

In anticipation of the lifting of restrictions on outsiders' interests in Stock Exchange firms, clearing banks, merchant banks and other organisations have indulged in a headlong rush to forge links with leading broking and jobbing firms. The aim is to emulate the highly capitalised US-style investment house, providing broking, dealing, fund management and corporate and personal financial services under one roof. These changes have far-reaching implications notably for the international competitiveness of the London market, its regulatory framework and economic efficiency, and for those many individuals whose careers are, for better or for worse, caught up in the re-organisation.

The Over-the-Counter market

An interesting development in the securities industry in recent years has been the growth in the OTC market of unquoted securities. This market is not conducted on an exchange floor, but is a telephone market operated from the offices of the various licensed dealers situated in London and the provinces. Over 40 stocks are dealt in by the OTC market and the list is continually growing. Most of the dealers act as market makers charging no commission but making their profit on the difference between their buying and selling prices. One major dealer (Granville), however, operates by matching buyer and seller. The establishment of the Business Expansion Scheme (BES) has given a considerable fillip to the OTC market. Under the BES, a taxpayer who invests in an unquoted trading company can obtain tax relief on the consideration paid for the shares, subject to certain conditions. One of these conditions is that the shares are not quoted or dealt in on the USM. But the fact that a company's shares are dealt in on the OTC market does not disqualify it as a BES investment. The existence of a market in the shares considerably enhances the investment attractions of the company.

To obtain an OTC price it is necessary to telephone the appropriate market maker. For many stocks there is only one market maker. There is no daily published price information for OTC stocks. Granville, however, publishes its prices every Saturday in the *Financial Times*, and bargains in some OTC stocks are also marked under Rule 535.2 and, therefore, appear in Saturday's *Financial Times* as well as in the Stock Exchange Weekly Intelligence.

The OTC market is separate from the Stock Exchange and not subject to its regulations. It is a new market and its regulatory framework is still evolving. There are currently two competing regulatory bodies: The National Association of Dealers and Investment Managers (NASDIM) and the British Institute of Dealers in Securities (BIDS).

The selection of comparable companies

The *Stock Exchange Official Year Book* provides a classification of quoted companies by sub-sector of the *FT*-Actuaries All-Share Index, and this is a convenient starting point in the search for comparable companies.[2] The Extel Cards for each company in the relevant sub-sector should then be consulted. This will enable the list to be narrowed down to manageable proportions — five or six comparable companies would be ample. It is inadvisable to rely on a single company as a bench-mark. A record should be kept of all companies rejected in this selection process and of the reasons for their rejection. If there are many companies operating in the same industry as the subject company, the valuer can be very selective and choose only those companies whose characteristics match the subject company's closely. If a close fit in terms of activity and size is not possible, the selection criteria will have to be broadened.

The valuer should prepare a table of comparative statistics covering the selected companies and the subject company. This should show the name of the company, a brief description of its activity, and an indication of its size as measured by turnover. Selected operating statistics, such as compound annual growth rates in turnover, trading profits and earnings, should be calculated for each company. Financial ratios covering gearing and liquidity should also be included. This type of analysis gives the valuer a feel for the performance of the quoted companies relative to each other and to the subject company, and, when combined with a consideration of their stock market ratings, forms the basis of his conclusion as to the appropriate capitalisation rate for the subject company.

The stock market ratings of quoted companies should never be taken secondhand from the financial press, investment circulars or other publications; they should always be calculated by the valuer. This precaution is necessary to avoid both errors of calculation — these occur particularly in newspaper sources — and inconsistencies in the basis of calculations. Published price-to-earnings (P/E) ratios, for example, may be calculated using the latest reported annual earnings per share, or, if interim half-yearly results have been published since the latest annual accounts, the earnings figure may refer to the latest available 12-monthly period. Although an accounting standard exists for the calculation of earnings per share, this is in no way binding on the investment professional. In practice, each organisation has its own conventions for the calculation of earnings per share. The treatment of the tax charge and exceptional, extraordinary and prior year items varies so much that no generally accepted earnings per share figure for a company is likely to exist. There are great dangers, therefore, in

---

[2] A subscriber to one of the computerised data banks, such as Extel or Datastream, will find the screening and selection of comparable companies infinitely quicker than the manual method described in the text.

taking published investment ratings, particularly from different sources. The analyst must do his own calculations on a consistent and appropriate basis.

Some valuers derive their capitalisation rate from an index, usually the appropriate sub-sector of the *FT*-Actuaries All-Share Index. This can be a misleading practice and should be avoided if possible. There are two reasons for this. First, a sub-sector may be compiled from as few as half-a-dozen companies. If one of these companies is very large and has very different investment characteristics from the others, the index average, which is a weighting by market capitalisation, may not be typical of the smaller companies. Second, and perhaps more importantly, those who use this method do not generally carry out any financial analysis of the constituent companies. Without some such analysis, the investment ratings of individual companies can be highly misleading. This is because both the P/E ratio and the dividend yield express the relationship of the share price to a single (the latest) year's earnings and dividend. This relationship cannot be properly understood without an appreciation of the prospects of the company, i.e., of the likely future relationship. Company A, for example, may be on a dividend yield of five per cent and Company B, ten per cent. Assuming both companies have the same market capitalisation the index average would be 7.5%. However, if investment analysis reveals that Company B is expected to halve its dividends making its expected yield five per cent, the use of the index yield of 7.5% would be incorrect. Thus, the investment significance of an index P/E ratio or yield is slight and it is inadvisable ever to base a market valuation solely on such criteria.

When valuing by analogy with comparable quoted companies allowance must be made for the advantages which stem from a listing and for the speculative element in share prices. The quoted company has easier access to equity finance and can acquire companies or businesses by offering its own shares or paper in exchange. In expanding companies these attributes confer a significant advantage. Share prices can be volatile and fickle on a day-to-day basis as market rumour, sentiment and speculation ebb and flow. It would not be appropriate to import this frothy overlay into the valuation of unquoted securities. Some of this volatility will be caused by the existence of a thin market in individual stocks. This is particularly true of USM and OTC companies, and the valuer must satisfy himself that the volume of transactions in the selected stocks is such that the share price is a reliable guide to market value. It is interesting to note in this connection that the Inland Revenue does not necessarily accept that a USM stock's price is conclusive of its open market value.[3]

[3] Inland Revenue Statement of Practice 18/80, published 23 December 1980.

Published share price information

The most convenient source of share price information for most valuers will be the *Financial Times*. The official source of share prices is, of course, the Stock Exchange Daily Official List and this is generally used for statutory valuations of quoted shares. However, the Official List prices are not necessarily closing prices and no investment statistics are provided, making it impossible to make quick comparisons. The *FT* Share Information Service is carried in a two-page spread at the back of the paper. Here can be found the prices and investment statistics for some 2,500 company securities covering almost every actively traded share on the Stock Exchange, together with gilt-edged securities.

Securities are grouped under various industry classifications. The service also covers the prices of shares which are dealt in under the Exchange's various special rules. USM stocks are classified under the appropriate industry sector alongside fully listed stocks but are identified by a symbol. The prices of stocks not covered by the *FT* Share Information Service can be found in the Daily Official List. The Saturday *FT* also contains a page headed 'Stock Exchange Dealings,' which shows in respect of any share not covered by the *FT* service the prices at which business was done in the 24 hours after 3.30 pm on the previous Thursday. This information is taken from the Official List.

The statistics for each share are presented in columnar form and comprise the price, the current dividend per share, and three standard investment ratings, namely, the cover, the gross dividend yield and the P/E ratio. The price of the security is the closing middle price taking account of inter-office dealings after the Stock Exchange closes. The middle price referred to is the mid-point in the range quoted by jobbers for buyers and sellers. In addition to the closing price the *Financial Times* also gives the highest and lowest price for the share during the year. The data straddles 15 or 16 months in the early months of the calendar year and a switch to current year figures is usually made around the time of the Spring Budget. The high and low prices are adjusted for the effect of any scrip or rights issues.

The dividend per share is shown net of tax. It is not necessarily the latest annual dividend. For example, if an interim dividend has been announced since the last final dividend, this interim dividend plus last year's final dividend will be the amount shown in the dividend column. A symbol alongside the dividend amount indicates whether this interim is different from the previous year's interim. Likewise, if a company has forecast a future dividend, then that, and not the historical dividend, is shown, again with an explanatory symbol. To calculate the dividend yield the net dividend is grossed up at the current rate of advanced corporation tax, now 29% and expressed as a percentage of the closing price.

The dividend cover and the P/E ratio are based on earnings per share calculated by the *FT* staff. There are three methods of calculating earnings: the 'nil' distribution method, the 'net' distribution method and the 'maximum' or full distribution method. The maximum distribution method is used for calculating dividend cover and the net method is used for the P/E ratio. If the P/E ratio calculated on the net basis is different by ten per cent or more from that calculated on the nil method, the net P/E ratio is placed inside brackets.

The distinction between the three methods of calculating earnings per share lies in the treatment of dividends and advanced corporation tax. This topic is considered in Chapter 10, but, briefly, the nil distribution method assumes that no dividends are declared, and earnings are, therefore, equivalent to the profit after tax and after adding back any unrecovered advance corporation tax (ACT). The net distribution method is based on the actual tax charge, including irrecoverable ACT, and the maximum distribution method defines earnings as the maximum gross dividend that could be declared out of profits for the year. Because the P/E ratio is based on net earnings and dividend cover is based on maximum distribution earnings, it will not generally be possible to verify the published dividend cover by dividing the net dividend per share into earnings per share implied by the P/E ratio and the closing price. It is important to realise, however, that whichever of these three methods is used, *FT* staff adjust the basic profits after tax for items considered to be of an exceptional and non-recurring nature. In making these adjustments *FT* staff exercise their own judgement and will not necessarily follow the treatment in the annual accounts. Unlike some investment professionals, the *FT* uses SSAP 15 earnings and not notionally fully-taxed earnings. As with dividends, earnings per share are updated for interim results.

It will be clear from this explanation of the *FT* Share Information Service that dividend yields may be based on:

(a) the latest annual dividend, i.e., the interim and final dividend appearing in the audited annual accounts;
(b) the latest 12 month dividend arrived at by aggregating the current interim dividend with last year's final dividend; or
(c) a forecast dividend such as one contained in an offer document.

Similar remarks apply *mutatis mutandis* to the published P/E ratio. Furthermore, reported earnings per share may be adjusted by *FT* staff to give a more accurate picture, entailing subjective judgements as to what is exceptional or non-recurring. It may well be misleading, therefore, to draw conclusions about relative investment ratings as shown by the *FT* Share Information Service without further enquiries.

The *FT* Share Information Service also includes a full list of gilt-edged securities classified by outstanding period to maturity. The Index-linked stocks are listed beneath the undated gilts. They differ fundamentally from conventional gilts in that both interest and principal are related to changes in the retail price index, subject to an eight month lag. Conventional gilts have a flat yield being the gross annual interest payment as a percentage of the price, and a gross yield to redemption. This is the discount rate which equates all interest payments plus the terminal value of the bond to the present price. It is analogous to the internal rate of return used in discounted cash flow appraisals. The gross redemption yield is of greater significance than the flat yield, mainly because the latter ignores the capital element. However, the gross redemption yield assumes that the bond will be held to maturity. Gilt prices fluctuate and the price of gilt-edged stock may not approach its redemption price until quite near its maturity date. It can, of course, fall below its present price.

The redemption yield on Index-linked gilts is calculated on an assumed rate of inflation over the life of the gilt. The *FT* provides prospective real rates of return on the assumption of two different rates of inflation: ten per cent and five per cent. The redemption yields are low compared to those on conventional gilts, but the investor in the Index-linked gilt has the assurance that the value of his investment will be preserved in real terms, whatever the inflation rate. The interest rate on conventional gilts does not allow for changes in the purchasing power of money and in times of high inflation such investments may well show a negative real rate of return.

Gilt-edged yields are not used directly in deriving capitalization rates from comparable listed companies. However, they will have already been impounded in the rate of return on equities — assuming that different investment opportunities are priced in terms of one another — and the valuer should always compare the rate of return implied by his valuation with the rate of return on gilts. Gilt-edged stock is one of the most liquid and safest forms of investment. Provided the stock is held to maturity, the gross redemption yield is virtually certain. In view of this, a valuation should never show a rate of return below that obtainable on gilts; in most cases it should be much higher.

Share price indices

The most popular index of share prices is the *Financial Times* Industrial Ordinary Shares Index, often referred to as the 30-Share Index. This index was started in 1935 and is based on 30 heavily traded 'blue chip' shares chosen as representative of British industry. There are no financial companies in the index and until the development of North Sea oil scheme an important element of the UK economy, thus justifying the inclusion of BP, there were no oil companies in the index. Mining companies are also excluded.

Each share counts equally in the index, no regard being paid to market capitalisation. The index is based on a geometric, rather than an arithmetic, mean. This has the advantage of damping down large rises in individual constituents. It tends, however, to bias the index downwards over the longer term and, because of this and the fact that it excludes certain sectors of the equity market, the 30-Share Index is not a suitable long-term measure of market levels or portfolio performance. Its main attraction is its simplicity and ease of calculation. Unlike the *FT*-Actuaries All-Share Index, it is calculated hourly and is widely available to the media. It performs well as a sensitive indicator of the mood of the market on a daily and hourly basis. In addition to the 30-Share Index the *FT* also calculates other specialist indices including the Gold Mines Index. This is based on 20 South African mines and is calculated in the same way as the 30-Share Index. The base date is 12 September 1955.

The *FT*-Actuaries All-Share Index is the professional investor's yardstick for the level of the whole UK equity market, and from the share valuer's angle this is the index of most use. With over 740 constituents, it embraces over 90% of the aggregate capitalisation of the market. As a weighted arithmetic index it is designed to behave as an actual portfolio would behave, and its analysis into some 35 component indices is of great use in sector analysis.

The *FT*-Actuaries indices began in 1962 and are compiled jointly by the *Financial Times* and the Institute of Actuaries in London and the Faculty of Actuaries in Edinburgh. The design and management of the indices is the responsibility of the actuaries' organisations while the *FT* carries out the day-to-day collection of prices and does the calculations. The committee of actuaries takes great care that the Index properly covers the market. Changes in the capital of companies have to be reflected in their weightings, and takeovers and mergers mean that constituents of the index have to be constantly changed. The allocation of companies to particular sectors is given careful thought, since this classification is widely accepted in the securities industry as the basis of investment analysis. As the economy changes, certain sectors disappear and new ones are created.

The calculation of the indices is complicated but the effect is simple: the total market capitalisation of the constituents for each index is divided by the adjusted base capitalisation for that index. The base capitalisation is either that of 10 April 1962 — the original base for all the indices — or some later date at which a particular newer index was split up. With frequent changes in the weights and a regular review of the constituents, the indices do not form a static series. One rule is that if the market capitalisation of a constituent has fallen below 0.005% of the aggregate capitalisation of the constituents of the All-Share Index and remains below that proportion for more than 12 months, then it is removed. A replacement company needs to be sufficiently large — with a market capitalisation of at least £12 million at present.

In addition to the index numbers, there is also calculated for each sector the P/E ratio, earnings yield and dividend yield. The P/E ratio is based on net earnings per share and the earnings yield on the maximum distribution basis. Both earnings and dividends per share are updated for interim changes and any firm forecasts. This data is the same as that used in the *FT* Share Information Service. Sector dividend cover can be calculated by dividing the earnings yield by the dividend yield.

The *Financial Times* also publishes the *FT*-Actuaries Fixed Interest Indices. These fall into two groups, namely, indices of prices and indices of gross redemption yields. Five of the price indices cover British Government securities and the remaining two indices cover, respectively, debentures and loans, and preference shares. The index of British government securities is based upon 31 December 1975 = 100. The base date for the debentures and preference share indices is 31 December 1977, the debentures starting with a value of 100 and the preference shares starting at 76.72.

The debenture and loan stock price index includes only those stocks with an outstanding nominal issue of not less than £11 million. Convertibles, stocks with warrant options and those with large sinking funds are excluded. The preference share index contains commercial, industrial and investment trust preference shares. To be eligible for inclusion in the index a preference stock must have an outstanding nominal issue of not less than £3 million; it must be normal i.e., cumulative but not redeemable, convertible or participating, and its voting rights must be restricted. There must also be sufficient dividend cover. The five gilt price indices comprise three different maturity classifications, i.e., five years, five to fifteen years, over fifteen years, plus irredeemables and all stocks.

These fixed interest price indices are accompanied by a series of 14 indices of gross redemption yields. The gilt yields are analysed by low, medium and high coupon stocks and by three maturity brackets within each of these coupon classifications. The three different coupon classifications are required because investors' individual tax positions are such that markedly different yields can occur on low, as opposed to high, coupon stocks. Together with the yield on irredeemables, which incidentally is a flat yield, these statistics provide a representative picture of rates of return across the spectrum of gilt-edged stocks. They are relevant to some degree in every valuation.

In February 1984, the Stock Exchange launched a new equity index known as the *FT*-SE 100 Index. It was designed as a minute-by-minute index suitable for use in futures market trading on the London International Financial Futures Exchange. A futures contract based on the All-Share Index was not feasible because practical problems in collecting the 740-odd required prices made it extremely difficult to calculate the All-Share Index more than once a day. Neither was the 30-Share Index particularly suitable as it was insufficiently closely correlated with the All-Share Index.

The *FT*-SE 100 Index is calculated in much the same way as the All-Share Index. With few exceptions, it covers the UK's 100 largest companies and accounts for 70% of the market capitalisation of all UK equities. The index has a base value of 1000 as of January 1984, and its components numbered 69 industrials, five oils, 21 financials, two investment trusts, two mining finance companies and one overseas trader. Studies show a correlation of 99.2% between the All-Share and the *FT*-SE 100 Index calculated back to January 1978.

Efficient capital markets and portfolio theory

The Efficient Market Hypothesis

An efficient capital market is one in which prices instantaneously reflect all currently available information and where expected future returns are reflected in share prices according to the riskiness of each share. Proponents of the Efficient Market Hypothesis (EMH) believe the New York and London Stock Exchanges to be broadly efficient in this technical sense. A brief review of the EMH's implications gives a good idea of its importance.

If all new price-sensitive information is instantaneously and fully impounded in share prices, there is no point in either technical or fundamental investment analysis. It is fruitless for the chartist to seek signs in the past sequence of share price movements as to the likely future course of the share price, since all information in the past sequence of prices if fully reflected in today's price. Diligent research into the fundamentals — the search for information that others have not found or fully appreciated — is equally pointless for the same reasons. Furthermore, if the EMH is valid and shares are correctly priced in terms of their relative riskiness, the portfolio manager cannot reasonably expect to achieve above average rates of return for the risk assumed. It is futile to attempt to beat the market in risk-adjusted terms, and the fund manager should devote his energies to the construction and maintenance of an efficient portfolio, which is defined as one which maximises the rate of return for a given degree of risk or, conversely, minimises the risk for a given rate of return, rather than trying to out-perform the market.

These are the major implications, but they are by no means the whole story. If the stock market is efficient, new issues are seen in a completely new light. The issuing house's concern with the correct timing is misplaced since any time is 'correct'. No advice is needed as to the best type of security to issue since the price per unit of risk is the same for all securities and, therefore, there can be no intrinsically superior security. In theory, a company's capital mix, i.e., its proportion of debt to equity, should not matter as the simple mixing of securities cannot reduce the cost of capital. Implications abound, too, in the realms of capital budgeting and financial reporting.

Although the share valuer is at one remove from the stock market, his craft is affected by new developments in it. The use of comparable quoted companies as valuation bench marks is seen in a different light if the EMH is assumed to be valid. According to efficient market theory, it matters not whether companies as diverse as an advertising agency or a steel company were valued in terms of each other. If all securities are priced in terms of each other and all price-sensitive information is impounded in share prices, any quoted company — and one would be sufficient — could be selected as a bench-mark.

The initial reaction to the EMH of anyone with practical experience of the securities industry is usually one of incredulity and often derision. The theory flies in the face of perceived reality. How can it be true? This question can only be answered by an examination of the arguments, reasoning and evidence adduced in support of the theory. The fact that appearances are not consistent with the theory is insufficient grounds on its own for rejecting it. Chapter 6 contains a detailed review of the EMH and of the empirical work carried out to test it. In the author's view these empirical tests, so far as he has examined them, do not provide the support claimed for the hypothesis; indeed, the hypothesis itself is so generally worded as to be incapable of either verification or falsification. It is, in the scientific sense, a meaningless hypothesis, which could be re-formulated with a good deal more clarity and much less effort in the definitional truism that 'on average every investor's performance will be average'.

Modern Portfolio Theory

Modern Portfolio Theory (MPT) is based on the concept of efficient markets but is a separate set of ideas. MPT sets out to tell the portfolio manager how he ought to act in an efficient market. As we have seen, there is no such thing in an efficient market as an under- or over-valued security, and the portfolio manager is misdirecting his efforts if he continues to seek above-average risk-adjusted rates of return. According to MPT, he should concentrate his energies on ensuring that he has an efficient portfolio. An efficient portfolio is one which maximises the rate of return for the level of risk assumed.

The major insight claimed by MPT is that by holding a portfolio of securities much of the riskiness of the individual securities can be diversified away with no adverse effects on the rate of return. Thus a combination of securities — a portfolio — will, if it is efficient, have an expected rate of return which is a weighted average of the rates of return on the constituent securities, but will have a level of risk lower than the weighted average risk of the individual constituent securities.

Risk is seen in MPT as having two components: systematic or market risk; and unsystematic or business risk. Market risk is unavoidable and arises from general economic and financial conditions affecting all companies, although to varying degrees. Business or unsystematic risk is specific to individual companies and is exemplified by fire hazard, labour disputes, law suits, success or failure in mineral exploration, and the like. Business risk, according to MPT, can be eliminated by diversification, the profits from such 'risk' being offset by the losses. If business or unsystematic risk can be eliminated by efficient diversification, then the rate of return on a security will be a function solely of its market risk. There will be no reward for assuming business risk which can be eliminated by holding an efficient portfolio of securities.

MPT defines risk as the variability of expected future rates of return, a stock whose rate of return could vary dramatically being considered as having a greater level of risk than one whose rate of return is likely to fluctuate within a narrow band. However, in order to construct his efficient portfolio, the exponent of MPT needs to know not total risk but market risk of a security since only this type of risk affects the riskiness of the portfolio. The market risk of an individual stock is given by its beta co-efficient. Thus a beta of 1.5 indicates a stock which will, on average, move 1.5% for each one per cent move in the market. A stock with a beta of 0.5 will, on average, move 0.5% for each one per cent move in the market. The beta co-efficient is the slope of the regression line correlating the rate of return on the security with that on the market. The beta of a portfolio is the weighted average of the betas of its constituent securities. Fund managers in this new scheme of things do not concern themselves with the traditional investment ratings, such as the P/E ratio and the dividend yield, but solely with a share's beta co-efficient.

A host of questions immediately come to mind, even on this briefest summary of MPT. Can risk really be measured by the play of a share's price? Is the distinction between business risk and market risk tenable, and what evidence is there that the rate of return on a security compensates for the market risk but not the specific risk? Why should investment performance be judged in risk-adjusted and not absolute terms? These and other issues arising from MPT are discussed in detail in Chapter 7.

Like the EMH, MPT cannot be ignored. If formulas such as the Capital Asset Pricing Model, which express the relationship between risk and the rate of return, are valid descriptions of share price determination in the quoted sector, they must have implications for the valuation of unquoted securities. As those who persevere with Chapter 7 will learn, MPT, despite its mathematical elegance and sophistication, is naive. The assumptions on which the theory is buttressed are so unrealistic as to discredit the conclusions, and the logical framework is flawed by circularity of reasoning.

This is not to say that modern investment theory has nothing of value. The notion of a rate of return consisting of a risk-free rate plus a premium for risk is a valuable insight, and the academic research into the size of this premium over the years[4] is of considerable interest to the share valuer. Undoubtedly, much of the criticism levelled at current investment yardsticks such as the P/E ratio is justified, and the results of the investment performance surveys carried out by academic researchers are of great interest in their own right, even if the claim that they support the new theories is not justified. Regrettably, however, MPT bears all the hallmarks of theory developed in isolation from practice. It has been evolved in the rarified world of the academic journals, where the language of mathematics and the use of statistical method have effectively barred from the debate he who has most to offer: the professional.

[4] Elroy Dimson and Richard A. Brealey, 'The Risk Premium on U.K. Equities', *The Investment Analyst*, no. 52 (1978), pp. 14–18.

6

The Efficient Market Hypothesis

The Efficient Market Hypothesis (EMH) is about the nature of share prices quoted on the Stock Exchange and of their relationship to each other. Quoted share prices have a profound influence on the valuation of unquoted shares. Often, this influence is direct, for example, when quoted companies are selected as benchmarks; at other times it is more general in nature. Any theory, therefore, which claims to throw new light on the process of share price determination and on the 'correctness' of share prices in general is of fundamental significance to the share valuer and deserves his closest attention. The EMH has many other implications briefly alluded to in the preceding chapter.

In general terms, the theory of efficient markets is concerned with whether share prices at any point in time 'fully reflect' available information.[1] The EMH states that, in general, they do. Three levels of efficiency are distinguished, namely, the weak level, the semi-strong level and the strong level, each corresponding to a different category of information. The weak form of the EMH asserts that share prices fully reflect the information contained in the sequence of past prices; the semi-strong form asserts that share prices fully reflect all publicly available information; and, according to the strong form, all relevant information, including inside information and the superior insights of the specialist, is fully impounded in share prices.

The weak form

In academic and scientific work, the formulation of an hypothesis usually precedes the empirical work of corroborating it: someone has an idea or theory and then sets out testing it in the real world. With the EMH, however, much of the empirical work preceded the development of the theory. Academic researchers in the 1950s and early 1960s observed that share prices, and also other speculative prices, such as commodities, tended to move in a random fashion. There was little or no statistical dependence between the change in a share's price one day

[1] Eugene F. Fama, 'Efficient Capital Markets: a Review of Theory and Empirical Work', *Journal of Finance*, 25 (May 1970), pp. 383–417, reprinted in Stephen H. Archer and Charles A. Ambrosio, *The Theory of Business Finance: A Book of Readings*, 3rd ed. (New York: Macmillan, 1983), p. 183.

with its change the next day. In the absence of statistical dependence, there could be no statistical technique for calculating from the sequence of past price movements what the share price would be in the future. But this is exactly what the chartist does. From graphs of the share's price history, often in conjunction with the trading volume, the chartist discerns familiar patterns and formations which repeat themselves. These patterns include the head and shoulders formation, triple bottoms, double tops and a host of other picturesque terms. When the price moves within a narrow band or range, the share is often said to be in a consolidation phase. Barriers below which the share price appears reluctant to descend are termed its resistance levels. And so on.

This activity, claim the adherents of the EMH, is pointless and a waste of effort. It is not possible to predict the future price simply from an analysis or extrapolation of the past price sequence. What serial correlation there is between successive share price movements is extremely low and of insufficient magnitude, when dealing costs are taken into account, to permit any profit in excess of that which could be obtained by a simple buy-and-hold strategy. In other words, current prices fully reflect all the information content of past prices. This is known as the weak form of the theory, the term referring to the restrictive category of information that is claimed to be fully reflected in the current price.

It is beyond the scope of the treatment here to review the considerable evidence that has been accumulated on the weak form of the EMH. An early example, however, illustrates the nature of the academic researcher's findings. In 1959, Harry V. Roberts published an article in the *Journal of Finance*[2] which showed comparisons between the graph of actual movements in share prices over a certain period with a graph of simulated or invented share prices. The simulated share prices were arrived at by cumulating random numbers. The actual share prices were the Friday closing levels of the Dow Jones Industrial Average Index for the New York Stock Exchange for each of the 52 weeks ended 28 December 1956. Roberts' graphs are shown in figure 1. Roberts pointed out that there was a similarity between the two graphs and that the chartists' well known formations and patterns could be detected in both graphs.

These findings were in no way conclusive of randomness but they nevertheless pointed to an interesting phenomenon. They led eventually to many other tests of greater depth and extent, using statistical techniques. With one or two exceptions, the researchers invariably concluded from these tests that the market was efficient in the weak sense.

[2] Harry V. Roberts, 'Stock Market "Patterns" and Financial Analysis: Methodological Suggestions', *Journal of Finance*, 4 (March 1959), pp. 1–10.

Figure 1: Actual and simulated levels of stock market prices for 52 weeks.

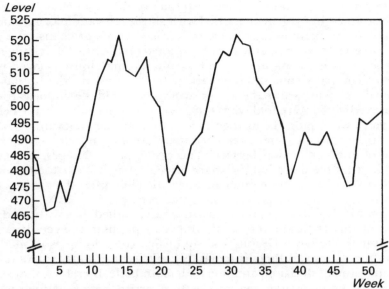

Friday closing levels, 30 December 1955–28 December 1956, Dow Jones industrial average.

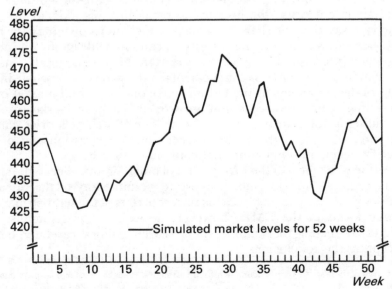

Simulated market levels for 52 weeks

Source: Roberts, *Stock Market Patterns*, pp. 5–6.

The absence of any statistical dependence in successive price changes does not mean that there is no connection or link between the share price today and the price yesterday or the day before. Imagine, for example, that you are supplied with all the relevant information for a quoted company except its current price and its price history. You have to guess the price at which it is quoted on the Stock Exchange. In essence, this is the nature of the task the Issuing House is faced with when a company comes to the market. It is beyond any doubt that the chances of your estimate being accurate would be immeasurably improved if you were told what the price was yesterday, the day before or even a week ago. The further back in time, the less relevant becomes the price. Statistical independence therefore does not deny the existence of any connection between successive price changes; it merely implies that the direction the share price is going to take tomorrow or further into the future cannot be inferred solely from the sequence of past prices. The chartist maintains that it can.

Technical analysis, as the chartists' craft is called, has withstood the blast of this criticism very well, and is as popular as ever. It is not difficult to see why. Despite the sophisticated techniques of modern investment analysis there is inevitably much uncertainty surrounding the investment decision, and it is understandable, therefore, that some investors should avail themselves of the chartists' services. If the charts confirm his fundamental analysis, the investor is more confident in his decision. A technical position which conflicts with the fundamental analysis might cause the investor to reconsider his judgement. And who is to say that the share price data, which on its own may (or may not) be useless in predicting the future, cannot yield significant meaning when interpreted by someone versed in the fundamentals? Just as one can interpret the broad movements in the market as a whole in the light of developments in the national economy — a bull market often preceding a phase of economic growth and a bear market usually heralding a down-turn — so the behaviour of a share's price can be interpreted in the light of the market's own progression and of the specific events impinging on that company's future.

As the weak form of the EMH is not of much significance to the share valuer, the author does not propose to examine any of the research studies in detail. Judging from his review of tests of the semi-strong and strong forms of the EMH, however, he would strongly advise the interested reader to examine the research studies carefully before accepting the conclusions.[3]

---

[3] A review of these studies can be found in most investment text books. See, for example, Simon M. Keane, *Stock Market Efficiency: Theory, Evidence and Implications* (Oxford: Philip Allan, 1983); and James Lorie and Mary Hamilton, *The Stock Market: Theories and Evidence* (Homewood, Ill.: Irwin, 1973).

The semi-strong form

From the restricted and easily tested hypothesis that successive share price movements are random, there has developed an infinitely more general and vastly stronger hypothesis that share prices fully reflect all relevant publicly available information. This is the semi-strong form of the EMH. It questions the usefulness of much of the investment analysis currently undertaken and it claims that the traditional approach to investment selection, i.e., that of beating the market, is futile. Instead of trying to pick winners, fund managers should devote their energies to ensuring that the rate of return on their portfolios is the maximum available in the market for the level of risk assumed.

As can be imagined, the semi-strong hypothesis is highly contentious — particularly amongst those who work in the securities industry. Investment professionals, such as stockbrokers who are in daily touch with buyers and sellers, know all too well how fickle and unstable people's views of the worth of a share are. Any suggestion that the current share price represents the market's last word on that company barring any new price sensitive information conflicts with appearances to say the least. The market itself can be fickle on a day-to-day basis without any change in the fundamentals, as witnessed for example by the following quotation from the Lex column of the *Financial Times* of 4 August 1984:

> A London market which awoke on Monday to fears of crashing oil prices, bringing in their wake a tumbling pound has ended the week in a mood of unbridled optimism . . . the capacity of financial markets to view their position as a bed of nails one day and a bed of roses the next is more breathtaking than ever.

The appearances therefore do not indicate market efficiency. This suggests the need to review the evidence very carefully.

First, however, we must be clear about one thing. The assertion that share prices 'fully reflect' all available information is an unrestricted generalised hypothesis which in the nature of things cannot be proved. To prove it in respect of a particular share price, let alone in respect of share prices generally, is an impossible task. It would entail identifying every piece of information conceivably relevant to an investment appraisal of the company. This would include the company's history, activities, products, market share, factories, plant and equipment, management and labour, trading record, balance sheet strengths and weaknesses, cash flow characteristics, its short-, medium- and long-term prospects in the light of the industry background, and the outlook for the national and perhaps international economy. Similar information would be required for comparable companies. It would then be necessary to prove:

(a) that every 'piece' of information has had an impact on the share price; and
(b) that the impact is no more nor less than it 'ought' to have been, i.e., that the piece of information was 'fully' reflected in the share price.

But just as the proponents of the EMH cannot prove their hypothesis empirically neither can the investment practitioner disprove it. For in order to disprove it he is set the same herculean task. This is, doubtless, one of the principal reasons for the incomprehension between practitioner and theoretician with regard to the EMH and the reason why it has failed to gain widespread acceptance in the investment world.

Investment theory is very much under the wing of economics, a discipline which considers itself a science and which espouses the scientific method. Science is characterised by the use of observation and experiment. A run of favourable observational data suggests an underlying law or state of affairs which is then formulated into a generalised hypothesis. However, a run of favourable data, no matter how long, is logically insufficient to establish the truth of an unrestricted generalisation. This is an accepted and well recognised aspect of the scientific method. But if logic is not to be the litmus test of a scientific hypothesis, what is? According to Sir Karl Popper, the philosopher of science, the hallmark of a truly scientific hypothesis is falsifiability. The scientist puts himself at risk, commits himself. It is open for anyone to try and refute the hypothesis by searching for contradictory evidence. The assertion that every atom has a nucleus can be tested, and the hypothesis destroyed if a single atom without a nucleus were found. As it is not possible to establish conclusively, or even beyond reasonable doubt, whether all public information is fully reflected in the share price or indeed in the market generally, the EMH in its semi-strong (and indeed strong) form does not have this hallmark of falsifiability. The fact that the EMH is only a null or bench-mark hypothesis and not one which is suggested by appearances is all the more reason why this criterion of falsifiability should be obligatory.

Ignoring for the moment this fundamental reservation let us examine the nature of the direct evidence adduced in support of the EMH in its semi-strong form. We notice immediately — and no doubt for the reasons already referred to — that not one of the tests of the semi-strong form has been designed to verify whether an individual share price or a group of different companies' share prices at any point in time fully reflects all the available information. Instead, the approach has been to select various types of information, such as scrip issues, earnings and dividend announcements, share placings and changes in interest rates, and to ascertain whether the market's reaction to such information is 'efficient'. This means that the share price reacts instantaneously to the publication of the information and that the magnitude of the change is no more nor less than it ought to be.

But how can the question of 'ought' be answered, other than by the academic researcher providing his own essentially subjective view of the effect that a particular piece of information should have on a share's price. This difficulty is circumvented by the introduction of a model of share price behaviour: an hypothesis as to how share prices are determined. The usefulness of such a model for the researcher lies in the fact that it is theoretically possible to specify what the rate of return on a share should be at a point in time. The rate of return on a share around the publication date of price sensitive information can then be observed to see whether it is significantly above or below what it ought to be as calculated by the model. The persistence of excess rates of return would imply inefficiency, i.e., the scope for above average performance. Inefficiency would also be implicit if rates of return were too low.

The model used throughout most of the tests of the semi-strong and the strong forms of the EMH is the Capital Asset Pricing Model (CAPM). The CAPM is a complicated piece of investment theory, which it would be inappropriate at this stage to set out in detail. Suffice it to say, however, that by assenting to the use of this model — as we do for the sake of argument — we are implicitly accepting a body of highly contentious theory about risk and the rate of return, which appears itself to be based on the assumption of an efficient market. In other words, a technique is being used in the verification of an hypothesis, which is itself dependent for its validity on the hypothesis being verified. It is also relevant to point out that the CAPM is based on expectational relationships, i.e., the expected rate of return is related to the expected risk. However, expectations cannot be observed. But it has apparently been demonstrated mathematically that the CAPM relationships hold for realised outcomes, i.e., that on average our expectations are realised! This so conflicts with everyday experience of life as to suggest that the mathematical manipulations are no more than an intellectual game. This reservation, too, we hold in abeyance.

The initial major work on evidencing the semi-strong form of the EMH was the study carried out by Messrs Fama, Fisher, Jensen and Roll (FFJR) on the effect of scrip issues on share prices.[4] This piece of

---

[4] Eugene F. Fama, Lawrence Fisher, Michael C. Jensen and Richard Roll, 'The Adjustment of Stock Prices to New Information', *International Economic Review*, 10, no 1 (February 1970), pp. 1–21.

research is generally acclaimed in the EMH literature as a comprehensive and rigorous scientific test, and its methodology was copied in later research studies. It is, therefore, worth examining in some detail.

The object of the FFJR study was '. . . to examine the process by which common stock prices adjust to the information (if any) that is implicit in a stock split'.[5] A scrip issue (in US terminology, a stock split) by itself has no economic significance. It affects neither the assets nor the profits of the company; it merely increases the number of shares. Despite this, the announcement of a scrip issue is traditionally regarded as a bull point, although whether it has ever been so regarded by professional investment managers is another matter. FFJR's approach was to examine the evidence on two related fronts:

(a) is there normally some 'unusual' [sic] behaviour in the rate of return on a security (i.e., its price) in the months surrounding a scrip; and

(b) if scrip issues are associated with 'unusual' price behaviour, to what extent can this be accounted for by relationships between scrips and changes in other more fundamental variables?

FFJR took 940 scrip issues on the New York Stock Exchange between 1927 and 1960. As some companies had scrip issues on more than one occasion, the number of companies included in the test was 622. For each of these companies, FFJR estimated the statistical relationship of the share's monthly rate of return (price level) with the rate of return on all quoted stocks on the Exchange using a regression technique. The estimated relationships were based on the 420 months during the period 1927 to 1959. For this purpose, the 15 months before and the 15 months after the split were excluded so that any unusual price behaviour in the months surrounding the split would not distort the long-term relationship. Unusual price behaviour would be reflected in deviations of the share's monthly rate of return from its theoretical level implied by the normal long-term relationship. FFJR calculated the average deviation of all 622 shares in each of the 29 months before and after the month of the scrip. The results are shown in figure 2.

The vertical axis measures the *cumulative* average deviations of returns (residuals) from the 'normal' relationships. A rising curve means that the deviations are positive, i.e., that the rates of return, and hence price, of the shares were more than they theoretically ought to

[5] Ibid., p. 1.

Figure 2: Cumulative average residuals — all splits.

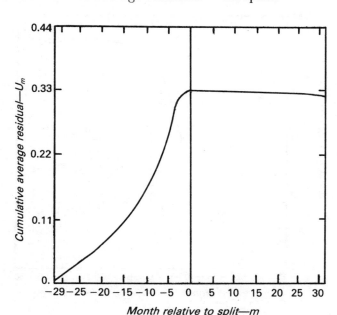

have been. After the scrip month the curve is fairly flat, indicating a return of the share price to its normal relationship. Figures 3 and 4 show the cumulative average deviations (residuals) for, respectively, scrip issues which were in due course followed by a rise in dividend and those which were followed by a fall in dividend. Increases and decreases for this purpose are defined relative to the market. Thus, if a dividend rose by eight per cent compared with an overall rise of the market of ten per cent, it would be classified as a decrease. The other point to bear in mind is that the scrip issues selected for the tests occurred at different times over a 33-year period although they are averaged into a single curve for the purpose at hand.

It is interesting to see how FFJR interpret the results of their work. They conclude that the rise in the average rates of return above their usual (i.e., longer-term) levels during the 29 months prior to the scrip cannot be attributed to the scrip issue itself, since in only about ten per cent of the cases is the period between the announcement date and the effective date of the scrip greater than four months. To continue in Fama's own words:

Figure 3: Cumulative average residuals for dividend 'increases'.

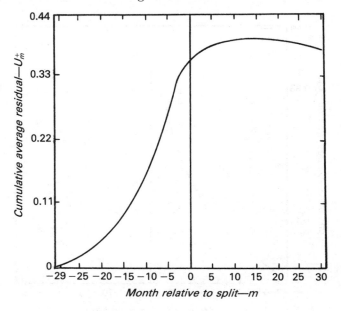

Figure 4: Cumulative average residuals for dividend 'decreases'.

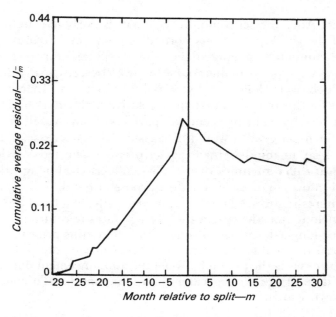

Rather it seems that firms tend to split their shares [make a scrip issue] during 'abnormally' good times — that is, during periods when the prices of their shares have increased more than would be implied by their normal relationships with general market prices, which itself probably reflects a sharp improvement, relative to the market, in the earnings prospects of these firms sometime during the years immediately preceding a split . . . when a split is announced the market interprets this (and correctly so) as a signal that the company's directors are probably confident that future earnings will be sufficient to maintain dividend payments at a higher level. Thus, the large price increases in the month immediately preceding a split may be due to an alteration in expectations concerning the future earnings potential of the firm, rather than to any intrinsic effects of the split itself. If this hypothesis is correct, return behaviour subsequent to splits (scrips) should be substantially different for the cases where the dividend increase materialises than for cases where it does not. FFJR argue that in fact the differences are in the directions that would be predicted.[6]

FFJR see their results as implying, 'that on the average the market makes unbiased dividend forecasts for split securities and these forecasts are fully reflected in the price of the security by the end of the split month'.[7]

Before considering whether FFJR's conclusions follow from the facts, it is worth considering whether in any event they throw much light on the efficiency of the market. The finding that scrip issues often presage a dividend increase is not new and has no implications for market efficiency. Market efficiency is about whether prices fully and instantaneously reflect information so as to preclude above-average performance. FFJR conclude that the share price on the effective date of the scrip reflects the dividend implications of the scrip. However, this does not imply efficiency since the effective date is not an information event. It is the announcement date which matters, not the effective date.

Incredible as it seems, the FFJR study did not focus on the announcement date but on a non-event — the date the shares actually went 'ex scrip'. The FFJR study ought to have examined 'unusual' price behaviour around the announcement date to see whether it was possible to profit thereby. The fact that it did not do so seems to have

6 Fama, p. 210.
7 FFJR, p. 17.

escaped some writers. For example, in a 'classic' article on the EMH in the *Investment Analyst* Henfrey, Albrecht and Richards stated: 'their [FFJR's] work showed that by the time the stock split was *announced* the market had fully rediscounted the fundamental information implicit in the stock split'.[8] Professor Keane, whose book provides an admirable non-mathematical discussion of the EMH, falls into the same trap: 'it [the FFJR study] has also found that market prices adjust to these potentially favourable signals [dividend increases] and that the adjustment appears to be sufficiently complete around the announcement date to prevent investors from profitably trading on the strength of the information'.[9] Fama, however, was careful not to make this mistake when summarising the results of the FFJR study.[10]

In fairness to FFJR, it should be pointed out that towards the end of their paper they addressed the problem of the announcement date versus the effective date. They say it is impossible to test fully the policy of buying a share as soon as a scrip issue is announced, since information often leaks into the market before the split is announced or even proposed to shareholders. (This may well be so and illustrates the point made at the outset about the unscientific nature of the EMH, i.e., the impossibility of verifying or falsifying it.) However, in opting for the effective date as opposed to the announcement date, FFJR have chosen an irrelevant date. Despite this difficulty with the announcement date, FFJR were not deterred from taking a random sample of 52 scrip issues out of their 940 and reworking the graph shown in figures 3 and 4 using month 0, first as the announcement date, and then as the effective date. FFJR gave no data on these 52 scrip issues and presented no graphs. They merely gave the following summary conclusion: 'in this sample the behaviour of the residuals after the announcement date is almost identical to the behaviour of the residuals after the split date . . . this suggests that one also cannot profit by buying after the announcement date'. Therefore, in the sample of 52 scrip issues the behaviour of the curve both after the announcement date and the effective date must have been flat, something like the curve in figure 5.

It is instructive to compare the behaviour of this curve with that of the curves for all 940 stocks in figures 2, 3 and 4. In none of the FFJR graphs is there any evidence of flatness prior to month 0, the curve in each case rising steeply up to that point. As graphs can be misleading when the scale is changed, it is perhaps safer to check this point by

---

[8] A. W. Henfrey, B. Albrecht and Paul Richards, 'The U.K. Stock Market and the Efficient Market Model', *The Investment Analyst*, no 48 (September 1977), p. 12.
[9] Keane, *Stock Market Efficiency: Theory, Evidence and Implications*, pp. 40–41.
[10] Eugene F. Fama, 'Efficient Capital Markets: a Review of Theory and Empirical Work', *Journal of Finance*, 25, p. 210.

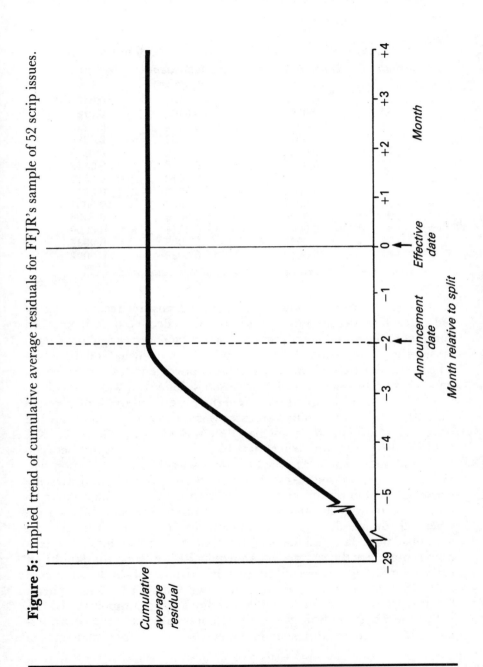

Figure 5: Implied trend of cumulative average residuals for FFJR's sample of 52 scrip issues.

referring to the values of the residuals (unusually high price levels) in and around the scrip month, as shown in the FFJR study. These were as follows:

Average residuals in month surrounding the split

Month	Splits/dividend increases	Split/dividend decreases	All splits
−6	0.0194	0.0106	0.0169
−5	0.0194	0.0100	0.0167
−4	0.0260	0.0104	0.0216
−3	0.0325	0.0204	0.0289
−2	0.0390	0.0296	0.0363
−1	0.0199	0.0176	0.0192
0	0.0131	0.0090	0.0068
+1	0.0016	0.0088	0.0014
+2	0.0052	0.0024	0.0031
+3	0.0024	0.0089	0.0008
+4	0.0045	0.0114	0.0000
+5	0.0048	0.0003	0.0033
+6	0.0012	0.0038	0.0002

Source: FFJR, *The Adjustment of Stock Prices to New Information*, p. 10.

The 'all splits' column shows that significant positive residuals occurred in each of the six months prior to the effective date in marked contrast to the month after that date, when there appears to have been no significant deviation of the share price from its 'usual' relationship. The average period of time between announcement date and effective date for the 940 stocks was not disclosed if, indeed, it was ever calculated. However, FFJR mention that in their random sample of 52 out of the 940 scrip issues, in only two cases was the period greater than 162 days (5.4 months) and the median time was 44.5 days (1.5 months).

FFJR also refer to an earlier study by Jaffe of 100 stock splits between 1946 and 1957 where the median time was 69 days (2.3 months). Whichever period one takes, therefore, the FFJR table indicates the existence of abnormally high rates of return between the announcement date and the effective date. FFJR's random sample of 52 scrips, where no unusually high rates of return were evident between the announcement date and the effective date, cannot therefore have been representative of the 940 stocks as a whole. In any event, the data FFJR present for all 940 scrip issues suggest the existence of abnormal rates of return for, on average, two months after the scrip announcement. Contrary to what is claimed, FFJR's findings do not support the EMH.

But the FFJR analysis raises other, potentially embarrassing questions. Do not their graphs show the persistence of abnormal rates of return over the 30-month period prior to the split? Did these not provide an opportunity for the investor to beat the market systematically? Unfortunately, no, because according to FFJR: '. . . the behavior of the average residuals is non-representative of the behavior of individual securities'.[11] But, surely, if the average is not representative of the typical it cannot be used to draw inferences about the behaviour of securities in general, or, alternatively, if generalisations can be drawn from the behaviour of the average residuals, they cannot be arbitrarily restricted to those which are consistent with the EMH.

The other difficulty which the FFJR study presents is the very behaviour of the average residuals around the effective date. Is it not strange that the average residuals in all three categories suddenly fall to insignificant levels in the month following the effective date — a non-event in terms of information? Why should the price suddenly fall back to its 'normal' level on that date? One would have expected some explanation of this apparent gross market inefficiency.[12]

There are two comments of a more general nature which need to be made on the FFJR study, and these may well be applicable to the various subsequent research studies which have been modelled on the FFJR one. First, the authors are highly proficient in their use of statistics and an inordinate amount of effort seems to be devoted to preening statistical feathers. The end result is an exercise which many finance practitioners would consider naive and meaningless. For example, the market model used by FFJR to estimate the 'normal' price level for a stock and hence the existence of any unusual price behaviour, is based on a calculated relationship of the individual security to that of the market over the period 1927 to 1960 — a span of 33 years during which the economic and financial background has changed beyond recognition. Any notion of such a relationship operating in real life over such a period would be laughed out of court. It is purely a creation of statistics, permitted for no better reason than that the regression line proved a good fit. It is doubtful whether the residuals mean anything.

Second, given the objective of gauging the reaction of share prices to scrip issues, one would have expected the analysis to focus on a much shorter period of time — a matter of weeks either side of the announcement date. To take a five year period was totally unnecessary and in fact counter-productive as the precise behaviour of the share price around the operative date could not clearly be observed as the lowest unit of time was the month.

---

[11] FFJR, *International Economic Review,* 10, no 1, p. 19.

[12] One obvious possibility comes to mind but it implies such an elementary blunder that it can hardly be true. This is that the mark-down in price when shares go 'ex scrip' has not been properly adjusted for, either in the sequence of earlier share prices or in the regressions.

Figure 6: Monthly stock returns and changes in annual earnings.

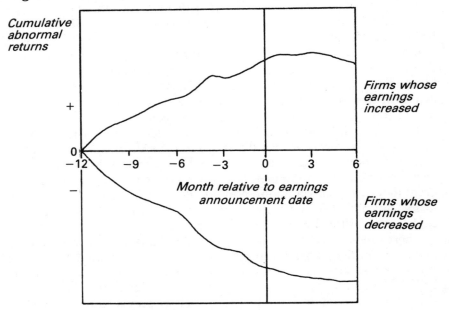

Source: Ball and Brown, p. 169.

The FFJR test has been followed by others, who have generally adopted the same approach of examining 'abnormal' share price behaviour around the time of different kinds of public announcements, 'abnormal' being defined in terms of the market model used. Thus Ball and Brown investigated the impact of earnings announcements on 261 US firms during the period 1957 to 1965.[13] Although their objective was to evaluate the usefulness of accounting earnings in establishing market prices, the study has been used to test the efficiency of the market.

Their study concluded that 85-90% of the price movement produced by earnings prospects was reflected in the share price by the announcement date. But, as we can see from the results in figure 6, there was ample opportunity to earn abnormal rates of return during the 12 months preceding the announcement.[14] This, too, fails to lend support to the EMH.

[13] R. Ball and P. Brown, 'An Empirical Evaluation of Accounting Income Numbers', *Journal of Accounting Research* (Autumn 1968), pp. 159–178.
[14] It is interesting to note that Fama in a review of the Ball and Brown study entered the same caveat as he did for the FFJR results, namely, that the persistence of abnormal returns as reflected in the average residuals did not imply opportunities for beating the market, since the behaviour of the average was not representative of the behaviour of individual securities.

The author has not reviewed the other tests and on the evidence so far does not feel inclined to do so. In any case, as Professor Keane, an adherent of the EMH, has remarked: '. . . the task of isolating the extent to which price movements can be attributed to a specific item or a group of items always presents a problem. The amount of direct research has therefore been, and is likely to remain, relatively restricted. Without the support of the indirect approach, the direct evidence is probably insufficient to convince investors of the market's efficiency.'[15] In the author's view, it is not only the limited extent of the direct tests which is likely to cause investors to be sceptical, but also the fact that on closer inspection the tests themselves do not support the hypothesis of an efficient market.

The strong form

The strong form of the EMH maintains that prices fully reflect all relevant information, whether publicly available or not. This is the most contentious form of the hypothesis and not even the most ardent adherent of the EMH would maintain that it is an exact description of the reality. Indeed, certain academic studies have indicated strong form inefficiencies. For example, specialists on the New York Stock Exchange apparently use their monopolistic access to information concerning unfulfilled limit orders to generate monopoly profits and, as everyone knows, officers of corporations may have inside information about their firms.[16]

Although the strong form is acknowledged to be not strictly valid, academic tests have been carried out to ascertain the extent to which it may be a true description of the reality. In Fama's words: 'Specifically, how far down through the investment community do deviations from the model permeate? Does it pay for the average investor (or the average economist) to expend resources searching out little known information? Are such activities even generally profitable for various groups of "market professionals"? More generally, who are the people in the investment community that have access to "special information"?'[17]

These questions are of great interest to the practitioner and if the EMH literature can throw some light on them a considerable service

[15] Keane, *Stock Market Efficiency: Theory, Evidence and Implications*, p. 41.
[16] Victor Niederhoffer and M. F. Osborne, 'Market Making and Reversals on the Stock Exchange', *Journal of the American Statistical Association*, 61 (December 1966), pp. 897–916; and Myron Scholes, 'A Test of the Competitive Hypothesis; the Market for New Issues and Secondary Offerings' (unpublished PhD thesis, Graduate School of Business, University of Chicago, 1969).
[17] Fama, *Journal of Finance*, 25, no 2, p. 213.

will have been rendered. As they are very much bound up with the question of investment performance, this has been the focus of the tests of the strong form of the EMH. Before we review these studies of investment performance, it is essential to be clear on their relevance to the EMH. The strong form of the EMH, more so than the semi-strong form, is an untestable hypothesis, and a little reflection on the difficulty of (a) identifying the existence of inside information, (b) detecting its use and (c) assessing whether it is fully reflected in the share price, will confirm that this is so.

The measurement of the investment performance of various institutional funds cannot, by itself, either prove or disprove the EMH. There are a number of reasons for this. First, the EMH does not maintain that shares are 'correctly' priced in absolute terms, i.e., with the benefit of hindsight. Rather it claims that they are 'correctly' priced in terms of the information available at the time. The actual outcome may be very different from what was expected from the available information. In the words of Henfrey, Albrecht and Richards: 'Market efficiency, however, does not imply that ex-ante expectations necessarily equal ex-post investments returns; it is possible with hindsight to show that most securities or funds have been "mispriced". However, this involves information not available at the time. Market efficiency only requires that currently available information be reflected in the price.'[18]

Second, conclusions relevant to the EMH can only be drawn from investment performance studies if the researcher knows the extent to which the fund used publicly available information, as opposed to inside or 'monopolistic' information. He must also be able to distinguish between performance based on fundamental analysis and that based on technical or chart analysis. Finally, and most importantly, measuring the performance of a large group of institutional funds says nothing about the behaviour of individual shares. An average across such a wide spectrum could well conceal a varied pattern of investment return behaviour, doubtless some of it for and some of it against the EMH.

The first so-called indirect test of the EMH was by Jensen in the 1960s.[19] He studied the performance of 115 mutual funds in the US over the period 1955 to 1964. He found that the funds on average were unable to out-perform a passive strategy based on holding the Index and that no individual fund was able to perform better than

[18] Henfrey, Albrecht and Richards, *The Investment Analyst*, no 48, pp. 14–15.
[19] Michael C. Jensen, 'The Performance of Mutual Funds in the Period 1945–1964', *Journal of Finance*, 23 (May 1968), pp. 389–416. Reprinted in James Lorie and Richard Brealey, eds., *Modern Developments in Investment Management*, 2nd ed. (Hinsdale, Ill.: The Dryden Press, 1978), pp. 231–258.

could be expected from random chance. After management expenses the performance of the majority was noticeably poorer. Other studies of mutual funds performance in the US include those by Sharpe, Williamson, Treynor and Friend Blume and Crockett.[20] According to Professor Keane, their respective findings were similar to those of Jensen.[21]

In the United Kingdom, the evidence points less uniformly in the one direction. The first published study of UK unit trust performance was that of Briscoe, Samuels and Smythe in 1969,[22] who examined the performance of 14 unit trusts over the period 1953 to 1963 and found that the UK investor behaved as if risk was not important. They concluded that the EMH was invalid — at least in its strong form. Subsequent work by Moles and Taylor[23] arrived at similar conclusions. They studied 86 UK unit trusts over the period 1966 to 1975 and apparently found that the average unit trust managed a return of a little over one per cent above a naive buy/hold strategy, and 'growth' funds a three per cent per annum excess rate of return. However, these results contrasted sharply with the findings of Firth, Ward and Saunders, and Cranshaw.[24] Firth, for example, concluded that the unit trusts in his sample earned on average 1.34% less per year in the period 1965 to 1975 than they should have done given their level of market risk.

At first sight, therefore, the evidence in the US seems to point uniformly to an embarrassing failure on the part of the mutual funds to provide their investors with a rate of return in excess of that which they could have obtained by buying the index. In the UK, the earlier studies indicate some success for unit trust fund managers in achieving above average performance. Later studies, however, show the opposite picture, although it is noteworthy that the studies by Moles and Taylor

[20] William F. Sharpe, 'Mutual Fund Performance', *Journal of Business*, 39 Supplement (January 1966), pp. 119–38; J. Williamson, 'Measuring Mutual Fund Performance', *Financial Analysts' Journal* (November/December 1972), pp. 78–84; J. Treynor, 'How to Rate Management of Investment Funds', *Harvard Business Review* (January 1965), pp. 63–75; and I. Friend, M. Blume and J. Crockett, *Mutual Funds and Other Institutional Investors: A New Perspective* (New York: McGraw-Hill, 1970).

[21] Keane, p. 43. However, neither the Williamson nor the Treynor articles contained any empirical studies of mutual fund performance or of efficient market behaviour. Both articles were merely expositions of a particular way of measuring fund performance.

[22] G. Briscoe, J. M. Samuels and D. J. Smythe, 'The Treatment of Risk in the Stock Market', *Journal of Finance*, 24 (September 1979), pp. 707–714.

[23] P. Moles and B. Taylor, 'Unit Trust Risk — Return Performance, 1966–1975', *The Investment Analyst*, no. 47 (May 1977), pp. 34–41.

[24] M. A. Firth, 'The Investment Performance of Unit Trusts in the Period 1965-1975', *Journal of Money, Credit and Banking*, 9 (November 1977), pp. 597–604; C. Ward and A. Saunders, 'U.K. Unit Trust Performance 1964–74', *Journal of Business Finance and Accounting* (Winter 1976), pp. 83–99; T. E. Cranshaw, 'The Evaluation of Investment Performance', *Journal of Business* (October 1977), pp. 462–485.

and the study by Firth all cover the same period, i.e., 1966 to 1975, but arrived at different conclusions.

However, as we have seen from our review of the FFJR study, closer examination of the facts behind the conclusions can put an entirely different perspective on the results. It is now proposed, therefore, to scrutinise the Jensen mutual fund study referred to earlier. Epithets such as 'classic', 'celebrated' and even 'trail blazing' have been accorded to this piece of research in the EMH literature, and we can be sure that there is no unfairness in selecting this study. Furthermore, the method employed by Jensen has been copied in most of the subsequent investment performance tests carried out both in the US and the UK.

Much of Jensen's paper is devoted to an explanation and justification of the model he uses for assessing investment performance of the selected mutual funds. Jensen used the CAPM and it is noteworthy that the CAPM has been used in most of the other investment performance studies. This model, and portfolio theory generally, are reviewed in Chapter 7, where it is shown conclusively that these theories are fundamentally unsound. It would not be appropriate to repeat all the arguments here but two of the more fundamental objections to the use of the CAPM should be registered at this stage:

(a) As mentioned earlier, the CAPM itself assumes an efficient market, indeed, a hyper-efficient market in which all investors have identical subjective estimates of the expected return on a security and choose between different securities on the basis of that return and the risk involved, risk being defined as the variability of the expected return. The CAPM cannot be used to test the EMH since it is itself dependent on the existence of an efficient market for its own validity.

(b) Any theory or model of share price determination such as the CAPM, which: (i) defines risk solely in terms of share price variability; and (ii) asserts that a share's rate of return is determined solely by its risk and by the rate of return on the market, is one which, taking securities as a whole, defines share prices in terms of themselves. At best, it is a definitional truism which tells us nothing. At worst, it is a pretentious and misleading sophistry.

Putting aside for the moment these fundamental reservations about the conceptual framework in Jensen's study, and accepting for the sake of argument the validity of his technique, let us examine his conclusions more closely and see how they correspond with the statistical data.

Jensen collected data on the performance of 115 open-ended mutual funds in the US over the period 1955 to 1964. In addition, he was able to obtain data for the period 1945 to 1954 for 56 out of the original 115 funds. Jensen's central conclusion was that the 115 mutual funds yielded a rate of return on average 1.1% per annum below what they 'ought' to have earned, given their level of risk. This was after payment of all their operating expenses and brokerage and related to a ten-year period for some companies and a 20-year period for others.

It is interesting to note that 76 funds under-performed on this measure and only 39 out-performed. When the funds' operating expenses are added back so as to obtain a measure of the performance of the funds' portfolios, the average under-performance was 0.4% per annum. Again, under-performers at 67 outnumbered over-performers at 48. Jensen points out, however, that the difficulties in accurately assessing the funds' expenses in the earlier ten-year period probably led to some understatement in the rate of return. Thus, when we look at the performance of the 115 funds for the period 1955 to 1964, where the expense data is more reliable, the average under performance falls to 0.1% per annum. Interestingly, 60 funds out-performed and only 43 under-performed on this basis. But here Jensen warns about placing too much significance on the seemingly large number of funds which out-performed because of the effect of undoubted measurement errors in the risk-free rate and the rate of return on the market. These measurement errors apparently have a tendency to understate beta and overstate alpha.

In any event, by applying the tests for statistical significance to the excess rates of return Jensen concludes that 'there is very little evidence that any of these 115 mutual funds . . . possessed substantial forecasting ability'. Jensen's further conclusion that 'there is very little evidence that any individual fund was able to do significantly better than could be expected from mere random chance' was the *coup de grâce*.

All this amounts to an apparently damning indictment of mutual fund performance over the review period. But what about the implications for the EMH? Apart from one isolated reference to '. . . the widespread interest in the theory of random walks and its implications regarding forecasting success', Jensen makes no reference to the EMH in his study of mutual fund performance. This is not all that surprising in view of the point made earlier that such studies cannot be regarded as tests of the EMH. But, despite this understandable reticence in the article, there can be no doubt that Jensen's central conclusions are regarded as a vindication of the EMH.[25]

If Jensen's study is regarded primarily as a review of mutual fund performance from the angle of the investor in such a fund, his concentration on their net of expenses performance is understandable and

---

[25] See, for example, Fama, p. 213, and Keane, p. 43.

justifiable. But as a test of the EMH, designed to gauge whether professional investors can consistently achieve above-average rates of return, the real interest and relevance must lie in the performance of the funds before management expenses. The level of these expenses has no influence whatsoever on the rate of return on securities and are irrelevant in assessing the portfolio manager's share selection skills. They can also vary from fund to fund. It is only the gross performance of the funds which is strictly relevant in the context of the EMH. Ideally, also, an adjustment should be made to the funds' gross performance for their transaction costs (e.g., brokerage, commissions, taxes etc.), since the CAPM assumes that there are no transaction costs. For practical reasons this was not possible.

The 115 funds on average under-performed by 0.1% per annum over the period 1955 to 1964. Thus, given the imprecision inherent in the data and the adjustment required for brokerage commission, it would be misleading to imply either under-performance or over-performance. Rather, we should conclude that the average performance of all funds was what could have been 'expected' given their degree of risk. The obverse of Jensen's conclusion that the funds were on average unable to out-perform a buy-the-market-and-hold strategy must now be stated; namely, the funds were, on average, unable to under-perform a buy-the-market-and-hold strategy. (Jensen concluded that the funds could most certainly under-perform on the net of expenses basis. He did not examine the possibility of under-performing on a gross basis. Any evidence that the funds could consistently under-perform on a gross basis, would of course, point to market inefficiency just as would superior performance.)

Finally, Jensen's suggestion that no individual fund 'was able to do significantly better than that which we expected from mere random chance' requires clarification. As Jensen admits, the evidence here is suggestive rather than conclusive of the point being made. Furthermore, Jensen's use of the word 'expected' is in the mathematical sense of the probability-weighted average of all possible future outcomes.[26] It does not follow, therefore, that any one by blindly selecting investments with a pin in one hand and a list of stocks in the other would have done no worse than the funds. It merely means that a sufficiently large number of persons selecting portfolios in this way would on average over the ten-years have performed no worse than the funds. As this could well mean hundreds, even thousands, of investors some of whom would have under-performed, others out-performed the market, and some having an average performance, it is a meaningless point to make.

---

[26] A critique of this concept can be found in Chapter 7.

Having narrowed Jensen's conclusions to those which might have a bearing on the EMH, it is appropriate to recall what the EMH maintains. According to the EMH, share prices fully reflect all available information. New information is instantaneously impounded in the share price and the magnitude of the price adjustment is no more nor less than it ought to be. It is, therefore, impossible to beat the market and futile to attempt to do so. Holding in abeyance the fundamental objections raised to the CAPM performance yardstick, let us examine how Jensen's conclusion could possibly throw any light on the EMH debate.

The finding that, over a ten-year period (20 years in some cases) the 115 mutual funds performed on average roughly in line with the Standard and Poors Composite 500 Price Index is not that surprising, since the funds' investments, being confined exclusively to domestic US stocks, will, taking the 115 funds as a whole, be broadly invested in index stocks. Clearly, the longer the period of time studied, the greater the tendency towards the average will be. And is this not the clue to the real significance of Jensen's findings? His research study, and indeed the subsequent studies of other researchers using his method and approach, if they do anything, do no more than provide a laborious proof of a definitional truism which could be addressed to fund managers everywhere in the following terms: *On average your funds' performance will be average.*

The EMH maintains that new information is fully and instantaneously reflected in share prices. Measuring investment performance at the end of ten years (20 years in some instances), says nothing about the instantaneous reaction of share prices to new information. It is entirely consistent with the existence of systematic inefficiencies.

Finally, Jensen's study and those of subsequent researchers in this field suffer from a further serious conceptual defect. Jensen's study concentrated on the performance of 115 mutual funds because this was the most representative sample given his resources. Doubtless, he would have preferred to study every investor's performance, but that quite clearly was impossible. Now it is axiomatic that a mere sample cannot reveal more about the characteristics of a population than can a survey of the whole population. But, although a survey of the entire population of investors was out of the question, it is not difficult to deduce what Jensen would have found if he had carried out such a survey. He would have had to conclude that, on the average, all investors achieve an average performance. In fact they must do so by definition, and it is as true of performance over a ten-minute period as it is of performances over a ten-year one. Given Jensen's averaging technique, which has been copied by subsequent researchers, any sample size drawn from any length of time could have only one and the same conclusion, i.e., that on average the funds performed in line with their average risk. Any other conclusion would be invalidated by sampling error: the sample could not have been representative. If the results of these tests are a foregone conclusion given the theoretical approach adopted, they can have no claim to be taken seriously.

This error of principle manifest in Jensen's approach is best illustrated by example from a totally different field. Imagine that a manufacturer has a batch of 5,000 light bulbs of uncertain quality and wants to know the extent to which bulbs in the batch have an expected working life above and below the average working life of all bulbs in the batch. Here we have a criterion in some degree analogous to the concept of superior and inferior performance in the investment world. It would be true but of no interest to the manufacturer if the quality controller, using Jensen's approach, reported to him that, from the random sample he took, it appeared that all the bulbs on average had an average expected life. He would have arrived at the same conclusion no matter what the size of the sample was. What the manufacturer wants to know is how many bulbs had an above average expected life and how many a below average expected life and the extent of the over- and under- average phenomenon. Similarly, to form an opinion on the EMH's claims we need to know the full range of rate of return behaviour. The average over a ten- or 20-year period is meaningless.

Part of the problem seems to be that in the EMH literature there is an equation of the term 'in general' with the term 'on average'. The statistical evidence is always 'on average' and the conclusions refer always to 'in general'. These two terms are not equivalent in meaning. The assertion that security prices in general fully reflect available information is much stronger than the assertion that they do so only on the average. In fact, given the nature of the average, an 'on the average' assertion would not necessarily imply that any individual share price fully reflected all available information.

A further point may have occurred to the reader who has followed the argument thus far. The assertion, indeed, assumption, that investment performance should be measured in risk-adjusted terms has not been questioned. So obvious is the point thought to be that no discussion is generally considered necessary. Yet the notion seems very strange when applied to other realms of risk taking. Nelson took a great risk at the battle of Copenhagen when he placed a telescope to his blind eye and ignored orders from his superiors. Had his judgement of the risk involved been in error, the battle could well have been lost and he would have doubtless been court martialled and his naval career would have come to a premature end. This situation exhibits the classic characteristics of risk, the possibility of victory and promotion on the one hand (the upside potential), and the possibility of defeat and ignominy (the downside potential) on the other. Commanders such as Nelson in all ages and in all countries have been successful risk takers, but it would be an odd country indeed which lowered them in public esteem to the level of the commander who plays safe because of the downside potential in imaginative military undertakings.

Yet this is very much the ethos of Modern Portfolio Theory (MPT). It is succinctly stated in a letter to the *Financial Times* on the subject of the usefulness of index funds:

> A portfolio which achieves a higher return than the index is not by definition a superior portfolio whenever its potential for under-performance is greater than that of the index. Consider, by way of simple example, that two alternative investments, cash and gold, had both experienced the same return over a given period. The cash fund would be superior because its downside risk is much lower.[27]

It is easy enough to see how MPT has led to this view of investment performance. If markets are assumed to be efficient, 'correctly' pricing shares in terms of their systematic or market risk, and this risk can be measured by beta, investment becomes a childishly simple game of computer-calculated regressions to establish beta and the selection of an efficient portfolio with the required beta. No need for painstaking research of the fundamentals, no exercise of judgement — in fact, no judgemental decision at all since the beta itself will be decided upon by the client. But, as we have seen, this is a make-believe world based on hopelessly unrealistic assumptions and a rationale defined in terms of itself. It is a defeatist view of the world which, if universally accepted, would mean the disappearance of investment analysis and the ultimate *reductio ad absurdam*: every fund manager spending all his time and energy creating and maintaining a portfolio based on what he believes to be the average portfolio of every other portfolio manager.

Nor does the point made about the superiority of the cash investment over the gold investment bear close examination. Could it not equally be argued that the gold fund was superior because of its greater upside potential? Where risk is measured by the variability of future returns, as it is in MPT, it is surely fallacious to categorise investments solely by their downside potential. If wealth maximisation is the sole aim of

---

[27] S. Glover, 'Usefulness of Index Funds in Portfolio Management', letter to *Financial Times*, 18 January 1984.

investment, then the absolute rate of increase in wealth must be the criterion of successful investment. Judged against this yardstick, there is no question of either fund being superior; they both yielded the same return. With the benefit of hindsight, which the analogy implies, it would have made no difference whether £100 had been invested in one fund or the other.

All investment is about risk, and this applies as much to gilts as it does to equities. The three month treasury bill, often used in CAPM theory as the risk-free investment, may yield a fixed return over three months, but its value fluctuates from day-to-day under the influence of interest rate movements. Changes in the purchasing power of money affect the real rate of return and, no matter how improbable, Governments have been known to renege on their obligations. All that can be said for the treasury bill, and to a lesser extent for other forms of government debt, is that, if, and only if, they are held to maturity, their nominal return is certain in amount and, for most practical purposes, sure to be received. The effects of inflation and high interest rates on the value of gilts is eloquent testimony to their riskiness as investments.

Success in investment, therefore, is essentially a question of success in risk taking. There is no suggestion, however, that the reckless, unthinking assumption of risk for risk's sake is a virtue. Sound judgement and the courage to back it is required. With this philosophy a person is happy to be assessed on his results, i.e., his ability to maximise the rate of return. To adjust such a return for the risk assumed is akin to discounting achievement for the labour and effort involved. If all seek to maximise their rate of return through judicious assessment of risk, the market may truly aspire to efficiency in the economic sense of the optimum allocation of resources. It is a policy more likely to raise the average rate of return than is an unworthy pursuit of the average itself.

The literature on the EMH is vast and the space available here is not adequate to do it full justice. Precisely because of this, the approach has been to choose less and review it in depth rather than to spread the analysis thinly over a wider front. The two studies investigated here were selected because of their impeccable academic credentials and because they apparently set the standard for further research efforts in this field. Both these studies have been widely acclaimed. They are invariably cited in textbooks when evidence is being adduced in support of the EMH.

If, as the author claims, these two studies prove nothing about the EMH, does that mean that the rest of the evidence presented by other researchers is similarly valueless? Without a detailed review of all the other studies no conclusive answer to this question can be given. However, the techniques used in these two studies are without doubt representative of those used in many subsequent studies. If these two studies do not stand up to close scrutiny, neither do many others. Furthermore, these two studies were the only ones selected for closer examination. It is not as if other research studies were investigated, found to be satisfactory and then ignored. In other words, the first two apples taken at random from the basket were bad. Equally disturbing is the fact that all this time, and despite continuous mention in the textbooks, no one seems to have noticed that there is anything wrong with these studies.[28]

In recent years, academic studies have identified inefficiencies in the market. These have been given labels such as the 'New Year effect', the 'week-end effect' and the 'size effect'. None of this is prayed in aid of the position taken here.[29] The EMH cannot be affirmed or falsified by an appeal to the evidence. It is an untestable hypothesis. Nor is the EMH a warranted inference from the fact that the aggregate performance of institutional investment funds tends to be broadly in line with the market when measured over a 20-year period.

Conclusion

The theory of efficient markets started life as the theory of random walks. Share prices were observed to fluctuate in a random manner so that knowledge of the past sequence of prices was no help in judging the likely direction of the share price in the future. This implied that technical or chart analysis had no hope of success.

The theory of random walks, known as the weak form of the EMH, is susceptible to statistical testing. Most of the tests carried out have apparently found no significant level of dependence, i.e., such dependence as was observed was of insufficient magnitude to permit any profit after transaction costs. The lack of serial correlation in successive price changes, however, does not imply the absence of any link or connection between successive share prices, but rather that future share price movements cannot be discovered merely from the sequence of past price numbers. There is no reason at all why past price movements cannot be interpreted in the light of fundamental investment analysis. Because the weak form of the EMH on its own is not of much significance to the share valuer, the author has not looked beyond the conclusions of various statistical studies to the underlying data. The

[28] See, for example, Richard A Brealey, *An Introduction to Risk and Return from Common Stocks*, 2nd ed. (Oxford: Basil Blackwell, 1983), pp. 33–35. It is interesting to compare Brealey's discussion of the FFJR test with the one given here.

[29] Although he has not read these studies, the author is deeply sceptical that any such thing as the 'New Year effect' or the 'week-end effect' exists in reality.

interested reader is strongly recommended to consult the research studies himself before forming an opinion.

The observation that share prices tended to move in a random fashion prompted the obvious question: 'why?' The line of enquiry produced by this question eventually led to what is now known as the strong and the semi-strong forms of the EMH. Random behaviour of share prices, deduced the researchers, is consistent with a market which instantaneously and fully reflects all new information. As new information can be randomly good or bad, so the resultant share price adjustments would be randomly up or down. Thus, the EMH asserts that share prices fully reflect all available information, and that prices adjust instantaneously to new information rendering it pointless to research the fundamentals for under- or over-valued stocks. It is equally futile for portfolio managers to spend time seeking abnormally high rates of return, since all shares are 'correctly' priced in terms of their risk. Adherents of the EMH recognise that some investors beat the market but they maintain, nevertheless, that the EMH is a good description of the behaviour of share prices in general. The distinction between the semi-strong form of efficiency and the strong form is that the former asserts that share prices fully reflect all publicly available information, whereas the latter is extended to cover all relevant information including inside information and the superior insights of investment professionals and specialists.

The EMH in its strong and semi-strong forms is an unrestricted generalised hypothesis. As it is not possible to prove, or disprove, the hypothesis in respect of any individual share or of share prices in general, the EMH is, in the positivist sense, neither true nor false but simply meaningless. In fairness, it has been recognised that the EMH in its generalised form has no empirically testable implications,[30] and the attempt to give it empirical content is centred around the need to define the term 'fully reflect'. According to Fama, information is fully reflected in share prices if it is 'fully utilised' in determining equilibrium expected returns. As the equilibrium expected return on a security is thought to be a function of its risk, a model of share price determination based on risk and the rate of return, such as the CAPM, is used to assess whether or not shares prices fully reflect all available information.

Such models are highly contentious. They are not generally accepted in the investment world, even if they are in the academic one. Their assumptions of markets in equilibrium, costless information available

[30] Fama, p. 184.

instantaneously to all, no transaction costs and no taxes, and homogeneous expectations of investors as to the expected returns, are so hopelessly unrealistic as to undermine the credibility or relevance of the derived theory. The theories themselves suffer from an inherent circularity of argument stemming from the fact that the two parameters — risk and the rate of return — are essentially defined in terms of the same phenomenon: the stock's price. The theories, therefore, have all the characteristics of the definitional statement — they generate their own truth and are impervious to 'exterior' logic. At all events, they do not enjoy a general degree of acceptance which would sanction their use for the purpose at hand. It may also be questioned whether the term 'fully utilised' throws any light on, or removes any of the subjectivity in, the term 'fully reflects'.

In view of the insurmountable difficulties in verifying that any particular share price, or indeed a group of share prices, fully reflects all the available information, the researchers' direct tests have focussed on the reaction of share prices to various types of information, such as, scrip issues, earnings announcements and the like. The studies have been designed to test the speed and the amplitude of the share price reaction. One such study, a 'pioneering' work by FFJR on the effect of scrip issues on share prices, was examined in detail to give the reader some idea of the reliability and significance of these tests. FFJR's finding that scrip issues often presage a dividend increase is not new and has no implications for market efficiency, which is about whether prices fully and instantaneously reflect new information. FFJR's conclusion that the share price reflects the dividend information implicit in the scrip issue by the effective date of the scrip does not imply efficiency since the effective date is not an information event. It is the announcement date which matters. Incredible though it seems, the FFJR study largely ignored the announcement date.

The statistical data indicate, however, the persistence of positive average residuals, i.e., abnormally high rates of return, between the announcement date and the effective date — a period on average of between one-and-a-half and two months. This is not consistent with market efficiency as defined. The FFJR study exhibits a number of disquieting features which cause one to have serious doubts about the reliability and significance of this type of test. It is noteworthy that the conclusions were based on the average price behaviour for 940 scrip issues during the period 1927–1959. Such an average is meaningless. The real point at issue is: how many stocks showed a 'full and instantaneous' adjustment to the new information? Of those which did not, what was the extent of the deviation from the predicted behaviour? These questions were never raised. The approach adopted in the FFJR study has been emulated by subsequent researchers in this field. The validity of their conclusions is, therefore, highly suspect.

The strong form of the EMH, even more so than the semi-strong form, is an untestable hypothesis. Nevertheless, various studies of institutional investment performance both in the US and the UK are cited by adherents of the EMH as giving considerable support to the validity of the hypothesis. Strictly speaking, these performance measurement studies are not tests of the EMH, since the EMH only maintains that shares are 'correctly' priced in relation to information available at the time and not necessarily that they are 'correctly' priced in terms of realised outcomes. Despite this objection, Jensen's classic study of mutual fund performance in the US was selected for closer examination in order to assess the merits of its claim, and that of other similarly designed studies, to support the EMH.

Jensen concluded that, net of expenses, the funds on average under-performed slightly over the ten-year period. Making allowances for expenses and brokerage, therefore, it is reasonable to assume that, on average, the funds neither under-performed nor over-performed. This is entirely to be expected given that the 115 funds were invested solely in domestic US stocks. Their portfolios in aggregate were unlikely to be very dissimilar to that of the market index they were judged against (the Standard & Poors' 500).

Jensen's technique of averaging every observation for each of the 115 funds over a ten-year period (20 years for some funds) proves nothing about the efficiency of the market in the sense of share prices in general and at all times fully reflecting all relevant information. It is quite consistent with the regular and frequent phenomenon of abnormal profits and losses on investment. His study, and the many similar ones based on it, do no more than prove (if they do even that) the truth of the definitional truism that on average every investor's performance will be average. Much of Jensen's study is devoted to his manipulation of the CAPM, a model based on *ex ante* expectations, for use in *ex post* realised outcomes. Readers will by now be familiar with inadequacies of this theory and its inherent circularity of thought.

The ubiquitous assumption that performance should always be measured in risk-adjusted terms was challenged. It was seen that success in investment is a function of success in risk-taking, no investment, least of all the so-called risk-free investment, being free of risk. Terminal wealth is the only logical criterion of investment performance. The attitude of modern portfolio theory as typified by Keane's assertion that '. . . the goodness of an individual decision cannot be judged simply by its outcome'[31] is the prescription for mediocrity.

[31.] Keane, p. 19.

Jensen's work, therefore, throws no light at all on the efficiency or otherwise of the market. In fact, given his approach and the averaging technique employed, the results of his tests were a foregone conclusion.

No professional worth his salt likes to admit that the market he works in is inefficient, and it is important to realise, therefore, that the term 'efficiency' as used in the EMH has a very specialised meaning. 'Efficiency' in this specialised sense has no implications for the skill or proficiency (or lack of it) with which the investment community operates. Indeed, the use of the term 'efficient' is much to be regretted since the adjective already had a precise meaning when applied to a market. It was used to denote a market which had breadth and depth and the procedures and structures to handle large lines of stock usually at or near the current price. The New York and London markets have a high degree of efficiency in the traditional sense, but the case for efficiency in the academic sense has not been made out. The hypothesis itself is incapable of proof or disproof and is, in a fundamental sense, meaningless.

7
Risk and the rate of return

Introduction

If risk did not exist and there were complete certainty as to future returns, money would be expected to earn just its time value or the pure rate of interest. According to the economist, this is the price demanded by lenders for forgoing present consumption. In such an abstract world, then, would one expect the rate of return to be identical for all investment opportunities? The answer is probably no, for at least two reasons. First, although risk has been assumed away, marketability or illiquidity has not. A building society or bank, for instance, would still offer a higher rate of interest on a time deposit than it would on a demand deposit because of the inferior liquidity of the former. Similarly, the poor marketability of an unquoted shareholding would be compensated for by a higher rate of return than that accorded to a similar shareholding in an identical, but marketable, quoted company.

Although some would consider marketability as part of risk, the two are distinct concepts. Marketability has no effect on a company's operations. It applies solely to the ease or otherwise of dealing in the shares. Risk on the other hand arises from the nature of the company's activities and is inherent in them; it directly affects the cash return on an investment, whereas marketability does not. Marketability is an important consideration in the valuation of unquoted shares and is discussed in Chapter 9. Second, administrative costs of financial institutions may have an effect on the rate of return. Thus, a substantial sum of money will usually earn a higher rate of interest than a smaller sum of the same maturity. For much the same reason, the money market is not available to the small investor.

Three elements can, therefore, be identified in the determination of the rate of return: the pure or risk-free rate of interest, the risk premium and a premium for inferior marketability. Additionally, the small investor may have to accept a reduction in the rate of return because of administration cost, although institutions such as unit trusts, money market funds and the like provide some means of mitigating this effect. In this chapter we consider the nature of risk, how it may be assessed and what evidence there is as to its relationship with the rate of return. Marketability, an important though lesser consideration, is discussed in Chapter 9. Modern Portfolio Theory (MPT) claims to have a precise measure of risk and to have established its relationship to the rate of return. This chapter also reviews this theoretical framework to see if it provides any useful insights.

The nature of risk

Risk arises from uncertainty, although it is more than mere uncertainty. As almost all outcomes of human existence are uncertain (save death), uncertainty, and hence risk, are concepts of which everyone has an intuitive knowledge or awareness. This is a consoling thought, as, in vain one scours the literature on economics and investment theory for an adequate definition of risk. Despite these difficulties, we are probably on safe ground in asserting that, in the world of investment at least, the notion of risk is closely linked to that of the likelihood or probability of loss. Loss, for this purpose includes not only loss of original capital but any shortfall in the actual rate of return from the risk-free rate.

Although uncertainty is the hallmark of risk, the two terms are not entirely synonymous. For example, most investors would regard outcomes in the distant future as more uncertain than nearer outcomes. In common parlance we might say that the more distant outcomes were riskier than the nearer ones, but this would serve to deprive the word 'risk' of its usual meaning. There is no reason to believe that oil exploration activity in Alaska will be any riskier two years hence than it is today. Risk proper does not increase or decrease with time. Uncertainty does. Thus, in evaluating a property investment, rental projections ten years from now are less certain than those one year from now. The uncertainty arises because of the many subjective assumptions which have to be made for such a projection. It is easy to make mistaken assumptions and the longer the period of the projection, the greater the effect of any errors.

If the present value of an investment is equal to the sum of the discounted expected future returns, risk, in the sense of the likelihood of loss, must originate from either a change in the expected cash return or an increase in the rate of return applied to it, or some combination of change in these two factors. The risk associated with the cash return stems from the risk inherent in the company's operations. Such risks are fairly well understood by most people. A speculative oil exploration venture is a good deal riskier than a building society paid up share account. A highly geared business is riskier than one funded entirely by equity.

The risk arising from changes in the discount rate or required rate of return is less well understood and may at first sight indicate a confusion of thought. Is not the rate of return supposed to provide appropriate compensation for risk? How then can it be a source of risk? This question can best be answered by considering the pricing of gilt-edged securities. Although in theory there must be some minimal default risk in such securities (e.g., from an economic collapse), it can be disregarded for all practical purposes. Any fall or rise in the value of government stocks must, therefore, be attributable solely to changes in the required rate of return. The rate of return an investor seeks on gilt-edged stock will change with the general level of interest rates in the economy, since no one will invest in gilts if a significantly higher rate of return can be obtained in the money market. Arbitrage will, therefore, ensure that gilt-edged yields are comparable with money market rates of return.

The fact that government securities can be a risky form of investment will come as no surprise to long term holders of War Loan or 2½% Consols, the current prices of which are at massive discounts to their original issue price. Only in the restricted sense of the gross redemption yield can the rate of return on gilts be considered risk-free. The gross redemption yield is that rate of interest at which the total discounted values of future payments of income and capital equate to the current price. It is not even a guaranteed compound rate of return to be earned from making an investment at that price, since it would be unlikely that each interest payment until maturity could be invested at the same rate of return. It also assumes retention of the stock until maturity — something which most investors in gilts would not countenance. Above all, however, it implies that an investor is not affected by a fall or rise in the value of his stock until such time as he sells it.

As the rate of return on equities is thought to consist of the pure rate of interest plus a premium for risk,[1] changes in the pure rate of interest should lead to changes in the required rate of return on equities. However, the effect is not as clear cut nor as easy to observe as it is with gilts since the cash return on equities is also a variable. In addition, the general level of interest rates in the economy will itself be an influence on the return on capital or vice versa. Disentangling the effect of changes in the cash return from the effect of changes in the capitalisation rate may, therefore, be well nigh impossible. But the basic proposition remains true nevertheless: changes in interest rates must lead to changes in the required rates of return on equities. An increase in interest rates, other than a temporary movement, will cause investors

---

[1] And perhaps, as noted earlier, a premium for inferior marketability.

to seek a higher rate of return on their equity investments and this will tend to depress prices. A sustained decrease in interest rates will have the opposite effect.

Modern theories of share price determination tend to ignore interest rate risk. For example, in the Capital Asset Pricing Model the risk-free interest rate is given; the model only explains how the risk premium is determined. It may well be that this type of risk gets no reward; it is, as it were, the price everyone has to pay or the hazard everyone has to face for stepping into the investment arena. It may also be argued that concentrating solely on the downside risk inherent in interest rate volatility ignores the equally great 'upside potential'. The latter could be regarded as the recompense for accepting the former. This might be an attractive line of argument were it not for the fact that it could equally well be applied to the assumption of business or commercial risk, for which theory tells us there is a definite reward in the rate of return.

Risk measurement

As an abstract quality risk exists to a large extent in the eye of the beholder. It does not admit of quantitative mathematical measurement and the riskiness of one investment can be discussed in terms of another only in a descriptive, qualitative way. At least, that is the author's view. Modern Portfolio Theory, however, claims to have a quantitative objective measure of risk. As such a development would be of fundamental significance, not least in the valuation of unquoted shares, this claim deserves to be investigated closely. This section also discusses some well known qualitative techniques for heightening one's awareness of risk.

MPT measures risk as the variability of the 'expected' rate of return. Here, the term 'expected' has a precise mathematical connotation and must not be confused with the popular usage of the word. Henceforth, the term will be in inverted commas whenever it is used in this technical sense. The 'expected' rate of return on a security is a probability-weighted average of possible future rates of return on that security. It is given by the following formula:

$$E(R) = \sum_{i=1}^{N} R_i p_i$$

where $E(R)$ = the 'expected' rate of return
R_i = the rate of return of the ith outcome

p_i = the probability of the ith outcome

N = the number of possible outcomes.

Two points should be noted. First, the mathematical 'expectation' is not necessarily what the individual investor expects, and, second, the assumption that there is a generally expected or 'expected' rate of return on a security in the sense of a consensus amongst investors, whilst intuitively appealing, has no evidential basis to it. It is more likely that share prices reflect a compromise between widely different perceptions of value.

Variability of the 'expected' rate of return, i.e., the risk, is measured by the standard deviation. This is a statistical measure of the dispersion of probable outcomes about the 'expected' outcome. An example will illustrate the concept. An investor is faced with a choice of investing in one of two companies. Company A is a food retailer operating a nationwide chain of supermarkets. Company B is a civil engineering contractor which undertakes large public works projects at home and abroad. The investment appraisal of Company A and Company B indicates the following outcomes and their respective probabilities:

Company A (Food retailer)

Assumed state of the economy (1)	Probability (2)	Rate of return (3) %	Probability-weighted outcome ((2) × (3)) %
Boom	0.3	35	10.5
Normal	0.4	27.5	11.0
Recession	0.3	20	6.0
	1.0		27.5

'Expected' rate of return = 27.5%

Company B (Civil engineering)

Assumed state of the economy (1)	Probability (2)	Rate of return (3) %	Probability-weighted outcome ((2) × (3)) %
Boom	0.3	95	28.5
Normal	0.4	35	14.0
Recession	0.3	−50	−15.0
	1.0		27.5

'Expected' rate of return = 27.5%

Clearly, an investment in Company B carries more risk than one in Company A. With Company B there is a 30% probability of losing money; with Company A the worst that can happen is that the rate of return falls to 20% instead of the 'expected' 27.5%. The standard deviation of Company A's rate of return is 5.8% and that of Company B, 56.5% (see Appendix 1).

If the probability distribution is normal, i.e., bell shaped when graphed, there is a 68% chance that the actual rate of return on Company A's shares will fall within one standard deviation of the 'expected' rate of return (see Figure 1). In other words there is a two out of three chance that Company A's realised rate of return will be between 21.7% and 33.3% (i.e., 27.5% plus or minus 5.8%). For Company B the range is much wider, −29% and 84% (i.e., 27.5% plus or minus 56.5%), and this indicates the extent to which Company B is a riskier investment than Company A.

The above example is modelled closely on those used in the MPT literature to illustrate the measurement of risk in individual securities and groups of securities, i.e. portfolios.[2] Even the most committed adherent of MPT would agree that these concepts are highly abstract. It is unrealistic to imagine that the possible outcomes can be portrayed in this manner, with a handful of probabilities summing to complete certainty. The judgemental process in the human mind is infinitely more subtle than these naive techniques would suggest and is incapable of being modelled by a probability distribution. Even if it were, is the standard deviation of 'expected' rates of return a logical criterion for measuring the risk?

As mentioned earlier, in portfolio theory risk is defined as the variability of the 'expected' rate of return. At first sight, this might strike the reader as odd. Surely the investor will be only too pleased if the rate of return turns out to be higher than 'expected'? Should not the investor's main concern be the probability that the outcome will be below the 'expected' level? However, if the probability distribution is normal, as shown in figure 1, the deviations above the 'expected' value are a mirror image of those below it, and, therefore, a list of stocks ordered on the basis of downside potential will differ little, or at all, from one ordered on the basis of standard deviation.

But what evidence is there that the probability distributions for individual stocks are invariably, or even usually, normal? In fact there

[2] See, for example, William F. Sharpe, *Investments*, 2nd ed. (Englewood Cliffs, N.J.: Prentice-Hall, 1981), pp. 120–121; Eugene F. Brigham, *Financial Management Theory and Practice*, 2nd ed. (Hinsdale, Ill.: The Dryden Press, 1979), pp. 97–104; Franco Modigliani and Gerald A. Pogue, 'An Introduction to Risk and Return: Concepts and Evidence, Part 1', *Financial Analysts Journal*, March–April 1974, pp. 68–80, re-printed in Eugene F. Brigham and Ramon E. Johnson, *Issues in Managerial Finance*, 2nd ed. (Hinsdale, Ill.: The Dryden Press, 1980), pp. 323–326; James H. Lorie and Mary T. Hamilton, *The Stockmarket: Theories and Evidence* (Homewood, Ill.: Irwin, 1973), pp. 174–175.

Figure 1: Normal probability distribution.

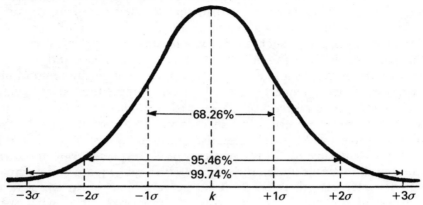

Notes:
(a) The area under the normal curve equals 1.0 or 100%. *Thus, the areas under any pair of normal curves drawn on the same scale, whether they are peaked or flat, must be equal.*
(b) Half of the area under a normal curve is to the left of the mean, indicating that there is a 50% probability that the actual outcome will be less than the mean, and a 50% probability that it will be greater than the mean, or to the right of k.
(c) Of the area under the curve, 68.26% is within $\pm 1\sigma$ of the mean, indicating that the probability is 68.26% that the actual outcome will be within the range $k-1\sigma$ to $k+1\sigma$.
(d) For a normal distribution, the larger the value of σ, the greater the probability that the actual outcome will vary widely from the expected, or most likely, outcome.

Source: Eugene F. Brigham, *Financial Management: Theory and Practice,* 2nd ed. (Hinsdale, Ill.: The Dryden Press, 1979), p. 103.

can be no evidence since expectations are formed in investors' minds and cannot be observed.[3] The claim that an ordering of stocks by standard deviation would be very similar to one ordered by deviations below the mean is, therefore, unsubstantiated.

The concept of the 'expected' rate of return i.e., a probability-weighted average of all possible outcomes, is itself unreal, and W. F. Sharpe's assertion that, 'when an analyst predicts that a stock will return 12% next year, he or she is presumably stating something comparable to an "expected" value' is true only in certain cases. For example, the analyst, having drawn up the probability distribution of Company B, would not predict a rate return of 27.5%. One obvious reason why he would never predict 27.5% is that he would be bound to be wrong, since none of the three possible outcomes include a rate of return of 27.5%. Rather, he would opt for that particular state of the economy which on balance he judges most likely. This would be the

[3] Empirical studies suggest, however, that for diversified portfolios the distribution of realised returns is reasonably symmetric about the mean. These studies are usually cited as evidence that 'expected' future rates of return are normally distributed. However, much as we would like our expectations to be realised, as often as not we are disappointed.

normal state, producing a rate of return of 35%. With Company A, which has a normal probability distribution, the most likely outcome coincides with the 'expected' value and here there is no difference.

However, criticism such as this would strike the practical man of investment as entirely missing the main point. Even if he could swallow his deep reservations about a concept which is not encountered in his own working experience, he is faced with the impossible task of having to observe the unobservable if he wishes to use it. Does not the 'expected' rate of return and hence its variability exist solely in the minds of investors? Here the theorist comes to his assistance with the soothing assurance that it is a property of the 'expected' rate of return that, on the average and in the long run, it should equate to the actual outcome. He can, therefore, look at the variability of rates of return realised in the past and treat this as the equivalent of what was 'expected'. In other words, where the realised rates of return exceed the 'expected' rates of return the excess will on average equal the shortfall occurring when realised rates of returns fall below the 'expected' level.[4] Few practitioners would have much faith in such an outcome. It seems more of an intellectual game than a search for the truth.

Undoubtedly, however, this risk measurement technique's most fundamental defect is its reliance on the rate of return, a major component of which is the risk premium. As the risk-free rate of return will not be expected to change much this technique measures risk in terms of the variability of the risk premium. It thus measures risk in terms of itself, which is a nonsense.

The absurdity of measuring risk by reference to rate of return behaviour can be easily demonstrated. It will be recalled from the earlier example that Company A and Company B both had the same 'expected' rate of return of 27.5% but different levels of risk. Investors would prefer Company A since they get the same 'expected' rate of return but with less risk. Capital market theory tells us that, for the market to be in equilibrium, investors would sell Company B's shares and buy Company A's until their respective rates of return reflect the relative riskiness of the two companies. It is instructive to see what happens once this process gets under way.

Let us assume that after the initial wave of buying and selling in this process of adjustment, Company A's shares have risen by 25% and Company B's fallen by 25%. Company A's 'expected' rate of return

---

[4] It is of course true that the proverbial dice thrower of textbook theory can expect to throw a six on average one in every six times, given a long enough go at it. But, the probability distributions we are concerned with are not 'objective' frequency-based ones. They are the subjective probabilities in individual investors' minds. There is no justification at all for asserting that such 'expected' outcomes will on average be equivalent to realised outcomes.

then falls to 22% (i.e., 27.5% × 100/125), and Company B's 'expected' rate of return rises to 37% (i.e., 27.5% × 100/75). But, this movement in price has caused the standard deviation to alter. Company B's rises from 56.5% to 75.3% and Company A's falls from 5.8% to 4.6% in direct inverse proportion to the movement in the share price. The calculation of the 'expected' rates of return is set out below:

Assumed state of the economy	Probability	Company A ROR %	Company A Probability-weighted ROR	Company B ROR %	Company B Probability-weighted ROR
Boom	0.3	28.0	8.4	126.6	38.0
Normal	0.4	22.0	8.8	46.6	18.6
Recession	0.3	16.0	4.8	−66.6	−20.0
			22.0		36.6

The standard deviation is then calculated as follows:

Company A

$k_i - \bar{k}$	$(k_i - \bar{k})$	$(k_i - \bar{k})^2$	$(k_i - \bar{k})^2 P_i$
28–22	6	36	36 × 0.3 = 10.8
22–22	—	—	0 × 0.4 = —
16–22	−6	36	36 × 0.3 = 10.8
			21.6

$\sigma = \sqrt{21.6} = 4.6\%$

Company B

$k_i - \bar{k}$	$(k_i - \bar{k})$	$(k_i - \bar{k})^2$	$(k_i - \bar{k})^2 P_i$
126.6–36.6	90	8,100	8,100 × 0.3 = 2,430
46.6–36.6	10	100	100 × 0.4 = 40
−66.6–36.6	−103.2	10,650	10,650 × 0.3 = 3,195
			5,665

$\sigma = \sqrt{5665} = 75.3\%$

Company B now appears to have even greater risk than before as a direct result of the price movement intended to compensate for its riskiness. Investors in Company A, whose share price has risen 25%, have the added bonus of seeing their stock rated as even less risky. Thus, riskier stocks are caught up in a vicious circle and safer ones in a virtuous circle. The more the riskier stocks are sold to adjust to equilibrium levels, the greater their risk appears; the more the safer stocks are bought in the equilibrium process, the safer they appear. In this absurd Alice-in-Wonderland environment, share prices are in the grip of forces forever pushing them into greater apparent disequilibrium.

It is interesting, none the less, to consider whether, shorn of its dependence on the share price/rate of return, this measure of risk might not be adapted to the valuation of unquoted shares. By shifting the focus of attention from the rate of return to the return itself, the valuer would concentrate on the extent to which the expected future cash returns (not rates of return) were likely to fluctuate. The valuer does this in any event, but not so as to list all possible outcomes and assign the appropriate probability to each one. An exhaustive probability distribution of future returns would be out of the question on the grounds of cost and practicality. However, some sort of crude scenario analysis may be feasible and useful. Assume, for example, that XYZ plc, a quoted company, is being used for comparison purposes in the valuation of ABC Ltd, an unquoted company. Three scenarios or outcomes only are specified — the most optimistic, the most likely and the most pessimistic — and probabilities are assigned to each one. If XYZ plc and ABC Ltd are fairly similar companies the result could well take the following form:

	XYZ plc		ABC Ltd	
Outcome	Return £000s	Probability %	Return £000s	Probability %
Optimistic	2,000	20	2,000	40
Likely	1,000	50	1,000	50
Pessimistic	(500)	30	(500)	10
		100		100

Here the simplifying assumption has been made that both companies have the same outcomes but different probabilities. If risk is defined as the probability of loss, XYZ plc is riskier than ABC Ltd since there is a 30% probability of it making a loss and only a ten per cent probability with ABC Ltd. Looked at from another angle, ABC Ltd appears the less risky since it has a 90% chance of achieving an annual profit of at least £1 million, whereas XYZ plc has only a 70% chance of achieving the same result. Other things being equal, ABC Ltd should have a higher value than XYZ plc.

Companies will rarely have the same likely future profits, and a more realistic example is required. Assume, therefore, that the valuer has selected another quoted company, QRS plc, in order to obtain a better feel for ABC Ltd's required rate of return. QRS plc's simplified outcomes are as follows:

	QRS plc			ABC Ltd		
	Return £'000	Probability %	'Expected' return £'000	Return £'000	Probability %	'Expected' return £'000
Optimistic	2,500	20	500	2,000	40	800
Likely	1,500	50	750	1,000	50	500
Pessimistic	(1,000)	30	(300)	(500)	10	(50)
		100	950		100	1,250

Clearly, QRS plc has a greater potential for both profit and loss than ABC Ltd. If we take MPT's measure of risk as the variability of future returns but apply it to the profit forecasts as opposed to the rate of return, we see that QRS plc's standard deviation is £1,331 and ABC Ltd's is £750 (see Appendix 2). These two figures cannot be compared with one another since they are based on different sets of outcomes. They become comparable, however, when expressed as a percentage of the probability-weighted average or 'expected' profit of each company, as set out below:

	QRS plc	ABC Ltd
(a) Standard deviation	£1,331	£750
(b) 'expected' (probability-weighted average) profit	£950	£1,250
Coefficient of variation (a) as a percentage of (b)	140%	60%

On this measure, QRS plc's future returns are over twice as variable as ABC Ltd's.

As mentioned earlier, however, variability of 'expected' or probability-weighted average returns is a flawed measure of risk where outcomes above the 'expected' value are not as equally probable as those below it. In any event, measuring risk as the likelihood that outcomes will be below the 'expected' value is not entirely consistent with the commonly accepted notion of risk as being the probability of loss. Even using the commonly accepted view of risk, however, QRS plc is still the riskier investment since it has a 30% probability of a loss, as opposed to ABC Ltd's ten per cent one, and the magnitude of that loss both in absolute and relative terms is greater. One measure of the relative magnitude is the impact or influence of each company's probable loss on its 'expected' outcome. Using the data above this works out as follows:

	QRS plc	ABC Ltd
Loss	−£1,000	−£500
Probability of loss	0.3	0.1
(a) Loss×probability	−£300	−£50
(b) 'Expected' value	£950	£1,250
(a) as a percentage of (b)	32%	4%

This seems to put QRS plc into a considerably riskier light *vis-à-vis* ABC Ltd than does the earlier measure of the total variability of returns.

No doubt many readers will find these efforts to extract something of use from the mistaken notion of MPT unsuccessful, and indeed the author must confess that he does not employ these probability distribution techniques in his own professional work. However, they are offered in the spirit that others may find them helpful or that someone may be able to improve on them and ultimately produce something of practical value. Certainly, techniques which require a more formal approach to the assessment of risk are much to be desired.

Although no satisfactory quantitative techniques exist for measuring a security's riskiness, there are a number of methods for improving one's qualitative assessment of risk. Probably the most widely used indicator of risk is the pay-back period. This measures the time it takes for future cash flows to recoup the cost of the investment. A project which is expected to pay for itself in three years is less risky on this count than one which is expected to pay for itself in five years. An investment decision would not be made solely on the basis of the pay-back period, but where other factors also indicate that there is a high degree of risk in the investment, the pay-back characteristics can become the deciding factor.

The pay-back period ignores the rate of return and, for this reason, should never be used as the sole investment criterion. The example below illustrates this point. Two investment proposals have the following characteristics:

	Proposal X	Proposal Y
Cost	1,000	1,000
Cash flows		
Year 1	400	200
2	600	400
3	400	800
4	300	800
5	200	800
Payback period	2 years	3 years
Rate of return	30%	40%

It would clearly be incorrect to opt for proposal X simply because of its pay-back period. Proposal Y has a higher rate of return and this, together with any other factors, has to be brought into the appraisal.

There are two other handy techniques which, despite their evident drawbacks, can be of practical assistance to the valuer in assessing the risk or uncertainty attaching to his estimate of future profits and dividends. These are sensitivity analysis and scenario analysis. Sensitivity analysis is useful where, as in most valuations, future profits are expressed as a single most likely outcome. It requires the valuer to explicitly consider the sensitivity of his forecast to changes in key variables or assumptions. An assumption or variable is important by virtue of the effect it has on the forecast outcome, i.e., it is an important assumption because a significant change in it would produce a significant change in the profit forecast. Therefore, in identifying the key assumptions and variables, the valuer is at the same time considering the variability of his forecast, and this is why this discipline is so worthwhile.

Failure to consider the sensitivity of a forecast to changes in key variables can undermine the credibility of a valuation. For example, few would have much confidence in the valuation of shares in a goldmining company which was based on a single projected price of gold and took no account of the effect of fluctuations in the price of gold. In more run-of-the-mill businesses the crucial assumptions or key variables may not be so obvious.

Sensitivity analysis has its limitations. For instance, in most cases it will be practical to consider only one variable at a time. In reality, however, one variable often affects another — for example, the level of sales usually affects the level of costs. But, the technique in any event can only give a rough idea of the variability of the outcomes, and so this particular blemish should not deter the valuer.

Scenario analysis consists simply of the specifying of the range of outcomes, usually in the form of the most optimistic and the most pessimistic. This technique is similar to that shown in the earlier examples of risk measurement but without the probabilities. Its usefulness depends entirely on the effort made in estimating the outcomes.

The risk premium

The concept of the rate of return consisting of the risk-free rate of interest plus a premium for risk led researchers to study the rates of return on equities so as to observe the size of the risk premium. The results of Dimson and Brealey's investigations in this area appeared in *The Investment Analyst* of December 1978.[5] They calculated that, over the period

[5] E. Dimson and R. A. Brealey, 'The Risk Premium on UK Equities', *The Investment Analyst*, no 52 (1978), pp. 14–18.

Table 1: The return on equities, the Treasury Bill rate and the excess return for the UK, 1919–1977.

Year	Return on equities	Treasury Bill rate	Excess return on equities	Year	Return on equities	Treasury Bill rate	Excess return on equities
	%	%	%		%	%	%
1919	42.0	3.9	38.1	1949	−6.8	0.5	−7.3
1920	−24.3	6.4	−30.7	1950	10.8	0.5	10.3
1921	−1.6	5.2	−6.8	1951	8.6	0.5	8.1
1922	49.9	2.6	47.3	1952	−0.1	2.1	−2.2
1923	11.9	2.6	9.3	1953	24.2	2.4	21.8
1924	21.9	3.4	18.5	1954	48.6	1.9	46.7
1925	31.7	4.1	27.6	1955	10.9	3.5	7.4
1926	3.2	4.5	−1.3	1956	−9.0	5.0	−14.0
1927	17.4	4.3	13.1	1957	−1.1	5.0	−6.1
1928	20.8	4.1	16.7	1958	47.8	5.1	42.7
1929	−12.2	5.3	−17.5	1959	54.8	3.4	51.4
1930	−11.6	2.5	−14.1	1960	1.7	5.0	−3.3
1931	−15.5	3.5	−19.0	1961	1.7	5.1	−3.4
1932	35.2	1.7	33.5	1962	0.4	4.5	−4.1
1933	31.2	0.6	30.6	1963	31.9	3.8	28.1
1934	24.3	0.7	23.6	1964	−4.1	4.4	−8.5
1935	14.0	0.5	13.5	1965	7.9	6.3	1.6
1936	19.1	0.6	18.5	1966	−6.2	6.1	−12.3
1937	−12.8	0.6	−13.4	1967	35.2	5.9	29.3
1938	−10.6	0.6	−11.2	1968	38.6	7.4	31.2
1939	2.2	1.2	1.0	1969	−14.3	7.9	−22.2
1940	−4.6	1.0	−5.6	1970	−8.4	7.5	−15.9
1941	22.9	1.0	21.9	1971	42.6	6.2	36.4
1942	17.9	1.0	16.9	1972	6.5	5.4	1.1
1943	11.5	1.0	10.5	1973	−25.2	9.0	−34.2
1944	12.5	1.0	11.5	1974	−47.4	12.6	−60.0
1945	5.9	0.9	5.0	1975	157.1	10.8	146.3
1946	17.9	0.5	17.4	1976	3.2	11.3	−8.1
1947	−2.3	0.5	−2.8	1977	43.0	9.4	33.6
1948	−4.8	0.5	−5.3				

Source: Dimson and Brealey, 'The Risk Premium on UK Equities', *The Investment Analyst,* no 52 (December 1978), p. 14.

1919 to 1977, the annual excess return on UK stocks averaged 9.2%. The corresponding figure for the US over the period 1926 to 1974 was 8.8%. The excess rate of return calculated by Dimson and Brealey was the difference between the rate of return realised on an equity index and the Treasury Bill rate. Rates of return were first calculated at annual intervals, and so the risk premium of nine per cent is the mean of the 59 annual risk premiums. These annual risk premiums are shown in Table 1.

The striking feature of this table is the erratic behaviour of the rate of return and the fact that in 25 of the 59 years under review the rate of return on equities was lower than the Treasury Bill rate. On the face of it, this conflicts with the theory that equity rates of return consist of the risk free rate of interest plus a premium for risk. However, the theory is about investors' expectations, not about realised outcomes. Dimson and Brealey's statistics show that equities lost money in 20 out of the 59 years. As no one invests in expectation of a loss, the realised outcomes of investment activity cannot be treated as the equivalent of investors' expectations at the time. Dimson and Brealey's work cannot, therefore, be regarded as an estimate of the risk premium expected by investors in ordinary shares over the period 1919 to 1977. It is rather an average of realised annual excess rates of return over more than half a century. Nevertheless, it is an interesting statistic and the share valuer, who can take a more settled long-term view divorced from the speculative gyrations of the stock market, will find it useful background information in the determination of risk premiums.

The risk premium undoubtedly varies from one period to another as well as from company to company. It is presumably at its highest in periods of high inflation and economic uncertainty. Thus, recent statistics show that over the period 1976 to 1985, the *FT*-Actuaries All-Share index averaged a return of 22.1% a year compared with 12.3% for three-month local authority bonds.[6] The author's experience is that rates of return expected on unquoted shares are never less than double, and are often as much as three times, those available on gilts. In many cases they are considerably more.

The relationship between risk and the rate of return

Although the average size of the risk premium over a period of time is useful to know, the valuer is more concerned with gauging the appropriate premium for a particular stock. How does the risk premium vary according to the company? As risk increases, for example, do investors require a commensurate increase in the risk premium? In other words, is the relationship between risk and the rate of return linear as shown by curve PB in figure 2, or does it take some other form such as curve PA which suggests that beyond a certain point the rewards for assuming risk become increasingly attractive? There are numerous possibilities.

A valid criticism of this sort of theorising is that it assumes that all investors have the same attitude to risk. They clearly do not. This is obvious to anyone who has attended an investment meeting. What one person may consider an exciting challenge, another may well regard as too risky. Rarely, if at all, does one find a unanimity of view at such gatherings.

[6] Lloyds Merchant Bank, *Gilts Market Letter*, February 1986.

Figure 2: Risk/rate of return trade-off.

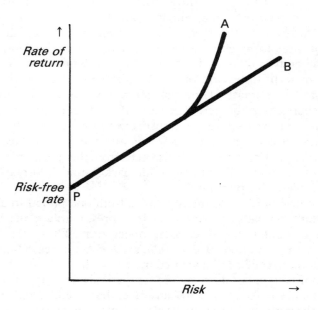

This is due not only to peoples' different attitudes towards risk but also to their different perceptions of it.

Economists recognise that people may differ in their attitude to risk and they explain it in terms of the utility function for wealth. Such a function describes the marginal increase in satisfaction or utility for a given increment in wealth. Figure 3 shows a textbook example of three different utility functions.

Curve C is reckoned to be typical of most investors. If C had £5,000 it would provide ten units of utility. If an additional £2,500 were received, utility would rise by two units to 12. However, if £2,500 were lost, utility would fall by four units to six. Thus, for C the potential gain in utility is not matched by the potential loss, and he would be unwilling to make a bet with a 50:50 chance of winning or losing £2,500. B would be indifferent to such a bet since the fall in utility if he lost £2,500 would be the same as the gain in utility if he won £2,500. A would be eager to make the bet since for him the potential gain in utility is greater than the potential loss. Most investors are assumed to have a diminishing marginal utility for money and are, therefore, seen as risk averters.

This form of marginal analysis has already been discussed in Chapter 1 and, despite its superficial attractions, found on closer investigation to be

Figure 3: Relationship between money and its utility.

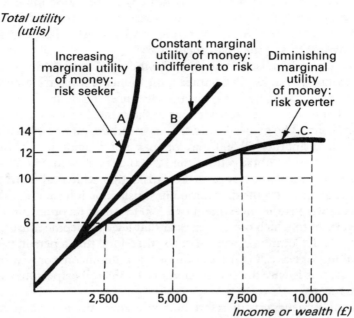

Source: Brigham, *Financial Management: Theory and Practice*, p. 133.

based on misconceived notions of human behaviour. It is true that as income or wealth rises its power to satisfy an individual's wants or desires declines, i.e., its utility diminishes. But far from pointing to greater risk aversion this indicates a greater willingness, or less reluctance, to invest in equity. This will become clear if we consider C's likely attitude to the same equity investment at two successive levels of income or wealth. At the £5,000 level an investment of £2,500 would entail a loss of four units of utility. However, the same investment made at the £7,500 wealth level would involve a sacrifice of only two units of utility. Therefore, as C's wealth rises the opportunity cost of equity investment becomes lower and risk assumption more attractive.

Thus, we would expect a man whose income barely provides him and his family with an average standard of living to be extremely risk-averse. To invest the mortgage money in speculative stocks would be unthinkable for such a person, since the threat of losing his home if the investment went wrong would be unacceptable. If this person's income were to double, however, it is more than likely that his attitude to risk would soften considerably. He may be persuaded to invest surplus funds in gilt-edged securities or even invest a modest sum in equities, perhaps through a unit trust or an investment trust. If we further assume that he receives a substantial legacy, it is not difficult to imagine him becoming an avid participator in the stock market, eager to assume investment risk — at the appropriate rate of return. As his income or wealth rises, therefore, so does his willingness to assume investment risk.

If this is so, where is the fallacy in the theory of diminishing marginal utility? Is it not, as shown in Chapter 1, the futility of comparing successive satisfactions of the same desire, in this instance, the desire for money or wealth? These successive satisfactions of the same desire are not alternatives for choice. The choice before C is to spend the money or to invest it. The fact that another £2,500 may or may not provide him with more satisfaction than he obtains from the £2,500 he wishes to invest, is of no relevance. He does not compare the satisfaction which an extra £2,500 would bring him with the diminution in satisfaction if he had £2,500 less. He merely weighs the investment of £2,500 against its opportunity cost, i.e., the extent to which other desires at that level of income must thereby go unsatisfied. Commonsense indicates, therefore, that a person becomes more willing, or less reluctant, to assume risk as his income or wealth rises. Doubtless, this is why the private investor is generally a person of above-average means.

This analysis suggests therefore that, as all investment is characterised by risk and as investors as a class have a low marginal utility of wealth, most investors actively seek risk. They are no more averse to risk than men are averse to work, but like men seeking work, they expect to be properly rewarded, and are attracted to risk by that higher reward. The art of investment, therefore, lies in the skilful assessment of risk so as to obtain the best possible return. There is an important difference of emphasis between this view and modern financial theory's obsession with risk aversion.

Given investors' different tolerance levels as regards risk, any notion of a generally accepted trade-off between risk and the rate of return must be recognised as a considerable abstraction from reality. It is helpful, nonetheless, to conceive of the rate of return as rising in line with increasing risk, and even if instances can be found where it fails to follow this rule rigidly, it may still prove a useful working assumption.

Abstractions such as these are necessary in valuation work if some semblance of order and rationality is to be imposed on the elusive, multi-faceted economic reality.

Finally, no discussion of the relationship between risk and the rate of return would be complete without reference to the claims of modern portfolio theory to have found the definitive answer to this relationship in the form of the Capital Asset Pricing Model.

The Capital Asset Pricing Model

The Capital Asset Pricing Model (CAPM) specifies the relationship between risk and the rate of return for efficient, well diversified portfolios. As it is not the role of the share valuer to advise on the construction of suitable portfolios of investments, one may well ask why this theory needs to be reviewed in this work. However, since a portfolio is merely a grouping of investments, a theory which claims to have established the precise relationship between risk and the rate of return for a portfolio must have implications for the same relationship as it applies to individual securities. As we shall see, Modern Portfolio Theory, through the CAPM, makes very definite assertions as to the relationship between risk and the rate of return on individual stocks.

It is a basic tenet of Modern Portfolio Theory that the riskiness of a stock held in isolation is different from its riskiness when held in a portfolio of stocks. According to MPT, the total risk in a portfolio is generally less than a weighted average of the risks of the individual constituent stocks, but the rate of return on that portfolio is always equal to the weighted average of the rates of return on the constituent stocks. Thus, by holding a portfolio of stocks, some of the risk of the constituent stocks is diversified away and the investor can obtain a level of risk which is lower than the risk of a security with the same rate of return but held in isolation. In view of this, claims MPT, the rate of return, or more specifically the risk premium, on an individual stock will reflect not its total risk but only that element of the risk which cannot be diversified away by holding a portfolio of shares. It would be illogical, argues MPT, for the rate of return to compensate the investor for assuming a risk he was not obliged to assume.

MPT, therefore, analyses the total risk of a security into diversifiable risk and non-diversifiable risk. These elements of risk are generally referred to as, respectively, unsystematic risk and systematic risk, or sometimes, non-market risk and market risk. Diversifiable risk is seen as emanating from factors specific to the particular company, such as, the Bhopal chemical disaster for Union Carbide or the Thalidomide drug for the Distillers Company. These 'unsystematic' factors are not restricted to adverse outcomes. They would include, for example, a highly profitable invention or the beneficial windfall effects on liquor stocks of an increase in excise duty. Indeed, it is the fact that these 'unsystematic' outcomes are, on the average, as likely to be good as they are bad that leads to the conclusion that this type of risk can be diversified away by holding a suitably large number of stocks. An efficient portfolio is one in which the diversifiable or unsystematic risk in the component stocks has been completely diversified away.

Undiversifiable or market risk is seen as stemming from influences to which all firms are to a greater or lesser extent exposed, such as, inflation, interest rates, fiscal policy — in other words, the general state of the economy. Conditions in the economy generally will affect different firms in different ways. The impact of a rise in interest rates on a property developer would not be the same as it would be on a retailer. Wage inflation has a greater impact on labour intensive firms than it does on capital intensive firms, and so on.

As this non-diversifiable or market risk varies with each company, and, according to the theory, is the only risk that is rewarded in the risk premium, the investor setting out on the task of constructing a portfolio needs to know what the level of market risk is in the various stocks.

As mentioned earlier, the standard deviation of the 'expected' rates of return is modern financial theory's measure of a share's total risk. To assess how much of that total risk is represented by non-diversifiable market risk a new technique has been devised: that of the beta co-efficient. In the CAPM, beta measures the sensitivity of a stock's 'expected' risk premium to movements in the market's 'expected' risk premium. A beta of 1.0, for example, indicates that a stock's risk premium will rise or fall by the same percentage as the market's risk premium rises or falls. A stock with a beta of 1.5 will see its 'expected' risk premium rise by one-and-a-half times the rise in the market's 'expected' risk premium.

The relationship between a share's risk premium and that of the market is given by the basic CAPM equation:

$$E(R_i) - R_F = \beta[E(R_M) - R_F]$$

Where $E(R_i)$ is the 'expected' rate of return on the security (or portfolio), R_F is the rate of return on a risk-free asset, such as, Treasury Bills, $E(R_M)$ is the 'expected' rate of return on the market and β is the measure of the security's (or portfolio's) sensitivity to movements in the market's 'expected' rate of return.

By adding the risk-free rate, R_F, to both sides of the equation the relationship can be expressed in the more familiar terms of the total rate of return, rather than the risk premium. That is:

$$E(R_i) = R_F + \beta[E(R_M) - R_F]$$

Thus, if the risk-free rate of interest were ten per cent, the 'expected' rate of return on the market 15%, and the beta of the stock 0.8, the 'expected' rate of return on that stock would be 14% as set out below:

$$E(R_i) = R_F + \beta[E(R_M) - R_F]$$
$$= 0.10 + 0.8\,(0.15 - 0.10)$$
$$= 0.10 + 0.04$$
$$= 0.14 \text{ or } 14\%$$

The assumptions on which the CAPM is based are:

(a) investors are risk averse and choose between different portfolios on the basis of 'expected' rates of return and the risk involved, risk being defined as the variability of the 'expected' rate of return;
(b) all investors have identical, subjective estimates of the 'expected' rate of return on a security and of the co-variance of the rates of return on all securities, i.e., investors have homogeneous expectations;
(c) there are no transaction costs and no taxes;
(d) all investors can borrow or lend an unlimited amount at a given risk-free rate of interest, and there are no restrictions on short sales of any securities;
(e) all investors asssume that their buying and selling will not affect the price.

Space does not permit us to set out the various steps which lead to the formulation of the equation and the interested reader is referred to a number of texts where this may be found.[7]

The relationships formulated by the theory apply to the unobservable world of 'expected' rates of return and risk. Despite this, beta co-efficients are calculated from historical data of the stock's rate of return and that of the market. Table 2 and Figure 4 are taken from a standard textbook and show how the beta co-efficient of a security is calculated from historical data.

Table 2: Returns on stock j and on the market 1974—1978

Year	Rate of return*	
	Stock j %	The market %
1978	11.55	7.11
1977	6.12	20.25
1976	2.72	1.44
1975	14.97	13.94
1974	(13.20)	(18.41)
Mean	4.43	4.87
Standard deviation	10.94	14.81

*Rate of return is equal to dividend yield plus any capital gain or minus any capital loss. The market is measured by an index such as the *FT*-Actuaries All Share Index.

Source: Brigham, *Financial Management: Theory and Practice,* p. 111.

Each dot on the graph in Figure 4 represents a different year. At that point, the realised excess rate of return can be read off for the security and for the market. A regression line is drawn through the set of dots in a way which

[7] See, for example, Lorie and Hamilton, pp. 171–210; Sharpe, pp. 116–185; and Brigham, pp. 96–173.

Figure 4: Relationship of stock j to the market.

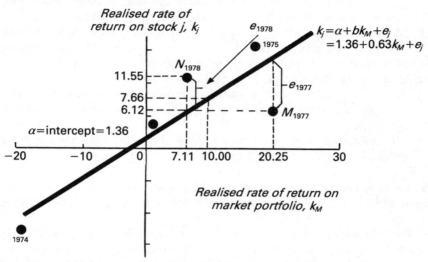

Source: Brigham, *Financial Management: Theory and Practice*, p. 112.

market. A regression line is drawn through the set of dots in a way which minimises the distance between the dots and the line. The slope of this line is the regression co-efficient, termed beta co-efficient, which measures the 'rise over-run' — in this case 0.63. This means that, on the average, for every one per cent increase in the rate of return on the market, there should be a 0.63% rise in the rate of return on a particular security. The vertical axis intercept is 1.36, indicating that if the market's rate of return were zero, this stock's rate of return would be 1.36%.[8]

With computers available to speedily regress the monthly rate of return of individual stocks against those of the market over an extended period (often five years), the calculation of beta factors for individual stocks is not an insuperable problem, and organisations now exist which provide this service to believers in MPT. Since the beta of a portfolio is a weighted average of the betas of the constituent stocks,[9] the investor is now in a position to construct a portfolio of stocks which will have the level of risk he desires. He need not consider whether the stocks he selects are under- or over-valued and, hence, a buy or a sell, since in the efficient market which MPT assumes, all securities are efficiently priced in terms of each other. Having constructed his portfolio with the desired level of risk, the investor

[8] This is the market model beta and not the CAPM beta. The CAPM beta is calculated using excess rates of return or risk premiums. There should not be any difference between the two but in fact there always is.

[9] The proof of this can also be found in the sources referred to in footnote 2 (p. 148).

retires to await his due reward in the form of a return which compensates him for the beta, i.e., market, risk assumed.

This body of investment theory can be considered from two angles, the practical one and the theoretical one. From the practical angle the sort of questions which should be asked are: is the theory intelligible to the typical investment professional whom it is presumably designed to assist? Are the assumptions realistic? Do aspects of it which the practical man can corroborate from his own experience agree or conflict with that experience? Above all, what is the evidence to suggest that these techniques lead to improved investment performance? From the theoretical angle, the enquiry should focus on the logic employed and the validity of the theory's concepts of risk and 'expected' rates of return. The theoretical aspects are considered first.

At the heart of MPT lies the belief that the risk of a share can be measured by the standard deviation of 'expected' future rates of return. The beta co-efficient, which measures a stock's systematic or market risk, is intimately linked to the standard deviation of returns. The relationship between the two is as follows:

$$\beta_{iM} = \frac{\varrho_{iM}\sigma_i\sigma_M}{\sigma_{M_2}}$$

β_{iM} is the beta co-efficient between security i and the market; ϱ_{iM} is the correlation co-efficient between security i and the market; σ_i is the standard deviation of security i's 'expected' rate of return; and σ_{M_2} is the variance (i.e., the square of the standard deviation) of the market's 'expected' rate of return.[10]

Provided the rates of return on the securities of a portfolio are not perfectly positively correlated, it is a mathematical necessity that the standard deviation of the portfolio's rate of return be less than the weighted average standard deviation of the constituent securities. It is on this fact alone that MPT bases its assertion that some risk can be eliminated by holding a portfolio of securities. It is this phenomenon which has led to the classification of diversifiable and non-diversifiable risk and to the intuitive explanations as to how these two types of risk arise.

The standard deviation of 'expected' or realised rates of return as a measure of risk has already been reviewed in detail earlier in this chapter. It was shown that this measure is flawed by fundamental circularity of reasoning. As the risk measure is a function of the share price which is itself a function of risk, risk is being measured in terms of itself. The root cause of this circularity is the use of a share's price or its rate of return to measure its risk. It leads to the absurdity of the 'expected' rate of return being

---

[10] For the derivation of this relationship, see Lorie and Hamilton, p. 204.

determined by its own variability. Put another way, any theory or model of share price determination which (a) defines risk solely in terms of the rate of return variability, i.e., the variability of the share price, and (b) asserts that a share's rate of return is determined solely by its risk and by the rate of return on the market, is one which defines security prices in terms of themselves.

Fundamental though this defect is, it is by no means the only significant objection to the standard deviation as a measure of a share's risk. Its use as a substitute for a measure of variability below the 'expected' rate of return is justified by the assumption that probability distributions for individual stocks are bell-shaped i.e., normal. This has never been evidenced, and, given that expectations are unobservable, it is not difficult to see why.[11]

There are many other inadequacies in this measure of risk notably the Alice-in-Wonderland effect mentioned on page 152. This throws risky stocks into a vortex where they get apparently riskier and riskier, and safe stocks into one where they get safer and safer. These defects deprive the standard deviation, and hence beta, of any significance as a measure of risk.

There is, therefore, no evidence to suggest that risk is eliminated, as opposed to being merely averaged, by diversification. The distinction between diversifiable and undiversifiable risk is spurious, a fact which is evident from the feeble examples of diversifiable risk found in literature on the subject. Sometimes it is a fire which damages factories or crops or a law suit for product liability; at other times it is the occurrence of strikes, the winning and losing of major contracts, successful and unsuccessful marketing programmes, higher than expected sales and so on.[12]

Many of these risks are insurable events, such as, fire, fraud, product liability, the loss of goods in transit and the like. When these extraneous examples are removed, the distinction between events which are the work of economic forces generally, and those which are independently generated and quite specific to the firm, is difficult to maintain. No man is an island and nor is any firm. It operates as one of the many cogs in the machine of the economy. Nothing happens to it, at least as regards its commercial operations, which has not been influenced or determined to some degree by the remainder of the economy. Workers strike for higher wages because inflation, devaluation or higher taxes have reduced their real pay. At other times, they strike in sympathy with workers in other industries. Why, for example, should there be a conceptual distinction between winning or losing major contracts and winning or losing the more run-of-the-mill contracts? Is it suggested that forces independent of the

[11] See footnote 3, p. 149.
[12] Brigham, p. 107; and Modigliani and Pogue, p. 334.

- economy determine the award of major contracts, but dependent forces determine the minor contracts? How can a marketing programme's success, or lack of it, be independent of the economy?

The classification of risk between a diversifiable and non-diversifiable element was doubtless introduced to explain the phenomenon of risk elimination apparent when securities were held in portfolios. It was not conceived *ab initio*. As has been demonstrated, however, the phenomenon of risk elimination is illusory and occurs solely when a misconceived and logically inconsistent measure of risk — the standard deviation of 'expected' rates of return — is employed. The notion of diversifiable and non-diversifiable risk has no theoretical foundation; nor is it supported by observation and an analysis of the circumstances in which companies operate. Above all, no one has questioned the assumption that the risk of the market, as measured by an appropriate index, is synonymous with the risk of the economy. In the United Kingdom, major sectors of the economy are not represented on the Stock Exchange. The public sector includes significant industries such as gas and electricity generation and distribution, coal, water supply, sewerage and drainage, rail and bus transport, health, education, aircraft and aerospace, shipbuilding and steel. Furthermore, many firms in the private sector do not have a Stock Exchange listing and these companies account for a significant proportion of economic activity. A recent estimate, based on statistics for 1975, puts the contribution of quoted companies to total GDP at only 22%.[13] This excludes the financial sector, but making generous allowance for this, one could hardly justify using the quoted company sector as a proxy for the economy as a whole.

There are many other misconceptions and illogicalities in MPT. To give them all an airing would require a much more comprehensive treatment of the subject than can be undertaken in a work of this size. However, it will be evident from the limited review carried out here that MPT has no firm, logical footing and is a seriously misleading set of ideas. From this critique of the logic of the theory, we now turn to a more commonsense appraisal from the perspective of the typical investor.

MPT is unintelligible to most practitioners. It is neither simple nor elegant but labyrinthine and abstruse. It takes a concentrated effort, usually accompanied by a refresher course in mathematics and statistics, to be able to follow the exposition. The individual with the strength to persevere in this endeavour finds to his astonishment that the equations used to represent relationships reveal a breath-taking naïveté and an utter lack of reality. He finds that the statistical techniques employed are more

[13] Donald A. Hay and Derek J. Morris, *Unquoted Companies: Their Contribution to the United Kingdom Economy* (London: Macmillan, 1984), p. 67.

suited to the quality control procedures of a packaging or bottling plant than they are to the untidy world of investment, where the rates of return are subject to wild, often emotionally-inspired, gyrations.

The example given earlier of the calculation of the beta co-efficient would for many people preclude the necessity to look any further into this theory. With the fore-knowledge that the stock's beta was 0.63 and with assumed knowledge of the rate of return on the market, the investor in this stock would not have been able to estimate the rate of return for any of the five years with any accuracy. Not one observation lies on the regression line. Like the EMH, this is another 'on the average' theory. If the investor throws the dice often enough, his number will come up in the statistically average way.

The assumptions of the theory are totally unrealistic and this presents one of the greatest difficulties for the practical man. Abstraction is necessary in all development of theory, but nothing in this theory seems to even faintly mirror reality. Everything that characterises investment and makes it so distinctive has been assumed away: there are no differences in outlook between investors; everyone has identical skills and judgement; each investor assesses the infinitely numerous possible outcomes of each investment and assigns probabilities to each one; no difference exists between each investor's assessment of these different possible outcomes or their probability; all investors base their assessments on the probability-weighted average or 'expected' rate of return; and all investors have the same time horizon or holding period. The other assumptions, which on their own might well have been seen as legitimate, i.e., no transaction costs, unlimited borrowing and lending at the risk-free rate, no restrictions on short selling and investors' assumptions that their own buying and selling will not affect the price, merely serve to convince the practitioner that nothing of practical relevance to investment can come from such an abstraction.

Most investors hold shares, either directly or indirectly, in portfolios. One of the few elements of MPT which might strike a cord of recognition with the practitioner is the emphasis on the value of the portfolio. Although the reasons why most investors hold portfolios are by no means as simple as MPT believes, risk reduction is certainly the most significant one. However, the investor would be surprised indeed to learn that, by the act of combining shares in a portfolio, some of the risk of the constituent stocks disappears; and that if the portfolio was split up into individual stocks, this risk would reappear. For him, the effect of a portfolio on risk is the same as its effect on the rate of return: it averages it out. Risk is something inherent in events impinging on the firm's business undertaking; it is not affected by changes in the ownership of the shares.

MPT is careful not to claim that its methods lead to improved performance. Indeed, if it appeared to produce better results than conventional techniques there can be little doubt that investors, whether believers or not, would be falling over themselves to adopt it. But, if it does not lead to improved performance, why should investors abandon the familiar, if imperfect, techniques for a new-fangled system in which they do not believe and which no one but an academic can fully understand?

It is over 20 years since Sharpe conceived the CAPM.[14] There has been ample time for this radical innovation, together with its accretions, to gain widespread acceptance in the investment world. Its failure to do so, despite the fact that throughout this time it has been the conventional academic wisdom inculcated into a generation of business school graduates, is its greatest indictment.

Conclusion

The rate of return on a security has to compensate the investor for:

(a) forgoing the pure or risk-free rate of interest;
(b) bearing the risk of equity investment; and
(c) suffering any lack of marketability.

Additionally small investors face a size penalty in that, owing to transaction costs, a small sum will earn a lower rate of interest than a larger sum, other things being equal. As the risk-free or pure rate of interest can be identified without much difficulty, it will be seen that valuation hinges in large part on the assessment of risk and its appropriate reflection in the risk premium. The question of marketability is considered in Chapter 9.

As the present value of a security is a function of its cash return and the discount rate applied to that return, risk, defined as the probability of loss, can arise from changes in the cash return or changes in the discount rate, or a combination of these two factors. For fixed-interest stocks such as gilts, local authority bonds and 'blue chip' loan stocks, where payment of the coupon is not in doubt, change in the general level of interest rates is the only source of risk. Interest rate risk has had a devastating effect on the value of gilts and other fixed-interest stocks over the years. It has also had an effect on equity prices since their rate of return, and hence price, cannot long withstand a rise in the rate of return on gilts. The effect on equities is masked by the risk premium and changes in dividends, but it exists nonetheless.

[14] William F. Sharpe, 'Capital Asset Prices: A Theory of Market Equilibrium under Conditions of Risk', *Journal of Finance*, 19 (September 1964), pp. 425–442.

As the rate of return on Government securities is by definition the pure or risk-free rate of interest, there appears to be no obvious reward for this type of risk. Variability, however, is two-sided and can just as easily result in a price rise as a price fall. Variability in the pure rate of interest provides an opportunity for wind-fall profit or loss, and it could be argued that it would be illogical to recompense for a downside risk without charging for the upside potential.

Business or commercial risk arises from the nature of a firm's operations and also from its capital structure. A gold mining company is riskier than a food manufacturer; a firm with a high level of debt is riskier than one funded entirely by equity. Measurement uncertainty is usually considered a part of business risk, but it may help to recognise it as a separate component. Distant outcomes are felt to be riskier than nearer ones when in reality they may be no riskier, but merely subject to more uncertainty. Ice cream sales five years hence may be no riskier than next year's sales, yet we have more confidence about our estimate for next year's figures than we do for those five years away. The more distant, but perhaps no less risky, outcomes are discounted at a higher rate than the nearer ones.

Risk is a quality of things which, like other abstract concepts such as truth and beauty, is instantly recognisable but defies numerical quantification or measurement. It is possible, none the less, to rank investments by their riskiness, but such an ordering is of the (perfectly legitimate) 'more or less' variety. Not everyone would agree that risk is not susceptible to accurate and precise measurement. Modern portfolio theory uses the standard deviation of 'expected' rates of return to measure risk. This concept was subjected to close scrutiny and found to be misconceived and based on circular reasoning. It defines risk in terms of itself and leads to absurdities in its application.

More conventional and less ambitious techniques which merely aim to heighten the awareness of risk were reviewed. These include the pay-back period, sensitivity analysis and crude scenario analysis. A variant of MPT's risk measure, but applied to the 'expected' cash return, not the rate of return, was discussed as a possible risk measure for the share valuer. It is very much a suggestion for discussion and development rather than a tried and tested technique.

It is one thing to state that the rate of return consists of the pure or risk-free rate of interest plus a risk premium, but quite another matter to specify precisely the relationship between the level of risk and the size of the risk premium. Modern financial theory asserts that the relationship is linear so that if the level of risk rises by, say, 20% so must the risk premium. This is based on the supposition of rational behaviour and is a perfectly acceptable position for the share valuer to take. In the

- stock market, however, it has not been established as a fact that the relationship between risk and the rate of return is linear in this way.

The individual's attitude to risk is conditioned by the well-documented phenomenon of the diminishing marginal utility of wealth. As wealth or income rises, the power of each additional £100 to satisfy desires diminishes. According to portfolio theory this makes the investor increasingly averse to risk. It was seen that this is a misconception and that in fact exactly the opposite is the case. Investors acquire a greater willingness, or alternatively they become less reluctant, to assume investment risk as their income or wealth increases. Modern financial theory's ubiquitous emphasis on investors' risk aversion is overplayed. Equity investors are, generally speaking, no more averse to risk than man is averse to work. He actively seeks it and is attracted to it by the reward. The art of investment lies in the skilful assessment of risk. Some people are better at this than others.

The theory of risk and the rate of return is an attempt to formalise the thought processes of the average or typical investor, so as to provide a useful explanation of share price formation and the behaviour of stock
- markets. It is an ambitious aim and is far from being achieved. Nonetheless, it provides some valuable insights which can help the share valuer. The notion that the rate of return consists of the pure rate of interest plus a premium for risk, uncertainty and marketability is useful. By explicitly considering these individual elements in every valuation, the valuer will become more aware of the subjectivity in his own judgements and, with practice, this will lead to greater consistency and objectivity in his own value determinations.

Finally, and purely for the sake of completeness, we examined the Capital Asset Pricing Model. At the heart of the CAPM lies the belief that the risk of a security can be measured by the standard deviation of its 'expected' rate of return. Portfolio theory's assertion that risk can be eliminated (as opposed to being merely averaged) by combining securities into portfolios is based on the mathematical properties of the standard deviation. Earlier in this chapter, it was shown that the standard deviation of 'expected' rates of return is an impossible measure of risk which stands condemned, not only by its inherent circularity of reasoning, but also by absurdities and anomalies in its practical application. There is no evidence, therefore, that combining securities into a portfolio does anything other than average or spread out the risk.

The assumptions of the CAPM emasculate reality beyond recognition and go far beyond the legitimate boundaries of abstraction. The notion that risk consists of a market or systematic element and a non-market or diversifiable component is not one which stands up to close scrutiny. It bears all the hallmarks, not of an observation of the real world, but of an invention to provide a superficially plausible explanation for the apparent elimination of risk in a well diversified portfolio.

The fundamental misconception of portfolio theory generally is that risk should be measured by the variability of 'expected' future rates of return, or share price volatility. The prices of unlisted shares tend to be highly volatile, but this is not because they are risky. Similarly on the Stock Exchange, the existence of a narrow market in a company's shares causes the share price to be volatile. The same company would be no less risky or safe if it had a wide spread of shareholders and a proper market in its shares. In the author's opinion, it is fundamentally wrong to make the measure of risk the chance play of a share's price — to make it the hostage of the ebb and flow of Stock Exchange rumour and sentiment. It is all the more surprising that portfolio theory should opt for this measure of risk, given its own belief that successive share price movements are entirely random.

Appendix 1

Formula for the calculation of the standard deviation

$$\sigma = \sum_{i=1}^{N=3} (k_i - \bar{k})^2 p_i$$

where σ = standard deviation
k_i = rate of return on ith outcome
$\bar{k}$ = 'expected' or probability-weighted average rate of return on the investment
p_i = the probability of the ith outcome
$\sum_{i=1}^{N=3}$ = summation sign for all possible (in this case, three) outcomes

For company A, the calculation is as follows:

$k_i - \bar{k}$	$(k_i - \bar{k})$	$(k_i - \bar{k})^2$	$(k_i - \bar{k})^2 p_i$
35.0−27.5	7.5	56.25	56.25 × 0.3 = 16.875
27.5−27.5	0	0	0 × 0.4 = —
20.0−27.5	−7.5	56.25	56.25 × 0.3 = 16.875
			33.75

$$\sigma = \sqrt{33.75} = 5.8$$

For company B, the calculation is:

$k_i - \bar{k}$	$(k_i - \bar{k})$	$(k_i - \bar{k})^2$	$(k_i - \bar{k})^2 p_i$
95.0−27.5	67.5	4,556.25	4,556.25 × 0.3 = 1,366.88
35.0−27.5	7.5	56.25	56.25 × 0.4 = 22.50
−50.0−27.5	−77.5	6,006.25	6,006.25 × 0.3 = 1,801.87
			3,191.25

$$\sigma = \sqrt{3,191} = 56.5$$

Appendix 2

Calculation of the standard deviation of returns

QRS plc

$k_i - \bar{k}$	$(k_i - \bar{k})$	$(k_i - \bar{k})^2$	$(k_i - \bar{k})^2 p_i$
$2,500 - 950$	$1,550$	$2,402,500$	$2,402,500 \times 0.2 = 480,500$
$1,500 - 950$	550	$302,500$	$302,500 \times 0.5 = 151,250$
$-1,000 - 950$	$-1,950$	$3,802,500$	$3,802,500 \times 0.3 = 1,140,750$
			$1,772,500$

$\sigma = \sqrt{1,772,500} = £1,331$

ABC Ltd

$k_i - \bar{k}$	$(k_i - \bar{k})$	$(k_i - \bar{k})^2$	$(k_i - \bar{k})^2 p_i$
$2,000 - 1,250$	750	$562,500$	$562,500 \times 0.4 = 225,000$
$1,000 - 1,250$	-250	$62,500$	$62,500 \times 0.5 = 31,250$
$-500 - 1,250$	$-1,750$	$3,062,500$	$3,062,500 \times 0.1 = 306,250$
			$562,500$

$\sigma = \sqrt{562,500} = £750$

8

Goodwill and other intangibles

If the adjectives 'tangible' and 'intangible' were given their proper dictionary definition, tangible assets would consist exclusively of assets with a physical substance capable of being touched and intangible assets would comprise solely incorporeal rights. In practice, however, tangibles include incorporeal assets such as debtors, loans and securities, whilst intangibles are restricted to non-current incorporeal assets, such as, goodwill, patents and trademarks. Deferred revenue expenditure, such as, research and development costs, is also considered an intangible asset.

Whatever the origins of the distinction between tangibles and intangibles — a distinction which is recognised in accounting, finance and investment — its main purpose today seems to be to delineate assets whose valuation is extremely subjective, often suspect (i.e., the intangibles), from those which are not. In Stock Exchange investment analysis, for example, intangibles are generally excluded from asset backing per share, implying that it would be imprudent to rely on their having any value. Similarly, most analysts exclude intangibles when calculating gearing ratios. In the accountancy profession it is considered prudent to write off 'purchased' goodwill as soon as possible and highly imprudent to recognise 'non-purchased' goodwill in the balance sheet. In practice, professional eyebrows are often raised where significant values are attributed to patents, trademarks and copyright in the accounts. The classification of assets between intangibles and tangibles seems to be based on the, perhaps unconscious, belief that value really only attaches to physical things.

As the value of a business is not the same as the value of its constituent parts (see Chapter 1), one may well question the need for a chapter devoted to the valuation of specific, albeit intangible, assets. One reason for this is that intangibles such as patents, licences, and trade marks can often be sold independently of the business as a whole, and it may, therefore, be necessary to value them separately, particularly if it seems that their value in exchange is much greater than their value to the business. Occasionally, too, companies have to be valued in expectation of a liquidation and then a valuation of the individual assets is required. Furthermore, goodwill, probably the most important intangible, is the subject of considerable mystery and misunderstanding. It is a term frequently encountered in finance, accounting and investment, and it often appears in valuation instructions such as where the assignment might be to value the 'net assets, including goodwill', of a company. Much of this chapter is therefore devoted to goodwill: what it is and whether and how it may be valued. This is followed by a discussion of the intellectual property rights in patents, trademarks, registered designs and copyright. Some possible valuation techniques are presented. The chapter ends with some remarks on deferred revenue expenditure.

Goodwill

The fact that the value of business cannot be reduced to the sum of the values of its constituent parts is a general characteristic of value and is found in realms other than economics. The value of a cinema film cannot be reduced to the sum of the values of each frame. In fact the film is much more than the sum of the value of each constituent frame. Similarly with a great painting or sculpture. Its value cannot be meaningfully expressed in terms of its constituent materials. It is the creative arrangement of these materials, as well as the materials themselves, which gives the painting or sculpture its visual appeal. In much the same way, it is the creative arrangement of the factors of production to form a unique business undertaking capable of satisfying economic demand which gives rise to goodwill, and, which gives the firm a value different from that of its constituent parts. The value of goodwill can no more be divorced from the value of the business than can the beauty of a painting be divorced from its canvas or the visual appeal of a building from the stone or the masonry out of which it is made. When a painting is defaced or a vase broken, its beauty disappears. In like manner, the business. When it is broken up into its constituent parts, its goodwill vanishes. Goodwill, therefore, may be regarded as that intangible quality which distinguishes a firm or enterprise from the collection of unrelated economic agents it would otherwise be.

This definition of goodwill is consistent with, although considerably wider than, Lord Eldon's definition in *Cruttwell* v. *Lye* (1810) 17 Ves Jr: '. . . nothing more than the probability that the old customers will resort to the old place even though the old trader or shopkeeper has gone'. It is in sympathy with Lord McNaghten's definition in *IRC* v. *Muller* [1901] AC 217: 'the benefit of the good name, reputation and connection of a business. It is the attractive force which brings in custom.' It is close to the definition formulated by the Research Committee of the now defunct Society of Incorporated Accountants: 'Goodwill consists of those elements in business relationships which make a continuance of such relationships probable notwithstanding a change in the ownership of the business'. Strictly speaking, however, the existence of goodwill does not depend on changes in the ownership of the business although its value might.

A firm cannot acquire its goodwill by purchase. It comes into being through the very forces which bring the firm into existence and by which it is built up. Although goodwill is an asset in the popular meaning of the word, it can hardly be considered an asset in the balance sheet sense of the word since it can never be acquired by purchase nor disposed of by sale. The only way a firm can dispose of its goodwill is by bringing to an end its own existence. It cannot confer that goodwill on another enterprise.

Goodwill, therefore, is not dependent on profits, still less on super-profits. In this it conflicts sharply with what goodwill is understood to be by most accountants. P. D. Leake, an early authority on the subject, held that 'the exchangeable value of the right [goodwill] depends on the probability of earning future super-profit; the term "super-profit" meaning the amount by which revenue, increase of value, or other advantage received exceeds any, or all, economic expenditure incidental to its production'.[1] Leake's subsequent definition of the term 'economic expenditure' makes it clear that his understanding of the super-profit concept is similar to that of H. E. Seed: 'Profits in excess of those required to provide an economic rate of remuneration for all labour and capital needed in a business'.[2] Although Leake allowed certain exceptions where goodwill could exist without prospect of super profits,[3] these have long since been forgotten. In the minds of most accountants goodwill exists only where there are super-profits, or at least profits.

The traditional definition of goodwill as a function of super-profits has to be understood in the context of the valuation of a business as a whole. The idea behind it is that there is a normal rate of return — the so-called economic rate of return — that can be earned on assets of a certain type. Where a business earns profits above this normal or economic rate, it is assumed the purchaser will pay the normalised value of the assets plus a number of years' purchase of the super-profits. The annual super-profits are calculated by deducting from maintainable profits a sum equivalent to the economic rate of return on the net assets. These super-profits are then multiplied by a factor representing the number of years' purchase. The value of super-profits is seen as

---

[1] P. D. Leake, *Commercial Goodwill*, 4th ed. (London: Gee & Co., 1948), p. 18.
[2] H. E. Seed, *Goodwill as a Business Asset* (London: Gee & Co., 1937), p. 8.
[3] Leake, pp. 20–21.

goodwill and is added to the value of the net assets to produce the value of the business as a whole.

As a technique for valuing a business in its entirety, the super-profits method has a long and ancient pedigree. The advantage claimed for it is that it recognises the transitory nature of above-average performance. However, a little reflection reveals logical inconsistencies in the concept. First, if profits at the economic rate of return are deducted from maintainable profits, any excess must be maintainable super-profits and not transitory super-profits. Second, there is not necessarily any relation between the balance sheet amount of an asset, whether based on historic or replacement cost, and its value. The value of assets used in a business are a function of their profit-earning capacity and not their cost. Third, goodwill in this scheme of things is a function of the assets. Thus, labour intensive service companies will tend to have lots of goodwill and capital intensive manufacturing companies, relatively little goodwill. Yet, there is no particular reason why capital intensive companies should have less goodwill than service companies. Furthermore, since dividends reduce the asset base, it would appear that a company can increase its goodwill by declaring a dividend.

Ignoring these serious conceptual shortcomings, it is impossible to measure goodwill on this definition with any degree of objectivity. How is one to know the going rate of return on net assets? How long are the super-profits going to last? What is the going rate for super-profits and how may it be ascertained? This valuation basis leads to highly esoteric arguments divorced from reality. It never features in descriptions of takeover deals and the author has never encountered it in commercial valuations or negotiations. Practical businessman do not use it. It seems to be a disappearing piece of accounting folklore which has a vestigial significance in the negotiation of share values with the Inland Revenue.[4]

The more modern view of goodwill is set out in accounting standard SSAP 22. In SSAP 22, goodwill is defined as 'the difference between the value of a business as a whole and the aggregate of the fair values of its separable net assets'. Fair value is defined as the amount for which an asset (or liability) could be exchanged in an arms-length transaction. SSAP 22 states that goodwill is by definition incapable of realisation separately from the business as a whole. It identifies four characteristics of goodwill:

(a) the value of goodwill has no reliable or predictable relationship to any costs which may have been incurred;

[4] See, for example, T. A. Hamilton Baynes, *Share Valuations*, 3rd ed. (London: Heinemann, 1984), pp. 197–201.

(b) individual intangible factors which may contribute to goodwill cannot be valued;

(c) the value of goodwill may fluctuate widely according to internal and external circumstances over relatively short periods of time; and

(d) the assessment of the value of goodwill is highly subjective.[5]

The weakness of SSAP 22's definition, as indeed of the traditional definition based on super-profits, lies in its failure to specify what goodwill, as valued, represents. Why is there a difference between the value of the business as a whole and the fair value of its net assets? Why should goodwill, in the sense of the established trading connections or relationships of a firm, have a value which, in all circumstances and at all times, is exactly equal to the difference between the value of the separable net assets and the value of the firm as a whole? Where the value of the business as a whole is less than the fair value (as defined) of the separable net assets, why is not the resultant 'negative' goodwill a liability of the business in the same way that positive goodwill is an asset of the business? Does the existence of 'negative' goodwill mean that the firm's existing trading connections and relationships have no value? Rolls Royce, to take a notable example, has made losses in recent years, but it would be naïve to maintain that it has no goodwill. At the other extreme, an insurance broking business dependent on the contacts and flair of one individual may well earn substantial super-profits but have a nil goodwill value. This is because the goodwill, which undoubtedly exists, is personal to the individual concerned. If he were to leave the business, the customers would follow him and a purchaser of the business would be left with just the assets and liabilities.

The definition of goodwill as the difference between the value of a business as a whole and the aggregate value of its separable net assets leads to the absurd conclusion that capital intensive companies have less goodwill than service companies. It has its origins in the widespread view of a business as a collection of assets which earns a return. This way of viewing a firm is particularly in evidence in the fields of accountancy, finance and investment. Financial statements buttress this belief. The balance sheet sets out the assets and liabilities, and the use of terms such as 'net worth' for equity funds shows that many people regard it as an indication of the business' value. The inclusion of intangibles in the balance sheet is frowned upon yet these intangibles are the vital ingredients in business success and, therefore, value.

[5] *Accounting for goodwill*, SSAP 22, paragraphs 1, 2, 21 and 25.

Each of the factors of production (i.e., land, labour and capital) is required in every form of economic enterprise. However, the balance sheet concerns itself solely with capital (and occasionally also with land), but ignores labour. As labour is the active element in production and capital and land are the passive elements, the balance sheet gives a one-sided view of a business and the less important side at that. The vital active force of the business, stemming from the quality of its employees, the reputation and standing of the firm, its products and customers, is not mentioned.

Given the present state of accounting theory and practice, these limitations in the presentation of accounts are unavoidable. However, when a business changes hands, the price reflects the full economic advantage gained, and this may exceed, or be exceeded by, the balance sheet equity funds. This difference, which is purely a hazard of the accounting conventions adopted and the proportion of labour and capital in the firm, has to be accounted for in the balance sheet of the acquiror. A label is therefore needed, but unfortunately a misleading description has been adopted. This difference does not represent goodwill nor is there any such thing as negative goodwill. A more appropriate description would be simply acquisition premium or acquisition discount.

Goodwill by its nature cannot be valued separately from the business, nor does it ever need to be valued separately. The purchaser of a business will enquire into the management and the work force, the company's marketing strengths and weaknesses, its technical expertise, the capacity of its plant, and so on. These factors are embraced in the concept of goodwill and are swept up in the valuation of the future earnings stream. In negotiations for the acquisition of a business, the value of goodwill is not a subject for consideration and it would be rare for the term even to enter into the discussion. As in commercial practice, so in theory: there are no techniques for establishing the separate value of goodwill since goodwill is never separately valued and the need for such techniques does not arise.

Although goodwill is not separately valued, the valuer must make careful enquiry as to the source and nature of goodwill in the firm being valued. This is because, in certain cases, the goodwill of a business does not pass with ownership of the shares. Many 'people' businesses such as advertising agencies, travel agents, professional firms — paradoxically those types of firms which according to the traditional definition have a high goodwill value — are susceptible to loss of business, and therefore goodwill, through the departure of key personnel. Reference has already been made to the one-man insurance broking business, but many other less obvious instances are encountered where a firm's goodwill could disappear suddenly. For example, a firm may do most of its business with a single customer to whom other sources of supply may be available. The sudden loss of the firm's customer would probably mean closure of the business and the disappearance of goodwill. Goodwill can also be jeopardised by undue reliance on a single supplier or a single product.

Where a business relies unduly on key individuals, it is usual for the purchaser to insist on service contracts to ensure their loyalty. Key employees are usually shareholders in this type of business, and it would be in their interests to enter into service contracts. Key employees who are not shareholders, however, may well insist on a substantially higher level of remuneration in return for entering into a service contract. This will depress the value of the equity. The going concern valuation of a business whose goodwill is highly personalised must carry the qualification that it assumes that appropriate service contracts will be in place. Similarly, the going concern valuation of a firm overly dependent on a single supplier or customer must refer to that fact and to the valuation assumption of continued customer or supplier loyalty.

Intellectual property rights

In its generally accepted sense this term embraces patents, trademarks, copyright, licences, know-how agreements, registered designs and allied rights. The licencing of these forms of property, by which the owner grants permission to another or others to make use of it, has become widespread over the years and has often proved a highly profitable activity for both parties. This type of asset is often extremely valuable. Furthermore, it may well be possible to dispose of such assets without prejudicing the firm's future as a going concern. Although it is rare for separate valuations of intangibles to be required, circumstances sometimes arise when the valuer has to form an opinion on the value of a trademark or patent, and knowledge of the general approach is necessary.

The truth of the dictum that valuation is essentially a bringing together of the economic concept of value and the legal concept of property, is particularly evident in the valuation of intellectual property where there is no physical attribute to cloud the issue. Property rights are all there is to value. An appreciation of the nature of the legal rights enshrined in patents, trademarks and the like is, therefore, vital. A detailed discussion of the legal rights and the various forms of intellectual property is a formidable undertaking and out of the question in the present context. All that can be attempted here is a brief résumé of the general nature of these rights with particular emphasis on patents and trademarks — two commonly encountered forms of intellectual property.

Patents

A patentable invention is a new and non-obvious industrially applicable idea. The applicant for a patent must file a detailed specification of the invention with the Patent Office and this is automatically made public 18 months after the initial filing. There is first a preliminary examination and search, the result of which is published with the specification, and then a substantive examination to ensure that the invention is a new, non-obvious inventive step (i.e., one which is not part of the published or freely known state of the art) and has an industrial or agricultural application. The patent itself is the document issued by the Patent Office which describes the invention and gives the patentee a right to take legal action against unauthorised use of the invention, called 'infringement', for a number of years.

For patents filed on or after 1 June 1978, the operative date of the Patent Act 1977, the period of exclusive right granted to the patentee for manufacturing and using the invention is up to 20 years, if the patentee pays the appropriate renewal fees. There is no right of extension. Patents issued under the Patent Act 1949 had a period of up to 16 years with the probability of extension on certain grounds. Any such patents which were 11 years old or more on 1 June 1978 kept to the 16 years, with the possibility of extension to a maximum of 20 years. Those with less than 11 years to run at 1 June 1978 were automatically extended to 20 years with no possibility of longer life. The law of 'old' patents — contained in the Act of 1949 as modified by the 1977 Act — will continue, therefore, to have an effect up to 1998.

Many patents are capable of use in a variety of ways, only one of which may be within the technological and marketing capacity of the patentee. Often, too, exploitation of the patent in other countries may be inconvenient for the patentee. For these and other reasons, it may be appropriate for the patentee to grant a licence to another firm to manufacture and sell the patented product or process. An exclusive licence gives the licensee assurance that no other licences will be granted in his territory and, also, that the patentee himself will not manufacture or sell within the licensee's province. It enables the licensee to sue infringers. Any other type of licence is known as a non-exclusive licence. It is noteworthy that the Comptroller General can order compulsory licensing if the patent has not been worked after a period of time. Many patents, notably those for intricate, complicated inventions, are inoperable without the technical know-how needed for their manufacture. This technical know-how is not covered by the patent and has to be separately licensed. As manufacturing techniques become increasingly sophisticated, the licensing of know-how assumes greater importance. Payment for the grant of a patent licence usually takes the form of a lump sum or a royalty on articles produced (normally calculated as a proportion of their net selling price), or both.

The normal method for protecting patent rights, as indeed for intellectual property rights in general, is by civil action for infringement of the right. All the normal rights are available including the right to sue for damages and to seek an injunction to prohibit continued infringement. On the other hand, however, any party can apply to the Patent Office or to a special Patents Court for revocation of the patent, usually on the grounds that the invention was not new or was obvious. It is quite common in an action for infringement of a patent for the defence to counterclaim by challenging the validity of the patent. Patent litigation has a reputation for being protracted and costly.

Trade mark

A trade mark is a sign used by a manufacturer or trader to distinguish his goods from similar goods of other firms. It is a badge of origin which:

(a) identifies in the mind of the consumer the manufacturer or supplier of the goods purchased; and
(b) protects the goodwill which has been built up by the supplier.

Registration of a trade mark establishes a right to take action against infringement of that mark, or use of a similar one that would lead to confusion in the minds of the public. An unregistered trade mark can, in certain circumstances, be protected by an action for 'passing off' as can a registered mark. This is the common law right of a manufacturer or trader to be protected against any person seeking to take unfair advantage of the product's prestige and reputation built up by the manufacturer often over many years.

The most recent legislation on trade marks is contained in the Trade Marks Act 1938. Registration of a mark, which is with the Patent Office (Trade Marks Registry), will be granted only after a further examination as to the mark's suitability to ensure that it is distinctive, is not deceptive, and is free from conflict with registered trade marks of others. Opportunity is given to third parties to oppose registration.

Unlike other forms of intellectual property, the duration of the protection afforded to trade marks can be indefinite, provided the renewal fees are paid when due. The Registrar is empowered to remove a trade mark from the register in certain circumstances. These are as follows:

(a) non-payment of fees;
(b) the mark has ceased to be distinctive through the owner's fault;
(c) there has been a breach of a condition appearing on the register;
(d) the mark has for one reason or another become deceptive;
(e) the proper significance of the mark has been destroyed by the owner, e.g., by allowing the mark to be used on inferior goods by a third party; and
(f) non-use.

Trade marks, like other forms of intellectual property, may be licensed for use by others. Although the proprietor of a trade mark usually keeps its use to himself within his own national boundary, he may well license it to a manufacturer of goods similar to his own in an overseas territory. This right is often combined with a patent licence and almost invariably with know-how, failing which the quality requirements will not be met. Payment for the licence is usually by way of a lump sum or periodical royalties, or some combination of the two. The fact that additional goodwill may accrue to the product because of their local manufacture is an added bonus for the licensor.

The advent of self-service shopping and advertising through the mass media has meant that some well-established trade marks are of great value. As from 1 October 1986, it will be possible to register a name used in offering services, as opposed to goods, to the public.

Registered designs

Registration under the Registered Designs Acts 1949–61 gives the registered owner of a design the sole right for an initial period of five years, with provision for renewal for two similar periods, to manufacture, sell or use products so designed. It is confined to designs for industrial use and the design must be new. As in the case of patents and trade marks, the certificate of registration issued by the Designs Registry at the Patent Office does not carry with it any guarantee of validity.

The Design Copyright Act 1968 extended the normal law of copyright to registerable industrial designs, whether or not the design is in fact registered. However, the period of protection is limited to 15 years. Non-registerable designs, such as, drawings and plans, enjoy copyright protection up to the full 50 years as for most copyright. There is an important difference between the protection afforded by copyright and that afforded by registration. Registration protects the design within the United Kingdom but not in foreign countries. Copyright protection extends solely to copying; it does not give any monopoly protection inasmuch as any person may arrive independently at the same work. There is no copyright in a mere idea. Registration, on the other hand, grants exclusive use.

The licensing of registered designs, e.g., between design consultants and industrial organisations, follows much the same pattern as in patent licensing.

Copyright

Copyright exists in original literary, artistic or dramatic works and gives protection against unlicensed use. Copyright and so-called neighbouring rights, such as performing rights, are automatic and, therefore, do not need to be conferred or registered in any way. In order to give notice that copyright protection is claimed, the practice of validating a document, design or whatever, with the name of the author or owner, the date and an international symbol, has grown up. Copyright lasts for the period of the author's remaining lifetime plus 50 years. As noted above, design copyright in three dimensional articles is restricted to 15 years as with registered designs.

The above highly abbreviated account merely scratches the surface of this topic.[6] It has ignored the very significant international aspects, such as the European Patent Convention and the European Patent Office, the 1883 Paris Convention, and the important effect of EEC competition rules on licensing agreements. However, it should serve as a general picture of the scope and nature of these rights and also as a warning: this is a highly specialised field, which the valuer would be ill-advised to enter without a patent agent or similar expert on one side and a patent lawyer on the other.

Valuation techniques

Before discussing some typical techniques in the valuation of intellectual property rights, it is appropriate to recall from Chapter 1 the cardinal rule of commercial share valuation: the value of something

---

[6] For further information the reader is referred to any good business library and to two works in particular: W. R. Cornish, *Intellectual Property: Patents, Copyright, Trade Marks and Allied Rights* (London: Sweet & Maxwell, 1981) and Patrick Hearn, *The Business of Industrial Licencing* (Farnborough: Gower Publishing Co., 1981).

cannot be stated in the abstract; all that can be stated is the value of a thing in a particular place, at a particular time, in particular circumstances. The questions 'to whom?' and 'for what purpose?' must always be asked before a valuation can be carried out. This rule is particularly significant as far as the valuation of intellectual property rights is concerned. More often than not, there will only be one or two possible interested parties, and the value of the patent to each of them will depend on their circumstances, e.g., their manufacturing capacity, existing product mix, marketing strengths, and so on. Failure to take these circumstances and those of the owner into account will result in a meaningless valuation. An example will illustrate the importance of considering the circumstances as well as describing a typical valuation approach.

N. Ose Ltd is one of the three snuff manufacturers in the country. Its main brand, Sneezy, generates sales of approximately £150,000 a year and has a market share of 30%. Demand for snuff has declined over the years and on this level of sales, the business can no longer make a profit. As N. Ose Ltd has valuable freehold property and marketable securities, its shareholders are considering putting the company into liquidation and have asked for a valuation on that basis. This entails, amongst other things, an assessment of the price which the Sneezy trade mark might fetch. Management accounts show that the gross profit margin on Sneezy is approximately 40%. In times of normal plant utilisation the Company could expect to make a net profit margin of ten per cent. Thus, the current gross profit on the Sneezy brand is in the region of £60,000, i.e., £150,000 at 40%, and the normal net profit, £15,000, i.e., £150,000 at ten per cent.

Subject to concern about the trend of demand for snuff and hence, capacity utilisation, N. Ose Ltd's competitors could expect to make pre-tax profits of at least £15,000 per year through the purchase of the Sneezy brand. As the industry generally has considerable surplus capacity from the period when the demand for snuff was much greater, the marginal profit on Sneezy will almost certainly be more than £15,000, although somewhat less than the full gross profit of £60,000. After discussing with management the likely additional overhead a competitor would incur in taking on the production and sale of the brand, it is estimated that the marginal profit should be in the order of £30,000 a year.

In the snuff industry everyone knows everyone else's business. If N. Ose Ltd were to put its main brand up for sale it would be seen as a sign of weakness, indicating that the company was in difficulty. Should N. Ose Ltd go out of business, the two remaining manufacturers would probably pick up much of the Sneezy customers in any event. They may well be disinclined, therefore, to pay for what would come to them anyway by doing nothing. On the other hand, each would be concerned to ensure that the brand did not fall into the hands of the other at a low price. These considerations, together with an appraisal of the financial position of the potential purchasers — what they can afford to pay and their borrowing capacity — must all enter into the valuation. At this end of the market, where the sums are small, the outlook depressed and the element of risk high, capitalisation rates would be very low, and in the circumstances, N. Ose Ltd may be unable to obtain more than £50,000 for its brand and might have to settle for considerably less.

At the other end of the scale is the multi-national pharmaceutical company with its drugs protected by patents and trade marks in most countries of the world. Such patents hardly ever come up for sale to third parties. The need to value them sometimes arises in an infringement action where damages have to be assessed, or for fiscal purposes when a transfer of patents between companies within the group crosses a tax jurisdiction, e.g., from a UK subsidiary to a French one. It is in valuations of this complexity and significance that the valuer will almost certainly need to take professional advice as to the strength of the patent. But, no matter how strong the patent may be, it will have little value if the commercial outlook for the drug is not promising.

In the early stages of a drug's commercial life the patent may have a very low value. Many highly promising drugs have had to be withdrawn because of unforeseen, or unacceptable, side effects. Adverse publicity, sometimes unjustified as, for instance, where doctors prescribe a drug in conditions for which it is not primarily intended, can lead to a collapse of demand and the withdrawal of the product. Heavy promotional and marketing expenditure is necessary, often over a period of years. It may well take five years before this expenditure begins to pay off. The patentee can then look forward to reaping the fruits of his endeavours. It is at this point that the patent begins to have a high value. Given the research resources of the pharmaceutical industry, the likelihood of the drug going unchallenged throughout the remainder of its patented life may be slim, and it would be prudent to expect profitability to tail off in due course.

One yardstick for assessing the value of a patent is to ascertain the royalty that the licensee would be prepared to pay for an exclusive licence. If the company has already granted a licence, the royalty rate provided therein may be an indicator of the likely rate. Otherwise, one must ascertain the rate of royalty usual in the industry. This notional royalty rate is then applied to the estimated sales the patentee would be likely to make during the remainder of the patent's life. The value of the patent is the present value of this stream of future royalties. The discount rate must reflect the strength of the patent and the risk of the introduction of new products which might displace the patented one. It will be a high rate.

Another approach is to carry out two forecasts of future sales of the product in question, one based on the continued exploitation of the patent and the other assuming that the patent is no longer valid and that competitors are free to copy the product. In the latter eventuality, the company's selling price will be determined by free market forces. The value of the monopoly rights conferred by the patent lies in the excess of the first turnover projection over the second. This should also be evaluated on the discounted cash flow basis, a method perhaps more suited to the calculation of owner value. The notional royalty technique is closer to the market value concept.

Inevitably, such a valuation would be a major undertaking and would involve much financial, commercial and legal investigation work. Even where the assumptions are completely realistic, the valuation would be highly subjective, and this should be reflected in a suitably wide valuation range.

Deferred revenue expenditure

On rare occasions a balance sheet may include deferred revenue expenditure as an asset. Examples of such assets are research and development costs, product launch costs entailing heavy initial advertising, and promotional costs for a new brand. These assets have no value independent of the business, and it is debatable whether they could be called assets at all. This is not to say that a firm does not derive great benefit from its research or development programme or from a major advertising campaign, but merely that a decision to write off expenditure over a number of years no more creates an asset than a policy of setting funds aside for future expenditure not yet incurred creates a liability. It is simply an accounting device to achieve a fairer picture of annual profit. Such intangibles are not valued as separate assets. Any value they generate will be reflected in the value of the business as a whole.

Conclusion

Goodwill arises through the combination of the factors of production (land, labour and capital) to form a unique business undertaking capable of satisfying economic demand. It is the intangible quality which distinguishes a firm or enterprise from the grouping of unrelated economic agents it would otherwise be. It is manifest in the very establishment of the business — the skills, diligence and resourcefulness of its employees (including management), the goods or services it offers, its customers and sources of supply, the condition of its assets and fitness for their purpose, and the firm's general reputation and standing in the marketplace.

The erroneous view of the firm as a collection of assets has led to the equally erroneous view that goodwill is the difference between the value of the firm as a whole and the sum of the fair values of its separable net assets. This produces the absurdity of negative goodwill and also implies that a firm can increase its goodwill, or reduce its negative goodwill, by declaring a dividend. It also suggests that service companies as a class have more goodwill than manufacturing (i.e., capital intensive) ones.

Goodwill is not dependent on profits, still less on super-profits. Examples were given in the text of how firms with no profits can have goodwill and how the goodwill in highly profitable firms may be worth very little, even nothing.

Goodwill is the very essence of the firm and cannot be valued separately from it. There are, therefore, no techniques for valuing goodwill separately, since goodwill as a separate asset does not exist. The 'value' placed on purchased goodwill in company balance sheets does not represent the value of goodwill; it is merely the difference between the price paid for a business and the balance sheet amount of its net assets. It is purely a hazard of the accounting conventions adopted and would be more accurately described as 'acquisition premium' or some such term.

The remainder of the chapter was devoted to a discussion of the general nature of the intellectual property rights included in patents, trade marks, registered designs and copyright. Some suggestions as to how they might be valued were put forward.

9

The dividend basis of valuation

The value of a financial asset is a function of the cash flows it provides and the discount rate applied to those flows. In a sense, this definition is no more than a postulate of rational behaviour, an ideal to which every investor and theorist would subscribe even though the ideal is sometimes lost sight of, or only very imperfectly reflected, in the investment appraisal techniques encountered in practice. No one imagines, for example, that investors everywhere carry out the same careful projection of the annual cash flows and rigorously apply their scientifically derived, risk-determined discount rates to those flows in evaluating an investment. But this is what they strive to do and it must, therefore, be the foundation for the development of valuation techniques.

There is only one form of cash flow which stems from ownership of shares in a limited company and that is dividends. It is for this reason that dividends play such a crucial role in the valuation of minority shareholdings. From the standpoint of the Stock Exchange investor, this may not be how it appears in practice. His return will consist of dividends plus a capital gain or minus a capital loss on disposal. If he is a speculator, he may only hold the shares for a few months and will be looking entirely to capital gain for his reward. Even if he takes a less short-term view, he will not expect to hold the shares forever, and it is quite likely that the dividend element of the total return will be dominated by the capital element, whether a loss or a gain. Dividends, it would seem, are not, therefore, the be-all and end-all of holding shares.

However, this argument ignores the factors which determine the capital gain or loss. By the time of sale the outlook for the company will have doubtless altered, hopefully in the direction of an improvement in dividend prospects. Alternatively, a change in the general level of interest rates may have taken place and this will alter the expected rate of return on the shares, and hence the present value of the future dividends. The point is, however, that the price realised for the shares will reflect the present value of the future dividend stream at that time (as with any subsequent disposal of the shares). For all present and future investors, expected cash flows consist of dividends.

This pre-occupation with dividends may strike some readers as unusual, given the prominence accorded to earnings in the market place and the widespread use of the P/E ratio in the evaluation of quoted shares.

However, the use of the P/E ratio does not by itself prove anything in this connection. As will be shown later in this chapter, the proportion of profits paid out in dividends is a key factor in determining the P/E ratio. Furthermore, where a comparable quoted company has the same pay-out ratio as the company being valued, the dividend yield basis will produce the same valuation as one based on the P/E ratio. Consider, for example, a fictitious quoted company having the following investment characteristics:

Share price	168p
Earnings per share (fully taxed)	30p
Dividend per share — net	10p
— gross	14.3p
Net assets per share	200p
Therefore:	
Dividend yield (gross)	8.5%
P/E ratio	5.6
Discount to net assets	16.0%
Dividend cover	3.0
Return on net assets	15.0%

If we were valuing an unquoted company by comparison with this quoted company and both companies' dividends were three times covered, there would be no difference between the dividend yield valuation and the valuation using the above P/E ratio. This is pure coincidence and does not mean that the P/E ratio can be relied on to give the right answer. For instance, if we additionally assume that the subject company also has the same rate of return on assets as the quoted company, we could simply apply the discount of 16% to its net assets and the same valuation would be produced. This is illustrated below:

Private company limited

Earnings per share	45p
Dividend per share — net	15p
Dividend per share — gross	21.4p
Net assets per share	300p
Therefore:	
Dividend cover	3.0
Return on assets	15.0%
Valuations	
Dividend yield 21.4p ÷ 8.5%	252p
P/E ratio 45p × 5.6	252p
Net assets: 300p less discount of 16%	252p

This convergence of the three valuations is a coincidence, but it under-lines, nevertheless, the fact that dividends, earnings and assets are all facets of the one reality. They are closely related to one another, but this relationship is highly unstable and one is prone to fall into serious error in valuing minority holdings on an earnings basis, just as one is by valuing such holdings on an assets basis. At best, one will obtain a correct valuation using incorrect methods. In practice, of course, companies do not have the same dividend cover. More often than not, the private company will have a much higher cover than the quoted analogue and, in these cases, the use of the P/E ratio will produce substantially higher valuations.

To the extent, therefore, that dividends are a function of earnings and an assessment of earnings growth is essential for a dividend-based valuation, there is no conflict between the two positions. However, until earnings are distributed by way of dividend they do not constitute the return on the shares, and it is incorrect to value them as if they do. The significance of non-distributed earnings lies in the implications for future growth in earnings and, thus, dividends. The position adopted here, which applies solely to the valuation of minority shareholdings for portfolio investment purposes, has been succinctly expressed in a classic text: 'Earnings are only a means to an end, and the means should not be mistaken for the end. Therefore, we must say that a stock derives its value from its dividends, and not its earnings. In short, a stock is worth only what you can get out of it.'[1]

This is an important topic which cannot be satisfactorily dealt with in isolation from the other valuation bases. In Chapter 12 the claims of the competing valuation bases are considered in detail and the opposing view that dividends are irrelevant is conclusively rebutted.

Basic approach

If a share derives its value from its dividends and the rate of return applied to those dividends, it is obvious that any valuation formula should explicitly consider these two variables. Thus, in the simplest case imaginable where dividends are expected to remain constant the valuation formula would be:

(1)
$$V = \frac{D}{r}$$

where,
V = the value of the share
D = the dividend per share (gross)
r = the required rate of return

[1] John B. Williams, *The Theory of Investment Value* (Cambridge, Mass.: Harvard University Press, 1938), reprinted in Lorie and Brealey, pp. 55–75.

Using this formula a share with a dividend of 20p gross and a required rate of return of 15% would be valued at 133p (i.e., 20/0.15). Where dividends are expected to remain unchanged, the rate of return is identical to the dividend yield.

However, dividends, like earnings, are never constant in amount, and the ability to put forward a convincing estimate of the likely future course of these two variables is essential in share valuation work. Uncertainty inevitably surrounds estimates of future earnings and dividends, and this uncertainty increases as the projections become more distant in time. Beyond a certain point, the estimates will inevitably degenerate into an assumption as to future growth, but provided the assumption is reasonable it is entirely legitimate. Indeed, the valuer should avoid employing estimating techniques which imply a greater degree of accuracy than is likely to be present, given all the circumstances including the length of the projections.

From the simple case of an unchanged dividend being paid in perpetuity, we turn to the formula for valuing a dividend stream increasing at a constant annual rate. This is as follows:

$$(2) \qquad\qquad V = \frac{D}{r-g}$$

where,
V = the value of the share
D = the prospective gross dividend per share
r = the required rate of return
g = the expected growth rate

Thus, a share with a prospective dividend of 20p gross, expected to grow at the rate of five per cent a year compound, would be valued at 200p using the required rate of return of 15%. The calculation is set out below:

$$V = \frac{20}{0.15 - 0.05} = \frac{20}{0.10} = 200p$$

The prospective dividend yield in the above example is ten per cent, i.e., 20/200. This must not be confused with the expected rate of return which is 15%. This equation, which is in effect the discounted cash flow formula for an income stream increasing at a constant annual rate, has many uses and the valuer should be aware of its derivation. The proof of this formula is as follows:

If D is the current (i.e., historic) dividend per share, g is the constant annual growth rate in dividends, and r is the discount rate or required rate of return to be applied to each year's dividend, the value of a share (V) can be represented as follows:

(1) $$V = \frac{D(1+g)}{1+r} + \frac{D(1+g)^2}{(1+r)^2} + \frac{D(1+g)^3}{(1+r)^3} + \ldots + \frac{D(1+g)^n}{(1+r)^n}$$

$$V = D\left[\frac{1+g}{1+r} + \frac{(1+g)^2}{(1+r)^2} + \frac{(1+r)^3}{(1+r)^3} + \ldots + \frac{(1+g)^n}{(1+r)^n}\right]$$

Multiply both sides by $\dfrac{1+r}{1+g}$

(2) $$V\left[\frac{1+r}{1+g}\right] = D\left[1 + \frac{1+g}{1+r} + \frac{(1+g)^2}{(1+r)^2} + \ldots + \frac{(1+g)^{n-1}}{(1+r)^{n-1}}\right]$$

Subtract equation (1) from equation (2) to obtain:

$$V\left[\frac{1+r}{1+g} - 1\right] = D\left[1 - \frac{(1+g)^n}{(1+r)^n}\right]$$

Express the bracketed term on the left hand side of the equation in terms of the common denominator $(1+g)$:

$$V\left[\frac{1+r-(1+g)}{(1+g)}\right] = D\left[1 - \frac{(1+g)^n}{(1+r)^n}\right]$$

Provided the rate of return (r) is greater than the growth rate (g), the bracketed term on the right-hand side of the equation approaches 1 as the number of years (n) approaches infinity, leaving:

$$V\left[\frac{(1+r)-(1+g)}{(1+g)}\right] = D$$

which simplifies to:

$$V(r-g) = D(1+g)$$

$$V = \frac{D(1+g)}{r-g}$$

$$V = \frac{D_1}{r-g}$$

D_1 is the prospective dividend, i.e., the current dividend D grossed up by the growth rate g.

Two points must be borne in mind when using this formula. First, the prospective and not the historic dividend must be used. Second, the formula is valid only if the discount rate/rate of return, r, exceeds the growth rate, g. Although in individual years g may well exceed r, it is inconceivable that it should do so indefinitely since this would produce an infinitely valuable share. In fact, above average growth is invariably a temporary phenomenon.

Temporary above (or below) average growth can be accommodated within the framework of equation (2). Assume, for example, that for a variety of reasons XYZ Ltd is barely profitable. However, under the influence of new management the appropriate remedial measures have been taken and, with a modest improvement in demand anticipated, you estimate that XYZ Ltd's recovery will be complete three years hence when dividends, assuming a 25% pay-out ratio, should be 30p per share. Growth prospects beyond that should be in line with the industry average, say, five per cent a year. However, the immediate prospect is for a dividend of 15p per share followed by one of 25p per share. A required rate of return of 15% a year is assumed.

The approach would be to use equation (2) to provide a notional value for the shares three years hence, when the company has assumed a 'normal' or constant growth rate pattern, and to discount this sum plus the dividends for years 1, 2 and 3 using the assumed rate of return of 15%. The general formula is as follows:

$$V = \frac{D_1}{1+r} + \frac{D_2}{(1+r)^2} \cdots \frac{D_n}{(1+r)^n} + \left[\frac{D_n(1+g)}{r-g} \times \frac{1}{(1+r)^n} \right]$$

Where D_1, D_2, . . ., D_n are the estimated dividends paid in each of the years of non-normal growth (in this case n is year 3), r is the required rate of return and g, the longer term growth rate. Using this formula, the present value of XYZ Ltd's shares work out at 260p each as set out below:

$$V = \frac{15}{1.15} + \frac{25}{(1.15)^2} \frac{30}{(1.15)^3} + \left[\frac{31.5}{0.15 - 0.05} \times \frac{1}{(1.15)^3} \right]$$

$$= 13.04 + 18.90 + 19.73 + (315 \times 0.66)$$

$$= 51.67 + 207.9$$

$$= 259.57, \text{ say, } 260\text{p}.$$

Finally, as earnings are the fund out of which dividends are paid and dividends in turn affect earnings by determining the amount of retained profit, one would expect a strong relationship between the dividend basis of valuation and the P/E ratio method. An idea of this relationship can be obtained by manipulating equation (2), the constant growth dividend discount formula:

(2)
$$V = \frac{D}{r-g}$$

Using the symbol k to denote the pay-out ratio and E_1 to denote prospective earnings per share, the prospective dividend, D, can be written E_1k and this term substituted for D in equation (2) as follows:

$$V = \frac{E_1k}{r-g}$$

If earnings are assumed to grow at the same constant rate as dividends, g also becomes the growth rate in earnings. Dividing both sides of the equation by the historic earnings per share E_0, we get:

$$\frac{V}{E_0} = \frac{k(1+g)}{r-g}$$

In other words, the historic P/E ratio, V/E_0, is determined by the earnings growth rate, g, the pay-out ratio, k, and the required rate of return, r.

In reality, earnings and dividends do not grow at the same constant rate forever, so the actual relationship will be different. Nevertheless, the factors will be the same. As k and g affect each other it would be wrong to interpret the relationship as implying that the P/E ratio could be increased by the simple expedient of raising the pay-out ratio; this would inevitably constrain growth in earnings.

The required rate of return

What is the rate of return required or expected for a particular investment? A short, but not entirely helpful, answer is that the same rate of return will be required as can be obtained on an investment of equal riskiness. Two practical difficulties stand in the way of the valuer or investor seeking to apply this principle. First, the assessment of risk is personal to the valuer and difficult to convey in quantitative terms. Second, the rate of return on comparable quoted companies (where these are regarded as the nearest alternatives) can be gauged only by estimating the likely future growth rate in dividends, and this too will be a matter of individual opinion.

As regards the first difficulty, the risk measurement techniques of modern portfolio theory offer little help. As shown in Chapter 7, the 'expected' value/standard deviation approach is unrealistic as well as being conceptually inadequate; and the beta coefficient of the Capital Asset Pricing Model is no better since it is founded on the same definition of risk. More importantly, the CAPM is responsible for the highly misleading and unfounded notion that in the valuation of securities only a part of the total risk — the so-called systematic risk measured by beta — is relevant to the determination of the rate of return.

Despite the lack of any satisfactory quantitative measure of risk, techniques exist for heightening one's awareness of risk and these are referred to in Chapter 7. Those attributes or characteristics of an investment which are indicative of risk can, in any event, be identified and described and a good qualitative 'feel' for the risk involved can be obtained. The absence of precise mathematical quantification of the risk involved does not mean that the degree of risk cannot be properly appreciated. It does, however, mean that the assessment of risk is inevitably subjective and open to different interpretations.

The second practical difficulty in assessing the required rate of return — estimating the cash return on alternative investments— is not a problem with fixed interest securities such as gilts, debentures and loan stocks, but is one as far as equities are concerned. Thus, if the valuer derives the required rate of return from comparable quoted companies, he must assess their prospects and the likely stream of future dividends.[2] This exercise need not be too onerous as far as quoted companies are concerned. There is usually no shortage of information. In addition to the annual and interim financial statements, conveniently summarised on Extel cards, there is the McCarthy press cutting service, which provides a copy of articles in the press relevant to the particular company and the industry. Brokers' circulars can often be obtained without too much difficulty. The valuer should thus be able to arrive at an informed estimate of future prospects for any quoted companies.

Having assessed likely growth rates for any selected quoted companies, the valuer can calculate the implied rate of return by solving r, the rate of return, in equation (2), as follows:

(2)
$$V = \frac{D}{r-g}$$

$$r-g = \frac{D}{V}$$

(3)
$$r = \frac{D}{V} + g$$

The rate of return on a security consists of the initial yield (the prospective

[2] The legitimacy of comparisons with quoted companies is discussed in Chapter 5 (The Stock Exchange and other Security Markets).

dividend as a percentage of the current price) plus the growth rate in future dividends. Table 1 shows how the result of such an exercise might be presented when four quoted analogues are chosen.

Table 1: Implied rates of return on selected quoted companies

Quoted company	Prospective dividend yield % (1)	Future growth rate % (2)	Implied rate of return % (1)+(2)
A Ltd	6.1	20.0	26.1
B Ltd	4.3	12.5	16.8
C Ltd	15.0	2.5	17.5
D Ltd	10.9	5.0	15.9

The implied rates of return can then be considered in the light of the perceived riskiness of each stock, and an appropriate rate of return selected.

Modern financial theory views the rate of return on equities as consisting of the so-called risk-free rate typically available on gilts, and a risk premium determined by the riskiness of the security. On this view, the implied rate of return should always exceed the risk-free rate, and in this form of analysis the valuer should make a point of setting out comparisons of the appropriate risk-free rates of return with the implied rates of return on the selected quoted securities. This is essential to ensure that the implied rates of return make sense. Typical risk-free rates would be the gross redemption yield on short, medium and long gilts, using high coupon stocks, and interest rates available in the money markets.

It may sometimes occur that the implied rate of return shows little or no risk premium — it may even be less than the risk-free rate. If this occurs, the phenomenon should be carefully investigated. A number of possibilities spring to mind. The valuer's estimate of the growth rate may be at fault. If this is understated, so will be the implied rate of return. Another possibility is that the company concerned is the subject of a take-over bid or of bid rumours. The price bid for the entire equity of a company is not based on its future dividend stream but on its earnings potential. If the share price reflects the control value of the company it must be rejected for comparison purposes.

Finally, there is always the possibility that the security is not priced in accordance with financial theory, i.e., it is irrationally priced. Not even the most fervent adherent of the Efficient Market Hypothesis — an hypothesis which Chapter 6 shows, in any event, to be devoid of meaning — maintains that all stocks are 'correctly' priced; for the smaller companies, with no great institutional following, shares may be 'inefficiently' priced.

Irrationality in pricing can reflect a variety of influences, such as emotion, ignorance, and the ebb and flow of rumour, sentiment and speculation. These influences may cause a security's price to be volatile and fickle on a day-to-day basis. It would not be appropriate to import this frothy overlay into the valuation of unquoted securities. To use an implied rate of return which is the same or lower than the risk-free rate of return is to subscribe to the 'bigger fool' theory of investment and valuation. This theory holds that, although a security's price cannot be justified in terms of the foreseeable future dividend stream, it is worth buying it in the hope or expectation that when it comes to be sold a buyer can be found, who will also pay a suitably inflated price. Doubtless, some people have made (and lost) money using this approach, but it can have no place in the art of valuation.

The steps in the technique outlined above can be carried out in reverse order, and some will find this a more helpful approach. Thus, one would start with a summary of the risk-free rates of return available on gilts, local authority deposits or bonds, money market instruments and the like. A suitable risk premium would be assessed in the light of the riskiness of the company and of the valuer's own experience of the risk premiums expected on other unquoted companies. This rate of return could then be applied to the comparable quoted stocks, which by definition will be stocks of similar riskiness to the subject company, and an implied rate of growth obtained. The valuer would then gauge whether this growth rate was feasible in the circumstances.

A simple transformation of equation (3) shows how the implied growth rate for a share may be derived:

(3)
$$r = \frac{D}{V} + g$$

Therefore,

(4)
$$g = r - \frac{D}{V}$$

The growth rate, g, is equal to the rate of return minus the prospective dividend yield, D/V. This formula can then be applied to comparable quoted companies. If the implied growth rate is reasonable, the required rate of return is indirectly confirmed. Assume, for example, that the valuer has provisionally determined a required rate of return of 15% for a company being valued. If a comparable quoted company of similar risk is on a prospective dividend yield of six per cent, its implied future growth rate in dividends is nine per cent (i.e., $r - D/V = 15 - 6 = 9$). The valuer must then consider whether this is likely in the circumstances.

Two important points should be borne in mind when deriving rates of return in this manner. First, no account is taken of the lack of marketability of the unquoted company. By convention, this is the last adjustment to be made and is generally expressed not as a percentage of the rate of return, but as a discount off the value arrived at after all other discounts have been made. Marketability discounts are discussed below. Second, estimates of future growth rates, no matter how well informed, entail subjective judgements; and the assumption of constant growth rates or, more properly, the averaging out of different annual growth rates into a single average annual rate is a crude approximation. For these and other reasons, the valuer is well-advised to use the term 'implied' to qualify rates of return or growth rates calculated by using, respectively, equations (3) and (4). Despite its shortcomings, equation (2) and its derivatives are probably the best practical means of deriving a credible rate of return in the present state of the art.

The initial yield method

This method consists of applying the appropriate initial yield to the current dividend. It is simple to use, has a wide following in practice, and is endorsed by various authorities on the subject.[3] A valuation arrived at by applying the appropriate initial yield will not differ from one using the dividend discount model of equation (2). This can be illustrated using the earlier example of the share with a prospective dividend of 20p gross, a growth rate of five per cent, and a required rate of return of 15%. If after proper enquiry the valuer concluded that the appropriate initial dividend yield was ten per cent, he would value the share at 200p. i.e., 20/0.10. This is identical to the valuation produced by the dividend discount model. In fact, a simple transformation of equation (2) shows why this is so:

(2)
$$V = \frac{D}{r-g}$$

Therefore,

$$\frac{D}{V} = r - g$$

Thus, the prospective dividend yield is determined by the required rate of return, r, and the growth rate in dividends, g. However, users of the initial yield method do not specifically consider these two vital determinants of

[3] For example, Hamilton Baynes, pp. 159–161, and Nigel A. Eastaway and Harry Booth, *Practical Share Valuation* (London: Butterworth & Co, 1983), pp. 86–92.

value. The initial yield, or any other indicator relating price to a single year's return, is a product or result of the forces determining value; it is not the prime mover. Using the initial yield method the client, and the valuer too, may well be unaware of the rate of return expected or implied by the valuation. The yield derived from the quoted company may provide an inadequate rate of return for the client, but this will not come to light with the initial yield method. In valuations where the reasoning is almost as important as the valuation conclusions — for example, valuations for legal purposes or for settling disputes — the initial yield method is at a disadvantage, since it is impossible to know how it is arrived at other than as an 'experience' judgement from a list of relevant factors. This point is not so important when the valuation is carried out for negotiating purposes, where the proof of the valuer's skill will be evidenced not so much by the quality of the reasoning as by the acceptability of the valuation figure to the negotiating parties.

Non-dividend paying companies

Many private companies do not pay dividends even though they make reasonable profits. The shareholders in such companies are usually also directors and the company is often their chief source of livelihood. For them, it may make sense to distribute the profits in the form of directors' remuneration rather than dividend. In other cases, wealthy shareholders, faced with high rates of tax on unearned income, may prefer to leave their funds in the company where they will ultimately accrue to their, or their successors', benefit. How should minority shareholdings in such companies be valued? Are we to conclude that because the company pays no dividends its shares have no value?

Before considering this matter in some detail, it is necessary to dispose of a valuation technique which is occasionally encountered, but which has no claim to be taken seriously. This is the hypothetical dividend yield method, whereby the valuer estimates the 'normal' dividend the company would declare if it were to pay dividends, and capitalises this on the basis of a required yield derived in the ordinary way. A discount would then be applied to the resultant figure to reflect the fact that the shares do not in fact pay a dividend. The discount is a matter of individual preference. Where this technique is used in fiscal valuations, the discount is not less than 50%.[4]

Although this method of valuing minority shareholdings in non-dividend paying companies may be permissible for fiscal valuations, it has no

[4] Eastaway and Booth, *Practical Share Valuation*, p. 218; and Hamilton Baynes, *Share Valuations*, p. 162.

place at all in the valuation of shares for commercial purposes. The fundamental objection to it is obvious. If the value of an asset is a function of its cash return, any valuation based on an imaginary cash return must itself be imaginary. The fact that there is a substantial discount merely makes it a discounted imaginary valuation. It is no more logical to value non-dividend paying shares on an imaginary dividend than it is to value shares in a loss-making company on an imaginary profit, say, the profit it would earn if it were properly managed or if the industry prospects were different. Shares must be valued on the basis of their actual not their hypothetical prospects.

The valuation of minority shareholdings in non-dividend paying private companies is an exacting and challenging task which requires experience and flair. These qualities cannot be conveyed in a book. Nevertheless, the following remarks may throw some light on an area of valuation which is generally shrouded in ambiguity and vagueness. Valuations required for portfolio investment purposes are considered first, then valuations for other purposes.

Valuation for portfolio investment purposes

A portfolio investor's interest in a company is that of the outside minority shareholder; he views his shareholding purely as an investment. There is no emotional commitment to the company such as might exist within members of a family, and there are no ties of employment. The hard-nosed portfolio investor would just as soon invest in quoted shares as unquoted shares, if he thought they offered a better rate of return given all the circumstances. Portfolio investors may be institutions or private individuals.

Until only a few years ago, it was comparatively rare for financial institutions to invest in unquoted companies, but all this has now changed and there has been a flood of new entrants to this market. According to one source, the number of venture capital management groups has grown over the last five years from 20 to over 100 and well over £500 million of venture capital has been raised during that period.[5] This does not include the substantial sums placed by 3i (formerly Investors in Industry) or by non-specialist investors. Institutional investment may take the form of replacement capital (where existing shareholders are bought out) or of injection of funds into the company by the subscription for new shares and possibly the provision of loans, the latter also frequently being termed venture capital.

Institutional investment invariably takes place with the active participation, and often at the request of, the controlling shareholders. It is

[5] *Financial Times,* 30 April 1985, Survey Venture Capital.

more than a straightforward purchase of a minority shareholding. The terms of the investment are usually negotiated in the light of a corporate plan showing the forecast profits and cash flow. The institution often has the right to appoint its own nominee to the board and regular management information will be available to it. Most important of all, the arrangements will make provision for the institution's ultimate 'exit route'. This may be a USM listing, the sale-on of the company, a buy-out of the equity by the management or a full Stock Exchange listing. Although some institutions insist on a running yield on their investment (i.e., dividends or loan interest), the typical venture capitalist investing in a high-growth start-up or expansion business does not. He looks for his return in the form of a capital gain on disposal of the shareholding.[6] The price for such a shareholding will be determined by the present value of the expected or estimated sale proceeds on ultimate disposal. There is, inevitably, much uncertainty and guesswork in such an evlation, not only because the actual trading results may be different from the expected ones but also because the terminal value is affected by the means of disposal. A USM listing, a full Stock Exchange listing and a sale of the company would all probably produce different sums. However, the basis of the investment is quite clear from the outset and this determines the valuation approach. Venture capital is very risky and there is a high failure rate. An expected rate of return of 50% per annum would not be unusual for this type of investment.

In practice, the problem for the venture capitalist is to know what percentage of the equity he should expect in return for investing the sum of money sought by the entrepreneur. Assume, for example, that the entrepreneur needs £500,000 of development capital. If everything goes according to plan, the company should be able to obtain a USM, if not an official, listing by year five. It is agreed that the likely issue price, based on the projections, should be in the order of £10 million. The present value of the company and the implied percentage of the value represented by the venture capitalist's injection of funds are set out below:

	Required rate of return		
	40%	*50%*	*60%*
Estimated value of the company in year five	£10m	£10m	£10m
Present value thereof at indicated rate of return	£1.86m	£1.32m	£0.95m
Required equity investment (£500,000) as percentage thereof	27%	38%	53%

[6] The provision of venture capital has an added attraction for some institutions, notably banks, which find it a useful means of introducing themselves to potential customers for their corporate finance and banking services.

With so many imponderables — the risk of the venture, the realism of the projections and the subjectivity of the 'exit' value — it is little wonder that such high rates of return have to be used. The actual percentage finally agreed will be a matter of negotiation in which other alternatives, e.g., debt finance, will be explored.

Although the provision of venture capital can properly be described as portfolio investment, it bears little resemblance to portfolio investment on the Stock Exchange where the investor buys his shares through a broker and, apart from the dividend cheque and the statutory notification of general meetings, never has any contact with the company. This type of investment is very rare in private companies, the vast majority of which do not welcome outside minority shareholders. Share transfer provisions in the articles of association are an effective means of restricting membership of the company. They are a great disincentive to investment, since they may block the 'exit' route even where no objection is made to the original purchase of shares.

A private individual who buys a minority shareholding in a non-dividend paying private company as a pure portfolio investment must do so on the basis of some prospect which, if realised, will provide him with the return he seeks. Where the valuer is advising an individual con-templating such an investment, he should discuss the likely possibilities with him. These will vary according to the circumstances. For example, there may be grounds for believing that dividends will be paid at some point in the future. If so, the shares can be valued on that expectancy. Alternatively, the company may be identified as being a likely subject of a successful take-over bid in due course. Such a likelihood would have to be carefully assessed and the estimated bid value suitably (i.e., heavily) discounted for risk, uncertainty and waiting time. Another possibility is that the shareholding may assume a 'strategic' significance to other shareholders in certain (likely) circumstances, i.e., the shares may be sought by other shareholders anxious either to protect their own position or to improve it. This may occur where the balance of power in a company is upset by the death of a shareholder and the transmission of his shares to others. These possibilities invariably point to a valuation of the company at some future time when disposal of the shares is considered likely. As the investor is faced with considerable uncertainty and invariably a long holding period with a high opportunity cost in terms of alternative invest-ment income forgone, the discount rate applied to such a valuation will inevitably be savage and at least as high as that applied by the venture capitalist.

The important point to bear in mind, however, is that the purchaser has some objective in mind on the basis of which the shares can be valued. The price a person pays who blindly purchases a minority shareholding in a non-dividend paying company, with not even a thought as to how he expects to profit from his investment, defies analysis and, like all irrational behaviour not motivated by self-interest, is outside the scope of investment and valuation theory. It would be naïve to pretend, however, that individuals never make ill-considered investments in private companies. In the *Financial Times* of 17 August 1985, there appeared a classic example of such an investment. It illustrates the pitfalls of portfolio investment in private companies so well that it is worth quoting from the article at length.

> Take the case of Mr 'A' who was looking for an investment for £50,000 from a property he had sold. He was introduced to a builder who had an option on a building plot suitable for flats. The builder proposed to form a company to exploit the situation; he and his family were able to put up £150,000 but they needed another £50,000 to meet the purchase price of the land: £200,000. The bank had agreed to lend funds to carry out the building works and at the end of the first year the company's capital would be doubled.
>
> Mr 'A' talked with friends in the housing business and decided the builder's statements were fair.
>
> So he took 25% of the share capital for £50,000. The builder, his wife, two sons and a daughter, each took 15%, making Mr 'A' the largest single shareholder. Everything went according to plan, and all the flats were sold.
>
> Mr 'A' was vaguely aware that there were five directors, all family names, well known, as explained. Nevertheless, he was a bit surprised when he received the first company accounts to find that the directors' fees of £50,000 were shown — £30,000 for the builder himself and £5,000 each for the other director shareholders. A five per cent dividend was proposed, but to conserve resources for future projects the directors magnanimously proposed to waive the dividend on their share.
>
> The promised profits were achieved but were depleted by the directors' fees, the dividend and Corporation Tax.
>
> Still, the company was worth £100,000 more than when it started. On the face of it, in the first year the investment had increased by 50% or had it?
>
> Mr 'A' did not mind the £30,000 fees for the builder although he thought that was enough. The other £20,000 directors' fees touched a raw nerve compared with his five percent dividend and the implication that no more directors were wanted. He decided to get out and sell his shareholding. This is when he

began to understand more fully the difference between owning shares in a public company and a private one.

Probably no ordinary investor ever looks at the memorandum and articles of a public company but an investor in a private company ought to review them carefully, always with professional advice. Although no longer a statutory requirement, the restriction on the transfer of shares is almost certain to be there. Thus even if Mr 'A' found a willing buyer for his shares the directors could refuse to register the transfer.

Mr 'A' was able to find a prospective buyer for his shares who was acceptable to the directors but the price offered was shocking. The prospective buyer's accountant pointed out various important factors which influenced the value of the shares:

(a) Although 25% was the largest shareholding, the other 75% were held by one family. They had control of the company day-to-day and the 25% shareholding could not by itself influence any of the company's policies so long as the family remained united.

(b) There was no way that the capital invested could be returned other than by a liquidation which was unlikely.

(c) There was no substantial established pattern to show that the company could achieve reasonable profits over a period of years. Although the value of the company had risen substantially in the first year, the company proposed to undertake further trading in speculative building ventures, that might or might not prove profitable.

(d) The family shareholders could and had paid themselves well.

(e) Although a dividend had been paid it was only minor reward for the investment and did not necessarily mean that future payments would be made.

(f) A speculative investment of this nature would look for a return of at least 20% and the dividend paid so far suggested a total value for the shareholding of up to £15,000.

What should the shareholder do? He did have statutory rights for the protection of minority shareholders but this means applying to the courts and the company's short life was probably not sufficient to establish that the minority shareholder was being unfairly treated.

The family shareholders might be persuaded to buy his

shares with a very large discount but they might be agreeable to offer a larger sum than the outsider's £15,000 — perhaps £20,000! They would probably pay themselves advance directors' fees to obtain the cash, on their accountant's advice.

A minority shareholder in a private company is obviously in an unenviable position. Even if there is a favourable takeover offer, or the company is in an exceptional cash situation from the disposal of its main business and liquidation is proposed, the majority shareholder(s) is unlikely to agree to a simple share by division.

It is not unusual in these cases for the major shareholder(s) to refuse to agree to any proposal unless the minority shareholders are prepared to enter into an agreement whereby the majority shareholder is entitled to a fractionally larger percentage per share of the takeover proceeds, or the amount available for distribution in the liquidation, than the minority shareholders receive.

The ordinary investor who buys shares in a private company but not a controlling interest has no practical method of recovering his investment. He has a few legal courses open to him but what is the worth of an investment that relies on legal action to gain a right to be treated fairly, and 'fairly' may not mean being treated equally with the majority?[7]

Valuation for other purposes

Where portfolio investment is not the purpose for which the valuation is required different considerations apply. Here the individual will be an insider — a term which would cover family, friends, employees, business associates or partners — and the transfer of shares will usually be from one shareholder to another.[8] Most minority shareholdings that come up for valuation fall into this category. In such cases everything depends on the circumstances and generalisations are impossible. The golden rule, however, is that the valuation should reflect the owner values of buyer and seller and their relative bargaining strengths. A valuation which does not follow this approach will lack credibility.

Chapters 1 and 2 contain many examples of how owner values affect

[7] R. B. Cannon, 'Share and Share — but not alike', *Financial Times,* 17 August 1985.
[8] The fact of kinship, employment etc. does not of itself make a person an insider but insiders are normally drawn from these groups. An influential minority shareholder can easily become an outside minority shareholder — by, for example, being voted off the board.

price. In many cases, the fact that dividends are or are not paid will be fairly unimportant since at least one of the parties will be viewing the transaction as a participator, if not as a controlling shareholder. The valuation will usually be arrived at on some discounted *pro rata* control basis. Exceptionally, where a small minority interest holds the balance of power, the value may even exceed the *pro rata* full control value. It will also be clear from Chapter 2 that values so arrived at will rarely be market values; they will be valid solely for specific transactions between stated parties.

The discount for lack of marketability

Compared with quoted shares, unquoted shares lack marketability. This lack of marketability arises in two ways. First, most unquoted companies have few shareholders. The resultant narrowness in the market for a company's shares makes it difficult, and sometimes impossible, to deal. Second, many private companies' articles of association contain share transfer restrictions. These typically provide that an intending seller must offer his shares to existing members who, if they do not like the intending seller's offer price, can elect to have the fair value of the shares determined by the company's auditors. Only if there are no buyers among existing members is the intending seller free to find a buyer outside the company. And in all private companies the directors have the right to refuse to register a transfer of shares.

Liquidity is a valuable attribute of an investment and the lack of it is a depreciatory factor. This has given rise to the practice of applying a discount for lack of marketability in the valuation of unquoted shares. It hardly needs saying that such a discount is only appropriate where a capitalisation rate has been selected from marketable investments such as quoted securities. Apart from the obvious fact that a large public unquoted company with many shareholders and regular, if infrequent, transactions in its shares will merit a much smaller discount than will the small private company with severe share transfer restrictions, the size of the discount is not a matter of calculation, or even perhaps of convention, but rather of individual preference.

An informal survey of investment practice carried out by the author in 1981 indicated no pattern at all in these discounts. Indeed, there was considerable irrationality. Some investors did not even apply discounts for lack of marketability; others applied them selectively, and none agreed on a common level of discount. The most popular discount level amongst those who felt strongly on this matter seemed to be 25%, although for some institutions it was as high as 50%. The position was further clouded by the practice amongst some professionals of including in this discount an allowance for other factors such as risk.

In the United States various studies have been carried out to gather empirical evidence on the discount for lack of marketability. These studies consisted of comparisons of the prices of letter stocks of US corporations with the prices of their quoted counterparts. Quoted US corporations frequently issue letter stocks when making acquisitions or raising capital. Letter stocks are identical to the company's stock already in issue except that they have not been registered with the Securities and Exchange Commission (SEC), and are therefore not quoted or marketable. Companies issue letter stocks because the time and cost of registering the new stock with the SEC would make registration impractical at the time of the transaction. In addition, founders' or large family shareholdings in quoted companies may never have been registered with the SEC and, like letter stocks, these too lack marketability. Although these restricted stocks cannot be sold to the public on the open market, they may be sold under certain circumstances in private transactions. Such transactions must be reported to the SEC, and so become a matter of public record.

The SEC Institutional Investor Study Report

The *SEC Institutional Investor Study Report* — the earliest of the US studies — analysed the discounts by trading market in which the counterpart quoted shares were dealt in.[9] There were four categories: the New York Stock Exchange (NYSE); the American Stock Exchange (ASE); Over-the-counter (reporting companies); and Over-the-Counter (non-reporting companies). An Over-the-Counter (OTC) company can avoid reporting to the SEC by maintaining its assets below $1 million, or by keeping its number of shareholders under 500. The SEC study showed that discounts in all markets varied considerably, some observations showing no discounts but a modest premium. However, discounts were lowest for NYSE quoted shares, and increased, in order, for ASE quoted stocks, OTC reporting companies and OTC non-reporting companies. For this last category, which has most in common with the typical unquoted company, the largest number of observations fell in the 30 to 40% discount range, and 56% by number and 52% by value of all such transactions showed discounts greater than 30%, as Table 2 shows:

[9] 'Discounts involved in Purchases of Common Stock' in US 92nd Congress, 1st Session, House. *Institutional Investor Study Report of the Securities and Exchange Commission* (Washington, DC: US Government Printing Office, 1971), 5:2444−2456 (Document no. 92−64, part 5).

Table 2: Discounts for lack of marketability.

OTC non-reporting companies

Discount category %	Number of transactions %	Value of transactions %
−15.0 to 0.0	4.5	8.0
0.1 to 10	8.0	5.0
10.1 to 20	16.0	24.0
20.1 to 30	15.0	11.0
30.1 to 40	22.5	28.0
40.1 to 50	18.0	11.0
50.1 to 80	16.0	13.0
	100.0	100.0
Totals	112.0	$104.0m

Source: SEC Institutional Investor Study Report, 1971.

The discounts were also analysed by annual sales volume of the subject companies. This showed a strong tendency for the companies with the largest sales to experience the smallest discounts.

The SEC Report raises a number of interesting questions. Why should discounts for lack of marketability be higher for smaller companies? Do investors see lack of marketability as something linked to, or inseparable from, a share's risk? Why do discounts vary so much even within a risk class such as companies of a certain size? In view of the diversity of discounts, is it realistic to think of marketability as a separately identifiable investment attribute which investors consciously buy or build into their reckoning of a reasonable purchase price?

Irrational though it seems, the evidence suggests that in the United States lack of marketability is a relatively greater disadvantage for the smaller company's shares than it is for the bigger company's shares. This may be because the letter stock of a large corporation is less illiquid than the letter stock of the smaller corporation. However, the fact that these discounts vary not only with the size of the corporation but also according to the trading market of the counterpart quoted stock suggests that the discount is risk sensitive. Assuming risk varies directly with size, US investors therefore appear to place a higher value on liquidity where a risky investment is concerned than they do when a relatively safe investment is concerned.

This state of affairs must be accepted as the judgement of the market place, but it can hardly be defended on logical grounds. Risk and liquidity are separate and distinct concepts. Other things being equal, a quoted company with a greater degree of risk will be valued less than a quoted company with a lower degree of risk. If both companies have letter stocks in issue, it is difficult to see the justification for anything but the same discount for lack of marketability in both cases; the relative riskiness of the two companies has already been taken into account in the quoted price.

Other US studies indicate an average discount for the lack of marketability of approximately 35% for letter or restricted stocks of quoted companies.[10] However, it is generally assumed that most such securities will eventually be registered and become quoted. This is not necessarily a valid assumption with unquoted shares. Furthermore, the unquoted companies' shares may be the subject of a buy-sell agreement (this is roughly equivalent to the pre-emption clauses often found in UK private company articles), which affects their marketability *vis-à-vis* that of letter stocks. These considerations suggest that the discount for lack of marketability in unquoted shares could well be in excess of 35%, and this has apparently been recognised in US Court rulings. More recently, Arneson has argued for marketability discounts of over 50%.[11]

An interesting point concerns the extent to which the discount for lack of marketability should change with the size of shareholding. Obviously, if the entire share capital of a company is being valued, there is no justification for a discount for lack of marketability, since the shares are not held as a portfolio investment and a company with only one shareholder cannot secure or maintain a listing. In other words, two companies identical in all respects save that one is quoted and the other is not, should have identical values as regards a purchaser of 100%, of the equity. The minority shareholder, on the other hand, suffers considerably from the lack of marketability, and for this reason, discounts must be at their greatest for the small, uninfluential shareholding. As it would not be unusual when valuing such shareholdings to use a dividend yield at least double that available in the stock market, a marketability discount of 50% may well be justified. With shareholdings over 50% but less than 100%, or even strategic minority holdings giving *de facto* control, the lack of marketability is less of an inhibiting factor since control of the company is the main objective and not portfolio investment. Here again, the shading of the discount to reflect these different situations must be a matter of individual judgement.

---

[10] Robert E. Moroney, 'Most Courts Overvalue Closely-held Stocks', *Taxes* (March 1973), pp. 144–154; J. Michael Maher, 'Discounts for Lack of Marketability for Closely-held Business Interests', *Taxes* (September 1976), pp. 562–571; and Thomas A. Solberg, 'Valuing Restricted Securities: What Factors do the Courts and the Service Look for?', *Journal of Taxation* (September 1979), pp. 150–154. Cited by Pratt, *Valuing a Business*, pp. 147–155.

[11] George S. Arneson, 'Nonmarketability Discounts Should Exceed Fifty Per Cent', *Taxes* (January 1981), pp. 25–31.

Dividend cover

Dividend cover is sometimes used as a crude indicator of the security of the current dividend and of the potential for further increases. Thus, a dividend covered only twice by profits will on the face of it be more vulnerable to a fall in profits than one covered three times.

Dividend cover is a dangerous criterion to apply blindly. Like the P/E ratio, it is a 'snapshot' device relating dividend to profit in a single year. The profit in that year may be lower or higher than normal; two companies with identical dividend cover may have very different prospects and, hence, different future dividend growth.

Before the introduction of the imputation system of taxation, dividend cover was calculated simply by dividing the attributable profits by the dividend declared. For many practical purposes, where scientific accuracy is not required, calculations on this basis may still be permissible. However, in more formal work it is essential to use the 'maximum distribution' method of computing earnings since this recognises that, under the imputation system, the size of the dividend can affect earnings through unrelieved ACT. Under the present system, ACT payable on dividends can be recouped by deduction against a company's mainstream corporation tax liability. If a company pays little or no corporation tax the ACT on dividends may not be recoverable and has to be written off, thus reducing earnings. This problem is likely to exist where a company's profits are largely earned overseas. It has also been a problem for a number of companies with UK profits for which generous tax allowances have made corporation tax virtually an optional impost.[12]

As the name implies, the maximum distribution method defines earnings as the maximum gross dividend payable out of the current year's results. Dividend cover is calculated by dividing this amount by the gross dividend declared for the year. A working example is the best way to illustrate the concept.

A company's results are summarised below:

		£000
Profit before tax		400
Tax		
UK corporation tax	96	
Overseas tax	50	146
Profit after tax		254
Minority interest	25	
Preference dividend (net)	20	45

[12] The abolition of stock appreciation relief and the phasing out of 100% first-year allowances has now brought an end to this tax holiday.

Attributable profit	209
Ordinary dividend (net)	100
Retained profit	109

The first step is to calculate how much of the corporation tax charge of £96,000 is recoverable by deduction of ACT. The amount of ACT which may be set off, it will be recalled, is limited to the amount which, with the relative dividend, absorbs all the taxable profit. The effect is that, with ACT assumed at 3/7ths and corporation tax at 50%, the set off may never reduce the 'mainstream' liability below 20%. The calculation is as follows:

	£000
Corporation tax charge	96
Taxable income 96×100/50	192
Minimum mainstream corporation tax — 192×20%	38
ACT recoverable 96−38	58

The maximum *net* dividend that could be paid without incurring any non-recoverable ACT is, therefore, £135,000, i.e., £58,000 × 7/3. However, the company's profit after tax is £254,000, and the difference of £119,000 (i.e., £254,000 − £135,000) is available for the payment of dividends. Any dividends thus paid will attract unrelieved ACT so that out of every £10 of profit only £7 of dividend can be paid. The maximum permitted distribution can now be calculated:

	£000
Dividend on which ACT is recoverable	135
Dividend on which ACT is not recoverable — £119,000×7/10	83
Notional profit after tax	218
Minority interest — 25×$^{218}/_{254}$	(21)
Preference dividend (net)	(20)
Maximum permitted dividend	177

The UK minority interest has been scaled down in line with profit after tax. This treatment would not be applicable for an overseas minority which is deducted before scaling down the profit for unrelieved ACT.

As the maximum permitted dividend is £177,000 and the actual dividend was £100,000, the cover works out at 1.8. The crude calculation of cover would have been 2.1, i.e., £209,000 divided by £100,000 — an appreciably higher cover than actually available. Dividend cover as shown in the Share Information Service of the *Financial Times* is calculated on the maximum distribution basis.

Conclusion

The future stream of dividends must determine the investment value of uninfluential minority holdings since this is the only form of return which portfolio investors, in aggregate, receive on their investment. Such holdings should, therefore, be valued on the stream of dividend basis. The use of the P/E ratio and the attention given to earnings per share in stock market circles does not invalidate this position.

If a share's investment value is determined by its future dividends and the rate of return at which they are discounted, a valuation technique which explicitly considers these factors is desirable. The dividend discount model, $V=D/(r-g)$ meets these requirements. It can be manipulated to provide a means of calculating implied growth rates in dividends for quoted companies (equation (3)), and this device can be used to check the reasonableness of the required rate of return.

The dividend discount model assumes a constant growth rate in dividends. However, it can easily be adjusted for above or below average growth immediately in prospect. As most Stock Exchange investment is based on a fairly detailed assessment of short- to medium-term prospects, with the longer term growth assumed at some norm, the dividend discount formula can be modelled closely on investor behaviour.

Although the dividend discount model is, in the author's view, the better technique, the initial yield method doubtless has a greater following. This method consists of applying the initial yield to the current dividend. It should yield the same results as the dividend discount formula, but it suffers from presentational defects and it does not explicitly consider the rate of return.

Many private companies do not pay dividends. Does this mean that their shares have no investment value? Two classes of portfolio investor were distinguished: the institutional investor, who frequently assumes the role of venture capitalist, and the private individual. The venture capitalist is an 'inside' minority shareholder who invariably invests on terms agreed with the controlling shareholders. He will have an agreed 'exit route' e.g., a USM listing or a management buy-out, on the basis of which the present value of the shares can be estimated.

The private individual is rarely a portfolio investor in unquoted companies, irrespective of whether or not they pay dividends. Private companies do not welcome outsiders as shareholders, and for his part the individual would find the illiquidity of such an investment unacceptable. In those rare cases where a private individual proposes to acquire a minority shareholding as a pure investment and the company does not pay a reasonable dividend or pays no dividend at all, the shares must be valued on the purchaser's expectations. He may foresee a bid for the company or the probability of a future quotation. Perhaps his shares might assume a strategic importance in certain circumstances, such as the death of another shareholder. Such valuations are inevitably highly subjective and heavily discounted, but they must have a rational basis to them. It makes no sense to value shares on a hypothetical dividend, nor in the commercial world is it ever necessary. In the investment world one does not usually find sane individuals prepared to part with substantial sums of money with no clear idea (albeit one difficult to put a figure on) as to how they may profit from their outlay.

Most transfers of minority shareholdings are between existing members of the company, and more often than not portfolio investment is not the main purpose. These are generally valuations as between stated parties, both of whom will often be insiders. In such cases the valuations should be on the basis of the owner values of both parties having due regard to the relative bargaining strengths of each side.

The size of marketability discounts which apply solely where the capitalisation rate has been selected directly from Stock Exchange data has traditionally been almost a matter of personal preference, and there is little reliable evidence in the UK as to the discounts applied in practice. The existence of letter stocks in the US has provided researchers with independent evidence as to the price of marketability. Studies of the discounts applied to letter stocks — discounts which seem to vary irrationally — indicate average discounts of at least 35%. Given the difference between letter stocks and unquoted shares, a higher discount would be appropriate for the latter. In some cases, discounts of as much as 50% may well be justifiable.

10

The earnings basis of valuation

Earnings are the bedrock of business values. They are the fund from which dividends are paid and they are ultimately the basis of all asset values. The word 'ultimately' is necessary here because in strict theory the value of an asset is a function of its future cash flows, and cash flow is not the same as earnings. Ultimately, of course, earnings or profit is transformed into cash flow but the timing of the two flows is different.[1] The use of profit and not cash flow in the evaluation of a business may, therefore, appear at first sight to be contrary to theory. However, the evaluation of a business in terms of its future cash flow is not generally practicable as the discussion of the DCF basis of valuation in Chapter 11 shows. Furthermore, the annual earnings of a company determine the maximum annual cash dividend that the ordinary shareholders could pay themselves. Barring a liquidation, this is the most they or any other owner of the entire share capital could expect to get out of the business. As such, it is a legitimate valuation basis.

The earnings basis is required for valuing controlling interests. The reason for this is quite simple. As shown in Chapter 3 the nature of a share changes fundamentally, as far as valuation is concerned, when the shareholding becomes big enough to confer control. Before that point is reached, the legal doctrine that a shareholder is not a part owner of the company's business undertaking accords with — indeed determines — the commercial reality. Such a shareholder must be content with what dividends the directors see fit to declare. Once control is obtained, however, the shareholder may distribute all the profits by way of dividend, should he so wish. The fact that he chooses to leave some, perhaps all, the profit in the business is neither here nor there; it is merely a way of investing the funds at his disposal. The meaning of control and the forms it can take are, therefore, of prime importance to the valuer. He also needs a sound grasp of the nature of profit, the problems in defining and measuring it, and the techniques for developing a reliable forecast of future earnings. Lastly, he needs a technical formula for transforming his earnings projection into a valuation.

[1] Failure to appreciate this point is a common cause of business failure.

The meaning of control

The essence of control is the ability to determine the composition of the board of directors since it is they who run the company's business on a day-to-day basis. A shareholding which carries over 50% of the votes is the minimum requirement for *de jure* control since it is sufficient to ensure the passage of an ordinary resolution and, thus, the appointment and removal of directors. A shareholding which does not command a majority of the votes may carry *de facto* control if the other shares are widely dispersed between unconnected parties. Consider, for example, a company with the following shareholdings:

Shareholder	No of shares
A	40
20 individuals each holding three per cent	60
Total	100

In order to prevent A from passing an ordinary resolution another shareholder would have to persuade at least 13 other shareholders to vote against the resolution. Unless he was connected with these shareholders this would probably be an impractical course, and A would be free to remain in control. In a quoted company with thousands of shareholders, a 40% shareholding would almost certainly give *de facto* control. If, at the other extreme, there were only two shareholders, A with 40% and B with 60%, A's shares would be a pure minority with little or no say in the affairs of the business.

Sometimes a minority holding which by itself is too small to ensure control may, nevertheless, have a strategic significance in that, when combined with another shareholding, it confers control. This would be the case in the following situation:

Shareholder	No of shares
A	34
B	33
C	33
Total	100

A and B are directors and together control the company. C is the widow of a former director and is now an outside minority shareholder. However, her shares would be valued on a controlling interest basis, i.e., by reference to earnings, since she holds the balance of power between A and B and can confer control of the company on either. The logic of this argument can be extended to very small shareholdings which hold the balance of power.

There are, therefore, degrees of control. Absolute control comes with ownership of all the equity. Day-to-day management control comes with over 50% of the votes, but in certain circumstances it can come with less. A bare majority, however, is insufficient to pass a special resolution. This comes with a 75% shareholding and marks the point where the degree of control increases appreciably between bare majority and absolute control.

The reflection of these different degrees of control in a valuation is an imprecise and subjective affair. In the normal run of things, a valuation of the entire equity produces the highest value per share. Between 75% and 90%, one would expect the per share value to be discounted somewhat to reflect the lack of complete freedom which the existence of a minority inevitably entails. This discount would be minimal for a shareholding of 90% or more, since s.428 of the Companies Act 1985 gives the purchaser of 90% or more the power to compulsorily acquire a dissenting minority's shareholding. For a shareholding between 50% and 75%, the discount off full *pro rata* value would be greater, since the inability to pass a special resolution is an important limitation of control. The discount off full control value in valuing a *de facto* controlling shareholding would be greater still.

However, everything depends on the circumstances and there is no general rule as to the absolute or relative size of these discounts. A purchaser who is not particularly concerned about the existence of a minority shareholder — perhaps even a purchaser who, say, for cash reasons prefers not to purchase outright control — may not seek to apply more than a token discount. On the other hand, some corporate purchasers are averse to outside minority interests as a matter of policy and would demand a significant reduction in the price for accepting less than full control. It is conceivable, too, that a shareholding may be valued at a premium to its full *pro rata* control value. This could occur where a small parcel of shares holds the balance of power. Assume for example that ABC Ltd is worth £500,000 and different percentage shareholdings have the following values:

Shareholding %	'Pro rata' full control Control value £000's	Actual value £000's	Discount to 'pro rata' Control value %
20	100	50	50
40	200	130	35
60	300	255	15
100	500	500	—

There are three shareholders, A, B and C. A and B each hold 40% and C holds 20%. A and B fall out and each bids for C's shares in an attempt to gain control. As a 60% shareholding is worth £255,000 and a 40% one, £130,000, A or B could, in theory, justify paying the difference of £125,000 for C's shares. As C's 20% stake has a *pro rata* control value of £100,000, a price of £125,000 would represent a premium of 25%. As always, everything depends on the circumstances. Thus, if A and B were the best of friends and were happy to continue running the company together, C's shareholding would be valued below its full *pro rata* control value. As a general rule, however, the smaller the shareholding, the greater the percentage premium in this situation.

A company with two shareholders each owning 50% presents a problem in valuing for control. If there is no casting vote, it would be illogical to value one shareholding on a control basis and not the other, and equally absurd to value them both as minority interests. In practice, the least objectionable course is to value both holdings on a full control basis, that is, at 50% of the value of the entire equity. The presence of a casting vote makes a difference. It means that the shareholder, X, who happens to be chairman of the board of directors can control the company and exclude the other shareholder, Y, from participation in the management of the company.

In these circumstances, X already has control and the argument for valuing Y's shareholding at its full *pro rata* control amount is difficult to sustain. Unless X behaves in a way which opens him to an action for the protection of minority rights, Y faces an indefinite period on the sidelines. It may then be in his interest to accept a price below the full control value. However, if X's objective in buying Y's 50% shareholding is to enable him to sell the entire company, then Y's stake should be valued at its full *pro rata* control amount. The reason for this is simple. X's control of the company comes not so much from his shareholding as from his position as chairman. X cannot sell the office of chairman and, therefore, he cannot sell control of the company. The price his shares would fetch in isolation would almost certainly be well below their *pro rata* control value.[2] X needs Y's shares in order to maximise the value of his own shares in any sale. X can, therefore, justify paying the full control value for Y's shares and Y, being on an equal footing with X as regards a sale of the entire company, should insist on no less.

Occasionally, the valuer encounters a capital structure in which voting rights are separated from the equity entitlement. This separation is achieved by having two classes of share, one which carries the

---

[2] This is a good example of owner value exceeding exchange value — see Chapter 1.

votes but has no entitlement to dividends or any surplus in a winding-up and the other which has no votes but otherwise has the normal equity rights. This type of capital structure has the advantage of enabling the existing shareholders to retain control of the company while still raising outside equity capital. Lloyd's underwriting agencies usually have this type of capital structure where it ensures that control of the agency is restricted to members of Lloyds or persons approved by the Committee of Lloyds. At the same time, non-voting equity investment is open to outsiders.

The value of voting shares with no equity entitlement must reflect the value of control and nothing else. But what value has control if it is not linked to an equity entitlement? What value is there in managing a business for the benefit of others? In short, none.[3] Doubtless, this is the main reason why the articles usually stipulate a transfer value of par for such shares. As every holder of voting shares is invariably a holder of the non-voting equity, it hardly ever happens that the voting shares change hands without the non-voting equity. The point made here is, therefore, somewhat academic. However, in allocating total value between the two classes of share, the principles established here can be used.

The question of control is intimately linked with the rights and duties of shareholders and directors — a subject which is discussed in some detail in Chapter 3. The reader is also referred to the first two chapters of this book which contain a number of illustrations of the effect of control.

Earnings

Earnings and profits are synonymous, earnings being defined for P/E ratio purposes as the profit after tax, minority interest and preference dividends, but before extraordinary items.[4] To understand the nature of earnings one, therefore, has to focus on the nature of profits. Although the law provides that the profit and loss account of a company should give a true and fair view of the profit and loss for the financial year,[5] it does not define profit. To get a better idea of what profit is we must consult the economist and the accountant. The

[3] The holder of these shares could elect himself to the board of directors and obtain a livelihood from the company. In practice, this might count for a lot but it is well nigh impossible to value this opportunity. To value it as a substantial amount would imply that the income derived from the position of employment exceeded the value of the services provided. The directors would be in breach of their duty to act in the best interests of the company if they charged more for their services than they were worth.

[4] *Earnings per Share*, SSAP 3, paragraph 2.

[5] Section 228(2) of the Companies Act 1985.

economist is interested in the definition of income or profit as a means of theorising about the economic behaviour of individuals. The accountant's concept of profit springs from his need to measure it. It is not surprising, therefore, if the two approaches have a different emphasis. At the risk of gross over-simplification, the economist defines profit or income as the increase in wealth or capital over a period (plus, of course, consumption/dividends), whereas the accountant regards profit as the excess of revenues over costs. In theory, there should not be any difference between the two definitions. In practice there often is, and in certain types of business the difference is marked.

Suppose, for example, that the aim is to determine the profit of a property investment company over the last year. The company's sole asset is a freehold building valued at the beginning of the year at £500,000. Its value 12 months later is £550,000. The lease was signed five years ago and has another two years to run. It provides for net rental income of £25,000 per year. Management expenses amount to £2,000 a year. The accountant would calculate the profit at £23,000 being revenue less costs. From the economist's point of view, however, the company made a profit of £73,000, set out as follows:

	£
Net worth at end of period	
Value of freehold building	550,000
Cash (profit)	23,000
	573,000
Deduct opening net worth	500,000
Profit	73,000

Few individuals, including accountants, would deny that the true measure of profit in this case is £73,000. Why, then, do accountants not switch to the economist's definition when measuring profits?

There are two main reasons for this. First, to measure profit as the increase in net worth requires a valuation of the firm's business at each year-end plus a valuation of any surplus assets. With a property company this would be difficult enough but not impossible. Property is a readily marketable commodity and there is no shortage of professional property valuers. Most people would accept the resultant profit or loss as an objective, professionally assessed figure.[6] It would be very different, however, for an industrial or commercial company. An independent professional valuation would be very expensive and problems would arise when a company had more than one business. Further-

---

[6] Those in the property world might be a little more sceptical. Different professional valuers sometimes produce widely divergent values for the same property.

more, the concept of market value would be difficult to apply since a business is often worth a different sum to different buyers. The directors would inevitably be closely involved in the valuation and this would hardly increase confidence in the objectivity of the eventual outcome. Thus, an income measure based purely on increase in the value of the business would be highly subjective and uncertain. With the exception of companies whose assets have a readily ascertainable market value, such as property companies, the resultant figure would probably lack credibility. The fickle nature and volatility of Stock Exchange prices would inevitably mean that, for quoted companies at least, profit measured by reference to their share price would be quite unpredictable.

The second reason why accountants stick to the revenue-less-costs concept of profit is one of prudence. As Professor Lee has pointed out, this is not a policy of deliberate understatement of profit so much as one of not counting one's chickens before they are hatched.[7] Thus, an unrealised gain is not treated as profit whereas an unrealised loss would generally be deducted in arriving at profit. Commendable though it is, this concern to be prudent makes it that much easier to manipulate profit. This manipulation of the earnings figure is easier in certain types of firm than in others. Contracting and construction companies, for example, are wide open to it. The assessment of uncompleted work on long-term contracts is, in any event, fairly subjective and there can be a legitimate difference of opinion amongst experts on the subject. If, in the name of prudence, the finance director decides to take an ultra cautious view of the final outcome or work-in-progress, it would be a brave auditor who stuck his neck out and disagreed. The following year, when a downturn is expected, a more generous view can be taken, and the reduction in the provisions will prove a useful boost to the results for the year. Little imagination is required to see the possibilities for this sort of thing in other industries.

The fact that, conservatism apart, the determination of profit according to accepted accounting conventions is sometimes a matter of highly subjective judgement, where differences of opinion amongst experts are to be expected, is itself a warning to the valuer against accepting reported earnings without enquiry. A vivid example of such a difference was brought to light when two firms of chartered accountants reported on a celebrated shortfall of £14.5m in a profit forecast made by AEI during the takeover by GEC in 1967. They found that £9.5m of the profit shortfall was attributable to adjustments which they

[7] T. A. Lee, *Income and Value Measurement: Theory and Practice,* 2nd ed. (Walton-on-Thames, Surrey: Nelson, 1980), p. 55.

regard as substantially matters of judgement.[8] This, admittedly, occurred before SSAPs were introduced, but there is still considerable scope for legitimate differences of opinion, both within the application of a particular accounting policy and between one policy and its alternative.

Although the economist's concept of profit is impractical for reporting purposes, it should not be ignored by the valuer. Value always reflects the underlying economic reality and this is unaffected by the vagaries of accounting conventions. Numerous instances of this can be found in Stock Exchange investment. An obvious one is investment in property shares where the net asset value of the share is an important criterion. Thus, investors realise that reported profit on its own is an inadequate measure of true profits and that growth in the value of the property portfolio must be considered. In the realm of private companies, excessive directors' remuneration may cause reported profits to understate economic profits. Where controlling interests are being valued, true earnings, after adding back any profit distributed in the form of directors' emoluments, must be used. Similarly, shareholder loans are sometimes *de facto* equity. If this is agreed to be the case, any interest charged on them must be added back to arrive at true profit for valuation purposes.[9]

As value looks to the future and not the past, the valuer's interest in historical earnings has only one aim: to predict the future course of earnings. A simple extrapolation of the historical earnings pattern is not adequate for this purpose. The fact that earnings have grown by, say, ten per cent a year in recent times is no guarantee that they will continue to grow at this rate. Indeed, some researchers in this field have come to the conclusion that historical rates of growth provide no clue whatsoever to future rates of growth. Professor Little, for example, found that changes in earnings per share for UK quoted companies were statistically independent, i.e., they followed a random walk, and that the study of the sequence of historical changes in earnings per share was useless as an aid in predicting future changes.[10] Similar studies in the US came up with the same conclusion: changes in the

---

[8] Robert Jones and Oliver Marriott, *Anatomy of a Merger* (London: Jonathan Cape, 1970), pp. 287–288. For a revealing discussion of the latitude afforded by generally accepted accounting principles in the US, see Lorie and Hamilton, Chapter 8.

[9] Interestingly, this point was given statutory recognition in the compensation provisions of the Aircraft and Shipbuilding Industries Act 1977. Under this nationalisation measure, repayment of inter-company indebtedness deemed to have the character of equity could be frozen by the issue of a notice under s.21 of the Act. The s.21 notice usually gave the loan the character of equity for compensation purposes.

[10] Ian M. D. Little and A. C. Raynor, *Higgledy Piggledy Growth Again* (Oxford: Basil Blackwell, 1966).

earnings of US corporations, like those of their UK counterparts, followed a random walk. Much is made of these findings in academic literature.[11]

There is insufficient space here to review in detail the various research studies, nor indeed is it necessary. Anyone who mindlessly extrapolates an historical earnings progression in order to obtain a forecast future earnings potential is not a valuer but a number cruncher. No investment analyst would dream of forecasting earnings in this way. The random walk of earnings (if such be the case) does not mean that past earnings are no guide to future earnings. On the contrary, they are the principle indicator of future potential. The academic research studies merely underline the need to interpret the earnings record in the light of the general economic and industry background and the circumstances of the firm. Only with an understanding of how the company has performed against its own particular background can the valuer make an intelligent forecast of future performance. A crucial factor in this forecast will of course be the valuer's own view of the industry background in the future.

The future must always remain unknown and uncertain; any attempt to forecast it must be based on the person's own experience since no other means, short of psychic powers, are available to him. No valuer or investment analysis need, therefore, be deterred by the findings of these studies from intelligently inferring future prospects from past performance.

Reported profit is a residual sum — the excess of revenues over associated costs. A small percentage change in either costs or revenue can produce a disproportionately large change in trading profit. This can be illustrated from the cost structure of a typical manufacturing company as shown in the *Corporate Report*.[12]

	£ million	%
Bought in materials and services	67.6	65
Employee costs	25.9	25
Taxation	3.9	4
Interest on loans	0.8	1
Depreciation	2.0	2
Profits (including dividends)	3.7	3
Total	103.9	100

[11] A review of this research is given in Lorie and Hamilton, Chapter 8. For a more recent survey see G. Foster, *Financial Statement Analysis* (Englewood Cliffs, N.J.: Prentice-Hall, 1978), pp. 97–107.

[12] Accounting Standards Steering Committee, *The Corporate Report: A Discussion Paper* (London: The Institute of Chartered Accountants in England and Wales, 1975), p. 50.

It will be seen that a ten per cent rise in employee costs would cut profit by 70% whilst a one per cent fall in sales value would reduce profits by 28%. Cost reductions and sales increases can have a similar disproportionate effect on profit. It is not surprising, therefore, if profit often fluctuates and rarely rises in a smooth, even progression.

The valuer may also find it useful to examine the sources of earnings growth from a statistical view point. Earnings growth can be seen as a function of the rate of return on equity and the amount of equity backing per share. This relationship is expressed algebraically as follows:

$$\text{Earnings per share} = \frac{\text{Total earnings}}{\text{Shareholders' funds}} \times \frac{\text{Shareholders' funds}}{\text{Number of shares in issue}}$$

Earnings growth can, therefore, come from an increase in the rate of return on equity funds or a rise in the equity funds per share, or from some combination of the two. The valuer, by assessing how these two variables are likely to perform, may be able to support his qualitative assessment of prospects with some, admittedly tentative, numbers.

Growth in equity funds per share comes chiefly from retained earnings. It can also come from the issue of shares at a premium to book equity per share, but for most unquoted companies share issues are rare. The effect of retained earnings on growth in earnings per share can be illustrated by a simple example. Assume that a company is earning 20% on shareholders' equity and that, generally, 25% of earnings is distributed. The retention rate is therefore 75%. If the company continues to earn 20% on equity, both on existing equity and any retained earnings, earnings per share will grow by 15% per year, as set out below:

		p
Equity assets per share, say		100
Earnings per share — 100 @ 20%		20
Retained earnings — 20×75%	15	
Earned thereon — 20%		3
Prospective earnings per share		23
Growth rate in earnings, 3/20		15%

The growth rate is, therefore, equal to the rate of return on equity (20%) multiplied by the retention rate (75%).

The valuer should not be deluded into thinking that techniques such as the above will necessarily give him a better perception of prospects than the qualitative assessment. Quantitative techniques can give an impression of accuracy and precision but they are no more accurate or precise than the assumptions on which they are based. For the company in the above illustration to show earnings per share growth of 15% per annum, as the calculation suggests, its rate of return on equity must remain at 20% and its dividend pay out ratio at 25%. The valuer will probably be well aware from his study of the company's past that such assumptions are unrealistic. Nevertheless, the technique has its uses and, provided its limitations are recognised, it can be helpful.

Great care must be taken in assessing a company's profit potential. Extensive enquiries will have to be made along with a thorough assessment of the business. There are various ways of tackling this, and a suggested method is set out in Chapter 17.

The discounted earnings method

Just as the value of a pure minority interest is the present value of the future dividend stream so, too, the value of a controlling interest should be the present value of the future earnings stream. The mathematical formula, which expresses the present value of the business in terms of its future earnings on the simplifying assumption of a normal long-term growth rate, is as follows:

$$V = \frac{E}{r-g}$$

where,
V = the value of the company
E = earnings
r = the required rate of return
g = the expected growth rate in earnings

This formula is the same as that used for dividend-based valuations but with the appropriate change of symbols. Its derivation is shown in Chapter 9.

The advantage of this formula is that it explicitly considers the growth rate in earnings and the expected rate of return — the two key factors determining value. Admittedly, profits do not grow at a steady annual rate *ad infinitum*; as the discussion here has shown, profits usually fluctuate. This is not as serious a drawback as it might appear at first sight, since some simplifying assumption about the longer-term growth rate has to be made whatever technique is used. Beyond the short-term, say, two or three years ahead, the valuer can never be very specific about the earnings performance in individual years. Specific profit forecasts in the short-term can easily be accommodated within the formula, as follows:

$$V = \frac{E_1}{1+r} + \frac{E_2}{(1+r)^2} + \ldots + \frac{E_n}{(1+r)^n} + \left[\frac{E_n(1+g)}{r-g} \times \frac{1}{(1+r)^n} \right]$$

where E_1, E_2 ... E_n are the estimated profits for each of the years specifically forecast, and g is the longer-term growth rate assumed beyond year n.

Should profits before tax or after tax be used in the above formula? If all companies and individuals bore tax at the same effective rate and the growth rate and the rate of return were all stated after tax, it should make no difference, since:

$$\frac{E}{r-g} = \frac{E(t)}{r(t)-g(t)}$$

where t is the uniform effective rate of tax and the other symbols are as previously indicated. However, individuals can have markedly differing effective rates of tax and so, too, can companies. Individuals' tax rates differ because personal taxation in the UK is progressive; companies' effective tax rates vary for a number of reasons, including differing entitlements to tax writing-down allowances and loss relief. It seems, therefore, that there would be a difference between using pre- and post-tax profits. As it is the net return to the investor which counts, in strict theory profits after tax should be used.

However, this theoretically desirable course is difficult to adhere to in practice. The main problem is that it is virtually impossible to establish a required after tax rate of return, since rates of return in the marketplace are invariably stated gross and, as has been shown, tax rates vary virtually according to the taxpayer. Gross rates of return are, therefore, much easier to handle and can be objectively assessed. For this reason, it is the author's practice to use gross rates of return, pre-tax profits and pre-tax growth rates in the discounted earnings formula. If the subject company has a pronounced tax peculiarity, for example, large unrelieved losses which are likely to shelter profits for some years, this can be separately valued on a DCF basis and given an appropriate weighting in the overall valuation. One of the other advantages of using pre-tax profits is that the resultant pre-tax profits yield, as adjusted for the growth rate, is directly comparable with the gross internal rate of return which the corporate vendor/purchaser has set for its own capital expenditure programme. It is also directly comparable with rates of return available in the capital markets.

As with dividend-based valuations, the required rate of return can be regarded as consisting of two elements: the basic or risk-free rate of interest, as typified by the rate of return on gilts, and a risk premium.[13] However, there is a difference. The risk premium evident on Stock Exchange investment will not have the same significance in the valuation of controlling interests as it does in the valuation of pure minority ones. This is because Stock Exchange prices reflect the market value of small parcels of shares — pure minority holdings — and not the value of controlling interests. Whenever a bidder appears for the entire equity of a quoted company, a substantial premium over the pre-bid price is usually exacted. This does not mean the bidder is prepared to accept a lower rate of return (by paying a higher price) than the average investor; the premium arises because the bidder is looking to the company's profits for his return and not to its dividends. Since dividends are usually covered two or three times over, and are, therefore, less risky as an income stream than the underlying earnings, the bidder in fact expects a higher rate of return than does the minority shareholder.

There are two approaches to the selection of the required rate of return — the comparable company method and the investment approach. If the valuer uses the comparable company approach, he derives his rate of return from the terms of recent take-over bids in the stock market. Put simply, if company X was successfully bid for on a prospective pre-tax profit yield of 20%, other things being equal, the subject company would be capitalised at the same rate. If the investment approach is used, the capitalisation rate is determined by reference to the rates of return on various alternative forms of investment, as adjusted for the perceived degree of risk. Alternatively, the purchaser's or vendor's own required rate of return may be used.

The comparable company method has many adherents but, in the author's view, the investment approach to selecting a capitalisation rate is superior. Unless one was actually privy to the confidential negotiations for a take-over, one can never be sure, from merely examining the public entrails of the bid, of having correctly identified the profits which the purchaser and vendor had in mind when they agreed the bid price. It could be misleading simply to take the published profit figure. Furthermore, the comparable company approach seems to be based on the somewhat artificial concept of an open market value for an entire company. Controlling interests in companies do not change hands with the frequency and facility of normal stock market trading. Potential buyers are few and far between and the subject company may have different values to

---

[13] Chapter 7 examines various techniques for assessing the degree of risk in an investment and reviews modern theories regarding the relationship of risk to the rate of return. The discussion here assumes Chapter 7 has been read.

each potential buyer. The price struck in a particular bargain is a function of two sets of values: those of the purchaser and those of the vendor. In routine portfolio investment on the stock market, the value gap between purchaser and vendor is so small that one can generally take the latest recorded price as an indication of market value and be sure of buying or selling at or near that price. This is not so with controlling interests. The comparable company approach does not identify the gap between each party's owner values and, therefore, ignores a potent influence on price. It could lead to negotiations being broken off because the price being asked is too high or it could induce a vendor to accept a needlessly low price.

Under the investment approach, the capitalisation rate is selected by reference to rates of return available in the market place, the degree of risk attaching to the company's operations, and the client's own required rate of return. One should be able to assess the value of the company to the client using this approach; it sets the highest price he should be prepared to pay if a buyer, or the minimum he should accept if a seller. The likely price for the company will depend on the value placed on the business by the other party to the transaction. For this reason, it is generally essential in the valuation of controlling interests to envisage a specific purchaser or class of purchaser. This is not as difficult as it sounds. Obvious potential purchasers can usually be found in the ranks of competitors or those in closely allied industries. More often than not, however, a client will already have a third party in mind.

It has to be admitted, nevertheless, that sometimes the client has no third party in mind and no obvious purchaser is around. The client wants to know what his company is worth and the valuer has to value in a vacuum. He then has to select the capitalisation rate purely from his own experience and judgement. Clearly, however, it cannot be less than the risk-free rate of return available on gilts. In the author's experience, profitable, established, well managed medium-sized companies are generally capitalised on pre-tax profit yields of 20–25%. Small, well-managed companies would sell on higher yields, generally around the 30% mark. These are only general indications. They would be lower for companies with superior management and above-average profits growth; they could well be much higher if management is bad, the industry background depressed and the profits outlook poor. These yields will not be valid for all times. The investment scene is constantly changing.

With inflation currently running at around five per cent a year, a firm must grow by at least this rate in order to maintain its position. Recalling from Chapter 9 that the growth rate when added to the initial yield gives the rate of return, it will be seen that the rates of return implied above, range from 25% for a well-managed, medium-sized company to 35% and more for the small company. In venture capital investments the expected rate of return is rarely less than 50%. These rates are over twice, and even three times, the rate of return on gilts and are eloquent testimony to the perceived riskiness of equity investment.

The P/E ratio

The price-to-earnings, or P/E ratio, is found by dividing a company's share price by its earnings per share. The latest published earnings per share figure is used to calculate the historic P/E ratio; the estimated current year's earnings per share is used to calculate the prospective P/E ratio. For example, XYZ plc reported earnings per share of 5p last year and you estimate it should earn 6p per share this year. If XYZ plc's shares stand at 60p, the historic P/E ratio is 12 (60 ÷ 5) and the prospective P/E ratio 10 (60 ÷ 6). It will be seen that the P/E ratio is just another way of expressing the earnings yield. XYZ plc's historic earnings yield is 8.3% (5 as a percentage of 60). The P/E ratio inverts this calculation: it is thus the reciprocal of the earnings yield.[14]

If the P/E ratio is merely the earnings yield in another guise, why the change? At least the earnings yield was expressed in a way in which it could be easily related to the dividend yield and the yield on other forms of investment such as gilts, Treasury bills, Eurobonds and money market deposits. There were probably at least two reasons for the changeover. First, as the post-war equity boom got under way and share prices rose to ever greater heights, it became increasingly difficult to differentiate between stocks on the basis of their earnings yields. It was much easier for the investment analyst to talk about ABC Co's P/E ratio of 30 in the light of RST Co's P/E ratio of 40, than to discuss why ABC Co had an earnings yield of 3.3% and RST Co one of only 2.5%.

Second, the initial yield (whether earnings or dividends) plus the estimated growth rate gives the estimated rate of return. This can then be compared with rates of return available on other forms of investment. It is, therefore, founded in some reality external to the equity market. The P/E ratio, however, is not. That the market is on a P/E ratio of, say, 12 means nothing and can only be judged in relation to some previous level of the market. The P/E ratio thus became a law unto itself and was increasingly seen as the determinant of a share's price instead of an inference to be drawn from it. The cult of the P/E ratio led to the concept of the relative P/E ratio. If a share's historic P/E ratio had been fluctuating between say 75% and 125% of the market P/E ratio or that for the industry sector, it

---

[14] This was invariably the case with the old system of corporation tax. Under the imputation system, it will not necessarily be true, since the dividend payment can affect earnings per share. But, for many companies it will be a reasonable approximation.

would be recommended as a buy, hold or sell if its relative P/E ratio were respectively at the bottom, middle or top of this range. This is another superficially attractive notion which, on closer inspection, turns out to be based on the assumption that the past will repeat itself without regard to changes in the fundamentals.[15]

But, it was not the P/E ratios flimsy theoretical basis which led investment professionals to question its usefulness so much as the growing inadequacy of earnings per share as a measure of performance. The rapid rise in the rate of inflation in the 1970s — the Index of Retail Prices rose from 70.6 in January 1970 to 275.6 in December 1980 — caused havoc with financial reporting. It became difficult to compare one year's results with another, since the pound sterling had a materially different purchasing power from one year to the next. Manufacturing and trading companies which valued their stocks on a First-in-First-out (FIFO) basis tended to have their reported profits swollen by a stock gains. Firms with fine earnings records found themselves in financial difficulties, unable to replace their stocks and to re-equip their factories. Historical cost earnings tended to seriously overstate true economic earnings in this inflationary period. It was obvious to all that an investment yardstick, which evaluated a share's price in terms of its reported earnings, was to some extent suspect.

But, inflation was not the only reason why earnings per share became increasingly unreliable as a performance measure. The introduction of a new accounting standard for deferred tax was also a contributory factor. While the accountancy profession grappled with the problems of devising a new standard for inflation accounting, the Government introduced tax reliefs to ease the corporate liquidity crisis. These reliefs tacitly recognised that reported profits were to a greater or lesser extent illusory. The most significant tax break in this connection was stock relief, but generous first-year allowances on capital expenditure were also of great importance. The effect of these reliefs, as originally conceived, was to defer tax for as long as stock levels increased and capital expenditure levels were maintained. Companies began to accumulate substantial deferred taxation reserves in their balance sheets, and in many instances there was little likelihood of the tax ever becoming payable. It was against this background that SSAP 15, *Accounting for Deferred Tax,* was issued in October 1978.

This accounting standard removed the obligation to provide for deferred tax on timing differences which were unlikely to be reversed for some considerable period ahead (at least three years). But it gave directors

[15] For more in this vein see Raymond L. Larcier, 'The Rise and Fall of the P/E Ratio', *The Investment Analyst,* no 48 (1977), pp. 25–30.

discretion to provide for such differences if they thought fit. The introduction of SSAP 15 led to a great disparity in the effective rate of tax, i.e., the tax charge as a percentage of the pre-tax profits, apparent in different companies' accounts. Some companies continued to provide in full for deferred tax; others provided the bare minimum and showed little or no corporation tax in their accounts. In between these two extremes there was a wide variety of behaviour.[16] This inconsistency in the provision for deferred tax meant that it became increasingly difficult to compare the P/E ratios of different companies. For some time it became the practice amongst investment analysts to use notional fully taxed earnings per share, and although this was a help, it did not reflect the often significant tax differences of individual companies.

P/E ratios in the *Financial Times* are based on the actual tax charge. To convert these into estimated fully taxed P/E ratios solve for x in the following equation:

$$x = P\left(1 + \frac{t-e}{t}\right)$$

where
x = the estimated fully taxed P/E ratio
P = the published P/E ratio in the *Financial Times*
t = the standard rate of corporation tax in the accounting period
e = the effective rate of tax, i.e., the actual tax charge as a percentage of pre-tax profits.

This shorthand method is considerably quicker than recalculating earnings per share on a full tax charge.

The introduction of the imputation system of company taxation in 1973 was also a source of confusion as regards earnings per share. Under the imputation system of taxation, the company's tax charge, and hence its earnings, can be affected by the level of its distributions. This has given rise to two possible ways of calculating earnings per share — the 'net' basis and the 'nil' basis. The net basis takes account of the actual tax charge whereas the nil basis excludes from the tax charge the dividend related amount, namely, any irrecoverable ACT and any unrelieved overseas tax arising from dividend payments. The nil basis produces an earnings figure which is not dependent on the level of distribution and so provides a better comparison between companies. But SSAP 3 recommends the net basis as

---

[16] The Accounting Standards Committee issued a revised version of SSAP 15 in May 1985. Amongst other things, this stipulates that deferred tax should only be provided to the extent that it is probable that a liability or asset will crystallise. This change in emphasis is designed to prevent the creation of unrealistically prudent deferred tax provisions.

this takes account of all relevant facts, including the additional tax liabilities inherent in the dividend policy, for which the directors should be accountable to the shareholders. In practice, the net basis is widely used. SSAP 3 encourages companies to disclose earnings per share on the nil basis when this is materially different from the net basis. In any event, the information necessary to calculate nil earnings is generally available in the notes to the accounts.

When the changeover to the imputation system took place in 1973, it was thought that after the transitional period few companies would have irrecoverable ACT and that for most companies there would be no difference between earnings per share calculated on the net basis and on the nil basis. Differences would be confined to a small minority of companies, mainly those with a large proportion of overseas earnings and those which, for one reason or another, paid little mainstream corporation tax. However, the introduction of stock appreciation relief and of ever more generous tax depreciation allowances meant that many companies could not recoup the ACT on their dividends, and this became part of their tax charge. Thus, net and nil earnings per share were often materially different for many companies.

Despite all these problems, the P/E ratio is still widely used. In this connection, the author well remembers a particular meeting of investment analysts in the City. The discussion turned to the usefulness of the P/E ratio. Speaker after speaker rose to voice some objection or other to its use. Such was the strength of feeling on the subject that the chairman decided to take a poll. The question was: 'Hands up those in favour of dropping the P/E ratio'. Not one hand was raised. So ingrained was the habit of looking at shares in terms of their P/E ratios, that everyone shrank instinctively from a step which threatened to leave them rudderless in a sea of Stock Exchange prices. Better to stick to the inadequate instruments to hand rather than to think radically and fundamentally about the valuation of shares.

Whatever one's views on the usefulness of the P/E ratio in Stock Exchange investment, the author's view is that it should be avoided when valuing unquoted shares. The reasons for this as regards the valuation of pure minority interests are given in Chapter 9. As regards the valuation of controlling interests, the objections to the use of the P/E ratio are the same as those to the use of the earnings yield. The earnings yield and the P/E ratio do not explicitly consider the expected growth rate in earnings and the required rate of return. The relationship of earnings for a particular year to the value of a business does not of itself mean very much. Its significance can only be assessed in the light of the earnings prospects and, to a certain extent, the trading record of the company. The fact that ABC Co's shares are on a P/E ratio of ten has a totally different significance if its profits are expected to double, than it does if its profits are unlikely to change. In contrast, rates of return as used in the discounted earnings method can be compared with rates of return on other stocks, gilt-edged securities and on non-Stock Exchange investments. Using the discounted earnings method, the valuer has to formalise his thinking and clearly identify the subjective judgements involved. The P/E ratio, although it can produce a reliable valuation in expert hands, tends to blur or fudge the uncomfortable uncertainty inherent in valuation by making one judgemental leap from the data to the valuation.

Conclusion

The controlling shareholder's position is analogous to that of the proprietor in that he can withdraw as much of the profit as he wishes. The fact that he chooses to leave some, perhaps all, the profit in the business is immaterial; for valuation purposes, he is regarded as withdrawing the profit and immediately re-investing it. Earnings are, therefore, the equivalent of the cash return for the proprietor and, hence, the appropriate basis for valuing controlling shareholdings.

There are various degrees of control which a shareholder, or group of shareholders, may exercise. The minimum requirement for control is the ability to determine the composition of the board of directors. Although *de jure* control requires over 50% of the votes, a lesser percentage may in certain circumstances suffice to confer *de facto* control. The various gradations in control corresponding to the legal rights which different percentage shareholdings enjoy are discussed in the text. The discussion also covers strategic shareholdings. These are small shareholdings which on their own do not control the company but which hold the balance of power. Companies where the equity is held 50–50, and classes of shares which have votes but no equity entitlement, can present difficulties. The view taken here is that, generally speaking, a shareholding in a 50–50 company should be valued at one half of the full control value of the company. Special considerations apply where one of the shareholders is chairman and has a casting vote. In theory, voting shares with no equity entitlement should have a low value if sold in isolation. In practice, they are rarely if ever sold without a matching equity entitlement, usually in the form of non-voting ordinary shares.

Before attempting an earnings based valuation the valuer must have an understanding of the nature of profit, the difficulties and pitfalls in measuring it and the problems in assessing prospective profits. Value always looks to the underlying economic reality, and this reality may not always be apparent from financial statements. Examples of how reported profits may differ from economic profits are given in the text. The inherent subjectivity in profit measurement and the ubiquitous exercise of prudence when accounting for profit — the understandable principle that it is better to understate than overstate profit — combine to vest in the directors considerable latitude in determining how much profit (or loss) will be recognised in a particular year.

In the assessment of future earnings, great care must be taken when extrapolating past growth rates into the future. This should only be done on the basis of a sympathetic understanding of the factors which have led to past growth and an appreciation of the extent to which these factors are likely to continue into the future. The unthinking extrapolation of the past into the future or the use of weighted averages of past earnings will not by themselves produce reliable forecasts. Profit as conventionally measured is a residual sum, the excess of revenue over costs. A small percentage change in revenue or costs produces a much greater percentage movement in profit. Fluctuations in profits are, therefore, more likely to be the rule than the exception.

The valuation technique recommended here is the discounted earnings method. This is the same formula as used for dividend-based valuations, but with the appropriate change of symbols. Apart from the fact that it is derived directly from the theory of investment value, its advantages are that it explicitly considers the expected rate of return and the forecast growth rate in earnings.

The P/E ratio is not recommended for valuing controlling interests although it can produce a reliable valuation in expert hands. Its main drawback, which it shares with the earnings yield, is its failure to explicitly consider the required rate of return and the growth rate. An additional disadvantage is that the P/E ratios evident from share prices generally cannot be used for valuing controlling interests. This is because share prices on the Stock Exchange are applicable to small parcels of shares and not to controlling interests. The valuer would have to calculate his P/E ratio from the terms of recent take-over bids.

11
Other valuation bases

Introduction

The dividend basis of valuation (dealt with in Chapter 9) and the earnings basis (dealt with in Chapter 10) are the two most widely used bases for valuing unquoted shares. However, there are other valuation techniques and these are examined in this chapter. The most well-known of these is the assets basis. The text sets out the general rules governing the use of this basis of valuation. It considers the disputed question of the significance of assets to the valuation of minority shareholdings in asset-based companies, such as property companies and investment trusts. It also challenges the generally held belief that, whatever a company's line of business, the higher the asset backing the safer the investment.

The discounted cash flow (DCF) basis of valuation is rarely used in valuing unquoted shares. Nevertheless, there are certain types of company for which it is suitable. When it is used, the valuation is generally an important one and the correct technique is essential. The reader will recall that a variant of the DCF formula is used in dividend-based valuations and that the same formula has been adapted for earnings-based valuations. This is because the DCF basis of valuation is closely modelled on the fundamental theory of investment value and, but for practical drawbacks in its application, it would be the preferred basis in all cases.

This discussion presupposes a familiarity with the DCF technique as applied to internal capital projects. It therefore focuses on the particular problems which arise when a company acquisition, as distinct from an internal capital project, is being evaluated. The chapter concludes with an examination of the 'weighted-average' valuation technique and a quick look at rules of thumb valuation formulae.

The assets basis

The general rule

Every business constitutes a combination of the factors of production — land, labour and capital. Capital is represented by the assets of the business. Since assets cannot work on their own but are there to assist

---

237

labour and make it more productive, assets are the passive element and labour the active one in a business. There is a tendency in many quarters to avoid the uncomfortable and unmanageable human element in the appraisal of business enterprises and to focus on the apparently more objective asset values. In the financial press, for example, business success, or the lack of it, is often expressed in terms of the need to make the assets work more effectively. Balance sheet asset values are commonly thought to underpin the share price, although there is no evidence that they do so, still less that the amounts at which assets are stated in the balance sheet can be regarded as realisable values. These habits of thought should be jettisoned; they are crutches for those who have not looked beyond appearances and lack true insight into the economic reality of the firm. The notion that a company is worth the sum of its individual asset values, less its liabilities, has no basis in theory or in fact. The value of a company's shares derives from its ability to earn profits and pay dividends i.e., from the joint application of capital and labour.

For this reason, the assets basis should never be used to determine the value of a company, other than one whose assets have a readily realisable exchange value, such as, property investment companies, investment trust companies and so-called 'money-box' businesses. Such companies are investment intermediaries and not economic enterprises. These remarks apply to controlling interests. Where minority interests are concerned, the assets basis should never be used, even where the company is an investment intermediary. This is because the asset values are out of reach of the minority shareholder. His interest in the company is restricted to dividends.

In a winding up things are different. The liquidator realises the assets and distributes the proceeds, net of any liabilities, to the members. The aggregate value of the net assets then becomes the return to the shareholders. Therefore, when a winding up is in prospect the assets basis must always be used irrespective of the size of the shareholding. Where liquidation value exceeds going concern value but there is no intention to liquidate, the liquidation value (and, therefore, asset value) determines the value of a controlling interest of 75% or more since such a shareholder can reach the assets by passing a special resolution. The minority shareholder cannot force a liquidation and if no liquidation is in prospect then liquidation value is irrelevant to the valuation of his shareholding, even where it exceeds the going concern value. A shareholder with bare control, i.e., one with between 50% and 75% of the votes, cannot compel a liquidation. However, even though he may be unable to force a liquidation, he can redeploy the company's assets. By selling off under-used or poorly performing businesses, i.e., by realising the liquidation values, he may be able to increase the profits of the company greatly. Where liquidation value exceeds going concern value, therefore, the former will have a considerable influence on the value to be placed on a controlling interest of less than 75%.

This does not mean that in the appraisal of a manufacturing or trading company one disregards the assets. In a manufacturing company, for example, the state of the plant and equipment and its suitability for the purpose at hand will be of great importance. If the plant is run down or obsolete, heavy capital expenditure may be necessary, and the injection of new capital this may require will affect the valuation. It may be, too, that the profit and loss account has not borne an economic depreciation charge, thus giving a false picture of true profits.

The foregoing could occur where a business uses old plant which is heavily depreciated or completely written down. In such a company the depreciation charge will not reflect the true cost of using the plant and economic profits will be overstated. This situation will only become apparent if enquiry is made about the age and condition of the assets.

The relevance of assets depends, therefore, on the type of business. In a capital intensive business these enquiries about the state of the plant will be of crucial importance; in a service company they will be a subsidiary factor. The point to remember, however, is that the significance of the assets lies in their physical condition and suitability for their purpose. Their balance sheet amount, determined as it is by historical cost, the particular depreciation policy in use and the accident of accounting convention, is unlikely to represent their value. Nor are these amounts intended to be values. As far as fixed assets are concerned, they are merely that part of the original cost not yet written off. As there is no necessary relation between cost and value (see Chapter 1), there is equally no necessary relation between written down cost and value. Nor is there any justification for regarding a business purely as a collection of assets.

Occasionally, purchaser and vendor agree to be bound by an independent valuation on the net assets basis. An agreement to be bound by an independently verified asset value may be seen as a useful device for removing the element of negotiation — and hence the possibility of the negotiations failing — from the final stages of agreeing a price. However, such a move should not be undertaken lightly. These full-scale asset valuations are often detailed, lengthy and costly exercises in which independent professional valuations of all properties, plant and machinery and other fixed assets are commissioned. Because of the contradiction in valuing a business by reference to the value of its individual assets and not by reference to the totality of its operation, numerous conceptual problems arise, and these can be the source of the very disputes which the adoption of this basis of valuation is designed to avoid.

These conceptual difficulties are likely to manifest themselves in the instructions given to the asset valuers. Suppose that a shipbuilding company is being valued on this agreed basis. Its fixed assets include the shipbuilding berths, dry docks, cranes, engineering workshops and associated equipment. A liquidation basis of valuation would be unacceptable to the vendor since the forced sale value of the plant and equipment would be ridiculously low. The shipbuilding facilities must, therefore, be valued on the basis of their existing use. But this entails an assessment of the profits they could generate and so becomes an earnings-based valuation in an indirect way. Furthermore, is the existing use valuation to be based on the assumption of adequate profitability or on the basis of existing profitability? In the present state of the shipbuilding industry there is a great difference. It is unlikely that any shipbuilder makes an adequate level of profits but it would be unfair, as far as the purchaser is concerned, to value the assets on a hypothetical level of profits. All that the vendor and purchaser have done, therefore, in agreeing to an asset valuation is to delegate consideration of the earnings potential of the business to the fixed asset valuers.

When these difficulties have been resolved and asset valuations determined, the question arises as to whether realisation expenses are to be taken into account and what deduction, if any, should be made for tax on any revaluation surpluses. Are taxation writing down allowances, and hence the deferred taxation provision, to be adjusted accordingly? The valuation of intangibles and of current assets, such as, stocks and debtors, can also present considerable difficulties. All in all, vendor and purchaser would be well advised to avoid this valuation basis and to persevere with an agreement on the earnings-related value of the business.

Minority shareholdings in property companies

The assertion that minority shareholdings should never be valued on an assets basis would not generally be contested as far as manufacturing, commercial or trading companies are concerned. Some would question, however, whether this rule applies to property companies, investment trusts and 'money box' companies. Professional investors on the Stock Exchange focus almost exclusively on net asset backing per share when appraising property companies and investment trusts. It is widely believed that share prices in these sectors are determined by net asset backing. Accordingly, it is unrealistic to ignore net asset value per share in the valuation of unquoted property investment companies and investment trusts.

The overriding point of principle here concerns whether, and to what extent, habits and conventions apparent in the evaluation of shares in Stock Exchange companies should be automatically and unthinkingly imported into the valuation of shares in equivalent unquoted companies. Clearly, they cannot. Every technique used in the valuation of unquoted shares must be justified on some rational basis founded on the theory of value, i.e., that the value of a financial asset is a function of the future cash returns and the expected rate of return. The net asset value of a company is relevant only to the extent that it throws some light on the cash return to be expected on the shares. As far as a minority shareholding is concerned, the value of the company's assets, even those of a property company or an investment trust, does not directly determine the return on the shares. In law, as in fact, the minority shareholder is entitled solely to dividends. These are not based on the net asset value of the company and, therefore, net asset value does not provide a logically justifiable basis of valuation.

It is true, nonetheless, that an irrational basis of valuation, if adhered to universally, will produce its own justification. If everyone (mistakenly) evaluates property shares solely in terms of net asset value per share then, ignoring the question of dividends, the capital gain on property shares, and hence the return, will be determined solely by asset values. However, this will only be true of a uniform, highly centralised market such as that provided by the Stock Exchange. As far as private company shares are concerned, there is no market and this 'Bigger Fool' theory of investment cannot be relied upon.

In the author's view, the attention given to net asset value per share of property companies — similarly the attention given to the earnings of manufacturing and trading companies — is consistent with the view of dividends as constituting the return on the investment. There are a number of reasons why appearances may belie the reality.

First, in order to gauge dividend prospects the outlook for profits or earnings has to be assessed. For a property company this entails an estimate of growth in net rental income. However, the capital value of a commercial property is assessed as a multiple of the current rent. This multiple reflects the expected growth in rent and the rate of return expected on the property. Indirectly, therefore, an assessment of the net asset value is analogous to an assessment of earnings growth, and hence dividend potential.

Second, as we saw in Chapter 10, accounting earnings are not always representative of economic earnings. This is particularly true of property companies. There is usually a ready market for commercial and industrial property. Growth in the value of the property portfolio should rightly be considered a component of earnings, since the surplus can be realised if desired and would in that event be available for the payment of dividends. Economic earnings of a property company (and also of an investment trust) therefore consist of reported accounting earnings and the increase or decrease in the value of the portfolio. By classifying their assets as fixed (when in fact the distinction between fixed and current assets has no meaning for a property company) and never realising their gains, property investment companies make considerable undisclosed profits. These profits come largely from growth in the portfolio, and the attention given to net asset value per share in the appraisal of quoted property companies can be explained as a shorthand technique (like the P/E ratio for the earnings of manufacturing and trading companies) for taking this important factor into consideration.

Third, as every property analyst is aware, the share price of a property company usually stands at a discount to net asset value per share. The existence of a discount to net assets is not consistent with net assets as constituting the return to the minority shareholder. Why should there be a discount? Furthermore, this discount varies from company to company. In some cases it may be 20%, in others, as much as 40%. As the professional valuation of property takes into account all advantages and disadvantages of the property, there can be no justification for variations in the discount if net assets are the return to shareholders.

Last, as we would expect from the above analysis, there is no statistical evidence that net asset values directly determine companies' stock market capitalisations. The evidence is purely anecdotal. Like other quoted companies, property companies pay dividends, and their pay-out ratio is well above the average. Dividends therefore constitute a part of the return, and net asset backing cannot in any event be the whole story. Shorthand methods which cut corners and fail to consider explicitly the true elements of value are best left to the Stock Exchange professional. The share valuer must base his valuation on the legal entitlement of the minority shareholder — what he can get out of the company. Net asset value per share is not directly relevant in such an exercise.

Asset backing and risk

Although the assets basis should not be used to value minority shareholdings, there is a commonly held view that asset backing per share has an influence on the required rate of return or capitalisation rate. A company with substantial asset backing is seen as a safer investment than one with slender asset backing, other things, i.e., earnings and dividend prospects, being equal.

This view, to which the author at one time subscribed,[1] is unsound. It is based on a calculation of what would be left for the shareholders in a liquidation. If no liquidation is in prospect, however, it makes no sense to rate shares on what would happen if a liquidation took place. Should the company subsequently be compelled to go into liquidation, its circumstances at that time are certain to be totally different from what they are today. It is rare for companies being compulsorily wound up to return anything to their ordinary shareholders. The reader is referred to Chapter 2 under 'liquidation value' for a fuller discussion of this misconception.

The discounted cash flow method

The discounted cash flow technique of valuation is derived directly from the fundamental theory of value. This states that the value of a financial asset is the sum of the present values of the future cash flows (dividends, profits, proceeds of sale) stemming from ownership. The DCF technique consists of two distinct parts. First, an estimate must be done of the amount and timing of all cash flows during the likely period of ownership. Second, a discount rate must be selected and applied to the cash flows to convert them into a present value. The sum of these present values is the value of the project or investment.

Investment projects versus company acquisitions

DCF techniques are commonly used in the appraisal of capital investment projects. Although the acquisition of a company may be viewed as just another, albeit more complex, capital investment, there are important differences between the two. For example, the cost of an internal project is known, the object of the DCF appraisal being to determine the likely rate of return. With the purchase of a company, the object of the DCF exercise is to determine what price it would be worth paying to acquire the business, not what the rate of return is.

Another important difference between the internal project and the acquisition of a company is the latter's status as a self-contained economic and legal entity. It is much more than just the purchase of

---

[1] Christopher G. Glover, 'The Valuation of Unlisted Shares', *Accountants Digest* no 132, Institute of Chartered Accountants in England and Wales, 1983, p. 23.

assets. The claims of other interest groups — preference shareholders, debtholders, creditors and employees — have to be taken into account. Where 100% of the equity is being acquired, the DCF appraisal may be carried out as if the buyer had legal ownership of the business and, hence, complete freedom to dispose of its cash. But, where a controlling interest of less than 100% is acquired, the buyer does not have unfettered discretion as to the use of the company's cash and adjustment must be made to reflect this fact.

The length of the projections is a much greater problem with company acquisitions than it is with capital projects. In the case of the latter, management has the necessary information at hand, backed up by professional experience. Cash flow projections over the longer-term can be made with much greater confidence. By contrast, in most company valuations profits beyond the short- to medium-term are assumed to grow at some reasonable longer-term rate. Precise numerical estimates of profit more than three to five years ahead are extremely difficult and often lack credibility. Furthermore, in the sale of a business the vendor may well be reluctant to divulge all the information required for a full DCF appraisal. This is particularly likely if vendor and purchaser are in the same industry, since disclosure of confidential information could compromise the vendor's position should negotiations fail. It may also weaken his bargaining position when the price is being negotiated.

Typical DCF situations

Despite these considerable practical drawbacks, pure DCF techniques are sometimes used in evaluating acquisitions. If Company A wishes to completely transform Company B or if Company B has a potential under A's ownership that cannot reasonably be evaluated from its historical trading results, full disclosure of information is the only way the price can be fairly determined and is consequently in the interests of both parties. However, DCF techniques are most commonly used where future cash flows can be estimated with some certainty. Companies in property investment and development, leasing and ship finance are obvious examples. The income of this type of business is usually determined on some contractual basis (e.g., tenancy or leasing agreements, charter parties and so on), which considerably simplifies the estimating. The main item of cost is usually interest on borrowings and as these, too, are on a contractual basis, the determination of net income and net cash flow should be straightforward.

The DCF basis is also used where the company is being wound up and all the assets are being converted into cash. The first step is to draw up a statement of affairs showing the estimated realisable asset values, net of realisation expenses and capital gains tax. The estimated liabilities must be deducted. Considerable time and effort may be required to produce reliable estimates and the advice of an insolvency practitioner may be needed where the amounts are substantial. Much uncertainty surrounds the amount and timing of the cash flows. This affects the riskiness of the investment and the timing of distributions. In this type of valuation it is not the cash flow within the company which is discounted but the distributions from the liquidator. The amount and timing of cash flows within the company are important because they indicate the cash surplus, if any, available for investment or distribution. In practice, it may be better to ignore interim distributions and to accrue interest on any cash surpluses. The one and final distribution is then the only cash flow to be discounted. Its net present value (NPV) indicates the value of the shares.

Net present value and price

The net present value (NPV) of the company will not be market value but owner value.[2] It denotes the price the owner, or assumed owner, could justify paying given the assumptions used in the cash flow projections.

A business will generally have a different value to different prospective owners. For example, an industry purchaser will usually view the company in a different light from a complete outsider. Not only will the industry purchaser have a better understanding of the business, but by merging the business with his own, he can expect cost savings or economies of scale. The industry purchaser is also better placed to identify ways of running the business more profitably. Taking these incremental gains into account the purchaser calculates the target company's NPV to him.

If the target company is quoted, its current stock market capitalisation must be below this NPV if the bid is to succeed. The appropriate price to offer is a matter of stock market tactics on which the advice of a merchant bank or stockbroker should be sought. In no circumstances should the offer exceed NPV. Where the subject company is not quoted, price will be a function of each side's owner value in the normal way. This means that the purchaser will have to assess as best he can the vendor's owner value. This will usually turn out to be some vaguely defined idea of what the generality of purchasers might offer for the company.

[2] As mentioned in Chapter 10, the notion of a market value for an entire business is suspect.

The financing of the acquisition — how the purchase consideration should be split between cash, debt and shares — should be seen as a separate exercise from the assessment of NPV. The amount of borrowed funds used should depend on the directors' perception of the level of debt it would be prudent to assume, taking into account the capital structure of the company being acquired. If it has a high proportion of borrowings and the purchaser has to borrow heavily to pay for the acquisition, the merged business may end up with a markedly higher gearing than the buyer had beforehand. If so, it may be better to make a share-for-share offer rather than a cash offer.

Information required

The basic information required for a DCF evaluation of a company is as follows:

(a) Estimates of future annual profits, depreciation and tax payable. As the valuation is intended to indicate the value of the company to the purchaser, profits for this purpose should be the incremental gain, i.e., the difference between the profits estimated to be made by the two businesses combined, and the profits which the purchaser would have made had the acquisition not occurred.
(b) Net movements in working capital in each year.
(c) The net realisable value of all surplus assets and an estimate of the likely delay in selling them.
(d) The amount and timing of capital expenditures.
(e) The amount and timing of loan or debt repayments.

A company's profits after adding back depreciation are rarely received entirely in cash in the year they are earned. They need to be adjusted for net movements in working capital, principally, stocks and work-in-progress, debtors and creditors. As a business grows it requires more and more working capital. Stock and work-in-progress levels rise, as do total customer balances. Supplier credit increases, but this rarely finances all the increase in current assets. In computing the net operating cash flows, therefore, a specific adjustment must be made for net movements in working capital.

This need not be the daunting task it appears at first sight. Rule of thumb methods exist for calculating the effect of expansion on working capital. The percentage of sales method is one of them. First, the approximate relationship of sales to the various components of working capital is established. This can be based on recent year's experience as shown by the firm's financial statements. For example, debtors may have averaged 15% of sales, stocks ten per cent and creditors eight per cent. It is a simple matter, and a revealing exercise, to apply these percentages to forecast sales in each of the years under review and produce a notional working capital requirement. Many companies make no formal estimates of future working capital needs. The results of a simple exercise such as this can come as quite a surprise.

Capital expenditure over the DCF review period must be carefully assessed as to its amount and timing, and brought into the projections in the years in which it occurs. It is advisable here to distinguish between routine replacement expenditure and major capital outlays, such as a new factory or the replacement of a major item of plant. The routine capital expenditures should be brought in as deductions from the annual cash flows. Those larger capital projects, which entail decisions as to the future course and direction of the business, should be discounted separately to form part of the cost of the investment. This in no way alters the total NPV of the investment; it merely highlights the important decision stages in the life of the investment.

Surplus assets, e.g., investments, bank deposits and property, usually produce income and this must be excluded from the net cash flows. Occasionally a whole segment of a business may be considered redundant. In the calculation of its net realisable value it may be necessary to take into account closure costs such as redundancy payments, pay in lieu of notice, loss of retention monies, etc. Any surplus assets or businesses should be evaluated separately from the net operating cash flows. There should be a separate NPV for the surplus assets and a separate NPV for the net operating cash flows.

The treatment of financing needs

Most companies have some form of loan finance in addition to equity funds. As the financing decisions of the company are distinct from its operational performance, it may be useful to evaluate the net operating cash flows separately from the debt finance. This also permits the effect of different financing assumptions to be more easily assessed. Assume, for example, that a company is being evaluated on the DCF basis and the discount rate is 15%. Its capital structure is set out on the following page:

	£000's
Ordinary shareholders' funds	3,000
7% (net) preference shares of £1 each	500
12% unsecured loan stock	1,000
	4,500

The loan stock is repayable at par in five years' time.

Its present value consists of two elements: the present value of £1 million payable five years hence and the present value of an annuity of £60,000 (i.e., £120,000 less 50% tax) for five years. The total NPV of the loan is £698,332 as set out below:

	£
Loan repayment	
£1 million × 0.4972	497,200
Annual interest	
£60,000 × 3.3522	201,132
	698,332

The effect on NPV of replacing the loan with a facility of similar amount but on different terms can easily be calculated. Assume that the loan is replaced on maturity by a medium-term bank loan repayable in equal annual instalments over seven years with a variable interest rate linked to bank base rates. In the absence of any indications to the contrary, interest rates seven years hence are assumed to be the same as now, i.e., 13%. The elements of present value therefore consist of:

(a) an annuity of £60,000 for five years (as before);
(b) interest for seven years on the reducing balance of the medium-term loan; and
(c) repayments of £142,857 at the end of each of years six to 12. The seven annual repayments total £1 million.

The calculation of NPV is set out below:

(a) Annuity of £60,000, NPV as above   £201,132

(b) Interest payments on the medium term loan:

Start of year	Principal outstanding	Interest at 6.5% net	Present value factor (15%)	Present value £
6	1,000,000	65,000	0.4323	28,100
7	857,143	55,714	0.3759	20,943
8	714,286	46,429	0.3269	15,178
9	571,429	37,143	0.2843	10,559
10	428,572	27,857	0.2472	6,886
11	285,715	18,571	0.2149	3,991
12	142,858	9,286	0.1869	1,736

                                                             87,393

(c) Loan repayments:
NPV as at the start of year six of an
annuity of £142,857 for seven years
at 15%

£142,857 × 4.1604   594,342

Present value factor for 5 years at 15%   0.4972

Current NPV   295,507

                                                         584,032

By refinancing the loan notes with a medium-term bank loan NPV increases by £114,300, i.e., £698,332 less £584,032.

The preference shares could be valued like the loan capital as the present value of the future net dividends payable. However, the preference dividend, like the ordinary dividend, is not a charge against profits and is, therefore, a discretionary payment. Where both preference and ordinary share capital is being acquired it may be simpler to include the preference dividend in the equity cash flows, i.e., not deduct it, the resultant NPV being attributable to both preference and ordinary share capital. The allocation of total NPV between preference and ordinary shares can then be decided by the parties to suit their own convenience. If the preference shares are not to be acquired, it would be advisable to deduct the net annual preference dividend from the operating cash flows. Admittedly, the preference dividend is still technically a discretionary payment, but unless the purchaser is prepared to run the risk of a minority action it obviously makes sense to allow for it. If the value of the preference shares is separately computed like the other constituents of capital employed, they would be valued as a perpetuity. Thus, 500,000 preference shares of £1 each would have a present value of £233,333, as set out below:

Net preference dividend	
£500,000 @ seven per cent	£35,000
Discount rate/yield	15%
Net present value	£233,333

If the NPV of the company's loan and preference share capital is computed in this net-of-tax way, care must be taken to ensure that the operating cash flows are stated before interest on borrowings and preference dividends. The tax charge will, in this case, be calculated on the profits before deduction of interest payable. This method, which is the one recommended by Merrett and Sykes,[3] has the advantage that it divorces questions of capital structure and surplus assets from the evaluation of the operating cash flow. However, this is purely a matter of convenience and if surplus assets, loan repayments, and interest charges were all brought into the main cash flow analysis in their appropriate years, the resultant NPV would be the same.

Allowing for a minority interest

Where a controlling interest of less than 100% is being acquired, the entitlement of the minority must be fully reflected. In such a case, the controlling shareholder is not free to use the company's cash resources entirely as he wishes. If cash is lent to one of the purchaser's other companies a market rate of interest must be charged in view of the directors' duty to act in the best interests of the company as a whole, i.e., that of all its shareholders. A proportion of any interest so received is attributable to the minority. Similarly, if cash is reinvested in the business some of the return will accrue to the minority. In the author's opinion, the correct way to take the minority interest into account is by deducting from the NPV of 100% of the equity the proportion attributable to the minority. Thus, if 80% of the equity were being acquired, it would have a NPV

[3] A. J. Merrett and Allen Sykes, *The Finance and Analysis of Capital Projects,* 2nd ed. (London: Longman, 1973), Ch. 13.

equal to 80% of the whole.[4] It may also be appropriate to apply a discount to the full *pro rata* control value to reflect the fact that the purchaser is not acquiring absolute control of the company. In Chapter 10 (under 'the meaning of control') these discounts are discussed. It all depends on the circumstances, including the attitude of the minority. It is not a matter of calculation but of judgement.

Terminal value

The value of the firm at the end of the DCF period has to be estimated and brought into the appraisal either at its discounted present value as a separate item, or by inclusion in the final year's cash flow. If the cash flow projections cover a long period, it may not be worthwhile to devote much time and effort to the assessment of terminal value. As an example, the present value factor for discounting a sum received in 20 years' time at 15% a year is 0.0611. In other words, just over six per cent of the terminal value ends up in NPV.

Where terminal value is material to the assessment of total NPV it should be taken as the going concern value of the firm at the end of the DCF period. The simplest way to estimate this is to value profits in the final year as a perpetuity unless, of course, there is good reason to believe that the firm's prospects at that time would not be worth very much. The discount rate can then be used as the valuation yield. A conservative practice is to value the business as though it were wound up at the end of the period.

The discount rate and the cost of capital

The discount rate transforms the future cash flows into net present value. Failure to choose the appropriate discount rate can be a very costly mistake. Yet there are few rules for determining the appropriate discount rate and the businessman or valuer must be guided largely by his own commonsense and knowledge of the basic principles of investment and valuation. Obviously, the discount rate should exceed the rate of return available on risk-free investments such as gilts. The

---

[4] In *The Finance and Analysis of Capital Projects,* Merrett and Sykes (p. 302) recommend that dividends payable to minority shareholders should be deducted in arriving at equity net cash flows. However, unless all the profits are paid out in dividends some of the cash flow will be attributable to the minority and it would be overstating the value of the majority shareholding to include therein the cash flow attributable to the minority's share of retained profits. If the minority interest is allowed for in the annual equity cash flows, the minority's full share thereof, and not just the amount withdrawn as dividends, should be deducted. In the method suggested in the text no deduction for the minority interest is made in the annual equity cash flows, the appropriate percentage deduction being made from the NPV of 100%.

excess return required will depend on the purchaser's attitude to the perceived degree of risk. Likewise, if a project or investment is to be financed by external debt, the rate of return before tax and interest payable must exceed the going rate of interest. Even where a project is not financed by external debt the rate of return should exceed the general level of interest rates. In practice, of course, the rate of return or discount rate will incorporate a substantial premium for risk and may be twice or three times the risk-free rate. All depends on the risk involved. In Chapter 7 the question of risk measurement and reward was discussed.

The use of a discount rate consisting of the risk-free rate plus a premium for risk has a minor theoretical blemish which should perhaps be mentioned here. The risk-free rate represents the time value of money. In theory, it is the compensation to the lender for forgoing the use of his money during the period of the loan. If the cash flows from a project or investment are of equal amount and riskiness, their risk-adjusted values should be the same. Their present value would then be calculated by applying the 'time preference' or risk-free rate to these risk-adjusted cash flows. However, where the discount rate includes a fixed percentage premium for risk, identical cash flows do not have identical risk-adjusted amounts. This is because of the discounting or compounding effect of the risk premium.[5] This is an interesting point to bear in mind although its practical relevance is probably slight. The notion of the risk-free rate of interest and the risk premium is no more than a helpful abstraction from reality. As shown in Chapter 6, the risk-free rate of return is not free of risk. The process of discount rate determination is not so sharply defined as to enable the risk element to be identified with exactness. Furthermore, the conceptual distinction between risk and uncertainty has not been fully explored. Many writers lump the two together but at least in everyday parlance it is a logically defensible position to argue that, although a project's cash flows are of uniform riskiness, later cash flows are bound to be more uncertain than nearer ones. As such they merit a higher discount rate.

Practical businessmen with extensive experience of their own industries and markets have an excellent understanding of the risks involved and of the rewards to be expected for assuming such risks. The valuer with his experience of valuing businesses in every sort of activity also has a contribution to make in guiding the businessman in making his decision. In practice, a range of net present values would be calculated

[5] See Michael Bromwich, *The Economics of Capital Budgeting* (Harmondsworth, Middlesex: Penguin Books Ltd, 1976), p. 248.

using different but acceptable rates of return. The highest NPV represents the maximum price the purchaser should pay.

If the purchaser is a company, the management might well argue that the discount rate should be determined in the same way as it would be for any other large capital project. Textbooks on capital budgeting and corporate finance are unanimous on this point: the discount rate for capital projects, as for company acquisitions, should be the buyer's cost of capital. What is the cost of capital and why should it be used and not the rate as determined by management in the manner just described?

The cost of capital is a weighted average of the firm's cost of debt and equity. The weights should be based on the target capital structure, that is, the firm's optimal mix of debt and equity. Note that it is not the firm's existing cost of debt or equity which is to be used but its marginal cost. The marginal cost of debt is the interest rate chargeable if the firm were to raise new debt in the market. Likewise, the marginal cost of equity is the rate of return that would have to be offered to investors if new equity were issued. For example, if a company's target capital structure consists of half equity and half debt and its cost of equity is 20% and its cost of debt 12%, the cost of capital is 13%, as follows:

		%
Cost of equity		
50% × 20%		10
Cost of debt		
Gross rate of interest	12	
less tax at 50%	6	
Net of tax rate	6	
50% thereof		3
		13

Interest payable is deductible for tax purposes. As cash flows are generally stated after tax in DCF work, the debt element of the cost of capital has to be expressed net of tax. This puts it on the same footing as the cost of equity. According to the textbooks, management ought to accept any project or investment which has a positive NPV using 13%, i.e. the cost of capital, as the discount rate.

The marginal cost of debt is not difficult to ascertain, particularly where existing borrowing facilities have not been fully drawn down. The cost of equity on the other hand is a different matter. The notion of equity as having a cost is a conceptual construct invented by economists. A company pays nothing for its equity nor does it have any legal liability to return the equity to its shareholders. However, from the shareholders' viewpoint (as the argument goes), equity has an opportunity cost being the rate of return the shareholders could obtain by investing their funds in a company of equal riskiness. By equating the company with the general body of shareholders a company can be said to have an opportunity cost of equity. The word 'opportunity' is dropped for convenience's sake and we are left with the cost of capital.

In theory, if the stock market does its job properly, a company's shares will be priced so that the expected rate of return fully reflects the company's degree of risk.[6] On this analysis the opportunity cost of equity is the rate of return currently available on the company's shares. As explained in Chapter 9, in order to obtain the expected rate of return on a company's shares we need to know the expected growth rate in dividends. But this information is not available — if it exists anywhere, it is in the minds of investors. We could ask a stockbroker or merchant banker but we might well get a different answer from each of them and their views could probably change from one week to the next. Lest we are prevented by this impasse from taking the analysis any further, let us assume for convenience's sake that the growth rate in dividends in recent years is a reliable indication of likely future growth.[7] Let us say, therefore, that over the last five years the dividend has grown at a compound annual rate of 15% and this, plus the current yield of five per cent, gives an estimated rate of return on equity of 20%. This becomes the cost of equity capital. If the firm had no debt and no intention of ever using debt, the textbooks tell us that this firm should invest in all projects with a rate of return of 20% and over.

The cost of equity invariably exceeds the rate of interest — if it did not, people would leave their money in the bank and not invest in equities. Therefore, as a firm increases the debt component in its target capital structure the cost of capital falls. Thus, if interest rates are assumed to be six per cent net of tax, as illustrated above, and the firm decides to increase its debt to one half of total capital, its cost of capital would fall from 20% to 13%, as calculated earlier. According to the theory it should now accept all projects returning 13% or more after tax. Taking this theory to its logical conclusion, the firm should clearly take on as much debt as possible as this can only reduce its cost of capital and bring more investment projects within its profitability criterion. Indeed, this is the remarkable conclusion reached by Miller

[6] According to the Capital Asset Pricing Model, only market risk is reflected in the rate of return. Non-market risk is diversifiable and therefore receives no reward. Chapter 7 provides a critique of the CAPM and modern portfolio theory generally. As to the evidence for efficient markets, see Chapter 6.

[7] *Pace* all those patient researchers whose rigorous academic studies have conclusively established the random walk of earnings and the futility of extrapolating historical trends into the future (see Chapters 6 and 10).

and Modigliani, two eminent American business economists, whose paper on this subject is regarded as a seminal contribution to the theory of the cost of capital.[8] Indeed, such is the prestige of these two economists that the absurdity of their conclusions has in no way cast doubts on the logic of their argument. The conclusions are clearly in flat contradiction to the facts. Every company must keep its borrowings within reasonable bounds. Failure to comply with this elementary rule of commonsense will lead to loss of confidence in the company, and hence a fall in its share price, and ultimately to bankruptcy.[9] The concept of the cost of capital as a weighted average of the cost of debt and equity, therefore, fails the elementary test of logic and practicality. Would it be true, nonetheless, that a firm should accept all investment projects showing a rate of return equal to or greater than the cost of equity? The short answer is no.

There are a number of fundamental objections to any stockmarket-based criterion for the selection of capital or investment projects. First, the Stock Exchange price of a share is not a consensus view, but merely a compromise between widely divergent views on value. Many investors have no informed view of the expected rate of return on a security and most are probably ignorant of the relationship between initial yield and the rate of return. Those who have informed views often differ in their opinions and their subjective evaluations are strongly influenced by their differing tax status. A pension fund, for example, is in a markedly different position from an investor liable to income tax and capital gains tax. Furthermore, there is more than a grain of truth in the Keynsian view of the Stock Exchange as something of a competition, where the object is not so much to invest for the long-term rate of return, but rather to invest on the basis of what one thinks others will think: to buy stocks before they become popular and to sell them before the fashion changes. The considerable resources devoted to fundamental research do not gainsay this view.

Second, inherent in the idea of equity having a cost is the assumption that the general body of shareholders and the company are one and the same. By imputing the typical investor's behaviour to the company the latter can be said to have an opportunity cost of equity. This tendency by economists to ignore the legal structures and 'see through' the company is a cardinal error which has led to numerous misconceptions. Financial assets are legal claims. Their economic nature is vitally

---

[8] Franco Modigliani and Merton H. Miller, 'The Cost of Capital, Corporation Finance and the Theory of Investment', *American Economic Review*, vol 48 (June 1958), pp. 261–297.

[9] These obvious points are acknowledged by most theorists, few of whom would subscribe to Modigliani and Miller's extreme position. What the author finds alarming, however, is that their position is seen as a theoretically respectable one.

affected by the legal structure and it is for this reason that two chapters of this book have been devoted to the legal aspects (Chapters 3 and 4). As these chapters are at pains to point out, a minority shareholder is not a part-owner of the company's business undertaking. The general body of shareholders consisting of a large number of investors, each with a tiny minority holding acting independently of each other, cannot be considered as a proxy for the company.

An individual owning 100% of the equity, however, is in a position analogous to the proprietor of the business and, subject to the claims of creditors and debtholders, his attitudes can be taken as the company's attitudes. He will set a higher value on each of his shares than will the minority shareholder. This reality is demonstrated time and again on the Stock Exchange when take-overs occur. The price bid for 100% of the equity invariably exceeds the minority-determined current share price by a substantial margin. Thus, the purchaser of a controlling interest appraises his investment in a different way from the minority portfolio investor. Likewise a company embarking on capital projects in which its interest will be absolute has a different angle or viewpoint from the portfolio investor. This difference is attributable primarily to the fact that for the minority investor dividends form the return on his shares, whereas for the controlling shareholder and the company itself the earnings of the investment or project are the return.[10]

Third, shareholders do not provide the equity capital in the commonly accepted meaning of the word 'provide'. Very few shareholders have ever subscribed any money for their shares or have ever attended an annual general meeting to see how 'their' directors are running the company and investing 'their' money. New money raised by public issues of shares accounts for a small proportion of the capital requirements of quoted companies. Retained profits are part of equity funds but they could not be withdrawn in practice without bankrupting the company. The idea that shareholders, either individually or collectively, could remove these funds and invest them elsewhere in the same way as money might be switched from one bank to another to take advantage of a higher rate of interest is pure fantasy.

The typical investor buys his shares from another investor whom he does not know and never sees. The Stock Exchange, therefore, is first and foremost a secondary market for investments. The attractiveness of a company's shares as an investment depends on its profitability. Investors seek out companies which make big profits and have bright prospects. Thus, it is the rate of return which a company obtains on its

---

[10] Miller and Modigliani hold the view that dividends and earnings are equivalent and the value of the company is the same, whichever basis of valuation is used. Their paper on this subject is reviewed in Chapter 12.

capital projects which influences the share price and not the share price which determines the rate of return on projects. The tail does not wag the dog.

The vast majority of companies are not quoted. Their cost of capital or cost of equity is not ascertainable even making the simplifying assumptions about dividend growth rates. In fact, the cost of equity in the stockmarket sense has no meaning whatsoever for them. As stated at the beginning of the section, the rate of return a board of directors should seek when appraising an acquisition on the DCF basis (or indeed when investing in an internal capital project) is essentially a matter for its own judgement in the light of borrowing costs, the perceived riskiness of the investment and conditions in the industry. The use of the cost of capital as the hurdle rate for DCF investments puts company acquisitions and project appraisal at the whim and fancy of stockmarket sentiment and confuses cause with effect. In any event, it is not susceptible to accurate calculation even for quoted companies and is meaningless for unquoted ones.

Weighted-average techniques

There sometimes creeps into valuation practice a tendency to hedge one's bets by valuing shares as a weighted average of valuations carried out on different bases. Suppose that a minority shareholding of 12% is being valued. The company makes good profits, pays a reasonable dividend, and has a substantial asset base. In recent years there have been a number of share transfers of small parcels of shares. The valuation is presented as follows:[11]

Valuation basis	Amount £000	Weighting %	Value £000
Assets	2174	15	326
Earnings	4156	20	831
Dividends	1905	55	1048
Prior sales	4125	10	412
			2617
Less discount for non-marketability, say, 35%			916
			1701
12% thereof			204

[11] This example is based on a model valuation in Nigel A. Eastaway and Harry Booth, *Practical Share Valuation* (London: Butterworths, 1983), p. 394. See also p. 329 for their rationale for this basis. A similar technique is advocated in Shannon P. Pratt, *Valuing a Business: The Analysis and Appraisal of Closely Held Companies* (Homewood, Ill.: Dow Jones-Irwin, 1981), p. 260.

The weightings are decided by the valuer bearing in mind the size of the shareholding. In this case the shares being valued are a minority interest of 12% and the heaviest weighting is given to dividends. Presumably, if a controlling interest were being valued earnings would receive the heaviest weighting, followed by assets.

This method of valuation is reminiscent of the Berliner method or dual capitalisation technique. The dual capitalisation approach has two components — the capitalisation of maintainable profits and the valuation of the net tangible assets on a going concern basis. The valuer then takes the average of these two. This technique is usually reserved for controlling shareholdings.

Neither the weighted-average technique nor the Berliner method is inspired by any theory. In what way can the company's assets be relevant to a minority shareholder? What justification is there for including an element of the earnings-based valuation when the outlook for earnings will have been taken into account when dividend growth was assessed? Can the effect of prior sales be disposed of in a mathematical way? Either the previous prices are relevant to today's value or they are not. If they are relevant, their significance will be dominant.

The arguments against the weighted average approach is convincingly stated in US Internal Revenue Service Ruling 59-60, s.7:

> Because valuations cannot be made on the basis of a prescribed formula, there is no means whereby the various applicable factors in a particular case can be assigned mathematical weights in deriving the fair market value. For this reason, no useful purpose is served by taking an average of several factors (for example, book value, capitalised earnings and capitalised dividends) and basing the valuation on the result. Such a process excludes active consideration of other pertinent factors, and the end result cannot be supported by a realistic application of the significant facts in the case except by mere chance.[12]

The rate of return implied by such a valuation is not explicitly considered. This makes it difficult to review the reasonableness of the valuation. Because the weights are purely at the whim of the valuer and cannot be justified by any independent evidence, a valuation presented in this way would be at a serious disadvantage in a court of law or before a tribunal.

---

[12] Reproduced in Eastaway and Booth, *Practical Share Valuation*, p. 456.

Rules of thumb

In certain types of business it may be customary to value using a rule of thumb formula. Examples of such businesses include public houses, petrol stations, small retail outlets and small professional firms. An insurance broker, for example, might seek to sell his business on a multiple of annual commissions; a small accountancy practice might change hands on a multiple of gross fees; a newsagent-cum-general store might be valued at a multiple of the gross profit plus stock at valuation.

Despite their lack of proper theoretical justification, these rule of thumb formulae can serve a useful purpose as a guide to value where the financial statements are unreliable or non-existent. It often happens that valuations thus calculated are difficult to justify on the conventional basis of the future returns. In many cases, this is because the price bid for such business reflects not only the economic profit of the business, i.e., the profit after charging for the working proprietor's reasonable remuneration, but also the purchaser's desire for a particular life style. For example, a village store in a charming but isolated rural spot making no more than a marginal profit may, nevertheless, have a strong attraction to a couple seeking self-employed status and refuge from city life. If the shop has its own accommodation and the couple have the proceeds of the sale of their house available to help with the purchase, the resultant price may well seem high when judged on a conventional basis of valuation. In effect, the return to the purchasers is not just the financial gain but also the highly prized intangible benefits. Where this sort of business requires valuing it is advisable to consult a specialist agency in close touch with the market.

Rule of thumb formulae should never be used to value substantial professionally-managed firms. On the rare occasions where a rule of thumb formula might be in use, this should be employed purely as a cross check against a conventional valuation technique based on the expected future return.

Conclusion

The instances where the assets basis will be appropriate for the valuation of a company as a going concern are rare. It will never be appropriate for a minority interest, since the isolated minority shareholder is in no position to reach the assets. As far as majority interests are concerned, a distinction must be drawn between manufacturing, trading and commercial companies on the one hand and property companies, investment trusts and 'money-box' companies on the other. As regards the former category the golden rule is that the value of a business is a function of its profit earning potential. The assets of a business are only one element in the equation and there is no necessary relation between their balance sheet amount and their separable values or the value of the business as a whole. Trading assets are worth what they can earn as part of a business. There is no justification for taking the aggregate of their individual values, less the liabilities, and treating this as the value of the business as a whole.

Majority interests in investment intermediaries will usually be valued on the assets basis. The reason for this is simple. The assets of such companies are marketable and have a value independent of the earnings of the company. They are purchased by the company precisely because they are marketable and the dealing in such assets is the main object of the company. The shares of a company in liquidation or of one where liquidation is in prospect should be valued on the asset basis. Here, the assets will be realised and the proceeds distributed to shareholders. It is the classic case where asset values form the return on the shares. In a winding up each share has a similar entitlement. Therefore, the value per share should not change with the size of shareholding.

It is popularly believed that asset backing is a measure of a share's risk and that minority interests in property and investment trust companies should be valued by reference to underlying asset values. Both these notions were examined and found to be mistaken or unwarranted.

The DCF basis of valuation is the one which most closely follows the theory of investment value, and as such it is the preferred basis in all cases. However, practical difficulties stand in the way of applying it in its pure form to most share valuations. The main problem lies in the difficulty of obtaining information. A DCF exercise usually entails cash flow projections for ten years or longer. Whilst this might be justifiable for an internal capital project where management have the experience and information to formulate credible long-term estimates, it is a different matter when an outsider examines the long-term future of a company in such a detailed manner. Nevertheless occasions arise where DCF valuations are feasible, particularly where income and expenditure are determined on some contractual basis as in certain property investment companies, leasing businesses and tanker finance companies. The DCF basis of valuation should not be used for valuing minority interests since corporate cash flows are not available to the minority.

Most of the work in a DCF valuation lies in estimating the cash flows. These must include not only profits but depreciation, working capital requirements, major capital outlays and terminal value. Where the aim of a DCF valuation is to show the value of the business to the prospective purchaser, as it normally will be, the cash flows must show the incremental gains and losses arising from the acquisition. Thus, any savings from merging the target firm with that of the purchaser must be included. In setting out the cash flows and calculating net present value it may help to separate the operating cash flows from the financing of the business. In this way the effect on NPV of different financing options can be more readily assessed.

The discount rate will normally be determined by the client in the light of interest rates generally and the degree of risk involved. In practice, a number of discount rates will be used, producing a range of values. The highest NPV should set the upper price limit in any acquisition negotiations. In the case of a corporate purchaser the discount rate should be comparable to the rate of return required on major capital projects, determined as above. According to textbook theory, however, the discount rate should be the firm's cost of capital. In other words, all projects, including acquisitions, which have a positive NPV when discounted at the cost of capital should be accepted.

Because of the crucial importance of the discount rate in DCF evaluations this concept of the cost of capital was examined. It has two components: the cost of debt and the cost of equity. In both cases it is the marginal cost which counts, i.e., the interest rate on new borrowings and the rate of return on fresh equity. The cost of capital is a weighted average of these two components, the weights being the proportions of debt and equity in the company's target capital structure. This concept was shown to be unsound in theory and virtually impossible to put into practice. The cost of debt does not present a problem, although not everyone shares the economist's obsession with what happens at the margin. It is at least an ascertainable figure which has a reality outside the hothouse of the Stock Exchange. The opportunity cost of equity, however, is a different matter. In the author's view, it is an unhelpful theoretical construct which puts a company's investment decisions at the whim and fancy of Stock Exchange prices. It is an unreal concept in that it confuses the investor or shareholder with the company and attributes to him attitudes which in practice he does not have. In claiming that Stock Exchange rates of return should determine the discount rate for capital projects it confuses cause with effect and puts the cart before the horse. It is the profitability of capital projects which determine the level of share prices and not vice versa.

The chapter ended with a brief reference to 'weighted-average' valuations techniques and to rule of thumb formulae. The former, despite their illogical basis, appear to have advocates on both sides of the Atlantic; the latter are mentioned purely for the sake of completeness. They are unlikely to have much practical relevance to the share valuer.

12

Choosing the appropriate valuation basis

In the three preceding chapters, the principal valuation techniques have been considered in detail from the point of view both of their logical justification and their practical application. The purpose of this chapter is to draw together from these and earlier chapters the rules for determining the appropriate basis of valuation for controlling and minority shareholdings. As there is comparatively little controversy as to the appropriate valuation basis for controlling interests, most of the discussion concerns the appropriate basis for valuing minority shareholdings. Although some new arguments are presented in this chapter most of the detailed justification for the positions taken here will be found in one form or another in earlier chapters. The chapter concludes with a discussion of the correct choice of valuation basis when a company purchases its own shares.

Controlling shareholdings

A controlling shareholding in a manufacturing, trading, or commercial company should be valued on the earnings basis since earnings form the return on the shares. The earnings basis is examined fully in Chapter 10 together with a discussion of the nature and various degrees of control. If a firm has surplus assets these should be valued separately and added to the earnings-based valuation. If circumstances permit, a controlling interest may be valued using the discounted cash flow technique explained in Chapter 11. This is in fact the preferred basis in view of its theoretical superiority, but more often than not practical difficulties stand in its way.

Earnings are not normally the most suitable basis for valuing property investment companies, investment trusts and similar 'money-box' companies. A controlling interest in this type of business should be valued on the assets basis since the assets are marketable and have a value independent of the profits of the company. These companies are merely investment intermediaries and a controlling interest, therefore, controls the investments. There is no hard and fast rule as to whether expenses of realisation and contingent capital gains tax on the sales of the assets at their revalued amount should be deducted in full. All will depend on the circumstances of buyer and seller. Where, for example, the purchase of an investment trust company is a 'back door' rights issue and the portfolio of securities will be sold on completion of the acquisition, the seller may have to accept the deduction of these items in full. On the other hand, if he can find a buyer interested in managing the funds he may be able to resist the deduction of at least the expenses of sale.

Sometimes, particularly when a company has been poorly-managed, or where its property has a much higher value than is warranted by the profitability of the business, the break-up value of the company may exceed its going concern value. If so, break-up value, which is calculated on an assets basis, will take precedence over the going concern earnings-based value. Even where the controlling interest carried less than 75% of the votes and cannot pass the special resolution needed to reach the assets, this rule is probably valid since it would still be open to the majority shareholder to have the company realise the break-up values and reinvest the proceeds at a higher return.

Apart from the exceptions noted, asset values, either those in the balance sheet or as individually revalued, are not strictly relevant to the valuation of a going concern. Even the popular notion that high asset backing reduces the risk of an investment and thereby increases going concern value is suspect.[1]

Minority shareholdings

Although valuations of controlling shareholdings often entail much detailed work they are conceptually fairly straightforward; they have many common features and there will usually be ample information available. The same cannot be said of valuations of minority shareholdings. Each minority valuation presents its own unique difficulties; conceptual problems often arise and the information available is frequently inadequate. In these circumstances, the valuer must maintain a rational approach even where this leads to uncomfortable conclusions. This rational approach must be informed by correct valuation principles.

The basic rule is that, in the absence of indications to the contrary, minority shareholdings in unquoted companies should be valued on the dividend basis. This method of valuation is described fully in Chapter 9. The justification for this rule is that the uninfluential minority shareholder in an unquoted company can expect nothing else but dividends by way of cash return on his shares. There is no market in the shares and, even if a buyer could be found, the directors' right to

[1] See Chapter 2, pp. 40–41 and Chapter 11 under 'Asset backing and risk'.

refuse to register the transfer and possibly the existence of fair value pre-emption clauses in the articles make it imprudent to count on much capital gain. If the opportunity of selling at a profit arises, it is a bonus. It will be valued like option money.

Because of these severe drawbacks no one in his right senses invests in a private company as an uninfluential outside minority shareholder. Even if someone were prepared to enter blindly into such a commitment it is hardly likely that the directors or controlling shareholders would sanction the transfer of the shares to him. Yet, despite this, some individuals end up as uninfluential minority shareholders. Almost invariably this is because they have inherited the shares or acquired them by way of gift. When the controlling shareholders retire or die, their shareholdings become divided amongst their children or other kin. The children may seek careers elsewhere and it is not long before their status in the company becomes that of the uninfluential minority shareholder.

Where a company pays no dividends, or where its dividends are purely nominal in amount, the rule that an uninfluential minority interest derives its value solely from the prospect of future dividends is tantamount to saying that such a shareholding is almost worthless. This uncomfortable conclusion is inescapable. Those who cannot accept it will find themselves driven to inventing circumstances or outcomes for which there is no solid basis. The acceptance of this strictly logical approach may become easier in the knowledge that its practical application is extremely limited. In the author's extensive experience of valuing minority interests in private companies — many of which pay little or no dividend — he has never had to conclude that a minority shareholding in a profitable company is virtually worthless.

There are a number of reasons for this. First, many minority interest valuations are required under a legal deed or contract, e.g., the articles of association, a shareholder's side agreement, court order or trust deed. If a fair value is required, then the harsh realities of the minority's position may be mitigated and some of the imbalance between controlling and minority shareholder redressed. At other times, the relevant agreement may stipulate a *pro rata* control value.

Second, hardly any minority interests are valued in a vacuum, i.e., without any purchaser or seller in mind. More often than not, a particular transaction is envisaged. The circumstances of buyer and seller then come into play. The fact that someone wishes to acquire the shares is indicative of a special purchaser since, as previously stated, no one in his right mind buys an uninfluential minority shareholding purely for its investment merits. Perhaps the purchaser is trying to build up a strategic shareholding. It may be that the controlling shareholder is unhappy about the existence of outside minority shareholdings and wants them all in his or his associates' control. Whatever the reason, where a specific transaction is contemplated the price will be a function of each party's owner values. In practice one of the parties, usually the purchaser, will have an owner valuation based on, or related to, control. He may not be prepared to pay this price in full but he certainly would not expect to obtain the shares for a pittance merely because he, the controlling shareholder, had not seen fit to declare dividends.

Third, many small private companies function, at least in economic terms, as partnerships. There will typically be three or more business associates working together, each holding shares in the company. No one shareholder has a controlling interest. Each shareholder regards himself as a partner and hence a part-owner of the undertaking. If this legally erroneous view is shared by all the members, shares will almost certainly change hands at a price based on full control. In any event, if a working proprietor's shares come up for sale other working shareholders will be anxious to ensure that no one member acquires the shares since this could upset the present, perhaps delicate, balance. The retiring member may, therefore, be in a position to hold out for a price well in excess of the bare minority value. Thus, a minority shareholding may have an influence which its legal rights and entitlement belie.

All this underlines that other guiding principle of share valuation: the value of something cannot be stated in the abstract, all that can be stated is the value of the thing in a particular place, at a particular time, in particular circumstances. The questions 'to whom?' and 'for what purpose?' must always be put. This principle is developed in Chapter 1 together with many examples of how it works in practice. Many of those examples are relevant to the valuation of minority interests. The reader is also referred to Chapter 9, under 'non-dividend paying companies', where the points made here are developed in greater depth.

Two further points require mention. First, should minority shareholdings in property investment companies, investment trust companies and similar 'money-box' businesses be valued on a net assets basis apparently like their quoted counterparts, or should they be valued by reference to dividends? Second, is there not a good case for valuing minority interests by reference to their earnings? The first point, and its related one of the relevance of asset backing to the valuation of minority interests, is considered in Chapter 11 under 'The Assets Basis'. It was concluded there that there is no justification for valuing minority shareholdings in property companies any differently from minority shareholdings in any other type of company.

As regards the second point, it was concluded in Chapter 9 that earnings are not the correct basis for valuing uninfluential minority holdings. Consideration of the earnings prospects is vital to a dividend-based valuation, since earnings are the fund out of which dividends are paid. But earnings do not constitute the return to the minority until they are distributed by way of dividend. The attention paid to earnings per share and the widespread use of the P/E ratio in Stock Exchange investment is usually cited as the justification for valuing minority holdings in unquoted companies on the earnings basis. As shown in Chapter 9, however, these appearances do not prove that share prices are determined on the basis that earnings form the return on the shares. They are in fact consistent with the assumption that dividends constitute the return, as indeed is the generally accepted accounting practice for recording investment income.

Investment trust companies, unit trusts and the like do not take credit in their income statements for the underlying earnings attributable to their minority shareholdings, but merely for their dividends. But even if it were proved indisputably that quoted companies' shares were priced by the market solely on the basis of their earnings, this in itself would not determine the point.[2] As stated in Chapter 11, when considering the applicability of the assets basis for minority interests in property companies, there can be no question of the blind unthinking adoption of Stock Exchange investment techniques to the valuation of unquoted shares. Every technique proposed must be justified on some rational basis. There is no justification in law or in fact for regarding earnings as the return to the minority shareholder.

The matter cannot be left entirely at this point, however, because there is a line of argument which holds that earnings 'correctly defined' have the same present value as dividends; that a company's dividend policy has no effect on the value of its shares; and that the whole valuation debate about earnings versus dividends is arid and unnecessary. The proponents of this view are Franco Modigliani and Merton Miller (MM), two financial economists, whose remarkable conclusions as to the optimum level of debt for a company we have already touched

---

[2] Attempts to relate earnings growth to P/E ratios and share prices using statistical techniques have failed to detect much linkage. In Raymond L. Larcier, 'The Rise and Fall of the P/E Ratio', *The Investment Analyst*, no 48 (1977), p. 28, one finds the following: 'Despite every analyst's intuitive feeling that earnings do matter, no positive correlation has been found between continuing earnings growth and prices, neither for a sample of stocks nor for a single share over time. But, on the contrary, there is some correlation with the trend of the index of industrial production and a definite one with the expected moves in interest rates. It can be demonstrated that earnings trends account at best for only 20–25% of the price movement of a given share, thus the P/E ratio, even in its most optimistic acceptance, gives only about one quarter of one's criteria when assessing the desirability of an equity investment.'

upon.[3] MM's paper on the dividend versus earnings question was published in 1963,[4] and despite strong challenges from other theorists,[5] their ideas are broadly accepted in the academic world and in the textbooks on corporate finance. The fact that they also coincide with the beliefs of many investment professionals, very few of whom will have heard of MM and even fewer of whom will have read their paper, is an added reason for subjecting the paper to close examination.

The dividend irrelevance proposition

MM's paper is lengthy, closely argued and, like so much of the 'literature' on finance, prefers the manipulation of mathematical symbols to the use of the English language. To deal with MM's paper satisfactorily it is necessary to provide a general overview and then to proceed to a detailed review of each of the main sections. These sections are as follows:

(a) Effect of dividend policy with perfect markets, rational behaviour, and perfect certainty.
(b) What does the market really capitalise?
(c) Earnings, dividends and growth rates.
(d) Effects of dividend policy under uncertainty.
(e) Dividend policy and market imperfections.

In section (a) MM show that in a perfect market — basically one in which there is no uncertainty about future returns, no tax distortions and no transaction costs — the dividend decision makes no difference to the market valuation of the company. In section (b) they claim to show that the same valuation is produced whether dividends or earnings are capitalised[6] and in section (c), the relations between share price, the rate of profits growth and the rate of growth of dividends are examined. Finally, sections (d) and (e) relax the restrictive assumptions of perfect markets and complete certainty adopted hitherto and

---

[3] See Chapter 11 under 'The discount rate and the cost of capital'.

[4] Merton H. Miller and Franco Modigliani, 'Dividend Policy, Growth, and the Valuation of Shares', *The Journal of Business of the University of Chicago*, 34 (October 1961), pp. 411–433; reprinted in Archer and Ambrosio, pp. 630–659.

[5] See, for example, Myron J. Gordon, 'Optimal Investment and Financing Policy', *The Journal of Finance*, 18 (May 1963), pp. 264–272; reprinted in Archer and Ambrosio, pp. 622–629.

[6] MM in this section broaden the analysis to include two other distinct approaches to the valuation of shares, namely, the discounted cash flow approach and the current earnings plus future investment opportunities approach. They claim that all four approaches produce the same valuation. As these two approaches do not concern us here they have been excluded from an already lengthy review.

attempts to show that the conclusions reached thus far remain valid. These sections are now considered in turn.

(a) Effect of dividend policy with perfect markets, rational behaviour and perfect certainty

Given the assumption that there is complete certainty about the future and hence no risk, every share must have the same expected rate of return throughout the market. As the return on a share consists of the dividends received plus any capital gain or minus any capital loss on sale, the value of a firm's capital can be expressed in simple equation form as follows:

$$(1) \qquad V(t) = \frac{1}{1+\varrho(t)} [D(t) + V(t+1)]$$

where,
  $V(t)$ = the value of the enterprise at time t
  $\varrho(t)$ = the rate of return at time t
  $D(t)$ = the total dividend paid during t to holders of record at the start of t
  $V(t+1)$ = value of the enterprise at the end of the period.

Thus, in the perfect world envisaged, the market capitalisation or share price would be equal to the dividend $D(t)$ plus the value at the end of the holding period $V(t+1)$ (this, of course, would be known in a perfect market), all discounted at the constant rate of return $\varrho(t)$.

This formula, however, overlooks the possibility that during the holding period the company may make a rights issue. MM make a simple adjustment to the formula to take this into account. Thus:

$$(2) \qquad V(t) = \frac{1}{1+\varrho(t)} [D(t) + V(t+1) - m(t+1)p(t+1)]$$

where,
  $m(t+1)$ = the number of new shares (if any) issued during t.
  $p(t+1)$ = the ex dividend closing price at which any new shares are issued.

This formula shows the three possible routes by which current dividends might affect the current market value of the firm $V(t)$, or equivalently the price of its individual shares, $p(t)$. Current dividends will clearly affect $V(t)$ via the first term in the brackets $D(t)$. They might also affect $V(t)$ via the second term, $V(t+1)$, the terminal value. MM insists, however, that since the terminal value must depend on future and not past events, such could be the case only if both:

(a) the terminal value were a function of future dividend policy; and
(b) the current dividend served to convey some otherwise unavailable information as to what future dividend policy would be.

MM assume that the future dividend policy of the firm, i.e., from $t+1$ onwards, is known and is independent of the actual dividend decision in t. (Clearly this is a highly restrictive assumption since a cut in the dividend would generally be interpreted by the market as a sure sign that the company has serious problems. However, let us accept it for the moment.) The terminal value, $V(t+1)$, therefore, is independent of the current dividend decision though it may very well be affected by subsequent dividends. Finally, current dividends can affect the rights issue term, $m(t+1)p(t+1)$, since the higher the dividend payout in any period the more new capital must be raised from external sources to maintain the desired level of investment.

The crux of MM's argument is that any increase in the dividend above the level set by the firm's investment decisions will necessitate a rights issue of an equal and compensating amount. Conversely (although this is not stated, but implied) any reduction in the current dividend would be used to buy in shares in the market.[7] In the perfect market which MM postulate, the amount paid to existing shareholders when their shares are repurchased on the market exactly equals the reduction in the dividend. Thus, in equation (2) altering the current dividend, $D(t)$, does not affect the value of the firm, $V(t)$.

MM prove this mathematically by reformulating the rights issue term, $m(t+1)p(t+1)$, in terms of $D(t)$. If the firm's profit in period t is $X(t)$ and its investment or increase in its holdings of physical assets in t is $I(t)$, the rights issue proceeds, being the excess of investment $I(t)$ over retained profits, $X(t)-D(t)$, become:

(3) $$m(t+1)p(t+1)=I(t)-[X(t)-D(t)]$$

Substituting (3) into (2), the $D(t)$ cancel out and the value of the firm at the start of t becomes:

---

[7] Until recently it has been illegal in the UK for a company to purchase its own shares, and many quoted companies still do not have the necessary powers in their articles of association. This alone invalidates MM's argument as far as UK companies are concerned.

$$(4) \qquad V(t) = \frac{1}{(1+\varrho(t))} [X(t) - I(t) + V(t+1)]$$

The current market value of the firm is equal to the terminal value, $V(t+1)$, plus the excess of profits over investment during the holding period, $X(t) - I(t)$, all discounted by the (universal) rate of return. Since the current dividend, $D(t)$, does not appear in (4) and profits, $X(t)$, investment, $I(t)$, terminal value, $V(t+1)$, and the rate of return, $\varrho(t)$, are all by their nature, or by assumption, independent of $D(t)$, it follows that the current value of the firm must be independent of the current dividend decision.

But what about future dividend decisions? As MM point out, future dividend decisions can only affect $V(t)$ via their effect on the terminal value, $V(t+1)$. It is a simple matter to repeat the reasoning above, showing that $V(t+1)$ — and hence $V(t)$ — is unaffected by dividend policy in $t+1$; that $V(t+2)$ — and hence $V(t+1)$ and $V(t)$ — is unaffected by dividend policy in $t+2$; and so on for as far into the future as we like. MM then conclude that, given a firm's investment policy, the dividend payout policy it chooses to follow will affect neither the current price of its shares not the total return to its shareholders. 'It is after all', affirm MM, 'merely one more instance of the general principle that there are no "financial illusions" in a rational and perfect economic environment. Values there are determined solely by "real" considerations — in this case the earning power of the firm's assets and its investment policy — and not by how the fruits of the earnings power are "packaged" for distribution.'

Because investors are not endowed with prophetic foresight, because equity investment is by definition risky, because the rate of return varies from company to company and from day to day, because companies can borrow funds as well as issue new equity, because issue costs are considerable and because taxes do exist and create significant distortions, it is tempting to dismiss MM's conclusions as an irrelevant abstraction meriting the rejoinder, 'true, but so what?' Although later on we examine MM's argument when they relax these other worldly assumptions and introduce uncertainty, it is as well, nevertheless, to ensure that this innocent and apparently obvious line of reasoning, which is an important first step, has no flaws in it.

It is of course true, and it needs no mathematical exposition to prove it, that if a board of directors makes a fixed and irrevocable decision to invest a certain sum and this can be met entirely out of retained profits given current dividend policy, any increase in the dividend will leave the company short of cash and, given all the other assumptions, necessitate a rights issue. But, is this equivalent to saying that dividend policy in general has no effect on the value of the shares?[8] MM concentrate on discrete time periods, t, $(t+1)$, $(t+2)$, etc., in which there always exists a terminal value which partly by definition and partly by assumption is invariably independent of the then current dividend. They go on to show that the dividend in each period has no affect on the share price at the beginning of the period. If the number of periods were extended infinitely in time, however, the absurd conclusion would be reached that, as no dividend can be found which affects the current share price, dividends in total have no effect on the value of the shares. However, this conclusion is flatly contradicted by equation (1) which shows that dividends form part of the return on shares and, hence, influence their value. MM's conclusion is, therefore, negated by the very equation on which it is premised.

Since the fifth century BC, Zeno's paradox of Achilles and the tortoise has stood as a reminder of the futility of viewing time (or space) as a series of extended units and not as a continuum.[9] MM's analysis is just another example of this absurd, misconceived line of reasoning. As will be seen later, this fundamentally erroneous conceptual framework is used to prove their proposition when the certainty assumption is relaxed. The conclusions of their paper are, therefore, vitiated by fundamental error. But this is not the only example of faulty reasoning. For instance, MM's conclusions depend on dividend policy in each period examined being independent of policy in the subsequent (or preceding) period. However, if we took time to be a yearly interval, as we are entitled to do, each year's dividend cannot be independent of every other year's dividend since 'policy' must by definition apply to more than one year and must indicate some continuity.

What MM seem to be saying, in a very tendentious and roundabout way, is that given dividend policy — not investment policy — it matters not if a firm reduces its dividend this year because in the abstract world assumed for this purpose, the present value of the increased dividends resulting from the higher retained profits will exactly equal the reduction in the current dividend. Assume, for example, that the current dividend is £100 and that ϱ, the rate of return available both to a company and investors, is ten per cent per annum. If the dividend is halved the firm will have an extra £50 which can be invested at ten per cent per annum *ad infinitum*. The increase in future dividends will,

---

[8] By dividend policy is meant the decision to reduce or increase the payout ratio; it is assumed that the policy is to pay out dividends. MM rule out in their analysis 'certain pathological extreme cases . . . the legendary company that is expected *never* to pay a dividend'.

[9] If Achilles gives a tortoise a handicap he can never overtake. For when Achilles reaches where the tortoise starts, then the tortoise will have moved on. When Achilles gets there, then the tortoise will have got a little further, and so on, indefinitely.

therefore, be £5 in perpetuity. This has a present value, using a discount rate of ten per cent, of £50 — exactly equal to the dividend cut. If the dividend were cut in any year there would be an equal and offsetting rise in the share price.

(b) What does the market 'really' capitalise?

In this section MM set out to demonstrate that four distinct approaches to the valuation of shares are in fact equivalent. These are:

(a) the discounted cash flow approach;
(b) the current earnings plus future investment opportunities approach;
(c) the stream of dividends approach; and
(d) the stream of earnings approach.

Of these only (c) and (d) directly concern us here. It is worth mentioning *en passant*, however, that as MM's earnings, X, in section (a) were assumed to be received in cash, proving the equivalence of their valuation formula to the DCF basis presented no great difficulty. Approach (b) is based on the super-profits concept. This views the worth of the enterprise as depending on the 'normal' return which can be earned on the firm's assets and any excess return or super-profits, the capitalised value of which is sometimes referred to as goodwill.[10] MM's proof of the equivalence of this approach is not reviewed here despite the reader's understandable curiosity as to how in a perfect market characterised by rational behaviour and complete certainty there could ever be projects offering rates of returns in excess of the one and only risk-free rate, ϱ.

The dividend approach values a company's shares as the present value of the future stream of dividends. Chapter 9 considers this valuation basis in detail, making it unnecessary to repeat MM's exposition here. What interests us, however, is MM's demonstration of the equivalence of the earnings approach and the dividend approach since, if MM's arguments are sound, the point repeatedly made in this book that dividends and not earnings are the return for the uninfluential minority is a confusing irrelevance to say the least.

MM's argument is disarmingly simple. First, we must be clear about earnings. 'Unfortunately', state MM, 'it is [also] extremely easy to mistake or misinterpret the earnings approach as would be the case of the value if the value of the firm were to be defined as simply the

---

[10] See Chapter 8.

discounted sum of future total earnings.[11] The trouble with such a definition is not, as is often suggested, that it overlooks the fact that the corporation is a separate entity and that these profits cannot freely be withdrawn by the shareholders, but rather that it neglects the fact that additional capital must be acquired at some cost to maintain the future earnings stream at its specified level. The capital to be raised in any future period is, of course, $I(t)$, and its opportunity cost, no matter how financed, is $\varrho\%$ per period thereafter'.[12] Hence, the current value of the firm under the earnings approach is stated by MM as:

$$(5) \qquad V(0)=\sum_{t=0}^{\infty}\frac{1}{(1+\varrho)^{t+1}}\left[X(t)-\sum_{t=0}^{t}\varrho I(t)\right]$$

This rather daunting equation expresses a very simple concept. It is that the current value of a company's shares, $V(0)$, is equal to the discounted future earnings, the discount rate being ϱ and earnings being the term in square brackets. The first summation sign indicates that the earnings stream to infinity is to be discounted. MM then proceed to show by mathematical manipulations, which need not concern us here, how this formula is equivalent to that used for the dividend valuation approach.

We can ignore the mathematical manipulations for the simple reason that, as we shall now see, the redefined earnings term in brackets in equation (5) is, by definition, always equal to the firm's dividend. By redefining earnings as dividends it is not altogether surprising, and needs no display of mathematical prowess to prove, that the stream of earnings approach 'as properly defined' is indeed equivalent to the stream of dividends approach.

The redefined earnings term in equation (5) consists of two parts: the by now familiar notation for the profit of the period, $X(t)$, and a summation sign of the cost, $\varrho\%$ per period, of financing the investment, $I(t)$, for ever more. We saw in section (a) that $I(t)$ must relate to investment expenditure in excess of the depreciation provision (investment here includes expenditure on both fixed and working capital). This $I(t)$ must be financed either by borrowings or by retained earnings.[13] However, to the extent that investment, $I(t)$, has been financed

[11] In a footnote MM state: 'In fairness, we should point out that there is no one, to our knowledge, who has seriously advanced this view'. The belief that the value of a company's entire equity, if not its stock market capitalisation, should be the discounted sum of its future total earnings is widely held in the investment and financial world. Such apparent ignorance of market realities does not augur well for an attempt to 'redefine what the market *really* capitalises'.

[12] Miller and Modigliani, p. 641.

[13] As $V(0)$ equals the current market capitalisation MM's formula excludes the possibility of a rights issue.

by borrowings, interest will have been paid and deducted in arriving at profits $X(t)$. The term $\varrho I(t)$ in equation (5) must, therefore, refer to that part of investment expenditure financed by retained profits. Now the present value of a perpetuity of $\varrho I(t)$ discounted at ϱ must be $I(t)$. The term,

$$\sum_{t=0}^{t} \varrho I(t),$$

is therefore identical to retained profits and MM have merely defined earnings as profits less retained earnings, i.e., dividends. This in fact is borne out by their subsequent manipulation of equation (5) to produce the following:

(6)
$$V(0) = \sum_{t=0}^{\infty} \frac{1}{(1+\varrho)^{t+1}} [X(t) - I(t)]$$

Comparison of equation (5) with (6) shows indeed that the term,

$$\sum_{t=0}^{t} \varrho I(t),$$

is equivalent to $I(t)$.

MM have merely indulged in a meaningless manipulation of accounting identities. They have proved nothing. The absurdity of their 'theorem' would have become immediately apparent had they descended from their rarified world of abstract theory and deigned to introduce a practical real world example. Any discussion of what the market 'really' capitalises must start with what the market 'really' understands by earnings and dividends. What evidence is there that the market thinks the earnings of a company are anything other than its audited reported results? These are the figures which analysts adjust in order to discern trends. It is these figures which determine what is available to the shareholder and influence his valuation. A share in a company is purely a creation of law conferring on the holder an entitlement specified by law. 'Real' earnings are the earnings the shareholder is legally entitled to; any arbitrary definition such as that introduced by MM has no legal, and therefore practical, significance.

(c) Earnings, dividends and growth rates

This section is in the nature of a digression in which, before moving on to relax the basic assumptions of sections (a) and (b) (perfect markets, certainty, etc.), MM 'clear up' a number of misunderstandings about the relation between the stream of profits and the stream of dividends per share, and settle scores with other theorists who take an opposing view. It in no way redeems the tautology of their dividend irrelevance proposition or the unsound reasoning of section (a), and no useful purpose would be served by reviewing it here.

(d) The effects of dividend policy under uncertainty

In this section MM consider the effect on their analysis of dropping the 'perfect certainty' assumption. Note that this still leaves in place the assumption of perfect markets and rational behaviour, the former indicating equal and costless access to information for all traders, no tax differentials between dividends and capital gains, and no transaction costs. As regards the latter, MM make the assumption that not only is the trader rational in the previous sense of preferring more wealth to less, irrespective of the form an increment in wealth may take, but he imputes rationality to the market. This rules out the possibility of speculative behaviour based on the 'Bigger Fool' theory of investment.

MM ask us to suppose that current investors believe that the future stream of total earnings and total investment, whatever actual values they may assume at different points in time, will be identical for two firms, 1 and 2. Total future dividends from period 1 onwards are also believed to be identical, so that the only way in which the two firms differ is possibly with respect to the prospective dividend in the current period 0. Using the previous notation the assumption is, therefore, that:

$$\tilde{X}_1(t) = \tilde{X}_2(t)$$

$$\tilde{I}_1(t) = \tilde{I}_2(t)$$

$$\tilde{D}_1(t) = \tilde{D}_2(t)$$

the subscripts 1 and 2 indicating the firms and the tildes ($\sim$) being added to the variables 'to indicate that these are to be regarded from the standpoint of current period, not as known numbers but as numbers that will be drawn in the future from the appropriate probability distributions'.[14]

According to MM, the return, $\tilde{R}_1(0)$ to the current shareholders in firm 1 during the current period will be:

(7) $$\tilde{R}_1(0) = \tilde{D}_1(0) + \tilde{V}_1(1) - \tilde{m}(1)\tilde{p}_1(1)$$

the terms on the right hand side being the current dividend $\tilde{D}_1(0)$, the terminal value $\tilde{V}_1(1)$ and any rights issue proceeds, $\tilde{m}_1(1)\tilde{p}_1(1)$. As the rights issue term must be equal to the excess of investment over retained profits, i.e., $\tilde{I}_1(0) - [\tilde{X}_1(0) - \tilde{D}_1(0)]$, equation (7) can be reformulated as follows to:

(8) $$\tilde{R}_1(0) = \tilde{X}_1(0) - \tilde{I}_1(0) + \tilde{V}_1(1)$$

(Recall that an identical transformation was made in section (a) when equation (4) was developed from equation (2).)

By a similar process the return to the current shareholders in firm 2 can be stated as:

(9) $$\tilde{R}_2(0) = \tilde{X}_2(0) - \tilde{I}_2(0) + \tilde{V}_2(1)$$

MM then compare $\tilde{R}_1(0)$ with $\tilde{R}_2(0)$. The terminal values, $\tilde{V}_1(1)$ and $\tilde{V}_2(1)$, can depend only on prospective future earnings, investment and dividends from period 1 onwards and these are by assumption identical for the two companies. Thus, every investor must expect $\tilde{V}_1(1) = \tilde{V}_2(1)$. As also by assumption, $\tilde{X}_1(0) = \tilde{X}_2(0)$ and $\tilde{I}_1(0) = \tilde{I}_2(0)$, $\tilde{R}_1(0)$ must equal $\tilde{R}_2(0)$. But, claim MM, if the return on two investments is the same, rationality requires that they have the same price so that $V_1(0)$ must equal $V_2(0)$ regardless of any difference in dividend payments during period 0.

This analysis is then extended to subsequent periods in a line of proof identical to that used in section (a) where perfect certainty was assumed. In MM's words:

> Suppose now that we allow dividends to differ not just in period 0 but in period 1 as well, but still retain the assumption of equal $\tilde{X}_i(t)$ and $\tilde{I}_i(t)$ in all periods and of equal $\tilde{D}_i(t)$ in period 2 and beyond. Clearly, the only way differences in dividends in period 1 can effect $\tilde{R}_i(0)$ and hence $V_i(0)$ is via

[14] MM, p. 651.

$\widetilde{V}_i(1)$. But, by the assumption of symmetric market rationality, current investors know that as of the start of period 1 the then investors will value the two firms rationally and we have already shown that differences in the current dividend do not affect current value. Thus we must have $\widetilde{V}_1(1) = \widetilde{V}_2(1)$ — and hence $V_1(0) = V_2(0)$ — regardless of any possible difference in dividend payments during period 1. By an obvious extension of the reasoning to $\widetilde{V}_i(2)$, $\widetilde{V}_i(3)$ and so on, it must follow that the current valuation is unaffected by differences in dividend payments in any future period and thus that dividend policy is irrelevant for the determination of market prices, given investment policy.[15]

The reader will recognise this line of argument as the fallacious 'Achilles and the tortoise' approach encountered in section (a). Here, as there, it produced the absurdity that as no single dividend payment can be found which influences the share price, dividends cannot form part of the return on the shares. But there are other equally damaging shortcomings in the analysis.

In section (b) MM introduced their definition of the earnings the market 'really' capitalises. This was as follows:

$$X(t) - \sum_{t=0}^{t} \varrho I(t)$$

as in equation (5).

As shown earlier, and as MM themselves demonstrate, this reduces to $X(t) - I(t)$. Accordingly, the earnings investors 'really' capitalise in period 0 are $\widetilde{X}(0) - \widetilde{I}(0)$. When the rights issue term in equation (7) is replaced by the accounting identity $\widetilde{I}_1(0) - [\widetilde{X}_1(0) - \widetilde{D}_1(0)]$, there must be substituted for the 'misunderstood' earnings, $\widetilde{X}_1(0)$, the earnings the market 'really' capitalises, i.e. $\widetilde{X}_1(0) - \widetilde{I}_1(0)$. This produces the formula:

$$(9) \qquad \widetilde{R}_1(0) = \widetilde{X}_1(0) - 2\widetilde{I}_1(0) + \widetilde{V}_1(1)$$

The same revision is necessary to equation (4) in the certainty world. It would be revealing to have MM's comments on this absurd formula which is derived from their definition of the earnings the market really capitalises.

[15] Ibid., p. 652.

The reader who has followed the reasoning thus far in an attempt to detect the logical consequences of dropping the vital certainty assumption is no doubt intrigued to see that the formulations and the proof are, as MM admit, essentially analogous to the proof for the certainty world. The only difference is that the same variables now have a tilde to denote the uncertainty. The reader may well be excused for questioning the necessity of the certainty assumption in the first place when an ubiquitous squiggle is all that is needed to transform the multi-faceted reality of the market place — the untidy world of investors' differing opinions, expertise, perceptions and sentiment — into the neat specific symbols of mathematical notation.

But can uncertainty be disposed of in such a sweeping, almost cavalier, fashion? MM state that the tildes indicate that the variables must be regarded not as known numbers but as numbers that will be drawn in the future from the appropriate probability distributions. However, by introducing the assumption that all investors believe that the future streams of earnings, dividends (except for period 0) and investment will be identical for the two firms, and by covering the variables with tildes, all that MM have done is to transfer the certainty assumption from the actual outcome to belief in the outcome. Conceptually, of course, no outcome can have complete certainty, save death; so the original certainty assumption must be about the certainty with which investors hold their beliefs about future outcomes. Thus in section (a) every investor was assumed to have 'complete assurance . . . as to the future investment program and the future profits of every corporation'.[16] But is this 'complete assurance' in the certainty world different in any important respect from the unanimous belief on the part of the investors as to the future for firms 1 and 2 in the uncertainty world? The fact that the numbers (for profit, investment, etc.) will be drawn from the appropriate probability distribution is neither here nor there if everyone believes that the particular variable will have one and the same value. One may well ask, in fact, what is meant by 'the appropriate probability distribution'. It suggests a set of objective, independently-determined probabilities for a given outcome, say, profits in year 2. They cannot be frequency-based probabilities since they are not repeated many times. They must, therefore, be the subjective probability distributions in the minds of current investors. If that is so, it is misleading to talk of these numbers as not known but drawn at random from the celestial tombola barrel by the hand of Fate.

What then is the key change when the certainty assumption is dropped? In a world of certainty, it will be recalled, there would be no

16 Ibid., p. 631.

risk and, consequently, there would be a uniform rate of return on all investment. It was this oddity which led to the conclusion that in such a theoretical world and given a target or policy pay-out ratio a cut in the dividend now would lead to an increase in future dividends, such that the present value of that increase would equal the current reduction. In the real world of uncertainty, where rates of return vary considerably over time and between companies, no such generalisation can be made. Furthermore, in the uncertainty world the cost of borrowing is usually well below the rate of return on equity; and, of course, interest is tax deductible. It may well pay a company to finance its growth in whole or in part by borrowings, thus releasing funds for the payment of dividends.

MM's analysis of dividend policy and leverage, and indeed their analysis ignoring leverage, still assume a perfect market, i.e., no tax differentials. Only the certainty assumption is dropped. Their 'proof' incorporating borrowing (leverage) is modelled on the 'Achilles and the tortoise' approach employed elsewhere in their paper, and, as in the immediately preceding analysis, the ubiquitous use of the tilde takes care of uncertainty. Instead of the total market value of the firm being equity alone, $\tilde{V}_1(1)$ and $\tilde{V}_2(1)$ are interpreted as debt plus equity.

Before moving on to the final stage of their paper in which the assumption of perfect markets is relaxed, MM consider what they term the informational content of dividends. In section (a), it will be recalled, MM made the assumption that dividend policy beyond the current period is independent of the dividend now. They acknowledge, however, that in practice a change in the dividend rate is often followed by a change in the market price. This, they say, does not negate the dividend irrelevance proposition since an unexpected cut in dividend often acts as a signal to investors that something is wrong of which they were not aware. The dividend change, in other words, provides the occasion for the price change though not its cause. This may well be so.

(e) Dividend policy and market imperfections

No doubt because they feel that their point has been adequately proved in their earlier sections, MM do not launch into a detailed analysis of the effect of the various departures from strict perfection and limit themselves to a few general observations about imperfect markets.

The first point they make is that what counts is not imperfection *per se*, but only imperfection that might lead an investor to have a systematic preference between a dollar of current dividends and a dollar of current capital gains. A tax differential in favour of capital gains at the expense of dividends is clearly a major systematic imperfection of this type. MM suggest here that a 'clientele effect' will be at work.

Each corporation will attract to itself a 'clientele' consisting of those preferring capital gain or income as the case may be, 'but one clientele would be entirely as good as another in terms of the valuation it would imply for the firm'.[17] But a preference for capital gain over income, or vice versa, is never absolute and it is naïve to imagine that investors can conveniently be herded into two distinct camps. Every investor wishes to maximise his rate of return and if he can make more money by investing in a growth stock, even though an income stock would be more tax efficient, he will do so.

But it is not just imperfections resulting in a systematic preference as between current dividend and current capital gain which count; any imperfection which upsets the theoretical equivalence of the dividend reduction and the present value of the resultant change in the dividend stream is also of relevance. Here we might mention the tax advantage of interest on debt. If the future dividend is increased and the firm makes up its cash requirement for investment by borrowing, the after tax cost of debt will almost certainly be less than the cost of equity and should, in theory, lead to an increase in value.

The possibility of the firm making good a dividend increase out of the proceeds of a rights issue features prominently in MM's arguments. Because of market imperfections, however, no firm would conceivably act in this manner. As a rights issue is expensive both in commissions and management time it would only be used to raise a substantial sum, and then only sparingly. In imperfect markets, transactions can have an appreciable effect on the market ruling price. Those investors who sell some shares to make up the shortfall in dividend may well drive the price down.

This necessarily detailed and lengthy examination of MM's paper has shown their dividend irrelevance proposition to be based on an unsound conceptual framework. The 'Achilles and the tortoise' approach used throughout their analysis leads to the absurd conclusion that, as no single dividend can be found which has influenced the share price, dividends cannot form part of the return on the shares. In demonstrating the equivalence of the earnings stream and dividend stream approaches to valuation, we saw that MM's proof rests on their own definition of earnings and not the one used by investors. It was shown that MM's redefined earnings are nothing more nor less than the dividend payments, rendering their conclusions totally meaningless.

[17] Ibid., p. 654.

When MM proceeded to drop the certainty assumption no real change took place since the assumption of a unanimously held opinion by rational investors as to the profits, dividends and investments of the two firms merely transferred the certainty from the actual outcomes to belief in the outcomes, these then assuming a tilde. This is a semantic distinction of no real difference. MM failed to address the problem which arises under uncertainty of a multiplicity of rates of return and in particular of the likelihood that the rate of return available to the company on its projects will be different from its cost of equity. Under uncertainty, too, the cost of borrowing will usually be lower than the cost of equity.

As for the effect of market imperfections, MM do not consider these in detail but they suggest that such imperfections that might cause investors to exhibit a systematic preference between dividend and capital gain could easily be counteracted by what they term the 'clientele' effect. However, as we saw, this is a rather naïve idea more appropriate to the world of certainty, perfect markets and robot-like rationality. MM ignored the important effect of tax-deductibility on the cost of borrowing (rendering it much cheaper than equity), and market imperfections in the real world (costs, time, adverse market reaction) which would preclude companies from continually raising money by rights issues.

MM's objective in their paper was not to develop a fully-fledged theory of what does determine market value under uncertainty, but to show at least that dividend policy is not one of the determinants. It will be abundantly clear by now that at every stage of their argument, even under the most restrictive, unrealistic assumptions, the analysis is fundamentally deficient and no helpful conclusion can be drawn from it. It stands as a classic example of the dangers of the modern approach to the development of theory — the theorist is given complete licence to introduce whatever assumptions he chooses; this enables him to transform the subject into something akin to a natural science, like physics or chemistry, where laws have immutable effect and mathematics is an ideal language. From this a theory is developed which, despite the incredible assumptions and doubtless because of the display of mathematical prowess, tends to impress. Finally, and very much as a secondary matter, the assumptions are 'relaxed'. The mathematical approach is retained despite its unsuitability for modelling the infinitely subtle world of investment and of the human mind. Thus, the most striking weaknesses of the MM paper lie in the two final sections where the effects of uncertainty and market imperfections are given such short shrift. No attempt was made to give practical, real world examples.

There is a commonsense view of dividend policy which can be expressed with greater economy and clarity, if not with the same degree of 'rigour'. It runs as follows. If a company is growing fast it will need extra capital. If the firm already has what it regards as its ideal mix of debt and equity, it will endeavour to fund its investment expenditure in these proportions. If likely future retained profits on the present payout policy are insufficient to provide in full the desired equity contribution to investment expenditure, it may make sense to reduce the payout ratio and thereby retain more profit. This will have two effects, both of which should exert an upward influence on the share price. First, failure to retain sufficient profit would force the firm to increase its debt: equity ratio or alternatively abandon its investment programme. Both of these outcomes would depress the share price. An appropriate increase in retentions avoids this. Second, if as assumed, the investment programme should generate a rate of return well in excess of the cost of equity, the incremental stream of dividends should have a net present value greater than the current dividend cutback.

On the other hand, when a firm with little or no growth in prospect reduces its dividend the opposite effect will take place. At best the cut in dividend will lead to a corresponding increase in cash balances; more likely, however, it will be insensibly absorbed in increased stocks, work-in-progress or debtors, or used to reduce creditors. Either way it will not produce an incremental stream of future dividends which compensate for the present cut. Lowering the payout ratio in such circumstances will have a downward influence on the share price. Dividend policy quite clearly has an effect on the share price.

As for the irrelevance proposition — the notion that the same valuation is produced whether using the dividends stream approach or the earning stream one — this is not true in the practical world (nor, indeed, in the world of theory). Earnings as generally understood, and not as redefined by MM, exceed dividends by a substantial margin. The same rate of return applied to the stream of earnings must, therefore, produce a higher figure than when it is applied to the dividend stream. As indicated in Chapter 9, the difference may not be so marked when the P/E ratio is used. This is because the P/E ratio is merely the ratio of price to a single year's earnings and is not a discounting mechanism. It will be very noticeable, however, where the stream of earnings approach is adopted.

MM's paper was published over two decades ago and we could be criticised for ignoring subsequent work in this field, some of which concedes a signalling role for dividends. However, MM's paper is regarded as a classic and it has had, and continues to have, a formative influence on the development of theory. By tackling this error at its source, we lay the axe to the root.

The purchase by a company of its own shares

In Chapter 3 a brief outline was given of the powers contained in the Companies Act 1985 which enable a company to purchase its own shares. These were first enacted in the Companies Act 1981. Although the introduction of this concession represented a legal landmark it would not have assumed much practical importance without the passing of the Finance Act 1982 which removed a serious tax disadvantage. Under s.233 of the Income and Corporation Taxes Act 1970, where a UK resident company purchases shares from one of its shareholders the company is regarded as making a 'qualifying distribution'. This means in effect that that part of the payment in excess of the original subscription price is treated as a dividend and the company must account for ACT on it. The distribution is treated as income in the hands of the shareholder in the same way as a dividend. The Finance Act 1982 made two important exceptions to this rule as it affects unquoted companies. Under s.53 the purchase by an unquoted company of its own shares will not be treated as a distribution where, either:

(a) the purchase is made wholly or mainly for the purpose of benefiting the trade; or
(b) the whole, or substantially the whole, of the payment is applied in discharging a liability for capital transfer tax charged on a death, and undue hardship would otherwise arise.

The Finance Act 1982 lays down a procedure for obtaining advance clearance that a proposed purchase meets one of these requirements.

Although this measure is still in its infancy it is hardly in doubt that it has made a major impact on the private company shareholder. It provides a useful new means whereby retiring shareholders can liquidate their investment and dissident minorities can be bought out. It also provides an important stimulus to the introduction of outside equity finance. However, our purpose here is not to review the legal and fiscal formalities[18] but to consider some of the novel valuation problems which can arise when a company purchases its own shares.

The fundamental rule that the owner values of buyer and seller should be taken into account when valuing shares in unquoted com-

---

[18] A detailed discussion of the legal procedures and taxation formalities of a company buying its own shares can be found in Michael Renshall and Roger White's 'Purchase of Own Shares', *Accountants Digest No. 136* (London: Institute of Chartered Accountants in England and Wales, 1983).

panies is difficult to apply when the company is the purchaser. From the company's standpoint, any sum paid out for the purchase of its own shares is pure loss. However, because the assent of the remaining shareholders is required and because the value of their shareholdings will be affected by the share purchase, their owner values will clearly be a major factor influencing the price. The other dominant influence is the company's financial position since this sets the upper limit on the price. If the company has not got sufficient cash resources the vendor may have to accept a lower amount.[19]

If a controlling interest is being bought in, the chances of receiving full value will diminish as the size of the shareholding increases. Obviously, no trading company can afford to buy in all its equity as this would leave it with no capital to trade. No company would be able to finance such a purchase, irrespective of the legal and fiscal problems of such a move. Most companies would be hard pressed to pay full value for a bare majority shareholding, but their chances of doing so are much greater for a 51% shareholding than they are, say, for a 75% one. Thus in valuing shares for a company buy-in there will normally be a 'reverse discount' for size, at least for controlling interests. In other words, the price per share is likely to fall off steeply as the size of the shareholding rises. This, of course, is the opposite of the effect one would normally expect. When this reverse discount operates, the value of the remaining shares will usually rise, producing an unintended but inevitable element of gift from vendor to the remaining shareholders.

When there are only two shareholders or where each of the remaining shareholders has the same number of shares, the valuation should proceed as if the vendor was selling his shares directly to the remaining shareholders, (subject, as always, to the financial position of the company and any constraints of the legal and fiscal requirements). The reason for this is that after the buy-in, the remaining shareholders will have the same position *vis-à-vis* each other as they had before it. Assume, for example, that a company has four shareholders each owning 25% of the equity. If the company purchases the shares of one of the members, the remaining shareholders will still be on equal terms with each other. The same effect would be achieved even where the vendor has a different size of shareholding than the others, For example, a company may have one controlling shareholder with 55% of the equity and three other shareholders with 15% each. If the company were to purchase the 55% shareholding the remaining shareholders would each have a one-third stake in the company.

[19] There may be other constraints, too, such as, the lack of sufficient distributable profits.

Where a company's shares are held in this convenient pattern each of the remaining shareholders has the same owner value and this simplifies considerably the assessment of a fair price. If the remaining shares are not held in equal amounts, the purchase by a company of its own shares can upset the existing relationships considerably. A first step, therefore, is to add up the remaining shares and express each member's holding as a percentage of this total. This will produce each remaining shareholder's percentage holding in the reduced share capital. This should then be compared with the existing percentage interest to ascertain the effect of the buy-in. Consider, for example, a company whose share capital consists of 100 ordinary shares with A holding 45 shares, B, 35 shares and C, 20 shares. B is approaching retirement and wants the company to purchase his shares, since neither A nor C has substantial private means. The ownership of the equity before and after the purchase is as follows:

	No of shares before	No of shares after	%
A	45	45	69
B	35	—	
C	20	20	31
	100	65	100

It is clear that C's position in the company is considerably weakened as a result of the buy-in and A's is correspondingly strengthened. A ends up with majority control whilst C, who held the balance of power previously, is now at the mercy of A. For this buy-in to go ahead, C's aquiescence is required, since the purchase contract must be voted by special resolution at which the vendor's shares do not count. C could, therefore, block the purchase. He should certainly use this power of veto to come to some satisfactory arrangement with A whereby the value of his shareholding is safeguarded and his future with the company assured. As far as B is concerned, he should hold out for a substantial value based on control, since his shareholding is sufficient to give control to either of the other two if a direct sale took place.

Because a company's financial position will change from time to time and because of the sometimes conflicting interests of different shareholders, it may be difficult to achieve consistency when valuing shares for successive buy-ins. A dissident minority shareholder may be such a thorn in the side of the directors that a substantial nuisance value may be reflected in the price at which he is bought out. On another occasion, perhaps when the company is not having a good year or is for some reason short of cash, a lower price for an equivalent minority shareholding might be paid. The essential point to bear in mind, however, is that the valuer must consider the effect of the buy-in not only on the company but also on the relative positions of the remaining shareholders.

Conclusion

Earnings are the appropriate basis for valuing controlling interests in most companies. The DCF basis, although theoretically superior to the stream of earnings approach, requires a lot more information than is likely to be available and can be extremely time-consuming. Its application will probably be limited to a few companies whose income and expenditure can be projected over the long term with confidence. The assets basis is appropriate for valuing controlling interests in property investment companies, investment trust companies and similar 'money-box' businesses. The assets basis should not be used for valuing manufacturing or trading companies as going concerns.

For minority shareholdings the general rule is that, in the absence of indications to the contrary, the dividend basis should be used. However many private companies pay little or no dividend. Although in theory this suggests a purely nominal value for the shares, in practice, other considerations mentioned in the text will often come into play. It would be rare to conclude that a minority shareholding in a successful but non-dividend paying private company was virtually worthless.

These remarks also apply to property investment companies, investment trusts and the like. Minority interests in such companies should not be valued on an assets basis since assets are not within the reach of the minority shareholder. The notion that asset backing in some way reduces the investment risk, and therefore justifies a higher value, is itself suspect.

Some practitioners and theorists advocate the use of the earnings basis for valuing minority shareholdings, citing Stock Exchange practice as the justification for this approach. This argument has been considered in detail in Chapter 9, where it was concluded that earnings are not the correct basis for valuing uninfluential minority holdings. However, two business economists, Modigliani and Miller (MM) have advanced the thesis that it matters not whether one uses the stream of earnings approach or the stream of dividends approach; both approaches should yield the same result. This thesis, which is still widely accepted in academic circles, has become known as the dividend irrelevance proposition and is in direct conflict with the position assumed here. In view of this, MM's original paper was reviewed in detail to establish whether the proposition was justified.

The review of MM's paper showed that their reasoning appears to be based on an unsound conceptual framework. The 'Achilles and the tortoise' approach used throughout the analysis leads to the absurd conclusion that, as no single dividend can be found which influences the share price, dividends cannot form part of the return on the shares. In demonstrating the equivalence of the earnings and the dividend streams, MM rely on their own definition of earnings and not the one commonly accepted. It was shown that MM's redefined earnings are no more nor less than the firm's dividend payments, rendering their conclusion tautologous and irrelevant. Their paper exhibited numerous other deficiencies which are discussed in the text. MM's proposition is not proved.

Lastly, this chapter briefly discussed some of the valuation problems which can arise when a company purchases its own shares. This relatively recent liberalisation of company law is of considerable significance to the private company shareholder. Valuation problems arise because the company is distinct from its shareholders and the shareholders themselves may have different attitudes towards a share buy-in. The resources of the company and the effect of the buy-in on the relative position of the remaining shareholders must be considered.

13

Options, warrants and convertibles

Options, warrants and convertibles have important features in common which justify grouping them together for valuation purposes. In formulating rules for the valuation of unquoted share options and convertibles it is first necessary to examine how their quoted counterparts function on the Stock Exchange. The Stock Exchange equivalents comprise not only traditional and traded options but also share warrants. Although for all practical purposes share warrants are never encountered outside the Stock Exchange, in many ways they are closer to the unquoted share option than are Stock Exchange share options. We also examine the techniques used by Stock Exchange professionals to evaluate options, warrants and convertibles and then consider how these may be adapted for use in the private company domain.

Stock Exchange options

In the traditional London options market, investors have the choice of a call option, a put option or a double option (sometimes termed a put and call option). Traditional options are for a period of three months and can be exercised only on expiry of the period, not during it. A call option entitles the holder to buy the shares at a stated price, known as the striking price; a put option entitles him to sell them at the striking price; and a double option entitles him to buy or sell at the striking price, but not both. The striking price is the current share price plus interest to meet carry over facilities during the option period. If the option holder does not exercise the option by the last declaration date, which is shown on the contract note and published in the *Financial Times,* he is deemed to have abandoned his option. Option money is paid at a rate per share as quoted by the option dealer.

Table 1 shows the three-month call rates (i.e., the cost of an option to buy shares three months hence) on 13 September 1985 as reported in the *Financial Times.* It will be seen that the option money as a percentage of the current share price averaged 9.3% for all 75 stocks. The lowest percentage was 5.2% (for T.I.) and the highest was 27.6% (for BSR). The standard deviation was 3.5% which may be interpreted as indicating a two out of three chance that the actual percentage will be 9.3% plus or minus 3.5%.

Table 1: Traditional options: three-month call rates at 13 September 1985

Stock	(a) Share price p	(b) Option money p	(b) as % of (a)
Industrials			
Allied-Lyons	280	16	5.7
BAT	278	32	11.5
BOC Group	284	25	8.8
BSR	58	16	27.6
BTR	363	52	14.3
Babcock	135xd	14	10.4
Barclays	385	48	12.5
Beecham	331	32	9.7
Blue Circle	500xd	45	9.0
Boots	203	15	7.4
Bowaters	337	20	5.9
British Aerospace	378	33	8.7
British Telecom	199	11	5.5
Brown (J)	28	3	10.7
Buton Ord.	505	39	7.7
Cadbury's	144	14	9.7
Charter Cons.	183	18	9.8
Commercial Union	224	19	8.5
Courtaulds	147	12½	8.5
Debenhams	355	17½	4.9
Distillers	390	28	7.2
FNFC	118	8½	7.2
General Accident	610	45	7.4
General Electric	164	17	10.4
Glaxo	£13¼	85	6.4
Grand Met	333	25	7.5
G.U.S. 'A'	790	60	7.6
Guardian	663	60	9.0
GKN	228	17	7.5
Hanson Trust	206	17½	8.5
Hawker Sidd	391	38	9.7
ICI	667	60	9.0
'Imps'	194	18	9.3
Jaguar	290	28	9.7
Ladbroke	285	24	8.4
Legal & General	665	50	7.5
Lex Services	225	28	12.4
Lloyds Bank	413	45	10.9
Lucas Inds	386	25	6.5
Marks & Spencer	152	11	7.2
Midland Bank	393	30	7.6
NEI	78½	8	10.2
Nat West Bank	645	60	9.3

Stock	(a) Share price p	(b) Option money p	(b) as % of (a)
P & O Defd.	421	36	8.6
Plessey	144xd	17	11.8
Polly Peck	218	26	11.9
Racal Elect	134	18	13.4
RHM	147	11	7.5
Rank Org Ord	400	32	8.0
Reed International	702	50	7.1
Sears	112	8	7.1
T.I.	386	20	5.2
Tesco	258	20	7.8
Thorn EMI	381	35	9.2
Trust Houses	144	13	9.0
Turner Newall	90	10	11.1
Unilever	£10⅝	85	8.0
Vickers	280	19	6.8

Property

Stock	(a) Share price p	(b) Option money p	(b) as % of (a)
Brit Land	152	12	7.9
Cap Counties	217	18	8.3
Land Secs	292	25	8.6
MEPC	292	28	9.6
Peachey	253	22	8.7
Samuel Props	166	14	8.4

Oils

Stock	(a) Share price p	(b) Option money p	(b) as % of (a)
Brist. Oil & Min	16	4	25.0
British Petroleum	543xd	42	7.7
Burmah Oil	304	18	5.9
Charterhall	34	6	17.6
Premier	46	5	10.9
Shell	705	60	8.5
Tricentrol	195	18	9.2
Ultramar	205xd	19	9.3

Mines

Stock	(a) Share price p	(b) Option money p	(b) as % of (a)
Cons Gold	430	44	10.2
Lonhro	151	14	9.3
Rio T Zinc	590	56	9.5

Source: Financial Times

Options serve a number of purposes. First, they can be used as a hedge to limit risk; second, they are a means of 'gearing up' an investment return, and third, they can be used as a speculative device.

When an option is combined with shares it reduces the risk to the investor of a major movement in the share price. Suppose, for example, that an investor has made a substantial capital gain on some shares. However, he is reluctant to sell the shares because there could well be a further significant rise in the share price. In such circumstances he may well take out a put option. This would lock in his present gain and leave him free to benefit from any further improvement in the share price. If the share price rises, as he expects, he will abandon the option. If the share price falls he will exercise the option enabling him to sell at the current price. Table 2 illustrates the effect of the option.

Table 2: Hedging effect of a put option

Basic data

No of shares	500
Current price	200p per share
Cost price	100p per share
Current gain	100p per share
Cost of put option	20p per share

	With option £	Without option £
(a) Share price rises to 250p		
Sale proceeds — 500×250p	1,250	1,250
Original cost — 500×100p	(500)	(500)
Option money	(100)	—
Gain	650	750
(b) Share price falls to 150p		
Sale proceeds — 500×150p	—	750
Exercise of option — 500×200p	1,000	—
Option money	(100)	—
Original cost	(500)	(500)
Gain	400	250

At the current share price of 200p the investor has the possibility of an immediately realisable profit of £500, i.e., the current value of £1,000 less the original cost. If he takes out a put option he locks in this gain while holding onto the shares for any subsequent rise in price. The effect is to reduce the gain he would otherwise have made by the amount of the option money, £100. Should the share price fall, he has the assurance of being able to sell his shares at £1,000. The profit will be

£100 less than he would have made if he had sold the shares in the first place, but considerably more than the £250 gain he would have made if he had retained the shares and not taken out a put option. The interesting feature of the hedge is that it guarantees the investor a profit of at least £400, no matter how low the share price falls. However, his potential profit is not limited to a fixed sum; it is merely restricted by £100.

Although the use of options to hedge risk is quite common, options are probably better known as a form of highly geared investment. This means that the percentage gain or loss is much higher than it would be on an investment in the underlying shares. Assume, for example, that an investor has good reason to believe that a particular share, currently priced at 100p, is likely to rise appreciably. He has £2,000 available and a call option would cost 10p per share. Table 3 compares the outcomes when a direct purchase of shares is made and when the sum available is used to purchase a call option, assuming in both cases that the share price rises to 125p. For an outlay of £2,000 the call option produces a profit of £3,000, and a direct purchase of the shares, a profit of only £500.

Table 3: Purchase of a call option compared with purchase of the underlying shares

	Call option £	Share purchase £
Investment		
2,000 shares at 100p each		2,000
Call option: 20,000 shares at 10p each	2,000	
Return		
2,000 shares at 125p each		2,500
20,000 shares at 125p each	25,000	
Cost of exercising call option:		
20,000 shares at 100p each	(20,000)	
	5,000	2,500
Gain	3,000	500
Rate of return	150%	25%

The reason why share options as a geared investment are not more popular is that the downside risk is often unacceptable. Looking at Table 3, if the share price had failed to rise above 100p the option would have become worthless and the investor would have lost his initial outlay completely. But for investors with the strength of their convictions and an appetite for risk the option on its own has a considerable attraction.

The purely speculative aspects of options are particularly evident in the double option. This costs nearly double a single option and is used to advantage where the share price is highly volatile. By trading against the option — taking a bull position when any downside risk is hedged by the put option or going short in the knowledge that the call option is available should the share price rise — it is possible to job in and out of the shares very profitably. However, this form of speculation requires a constant vigilance for price movements and no little skill or luck in judging the market.

In April 1978 a traded options market was established under the auspices of the London Stock Exchange. Unlike the traditional option, a traded option can be bought and sold before its expiry date. It can also be exercised before the expiry date, although it is usually more profitable to sell it rather than exercise it. The expiry date and exercise price for each class of traded option is fixed by the Stock Exchange. Traded options have a maximum life of nine months, with expiry dates fixed on a three-monthly cycle so that there is a choice of three expiry dates: three, six and nine months ahead. Particulars of GEC's traded options are shown in Table 4:

Table 4: GEC's traded options — 13 September 1985

Share price	Exercise price	Oct	Calls Jan	April	Oct	Puts Jan	April
	160	16	24	30	4	6	10
164	180	5	10	18	16	19	22
	200	1	4	10	38	38	38

Source: Financial Times

When the October 'series' expires a new nine-month series, expiring in July, will be opened for trading. There are three different exercise prices. Where the price of the underlying shares moves above the highest exercise price or below the lowest, new series at different exercise prices are added. There can be as many as five or six exercise prices operating at any time in respect of the shares of a particular company.

The price of a traded option is a function of supply and demand in the market, which is not a very helpful statement. The factors generally believed to affect the value of an option are:

(a) the underlying share price;
(b) the exercise or striking price;
(c) the period to expiry;
(d) the riskiness of the underlying share;
(e) the general level of interest rates.[1]

A call option is 'in the money' if the share price is greater than the exercise price. A put option is 'in the money' when the share price falls below the exercise price. The profit which can be realised when a share option is 'in the money' is termed its intrinsic value.

Unexpired options also have a time value, reflecting the possibility of a further increase in the underlying share price during the remainder of the option period. Thus the GEC October 160 call option worth 16p has an intrinsic value of 4p, since the holder could buy shares at the exercise price of 160p and sell them in the market at 164p. The balance of the option price, 12p, reflects the time value of the option. The longer the unexpired period the greater the time value. This rule can be seen at work in the GEC January 160 and April 160 call options, priced respectively at 24p and 30p. As their intrinsic value is 4p, the same as that of the October 160's, the increased price must reflect the greater unexpired period or time value.

Although the riskiness of a share is, in theory, fully reflected in its price, the share's risk also influences the price of the option. The option price is a reflection of the likelihood or risk that the option will be exercised, and this depends on the volatility of the share price. Obviously a share which could well move up (or down) 20% from its current level would require a higher option price in percentage terms than one which would be unlikely to move more than ten per cent. As the more volatile stocks are reckoned to be the riskier ones, the higher the risk of the share, the more expensive the option. This can be seen from Table 1. A British Telecom call option cost only 5.5% of the current share price whereas a call option for Charterhall cost 17.6%.

The influence of the general level of interest rates is somewhat more theoretical and applies to traditional and not traded options. In theory, a traditional call option must be worth at least the current share price

---

[1] These factors are all incorporated in the Black–Scholes option valuation model. This model is widely used by professionals in traded options markets. It requires as assessment of share price volatility and is therefore unsuitable for unquoted share options. The interested reader is referred to Fischer Black and Myron Scholes, 'The Pricing of Options and Corporate Liabilities', *Journal of Political Economy*, 81, (May/June 1973), pp. 637–654. A more accessible discussion of the Black–Scholes call option valuation formula can be found in William F. Sharpe, *Investments*, 2nd ed. (Englewood Cliffs, N.J.: Prentice-Hall, 1981), p. 438.

less the present value of the exercise price. This is because the call option acts as a hedge guaranteeing the investor any growth in the share price while allowing him to invest his funds at the risk-free rate in the meantime. If the share price goes up, he can make a profit by exercising the option. If the share price falls, he is left with the exercise price, i.e., the current share price. A direct investment in the shares would reap the same rewards if the shares rose but it would produce a loss if the shares fell. Therefore, an investment consisting of a call option in the shares and a cash deposit of the present value of the exercise price must be worth more than a direct investment in the shares.

Thus,

$$S \leqslant M + PV(E)$$

where S is the current share price, M is the option money and $PV(E)$ is the present value of the exercise price.

Therefore,

$$M \geqslant S - PV(E)$$

The call rates for traditional options shown in Table 1 all exceed this minimum or lower limit by a substantial margin. This rule does not apply to traded options since they can be exercised at any time during their currency. Their minimum price is their intrinsic value, which is the extent to which they are 'in the money'.

The traditional options market is still alive and well as the list of companies in Table 1 testifies. The traded options market has not developed as its promoters had hoped and the number of companies with traded options is comparatively small.

Stock Exchange warrants

A warrant is a form of option which gives the holder the right to buy a stated number of shares at a specified price at some future time. Unlike options, warrants are issued by companies and when the warrant is exercised the warrant holder subscribes for shares in the company. The subscription or exercise price is usually set above the current share price and is protected against subsequent scrip or rights issues. Under current Stock Exchange regulations a quoted company may not issue warrants in excess of ten per cent of its outstanding share capital.

Warrants are more common in the United States than they are in this country. In the early 1970s a number of property companies and 'high-fliers' issued share warrants. They were particularly popular with investment trusts who found it difficult to persuade investors to subscribe for shares because of the discount to net asset value to which the shares would inevitably fall. Investment trusts used share warrants as a 'sweetener'. Warrants are often attached to loan stocks. In some issues they are detachable.

Warrants have the reputation of being a highly specialised gamblers' market for experts only. Doubtless, this is because of the volatility of warrant prices. But some of the mystique of warrants is attributable to the jargon used by professionals. We shall now examine three of these terms: gearing ratios, conversion premiums and volatility factors. The gearing effect of a warrant is similar to that of an option. Assume that a share worth 200p in the market has related warrants entitling the holder to subscribe for shares at 220p and these warrants are quoted at 80p. If the ordinary share price rises to 220p — a rise of ten per cent — the warrant may well rise to 95p — a rise of 18.8%. The gearing ratio is found by dividing the share price by the price of the warrants. If the share price is 200p and the warrants are quoted at 80p, the gearing ratio is 2.5.[2]

The conversion premium is the theoretical extra price over and above the underlying share price which the investor pays when he buys a share warrant. It assumes he holds the warrant to maturity and then exercises his conversion rights. In the example in the preceding paragraph, the conversion premium works out at 50%, as set out below:

	p
Market price of warrant	80
Warrant exercise price	220
	300
Less current share price	200
	100
Conversion premium $\dfrac{100}{200}$	= 50%

The volatility factor refers to the behaviour of the underlying share price and is supposed to provide some indication of how speculative the warrants are. If the share price fluctuates considerably the warrant is more attractive since it provides more opportunities for gain (and loss!).

[2] For a critique of this particular investment yardstick and a more detailed discussion of warrant pricing generally see James O'Horrigan, 'Some Hypotheses on the Valuation of Stock Warrants', *Journal of Business Finance and Accounting*, 1 (Summer 1974), pp. 239–247; and A. P. Bird, 'Some Hypotheses on the Valuation of Stock Warrants: A Comment', *Journal of Business Finance and Accounting*, 2 (Summer 1975), pp. 219–232.

When warrants are issued the subscription or exercise price is usually set at a small premium to the current share price. The warrants are usually exercisable in a particular month in each year, there being a final year when the warrants expire. Like an option, a warrant has an intrinsic value — sometimes called a formula value — when the underlying share price exceeds the exercise price. This excess sets the lower limit on value. As with an option, the value of a warrant cannot exceed the value of the underlying share.

The reader may find it helpful if some of these notions are related to actual warrant issues. The warrants of United Biscuits and J Rothschild Holdings have been selected for this purpose. Relevant particulars, as of 13 September 1985, were as follows:

	United Biscuits	Rothschild Holdings
Warrant price (W)	59p	40p
Exercise price (E)	149p	86.34p
Share price (P)	185p	100p
Life	3½ years	7 years
Gearing ratio P/W	3.1	2.5
Conversion premium $\dfrac{W+E-P}{P}$	12.4%	26.3%
Minimum or intrinsic value P−E	36p	13.7p
Maximum value, P	185p	100p

As a warrant is essentially a longer-term option the factors influencing its price will be much the same as those affecting option prices. Warrants, however, exhibit a few distinctive features which are worth mentioning. When a warrant is on its minimum or intrinsic value, it will rise by 1p for every 1p rise in the ordinary share. In such a case, the nominal gearing ratio is an accurate guide to the actual gearing. When the warrant is above its minimum value the warrant will not rise by as much as the ordinary share price, and the nominal gearing ratio is an unreliable guide.

Interestingly, empirical studies show that warrants tend to stand on their minimum value once the share price is more than about twice the exercise price, whatever the life of the warrant. The same studies show that the importance attached by the market to the life of the warrant is nothing like as much as it should be and that warrant investors are irrationally shortsighted.[3] Finally, because of the Stock Exchange restrictions on the size of a company's warrant issues, markets tend to

[3] Bird, *Valuation of Warrants,* pp. 224 and 231.

be thin and many issues can be dominated by a single investor. Some warrants may, therefore, have exceptionally high spreads and be difficult to deal in. Their prices may not be indicative of market value.

Quoted convertible loan stocks

Convertible loans stocks ('convertibles') are a cross between a fixed-interest security and an equity investment. They provide the holder with a fixed annual return in the form of interest on the nominal amount of stock held and also the option to convert the loan stock into ordinary shares of the company at a pre-determined rate. The loan stock is redeemable, usually at par, at a stated date. For example, the Habitat 9½% convertible unsecured loan stock 1998/2001 pays the fixed sum of £9.50 per £100 of nominal stock and is redeemable between 1998 and 2001 by four equal instalments. The stock is convertible into ordinary shares during August in any of the years 1985 to 1998 inclusive on the basis of 100 shares per £145 nominal of stock.

A convertible, therefore, has two elements of value: first, its value as a debt instrument and, second, the value of the option to convert into equity. Unlike the share option or warrant, the exercise price is not fixed but depends on the value of the convertible. The Habitat loan stock can be converted into 69 ordinary shares per £100 of stock, i.e., $100 \times 100/145$. On 13 September 1985, £100 of stock had a market value of £305. The exercise price was, therefore, 442p (£305 divided by 69) which was 16p below the share price of 458p on 13 September 1985. However, as conversion can take place only in August and the convertible price of £305 was a September price, the purchaser would have to wait another 11 months before being able to convert.

As the convertible had a flat or running yield of 3.1% (i.e., £9.50 divided by £305) and the shares yielded 2.5%, the income differential was slight and conversion into the higher value, more marketable equity would have been attractive. In fact convertibles have been traditionally evaluated by reference to the income differential compared with the underlying shares. The interest receivable on the convertible usually exceeds the dividends on the equivalent ordinary shares and this is a major feature of the convertible's attraction. By estimating future dividend growth the investor can identify the year in which this differential is likely to disappear and when it would, in theory, be advantageous to switch into the ordinary shares. The net present value of these annual income differentials is then added to the market value of the equivalent ordinary shares to arrive at the notional value of the convertible.

It is interesting to try this method on the Habitat convertible. The dividend on the equivalent ordinary shares amounted to £7.89, being 69 shares at 11.43p per share. If the Habitat dividend were expected to grow at 20% per annum in the coming year the dividend on the 69 underlying ordinary shares would rise to £9.47. As this is virtually the same sum as the annual interest on the convertible loan stock, conversion would be desirable in 12 months' time. The present value of the convertible then becomes:

69 shares at 458p each		£316.02
Present value of income differential		
Loan stock interest	£9.50	
Dividend on 69 ordinary shares	7.89	
Difference	£1.61	
Discounted for 12 months at, say, 12%		1.44
Present value of convertible		£317.46

This suggests that at a price of £305 the Habitat convertible was 'cheap' and therefore a buy.

No one pretends that this is more than a quick guide — a rough and ready rule of thumb. One obvious shortcoming is that it assumes the stock is immediately convertible. This is not true of the Habitat issue since the holder must wait another 11 months to the following August, by which time the share price and the price of the convertible will almost certainly have changed. Equally important, it ignores the value of the option to convert.

Another approach is to value the convertible's element of pure debt to see whether the implied value of the conversion rights is reasonable. On the date in question the average gross redemption yield for 15-year debentures and loan stocks, as shown by the *FT*-Actuaries Index was 11.45%, say, 11.5%. The pure loan stock element in the Habitat convertible might therefore be approximately evaluated as follows:

Present value of £9.50 a year for 13 years at 11.5% (annuity factor 6.5835)	62.54
Present value of redemption proceeds of £100 in 13 years' time at 11.5% (discount factor 0.2429).	24.29
	86.83
say,	£87.00

If the straight debt is worth £87 and the market price of the convertible is £305 the difference of £218 is the implied value of the option to convert. The cost of conversion — there is no exercise price — is the value of the straight debt renounced, currently £87. This is analogous, therefore, to a warrant or option costing £218 to subscribe for 69 shares at a price of £87 in total at any time within the next 13 years.

The underlying shares are currently worth £316 (i.e., 69 shares at 458p each) which gives the option or conversion right an 'intrinsic' value of £229. The fact that this exceeds the implied value of £218 suggests that the redemption yield selected for evaluating the pure debt ought to have been higher. It also suggests that there is little or no time value in the option. This corroborates the phenomenon identified earlier as regards warrant pricing: when the share price is more than twice the exercise price the warrant tends to stand on its minimum or intrinsic value, whatever its life.

Unquoted share options

The preceding discussion of how share options, warrants and convertibles are priced on the Stock Exchange is a necessary preliminary to an enquiry into the most appropriate methods for valuing their unquoted equivalents. First, we consider unquoted companies' share options. These remarks may also apply to share options which quoted companies grant their employees under various executive or employee incentive schemes. As such options cannot generally be traded, they have much in common with private company share options.

Unquoted share options are very different creatures from their Stock Exchange counterparts in that they are not instruments of speculation or hedging and provide no possibilities for jobbing in and out of the underlying shares. Ownership is restricted to the grantee. The typical share option found in the private company sector and in the share incentive schemes of quoted companies is more akin to a warrant than an option, in that the option holder exercises his option by subscribing for shares in the company. The life of the unquoted share option is closer to the life of a warrant than a Stock Exchange option.[4]

Whatever the circumstances surrounding the grant of an option its value must derive from the expected gain on exercise. The expected gain on exercise is the difference between the exercise price, E, and the share price, P, on the exercise date. The share price on the exercise date can be expressed in terms of the current share price, P, by means of the expected compound annual growth rate, g, in the share price over the

---

[4] One of the conditions of Inland Revenue approval of a share option scheme is that the option cannot be exercised earlier than three years, or later than ten years, after it was granted.

number of years, n, before expiry of the option. The relationship between the option value today and the expected gain on exercise can, therefore, be formulated as follows:

(1)
$$C=\frac{P(1+g)^n-E}{(1+k)^n}$$

C is the value of the call option, k is the required rate of return and the other symbols are as indicated above.

The value of an option depends therefore on the current value of the underlying shares and it requires an estimate of the likely growth in the value of the shares and of the required rate of return. Where the company is quoted, the current share price presents no problem (this can be read off from the *Financial Times*). For an unquoted company, however, it will be necessary to value the shares. The required rate of return used in valuing the shares can then be used for k in equation (1). The fact that the risk of the option is not identical to the risk of the share may cause the theorist to part company with us on this recommendation, but given the inevitable imprecision of the exercise it should make little difference. The nub of the matter is the growth rate since this determines what the share price is estimated to be on the exercise date. This is completely unknown and all that can be attempted is an informed projection based on all relevant factors.

Another way of approaching the problem is to re-express equation (1) in terms of the growth rate:

(2)
$$g=\sqrt[n]{\frac{C(1+k)^n+E}{P}}-1$$

Applying this equation to the share warrants for United Biscuits and Rothschild Holdings (see under 'Stock Exchange warrants' in this chapter) and using a 20% rate of return (k), the implied growth rates in the underlying share price work out at, respectively, 10.3% and 12.6% a year. Using different growth rates and rates of return, it should be possible by trial and error, to obtain a fairly reliable feel for the value of the option.

In view of the subjectivity involved in this method it would be advisable to cross check the results by reference to any available evidence on the Stock Exchange. The traditional options market is not a good guide here since traditional options have a life of only three months. Traded options with a maximum life of nine months are not much better. The closest parallel on the Stock Exchange seems to be the quoted share warrant. Like the unquoted share option it has a long life and is exercised by subscribing for shares in the company. Convertible loan stocks may be of some help. These can be analysed to find the implied value of the option to convert. It would be wrong, however, to read too much significance into the prices of quoted share options and warrants. These have distinctive features and attractions not shared by their unquoted counterparts. Stock Exchange options and warrants have a strong speculative attraction and are rarely held to expiry. This speculative attraction would disappear if the warrants and options could not be bought and sold easily. In short, marketability is everything.

Unquoted convertible loan stock

Two methods of valuing unquoted convertibles come to mind: first, the income differential method used in the appraisal of quoted convertibles and, second, valuing the straight debt and the conversion rights separately. In both cases it will be necessary to value the underlying ordinary shares.

The income differential method has already been illustrated using the Habitat convertible (see page 300). It assumes that the loan stock can be converted into equity at the present time which, in many instances, will not be a valid assumption. It also ignores the value of the option.

As many private companies do not pay dividends, the income differential method will produce a value for the convertible equal to its value as straight debt plus the current value of the underlying shares. Take as an example a private company loan stock issue paying interest at 9½%. Each £100 nominal of stock is convertible into 25 ordinary shares from year five onwards. The stock is redeemable 20 years hence. The ordinary shares are currently valued at £2.50 each and do not pay any dividend. As the ordinary shares yield nothing there will never be a point at which on income grounds it would pay the holder of the loan stock to convert into ordinary shares. One hundred pounds of stock will always yield £9.50 a year more than the underlying shares, and the investor would hold onto the convertible until the redemption date 20 years hence. The value of the convertible, discounting the income differential at 15% per annum, then works out at £121.96 per £100 of stock, as set out below:

Interest per £100 of loan stock	£9.50
Dividend on 25 ordinary shares	—
Income differential per annum	£9.50
Optimum conversion date	year 20
Present value of an annuity of £9.50 at 15% (factor 6.2593)	£59.46
Add current value of 25 ordinary shares 25×£2.50	£62.50
	£121.96

The straight debt element of the convertible would be valued as follows:

	£
Present value of an annuity of £9.50 for 20 years (as above)	59.46
Present value of redemption proceeds 20 years hence, at 15% £100×0.0611	6.11
	65.57

The value of the income differential, £59.46, is very close to the full value of the straight debt, £65.57. The implied value of the option to convert is therefore £56.39, i.e., £121.96 less £65.57. However, the maximum value of an option or warrant is the current share price — in this case £62.50. The income differential method has therefore valued the option to convert at 90% of its maximum value.

Although in theory the longer the option period the greater the option's value, in the case of warrants, as we saw earlier, the time factor ceases to have a perceptible effect beyond a certain period. And this is probably true in the present example. No one would be particularly attracted by an option to acquire shares in 20 years' time, at whatever price. Investors' time horizons are short. Most investors would probably appraise this convertible on the prospects for the ordinary shares five years hence i.e., the first possible conversion date. The evaluation in that case would be as follows:

Present value of an annuity of £9.50 for 5 years at 15% (9.50×3.3522)	£31.85
Current value of ordinary shares (25×£2.50	£62.50
	£94.35

This implies a value for the conversion rights of £28.78 (i.e., £94.35 less the value of the straight debt, £65.57). This is roughly half the implied option value in the earlier calculation. In any event, using the income differential method the convertible has a value of between £94.35 and £121.96, depending on the conversion date assumed.

If the convertible were to be valued using the second method, the conversion rights would be evaluated separately from the straight debt. This too can only be a rough and ready guide, mainly because of the simplifying assumptions that have to be made about the future growth in the share price and the value of the loan stock on exercise. If, for example, we assume that the share price will rise by 15% a year over the next five years and that the value of the straight debt remains at £65.57, the option value, using equation (1), works out at £24.17, as set out below:

(1)
$$C = \frac{P(1+g)^n - E}{(1+k)^n}$$

$$= \frac{62.50(1.15)^5 - 65.57}{(1.20)^5}$$

$$= \frac{62.50(2.0114) - 65.57}{2.4883}$$

$$= £24.17$$

As the value of the conversion rights is £24.17 and the value of the straight debt £65.57, the value of the convertible becomes £89.74. The required rate of return, 20%, is that used in valuing the ordinary shares. (There is no rule that it should be; all that is necessary is that the rate used is the rate required by the investor concerned.) The valuation produced by this method, £89.74, is reasonably close to the valuation of £94.35 produced by the income differential method. However, had equation (1) been calculated on the assumption that conversion took place in 20 years' time, the option value would have risen only marginally to £24.97 pushing the convertible's value up slightly to £90.54. The effect of using a 20-year period on the income differential method was much greater. The convertible's value rose from £94.35 to £121.96.

However, it is unrealistic to assume that a growth rate of 15% a year, well above the current inflation rate, could be sustained for 20 years, and a growth rate of, say, ten per cent would be more plausible. But this eminently justifiable change to the assumptions has a very marked effect on the value of the conversion rights. These are now worth £9.26 as calculated below:

(1)
$$C = \frac{P(1+g)^n - E}{(1+k)^n}$$

$$= \frac{62.50(1.10)^{20} - 65.57}{(1.20)^{20}}$$

$$= \frac{62.50(6.7275) - 65.57}{38.3376}$$

$$= £9.26$$

All depends therefore on the realism of the assumptions.

Conclusion

In this chapter we have discussed the valuation of unquoted share options and convertible loan stocks, the former being an increasingly popular executive incentive and the latter an uncommon type of security for an unquoted company. The approach was to examine Stock Exchange share options, share warrants and convertibles — three related investment instruments with common features of relevance to their unquoted counterparts — and to formulate a logical approach to the valuation of unquoted share options and convertibles.

The value of a share option derives essentially from the expected gain on exercise. The formula which expresses the relationship of the different variables (the share price, exercise price, growth rate and rates of return) is given in the text. The maximum value of an option is the current share price. Its minimum value is the difference between the current share price and the discounted exercise price. This is known as the intrinsic value. The suggested valuation formula requires a number of subjective judgements and can only give a rough guide to value. However, by varying the assumptions and comparing the results with the prices of Stock Exchange warrants and options, and also the value of conversion rights implied by convertible loan stocks, the valuer should be able to obtain a reliable 'feel' for the value of the option. However, much of the attraction of quoted options and warrants lies in their suitability for speculation and hedging. Shorn of these attractions, which they do not share with their unquoted counterparts, they would be worth much less. This important point should be borne in mind when making comparisons.

Two methods are suggested for valuing convertibles. First, there is the traditional income differential method used on the Stock Exchange. Alternatively, the convertible may be valued by means of its two elements considered separately, namely, the value of the straight debt instrument and the value of the conversion rights. Examples are given in the text of both these techniques and how they may complement one another. The shortcomings of the valuation methods were discussed.

14

Fixed interest securities and miscellaneous valuation topics

Compared to the valuation of equities the valuation of fixed interest securities is straightforward and uncomplicated. Most of the problems of valuing equity arise from the indeterminate nature of the future return. The return on fixed interest securities is much easier to estimate being in large part known in advance. Valuation then becomes principally a question of the relative security of income and capital. For a 'blue chip' company whose ability to meet its financial obligations is virtually undoubted the question becomes academic. A fixed interest security in such a company is virtually risk free and may not yield much more than a government stock. The relative security of income and capital will begin to count further down the credit rating scale and this will be reflected in higher yields. In broad terms, fixed interest securities comprise preference shares, debentures and loan stocks.

Various valuation topics or difficulties which do not fit conveniently into earlier chapters are also considered here. These include the valuation of deferred shares — shares with deferred equity rights — and the valuation of non-voting ordinary shares. This chapter also considers the *cum div/ex div* point in relation to the valuation of unquoted shares and the relevance of prior sales.

Fixed interest securities

Preference shares are part of a company's share capital and preference shareholders are members of the company. If there are no profits they may well receive no dividend in which case there is little they can do. Debenture holders and loan stockholders on the other hand are creditors of the company and can enforce their claim in law. Interest on debentures and loan stocks is a cost of the business and is payable irrespective of profits. In a winding up, the preference shareholders rank after the debenture and loan stockholders. The different legal characteristics of the various forms of fixed interest securities are considered in detail in Chapter 3. However, even from this brief summary it is clear that there are significant differences affecting the relative security of income and capital. These must be reflected in the rate of return.

The required rate of return on unquoted fixed interest securities, as on equities, consists of the risk-free rate of return on government bonds plus a premium for risk and poor marketability. The yields on quoted preference shares and debentures are also a strong influence. No one would invest at ten per cent in private company preference shares if he could obtain the same rate of return on gilts or on quoted preference shares. As fixed interest securities have no votes they generally have the same value whoever the purchaser or vendor. They may therefore be valued in the abstract. A convenient starting point would be a list of Stock Exchange yields such as that shown in Table 1:

Table 1: Average gross redemption yields at 13 September 1985

FT-Actuaries Index	%
Gilts (high coupon)	
5 years	10.99
15 years	10.78
25 years	10.43
Debentures and loans	
5 years	11.57
15 years	11.45
25 years	11.32
Preference shares (flat yield)	12.14

Source: *Financial Times*

The detailed qualifications for inclusion in the relevant *FT*-Actuaries Index are set out in Chapter 5. In brief, however, debentures and loan stocks must have an outstanding nominal issue of not less than £11 million; interest must be covered by the profits shown in the previous two years' published accounts, and the coupon must not be unusually low. A preference share issue must have an outstanding nominal issue of not less than £3 million. It must be a normal stock, i.e., cumulative, not redeemable, not convertible, not participating and with normal (limited) voting rights.

The fixed interest securities of the typical private company would not qualify for inclusion in these indices, and in basing a required yield on these figures a substantial premium has to be added to reflect the higher risk and the lack of marketability. In the author's experience, yields of between 15% and 20% would not be inconsistent with the Index figures quoted in Table 1.

The arithmetic of investment is such that value is reduced when the yield is raised and is increased when the yield is lowered. This is generally accepted by the investment professional but appears sometimes strange to the newcomer. The dividend yield on a preference share is given by the following expression:

$$x = \frac{D}{P}$$

where x is the dividend yield, D is the gross dividend per share and P is the share price. Switching this expression around we obtain:

$$P = \frac{D}{x}$$

It is easy to see from this equation that if the yield x is increased the share price P must fall. If x is reduced P will rise.

As just mentioned, the required rate of return is a function of the risk-free gilts rate. Therefore, if the return on gilts rises, so must the return on preference shares, debentures and loans. Because of the inverse relationship noted above, this will be accompanied by a fall in prices. If the return on gilts falls so must the return on other fixed interest securities. This will be accompanied by a rise in prices. What then causes the return on gilts to vary? It would be interesting to know this since changes in the rate of return on gilts produce consequential changes in the rate of return on all financial assets. The answer is that gilt prices are highly sensitive to changes in interest rates. Again, the relationship is an inverse one. As interest rates rise, gilt prices fall and vice versa.[1]

Irredeemable gilts, such as Consols or War Loan, and non-redeemable preference shares are regarded as perpetuities. They are expected to pay a fixed and constant amount each year for an indefinite time period. Their value is found as the present value of the infinite series, as follows:

$$\text{Price} = PV = \frac{D}{(1+r)} + \frac{D}{(1+r)^2} + \frac{D}{(1+r)^3} + \ldots + \frac{D}{(1+r)^\infty}$$

D is the fixed annual return and r is the required rate of return. This expression resolves to the following:

$$PV = \frac{D}{r}$$

In other words, the rate of return on a perpetuity is simply the fixed annual income as a percentage of the price. Normally, however, there is some redemption or repayment date. If so, the flat yield (sometimes called the running yield) will not necessarily equal the true rate of

[1] The really interesting question, which we duck here, is what causes interest rates to change.

return or yield to redemption. The redemption yield is the annual discount rate which when applied to the future dividends or interest and the eventual redemption proceeds produces a net present value equal to the current price. It is r in the following equation:

$$\text{Price} = \frac{D}{(1+r)} + \frac{D}{(1+r)^2} + \ldots + \frac{D}{(1+r)^n} + \frac{M}{(1+r)^n}$$

where D is the annual dividend and M is the redemption money payable in year n. Gross redemption yields on fixed interest securities are published daily in the *Financial Times*. An example of the index averages is given in Table 1.

It may help to illustrate the application of this formula. Suppose that you are asked to value a holding of ten per cent loan stock redeemable at par in two years' time. The required rate of return, selected after appraising the risk involved and the gross redemption yields available on the Stock Exchange, is 17.5%. The valuation of £100 nominal of stock would proceed as follows:

	£
Present value of annual interest of £10 for two years (annuity factor: 1.5754)	15.75
Present value of £100 paid in two years' time (discount factor: 0.7243)	72.43
Value	88.18

Participating preference shares have a supplementary profit entitlement. This is akin to an equity interest and should be valued as such. It is advisable to value the straight preference element separately. Similarly, any arrears of dividend on cumulative preference shares should be brought into the valuation separately at their net of tax amount as suitably discounted to reflect the probability of payment. When the preference dividend falls into arrears the preference shares usually become entitled to vote. The valuer should ensure that any such entitlement is reflected in the valuation. The articles may specify other circumstances which may trigger off preference share votes. The valuer must ensure that he is aware of these.

Deferred shares

A deferred share is one where part or whole of the equity entitlement (or rights) is deferred for a stated period. Examples of this type of share can be found on the Stock Exchange although they are fairly rare. These deferred shares rank *pari passu* with the ordinary shares except as regards dividends. Croda International, for example, made a scrip issue of deferred ordinary shares in 1978. The deferred shares ranked equally with the ordinary shares but were not entitled to receive any dividends until after 1988. London & Midland Industrials created a similar type of deferred ordinary share in 1983 but with the dividend entitlement deferred for eight years.

These deferred ordinary shares are presumably designed to appeal to investors with a strong preference for capital gain over income. The reason they are not more popular is probably because of the familiar effect of the scrip issue. A scrip issue is purely a paper transaction and does not increase shareholders' wealth. Any value the deferred shares attract on issue must be at the expense of the existing ordinary shares. The effect on the tax position of the ordinary shareholder who took up his scrip entitlement was therefore neutral. As far as purchase of the deferred share is concerned, the investor has to weigh the capital gains tax advantage of a non-income producing share against the disadvantage of investing in a company which is continually paying out a substantial proportion of its profits in dividends — as far as he is concerned this would be a dead loss and a constraint on growth.

Table 2: Comparison of ordinary and deferred share prices for two quoted companies as at 13 September 1985

	Croda International	*London & Midland Industrials*
	p	*p*
(a) Ordinary shares	129	204
(b) Deferred shares	89	122
(c) Discount on deferred shares	40	82
(d) Ordinary dividend (net)	7	9½
(e) Dividend deferral period unexpired	4 years	7 years
(f) Assumed present value of dividends foregone by deferred shareholders — (d)×(e)	28	66½
(g) Unexplained difference — (c)−(f)	12	15½
(h) (g) as % of (a)	9.3%	7.6%
(g) as % of (b)	13.5%	12.7%

The discount on the deferred shares compared to the ordinary shares should be the present value of the dividends foregone, since dividend entitlement is the only difference between the two classes of share. Table 2 compares the prices of the ordinary and deferred shares of Croda International and London & Midland Industrials as at 13 September 1985. Croda's ordinary share price was 40p above the price of its deferred shares and London & Midland's was 82p above. As we do not know the expected growth rate in dividends or the expected rate of return we cannot be sure whether these differences represent the present value of dividends forgone. However, we can indulge in some intelligent guesswork.

First, the risk-free rate of return on gilts at the time was approximately 11% as shown in Table 1. The risk premium for index stocks over a long period has averaged nine per cent as calculated by Dimson and Brealey.[2] It is reasonable to assume, therefore, that a net rate of return of, say, 17.5% would have been required on an equity investment in either of these two companies. If the dividend was also expected to grow at 17.5% the present value would simply be the current dividend multiplied by the number of years' dividends foregone. However, as shown in Table 2, this still leaves a lot of the difference unexplained. So the implied growth rate in dividends must be considerably higher than 17.5%. In fact for Croda it is 35% and London & Midland, 24%. These are conservative estimates since the required rate of return, 17.5%, is, if anything, understated. Clearly, growth rates of this order, even over a four-year period, are unrealistic. The discount is, therefore, significantly higher than one would expect on dividend grounds. This may be another example of market mispricing or it may provide evidence of the bird-in-hand theory of Myron Gordon.[3]

Moving from the Stock Exchange to the private company, one generally finds that the deferred ordinary share is deprived not only of dividends but also of a vote and the right to any surplus in a winding up. If the deferral is for a sufficiently long period the present value will be very low and a gift can be made which attracts little or no capital transfer tax and capital gains tax. Eventually, often many years hence, the shares will assume a substantial value. But tax considerations are not the only reasons for the creation of deferred shares. Sometimes they are issued to employees as an incentive to work hard and stay with the company. In this respect they are akin to share options. In such cases, the deferral period will be fairly short — almost certainly under five years if the shares are to act as an incentive. The articles usually provide that an employee must sell his deferred shares on leaving the firm.

In the valuation of unquoted deferred shares there is no objective

[2] E. Dimson and Richard A. Brealey, 'The Risk Premium on UK Equities', *The Investment Analyst*, no 52 (1978), pp. 14–18.

[3] Gordon argues that investors prefer a dollar of dividend now to a dollar of retained profit. Although profit when reinvested in the business produces dividend growth, those future dividends suffer from increasing uncertainty as they extend to the future. They are therefore discounted at an increasingly higher rate and this upsets the equivalence between a dollar of dividend now and a dollar of retained profit. See Myron J. Gordon, 'Optimal Investment and Financing Policy', *The Journal of Finance*, 18 (May 1963), pp. 264–272. Reprinted in Archer and Ambrosio.

market price from which the value of the deferred shares may be imputed. The valuer therefore has to value the deferred shares from first principles. When the deferred shares come into their full equity rights, value will flow out of the existing ordinary shares. This happens because the profits and dividends will then be divided up amongst a greater number of shares. For Croda and London & Midland, the deferred shares represented only ten per cent of the equity. But, in private companies the dilution effect may be much greater. Consequently, the valuer must start with a valuation of the total equity as at the date when the deferred shares assume full equity rights. This value will be computed on the minority basis or the controlling interest basis as appropriate. The valuer should then allocate it between ordinary shares and deferred shares. This is just an arithmetical exercise since an ordinary and a deferred share will by then be of equal value. The value of the deferred shares should then be discounted at the required rate of return to arrive at the present value.

This technique is best illustrated by an example. A company whose issued share capital consists of 100,000 ordinary shares of £1 each plans to issue 900,000 deferred ordinary shares by way of a nine for one scrip. The deferred shares have no entitlement to dividends, profits or votes until 15 years' time when they will rank equally with the ordinary shares. You are asked for your opinion as to the value of the deferred shares immediately after their issue.

The value of the company in 15 years' time is unknown and can only be surmised. However, the value of the company today can be estimated with reasonable confidence. Let us assume that, using a rate of return of 20%, the ordinary shares are worth £5 each, indicating a value for the entire equity of £500,000. We now need a long term average growth rate to guess the value of the company 15 years hence. You opt for ten per cent, this being the dividend growth rate assumed in valuing the ordinary shares. The valuation of the deferred shares then proceeds as follows:

Current value of the company		£500,000
Compound interest factor for growth at ten per cent over 15 years		4.1772
Theoretical value of the equity in year 15		£2,088,600
Share in issue in year 15 (ranking equally)		
ordinary shares	100,000	
deferred shares	900,000	1,000,000
Value per deferred share/ordinary share in year 15		£2.09
Discount factor, 15 years at 20%		0.0649
Present value of deferred shares		£0.1356
say,		13½p

The valuation of uncertain entitlements far into the distant future is highly subjective hence the 'theoretical' value in 15 years' time. It is extremely sensitive to the growth rate and discount rate assumptions. The most the valuer can do is to ensure that his assumptions are justifiable and consistent with each other. It would not be consistent, for instance, for the long-term growth rate to exceed the required rate of return, since this would produce an infinitely valuable stream of earnings whereas all financial assets have finite values. Likewise, in the above example it would have been inconsistent to use a long-term growth rate different from that assumed in valuing the ordinary shares.

Despite the precision implied by discount and compound interest factors expressed to four decimal points, this valuation technique is extremely broad brush and sweeping. It can give no more than a rough guide.

Some authorities recommend that the current, as opposed to the future, value of the ordinary shares should be discounted over the deferral period to arrive at the value of the deferred shares.[4] In the above example, this would have produced a value of 32½p for each deferred share, as set out below:

Current value of ordinary share	£5.00
Discounted at 20% per annum over 15 years (factor 0.0649)	32½p

This is more than double the earlier value of 13½p per share. This technique is unsound for two reasons. First, it ignores the growth in value and second, it ignores the dilution effect.

Non-voting ordinary shares

The valuation of non-voting ordinary shares raises the question of the value of a vote. A number of quoted companies have non-voting ordinary shares and we start by comparing the prices of quoted voting and non-voting shares in the same company. Table 3 sets out such a comparison in respect of a random selection of six quoted companies having non-voting ordinary shares.

[4] As in Eastaway and Booth, *Practical Share Valuation*, p. 5 and pp. 374–376, and B. W. Sutherland, *Principles of Share Valuation for Fiscal Purposes* (London: The Institute of Chartered Accountants in England and Wales, 1985), p. 66.

Table 3: A comparison of voting and non-voting ordinary share prices for six quoted companies

	Voting ordinary shares	Non-voting ordinary shares	Discount	
	p	p	p	%
Clifford Dairies	145	135	10	7
Coates Bros	138	126	12	9
Liberty's	805	570	235	29
Thomas Locker (Holdings)	29½	26	3½	12
Young & Co Brewers	215	170	45	21
Horne (Robert)	170	160	10	6

Source: Financial Times

Table 3 shows that:

(a) non-voting ordinary shares stand at a discount to the voting ordinary shares;

(b) there is no single amount which could be considered as the price of a vote in all cases;

(c) the discount seems to be related to the value of the share in that the 'heavier' the share the larger the discount in absolute terms; and

(d) the percentage discount varies from company to company.

Two percentage discounts, those for Liberty's and Young & Co, stand out as being significantly higher than the other four.

The typical Stock Exchange investor is a minority shareholder. He never attends an annual general meeting and it would probably not cross his mind that he has a vote. If he disapproves of how the company is run, he 'votes with his feet' and sells his shares. On this analysis it is difficult to justify anything other than a purely nominal discount for the lack of a vote. The probability of a bid for the company might justify a more substantial discount since the non-voting shares would be of less value to a bidder than the voting shares, and this would be reflected in the offer terms. However, the City Code on Takeovers and Mergers stipulates that where a company has more than one class of equity share capital a comparable offer must be made for each class, whether such capital carries voting rights or not.[5] But a comparable offer need not be an identical offer. The Panel had no hard and fast rule for deciding what is a comparable offer but professional advisers must be able to justify the difference. The discount current in the market will obviously be a relevant factor.

[5] Rule 14.1, *The City Code on Takeovers and Mergers*, April 1985 edition.

If we accept that non-voting ordinary shares should stand at a discount to the voting ordinary shares, (a) merely to recognise the point, and (b) to reflect the former's disadvantage over the latter in any bid terms, the discount in four out of the six companies in Table 3 — Clifford Dairies, Coates Bros, Thomas Locker and Robert Horne — can be explained. The fact that the discount varies from 6% to 12% may trouble the efficient marketeer but it will not seem unusual to those of us who have never doubted that Stock Exchange pricing is anything other than a rough and ready, hit and miss affair. As to the big discounts for the non-voting shares in Young & Co. and Liberty's we can only surmise, on the basis of press reports and market rumour, that both these companies are viewed as highly attractive acquisitions and that their voting shares, which are tightly held, are keenly sought by interested parties anxious to build up or protect their positions.

Where the voting ordinary shares are numerous, a small minority interest in the voting shares is almost as uninfluential as a small minority holding of the non-voting shares. In such a case, it seems reasonable to apply a discount based on Stock Exchange comparisons. The comparisions in Table 3 could justify a discount of, say, ten per cent. However, where there is only a small number of voting ordinary shares the price differential between voting and non-voting shares will be substantial. Consider, for example, the following capital structure:

	£
100 ordinary shares of £1 each	100
10,900 'A' non-voting ordinary shares of £1 each	10,900
	11,000

Ownership of the ordinary shares will be highly prized and almost any holding of whatever size will be influential. There will, therefore, be a big difference between the value of the ordinary shares and the 'A' non-voting ordinary shares. In this case it would be wrong to think of the value of the two classes of shares as being related by some Stock Exchange-derived discount.[6] As always in share valuation, much depends on the circumstances. If the company is in trouble or conflicts develop between the shareholders the voting rights may assume a value they would not attract in quieter times.

Valuations *cum div* and *ex div*

The terms *cum div* and *ex div* are used in the Stock Exchange to denote

[6] See Chapter 10, under 'the meaning of control' for a discussion of valuation considerations in this type of capital structure.

that the price of a stock respectively includes or excludes the forthcoming, recently announced dividend. A share usually goes *ex div* on the first day of the account following a dividend announcement. This means that the seller and not the buyer is due to receive the distribution. If the share is not quoted *ex div*, the buyer is entitled to the dividend to come. If, because of the delay in registration, the dividend is actually paid to the seller, the buyer is entitled to recover it from him. Fixed interest stocks usually go *ex* some four to six weeks ahead of the actual payment.

The price of a share on the Stock Exchange therefore includes the right to the forthcoming dividend unless the price is explicitly stated to be *ex div*. When a share goes *ex div* the forthcoming net dividend is deducted from the *cum div* price. Thus, if a company's shares are priced at 150p and a net dividend of 7p (10p gross) is announced the *ex div* price will be 143p. However, when gilts go *ex*, the *gross* interest payment is deducted. When deriving capitalisation rates from quoted shares which have gone *ex div* the purist would argue that the net dividend should be added back to arrive at the *cum div* price. But, unless the quoted company has a very high dividend yield, the adjustment will be of only marginal significance, and in most instances can be ignored.

The *cum div/ex div* point rarely arises in share valuation but when it does it usually embarrasses the unprepared valuer. If a valuation is done just before a dividend payment, one of the first things vendor and purchaser will want to know is whether the price includes or excludes the right to the forthcoming dividend. It clearly does not enhance the parties' confidence in the valuation if the valuer is at a loss for a reply.

The valuer should make it a rule, therefore, to consider the timing of dividend payments in all valuations. If a dividend has just been declared but not yet paid, he should qualify his valuation with words such as '*ex* the final dividend of xp per share in respect of the year ended———'. By consent between the parties, of course, the valuation could be *cum* the recently declared dividend. In that case the full amount of the net dividend would have to be added to the valuation.

Where the valuation does not fall between the declaration of a dividend and its payment there is no call for the *ex div* appendage. All valuations are *cum div*, although as mentioned above, the words *cum div* would only be used where shares would normally be *ex div* but are *cum div* by arrangement. The DCF-derived dividend valuation formula in Chapter 9 assumes receipt of the first dividend 12 months from the valuation date. In reality the dividend payment will only by accident fall on that date. Strictly speaking, therefore, the valuer should make an adjustment where dividends are likely to be paid early on in the year. All depends on the size of the dividend. A token dividend such as many private companies pay would not be worth the bother. Where the dividend payment is significant, however, the valuer should consider increasing the valuation to reflect the appropriate proportion of the likely net dividend. He can then give the parties his assurance, should it be sought, that the timing of dividends has been taken into account.

Prior sales

Transactions in unquoted company shares are so rare that the valuer can easily overlook the fact that shares may have changed hands in the past at prices which throw some light on the current value of the shares. The valuer should always enquire about past transactions in the company's shares and any previous valuations. Unless transactions are so frequent as to constitute a market, the prices of isolated transactions in the past should not directly influence the current valuation. There will usually be many good reasons why the current valuation should be significantly different from earlier prices. The trading prospects and financial position of the company may have changed considerably in the intervening period, as may have capital market conditions, in particular, interest rates and required rates of return. Earlier prices, like the present one, reflect the owner values of buyer and seller as well as the circumstances of the transaction. These will hardly be the same today. It should not be forgotten, too, that many private company share transactions are not at arms-length.

If previous transactions in the shares have taken place the valuer should, nevertheless, analyse them carefully and endeavour as best he can to reconcile them with the current valuation. If a particular transaction was concluded at a price which defies rational explanation he may ignore the price, but at least he has not overlooked it.

As to whether the transactions in a company's shares constitute a market or not is a question of judgement. For the overwhelming majority of unquoted companies there exists no market in their shares. The question arises for a small number of large, unquoted, usually public companies with a wide spread of shareholders. Shares in such companies may be traded under Rule 535.2 of the Stock Exchange or even on the OTC market.[7] The valuer must enquire closely into recent prices. If the shares are regularly traded at prices which do not fluctuate too widely, the trading price will exert a considerable influence on the valuation in hand. If a true market exists, of course, there is no need for the valuer since recent prices are by definition a good indication of market value. But even the Stock Exchange's USM is an imperfect

[7] See Chapter 5 for a description of these markets.

market and instances can be cited of USM companies which have accepted bid terms below their current USM capitalisation. Where shares are tightly held and markets thin, as they are for many USM and OTC companies, the current share price may not be a good indication of market value. It is noteworthy in this respect that the Inland Revenue will not necessarily accept a USM price as conclusive evidence of market value.

Conclusion

Unquoted fixed interest securities comprise preference shares, debentures and loan stocks. Broadly speaking, their value is a function of the risk-free rate of interest as adjusted for the relative security of income and capital. In normal circumstances none of these fixed income securities has voting rights. This means that the value per share should generally be the same irrespective of the size of the holding. As it would be unusual for a fixed interest security to have a different value to different persons, this type of investment can be valued in the abstract by reference to the yields on gilts and quoted preference shares, debentures and loans. Appropriate allowance must be made for the higher risk and inferior marketability of the unquoted investment.

The typical deferred share in a private company is a form of ordinary share with deferred or postponed equity rights. Some quoted companies have deferred ordinary shares and two such companies were selected in order to examine the price differential between the deferred ordinary shares and the ordinary shares. In the case of these two companies the only difference between the deferred ordinary shares and the ordinary shares lay in the former's deferred dividend entitlement. However, the discount to the ordinary shares seemed excessive when measured by likely future dividends forgone. Valuing deferred shares solely by reference to dividends forgone would, in any event, ignore the dilution effect when the deferred shares become enfranchised. Unquoted deferred shares should, therefore, be valued from first principles. The technique suggested here involves a current valuation of the equity and estimates of the long-term growth rate and the rate of return. It inevitably entails highly subjective judgements and can only give a very approximate answer.

In valuing non-voting ordinary shares the valuer has to assess the value of a vote. As far as uninfluential minority interests are concerned, the value of a vote is not very high. Comparison of the prices of quoted voting and non-voting ordinary shares lends broad support to this view. A discount of ten per cent or thereabouts is suggested on the basis of current evidence.

Where dividend payments fall shortly after a valuation is issued, that valuation should specify whether it is *cum* or *ex* the forthcoming dividend. The valuer should in any event consider the timing of dividend payments and make any appropriate adjustment to his valuation to reflect dividends received much sooner in the year than implied by his valuation method.

The chapter was concluded with a discussion of the relevance of previous transaction prices to the current valuation of a company's shares. Although their relevance may be slight, as where transactions are few and far between, past prices should be examined and, if possible, reconciled with the current valuation.

15

Legal or binding valuations

Introduction

This chapter is concerned with valuations which are expressed as binding on the parties involved. They are loosely termed legal valuations to indicate the existence of some form of contract under which the valuation is required. The most commonly encountered legal valuation is probably the determination of the fair value of shares under the share transfer provisions of a company's articles of association. This task is usually carried out by the company's auditors. Sometimes shareholders enter into a side agreement which provides for the independent valuation of shares for the purposes of a sale. From time to time and with increasing frequency, disputes between shareholders come before the courts. These disputes often result in an order by the court for the shareholding of one party to be bought out by the other at an independent valuation. The essential feature of all these valuations for the purposes of this chapter is their binding nature: that is, the valuer is not acting in an advisory capacity where his client is free to accept or reject his advice, but rather he makes a determination of value which both sides are obliged to accept. This is a very significant difference and affects the valuer's legal position, the valuation approach and the work involved.

The valuer's position in law and the status of his valuation certificate is of considerable practical importance since, where the parties are in dispute, it is more than likely that at least one of them will disagree with the value. If that party is disputacious by nature, he may seek to upset the valuation. If unsuccessful in this, he may consider sueing the valuer for damages in negligence. The valuer should therefore know how to ensure as far as possible that his certificate remains conclusive and not open to question. He should also be aware of his potential liability to a claim for damages for negligence. The detailed consideration of these topics is followed by a discussion of the meaning of the valuation bases sometimes stipulated in the underlying agreements. Some remarks on the appropriate working method for legal valuations conclude the chapter.

The binding force of the valuation

The fundamental rule of law is that if the parties to a contract agree to refer the determination of value (or of any other matter) to a third party and to be bound thereby, then the value so determined is final and binding, whether one or the other party likes it or not. This rule was first enunciated in *Collier* v. *Mason* (1858) 119 RR 394, where Mr Mason had agreed to buy a house from Mr Collier at an independent valuation which in the event seemed to Mr Mason — and the judge — to be exorbitant. The judge, nevertheless, refused to set aside the valuation. The principle has been confirmed in subsequent cases and is undisputed. In *Arenson* v. *Arenson* [1973] Ch 346 Lord Denning MR summed up the position thus:

> On reading all the cases it seems to me there is one dominant theme running through them. It is this. Whenever two persons agree together to refer a matter to a third person for decision, and further agree that his decision is to be final and binding on them, then, so long as he arrives at his decision honestly and in good faith, the two parties are bound by it. They cannot reopen it for mistake or error on his part or for any reason other than fraud or collusion.

Thus, in *Campbell* v. *Edwards* [1976] 1 WLR 403, CA, the lease of a Mayfair flat contained a special provision that if the tenant desired to assign the premises she had first to offer to surrender them to the landlord and the price was to be fixed by a surveyor to be agreed by the parties. The tenant decided to assign the lease and first offered to surrender it to the landlord, who accepted the offer. The parties eventually agreed to appoint a well-known firm of surveyors (Chestertons) to determine the price payable. The surveyors in due course determined the price payable by the landlord at £10,000. The tenant gave up the premises but the landlord disputed the assessment of the price. He obtained valuations from two other firms of surveyors, one for £3,500 and the other for £1,250, and issued a writ claiming he was not bound by the original valuation. In the statement of claim he said:

> The valuation was incorrect in that the true surrender value of the lease at the specified date was under £4,000. In the circumstances, Messrs Chesterton must be presumed to have assessed the price in an incorrect manner and their valuation is therefore vitiated.

The landlord's claim for a declaration that he was not bound by the valuation came before the master and the judge both of whom ruled that the claim disclosed no reasonable cause of action. In dismissing the appeal against this decision Geoffrey Lane LJ said:

> In this case counsel for the landlord has argued that there is sufficient discrepancy between the valuer's report and the subsequent valuations obtained by his client to indicate that the valuers, Chestertons, must have acted on a wrong principle. He says that, despite the fact that this is not a speaking report, that wide discrepancy is sufficient to cast doubt on the valuation. I disagree. There is nothing to suggest that the valuer here did not take into consideration all the matters which he should have taken into consideration, and where the only basis of criticism is that another valuer has subsequently produced a valuation a third of the original one it does not afford, in my view, any ground for saying that Chestertons' valuation must have been or may have been wrong.

Baber v. *Kenwood Manufacturing Co Ltd* [1978] 1 Lloyds Rep 175 was another case in which the court declared that an expert's valuation — this time it concerned the valuation of shares by the company's auditors — could not be impeached for mistake. Baber held 2400 shares in a company called Millwall Engineering Ltd and agreed to sell these to Kenwood Manufacturing. Under the contract of sale the price was to be agreed between the parties, or in default of agreement to be determined by Millwall's auditors valuing under the procedure in the articles of association. Under this procedure, the auditors, acting as experts and not as arbitrators, had to arrive at the fair selling value of the whole of Millwall's equity as between a willing vendor and a willing purchaser, and the shares in question were to be valued *pro rata*.

Baber and Kenwood were unable to agree on a price so the auditors were appointed to determine the value. This they duly did in the form of a 'non-speaking' certificate. Baber, however, was dissatisfied with the valuation and brought an action against the purchaser to have the valuation set aside as invalid and not binding, and, depending on this, to claim damages against the auditors. The valuation was attacked in the following terms:

> The said valuation . . . was not a proper valuation in accordance with the relevant provisions of the Agreement . . . and the Articles . . . in that the same was vitiated by

fundamental errors of principle in that the Second Defendants (the auditors): (i) omitted to obtain any or any proper or sufficient valuation of the plant and machinery of the company; (ii) acted upon an inaccurate record namely the Plant audit in ascertaining the value of the plant and machinery of the Company; (iii) failed to take into account the break-up value of the Company in valuing its entire share capital; (iv) failed to value the shares in accordance with the provisions of . . . Article 7(2).

Kenwood Manufacturing appealed to the court to have the action struck out as disclosing no reasonable cause of action against them. The question before the court therefore was not whether a mistake had been made, but whether, assuming the alleged mistakes were proven, there would be a cause of action against Kenwood.[1] The trial judge decided in favour of Kenwood and this was upheld in the Court of Appeal. The statement of claim was struck out as disclosing no reasonable cause of action. Megaw LJ's reasoning is of considerable interest:

> The point of law agreed upon by Counsel on behalf of the parties to the appeal is as follows:
>
> Whether the valuation . . . can be impeached by the plaintiff on the ground of mistake by the valuers?
>
> . . . In my judgment the answer to the question framed is 'No'. I give this answer with reference to any or all of the mistakes averred in para. 37 of the statement of claim [cited above]. I make that qualification because I should take a different view if there were to be alleged or proved facts of a nature not here accepted, but which might be regarded as falling within the meaning of the word 'mistake'. Thus if in the present case, it had been averred and proved that the second defendants had in error valued the shares of some different company or had given their valuation by reference to some different number of shares than 2400, the plaintiff in my opinion would not be bound by the valuation. But the reason for that is that the purported valuation would be shown to be a valuation which was not in accordance with the express terms of the contract.

[1] The auditors, who vigorously denied any negligence, did not desire to be heard on the application.

And also:

> Why do the parties provide that the auditors 'shall be considered to be acting as experts and not as arbitrators?' For the single reason that, if they were to be considered as arbitrators, there would at least be a danger that one party or the other might be able to require a case to be stated before a Court of Law, by which means it could be suggested that the award was not binding because of some error in it. If that is what the parties sought to prevent each other from doing by using the words which I have quoted, it would, in my judgment, be entirely wrong in principle that one party, having so agreed, should be entitled in law to frustrate the agreement by alleging mistake in the experts' opinion.

This fundamental rule, like all fundamental legal rules, has its exceptions. The existence of fraud or collusion would be grounds for setting aside the valuation — 'If there were fraud or collusion, of course, it would be very different. Fraud or collusion unravels everything'.[2] Second, if the valuer issues a 'speaking' certificate, in other words, if he discloses how he has arrived at his valuation, the Court may examine his reasoning and calculations and, if found wrong, the valuation might be upset. Third, if the valuation was made on an erroneous principle, e.g., a valuation of the wrong subject matter, it can be set aside.

Fraud or collusion

Fraud will hardly be a concern for the honest valuer, nor in fact should collusion. However, where the valuer already has a professional relationship with one of the parties the borderline between collusion and the lack of the proper degree of professional independence may be extremely difficult to draw. The auditor of a company may be in such a position. Suppose that his accountancy firm provides a wide range of accounting and taxation services to the company and that he personally advises the directors on financial and even commercial policy. If he is appointed under the articles to make a binding determination of the value of a retiring member's shares and he knows that the directors, with whom he may have a close personal relationship as well as professional relationship, want a low value, he may find his professional independence an embarrassment and it may cost him dearly. In such circumstances, the valuer must never give any prior indication of his

2 Per Lord Denning MR in *Campbell* v. *Edwards*, supra.

valuation to either party. He must keep his own counsel and his independence must be beyond question or reproach. Some inconvenient practical implications of this standard of conduct are discussed later on in this chapter under 'procedure'.

The speaking certificate

The important case here is *Dean* v. *Prince* [1954] Ch 409. A small light engineering company with an issued share capital of 200 £1 ordinary shares was owned by its three directors. One of the directors, who held 140 shares, died. The other two each held 30 shares. Article 9(g) of the company's articles of association provided that, if a member died 'his shares shall be purchased and taken by the directors at such price as is certified in writing by the auditor to be in his opinion the fair value thereof at the date of death and in so certifying the auditor shall be considered to act as an expert and not an [arbitrator] . . .'. The auditor duly certified a fair value of £7 each for the shares. The director's widow, Mrs Dean, was dissatisfied with the value and her solicitors succeeded in persuading the auditors to disclose how they had arrived at their valuation. The auditors wrote:

> We enclose a few notes which we have prepared to show you how the points you raised at our discussion last week have been allowed for in our valuation insofar as we considered them appropriate. We trust that they will enable you to satisfy [Mrs Dean] that £7 a share represented a fair value.

This disclosure, on the face of it innocuous and almost certainly intended to be helpful, opened the road to legal action to have the certificate set aside. The notes showed amongst other things that the company had been valued on a break-up basis. Mrs Dean thereupon brought an action seeking a declaration that the auditors' valuation of the company's shares was arrived at on the wrong basis and was not binding. She also sought an injunction restraining the remaining directors from transferring the shares.

The defendant directors claimed as a point of law that the certificate was final and binding, that on the face of the certificate there was nothing wrong with the valuation, and that it was not legitimate to go beyond the certificate and to look at explanations subsequently offered by the auditors to show that they proceeded on a wrong basis. Harman J, the trial judge, overruled this objection, saying:

In my judgment there is nothing in that point. It is well settled that those who have a discretion, e.g., trustees who have powers to apply income for maintenance and directors who have powers to admit members to a company, can maintain a silence in regard to the reason for their decision which the court will not oblige them to break, and that, if they do maintain silence, no action will lie against them, but, if they choose, for whatever reason, to disclose the motives which impelled them to their decision, the plaintiff may come to the court to impeach those motives. That seems to me to be analogous to what has happened here. It is true that the auditors are dealing as experts and that they have to arrive at what is their opinion about the fair value. It may well be that their opinion, although wrong in the eyes of others, may prevail, but if they have founded themselves on an entirely wrong basis, I cannot see that the provisions of article 9(g) of the company's articles preclude the plaintiff from attacking it.

Harman J also relied upon the decision in *Johnston* v. *Chestergate Hat Manufacturing Co Ltd* [1915] 2 Ch 338. In that case a manager was entitled to a certain percentage of the net profits of the company. The agreement defined 'net profits' and provided for a binding certificate of net profits by the auditors. The manager sought a declaration that on a true construction of the agreement 'net profits' were before deduction of tax and not, as shown in the auditors' certificate, profits after tax. The company argued as a preliminary point that the auditors' certificate was binding and conclusive. The judge (Sargant J) held that as the certificate was based on a wrong principle the court was not bound by it. Just as Sargant J did not confine himself to the certificate but looked at the balance sheet on which it was based, so, Harman J concluded, he was not precluded from looking at the documents other than the certificate, i.e., at the notes disclosed by the auditors.

The reader will be interested to know that Harman J's subsequent finding that the valuation was made on erroneous principles was overturned by the Court of Appeal and the auditors' valuation was upheld. This, of course, was a separate matter from the one of whether the certificate could be challenged in the first place. Lord Denning's remarks in the Court of Appeal throw some interesting light on the fair value concept. These, and the views of the other judges, are discussed later under 'fair value'.

In the recent case of *Burgess* v. *Purchase & Sons (Farms) Ltd* [1983] 2 All ER 4 the court upheld this distinction in law between a speaking and a non-speaking certificate. There, on Mr William Purchase's death his personal representatives, the plaintiffs, gave the company notice that they desired to sell his ordinary and preference shares in the company. Under the articles the shares were to be offered to any member 'at the fair value', this to be fixed by the auditors whose decision was to be 'final, binding and conclusive.' However, in the letter setting out the values so fixed, the auditors explained how they had arrived at their figures. It was therefore a speaking certificate. The plaintiffs alleged that the valuations had been prepared on a fundamentally erroneous basis and sought a declaration setting aside the valuation. The defendants argued that in view of 'dicta' in recent cases in the Court of Appeal, notably *Campbell* v. *Edwards* and *Baber* v. *Kenwood* it was no longer the law, if it ever had been, that a speaking valuation could be challenged. There was now no difference between a speaking and a non-speaking valuation and the defendants applied to have the plaintiffs' case struck out as showing no reasonable cause of action. In other words, a speaking valuation, too, could not be challenged.

Nourse J dismissed the application.

> It seems to me that I could not tread that path without trespassing on the rarest ethers of speculation. The function of a judge of first instance is to apply the law as it stands. He is not to speculate on what some higher court may one day declare it to be. If the law is declared by earlier decisions at first instance he ought to follow them unless he is satisfied that they are wrong. In this case the law is declared by three earlier decisions at first instance. I am certainly not satisfied that they are wrong. I must therefore follow and apply them.

He also gave his views on the present state of the law:

> In my judgment the present state of the law can be summarised as follows. The question whether a valuation made by an expert on a fundamentally erroneous basis can be impugned or not depends on the terms expressed or to be implied in the contract pursuant to which it is made. A non-speaking valuation made of the right property by the right man and in good faith cannot be impugned, although it may still be possible, in the case of an uncompleted transaction, for equitable relief (as opposed to damages) to be refused to the party who wishes to sustain the valuation. On the other hand, there are at least three decisions at first instance to the

effect that a speaking valuation which demonstrates that it has been made on a fundamentally erroneous basis can be impugned. In such a case the completion of the transaction does not necessarily defeat the party who wish to impugn the valuation.

Nourse J was well aware of the inconsistency of a principle which holds that the test of whether a certificate can be upset depends solely on whether or not the evidence to challenge it is disclosed. His judgment also considered whether the existence now of a remedy against the valuer for negligence had any relevance to the binding force of the certificate. His observations are reproduced below:

Whether this will hereafter be found to be the law to be applied to speaking valuations by some higher court is not for me to say: I merely proffer the following observations. It may be that the rule can be justified on the footing that a valuation made on a fundamentally erroneous basis is no more that for which the parties have contracted than one made of the wrong property by the wrong man or in bad faith. The possibility of there being an implied term to that effect was discussed by Sir David Cairns in *Baber* v. *Kenwood Manufacturing Co* [1978] 1 Lloyd's Rep 175 at 181. Where the contract provides for the valuation to be fair it might often be said that there was a breach of an express term. In either event there must remain something of an anomaly in that the right to impugn a valuation for fundamental error, as opposed to bad faith for example, depends solely on whether the evidence which makes the attack possible is or is not voiced by the valuation itself. The reconciliation may be that the law ought not to shrink from an anomaly where the court can see for itself a fundamental error on the face of the very exercise for which the parties have contracted. It may be that Harman J's analogy with trustees and directors is after all a sound basis for the rule.

As for the suggestion that the rule, if otherwise soundly based, ought now to be reconsidered in the light of *Arenson* v. *Arenson* and *Sutcliffe* v. *Thackrah* I must, with the greatest respect to the views of Lord Denning MR and Megaw LJ, if indeed they went that far, express my own view that that cannot be correct. Like Buckley LJ and Sir Seymour Karminski in *Arenson* v. *Arenson* when dealing with the converse, I do not think that the question of what remedy, if any, the plaintiff may have against the valuers has any relevance to the question of what is his remedy against the other party to the contract. That course is charted between the Scylla of leaving the plaintiff with no remedy at all and the Charybdis of assuming that every valuation made on a fundamentally erroneous basis involves negligence on the part of the valuer, an assumption which no court of justice could make. Take, for example, the valuer who proceeds on a fundamentally erroneous construction of the agreement which it is not within his professional competence to detect. In such case there could be no invariable rule that the valuer was liable in negligence. Of greater practical significance, take the valuer who only agrees to act on terms that he is not to be liable in negligence, a protection which the law does not deny him. That example seems to be the clearest exposure of the plaintiff's plight and the surest ground for saying the suggestion cannot be correct.

An erroneous principle

If a valuation is made on a fundamentally erroneous principle it can be upset. This of course would be the grounds for challenging a speaking certificate but it can also be the grounds for impugning a non-speaking certificate. If, for example, the valuer made a valuation of the wrong thing or at the wrong date or failed to proceed on the basis agreed, there would be grounds for setting aside the valuation. In *Jones* v. *Jones* [1971] 1 WLR 840, the parties had agreed that D should value the company 'on an assets basis as between a willing vendor and a willing purchaser of a business being carried on as a going concern'.[3] The agreement also provided that, in valuing any land or premises D should employ DC, and in valuing any stock or machinery he should employ an expert valuer. In the event, D instructed DC to value the premises at 'break-up' value and did not employ an expert valuer for the machinery. Ungoed-Thomas J concluded that on both these counts, the valuation had been rendered erroneous in principle and should be set aside.

The justification for this rule lies in the law of contract. A valuation on a fundamentally erroneous principle, such as one at the wrong date or not on the agreed basis, is not what the parties agreed to be bound by. An immaterial error such as a clerical slip on the face of the certificate which does not affect the result will not vitiate the valuation

[3] See 'Interpreting the terms of reference' for a discussion of the meaning of this valuation formula.

although an error, no matter how small, in what has to be certified is apparently a material error.[4]

The defendants in *Jones* v. *Jones* claimed that an error in principle does not vitiate a valuation unless the person relying on it can show that it results in a materially different valuation both in the part of the valuation subject to error and the overall valuation. Ungoed-Thomas J rejected this argument:

> . . . I do not conclude that there is any requirement of general application that where a valuation is made on an erroneous principle, yet the valuation nevertheless stands unless it is shown that a valuation on the right principle would produce a materially different figure from the figure of the valuation that he made. (This would incidentally place on the objector the onus, not only of proving that the selected expert has acted on a wrong principle, but of incurring what might be the very heavy burden and expense of a completely new valuation, which itself might not be accepted as conclusive between the parties and merely leading to yet another valuation.) The authorities thus to my mind establish that if a valuation is erroneous in principle, it is vitiated and cannot be relied on even though it is not established that the valuation figure is wrong.

As it happened the judge also concluded that, on the evidence before him, a valuation on the correct principle would have shown a substantially higher figure.

Valuer's liability for negligence

The valuer, like any other professional or business person, owes a duty of care to those who employ his services and he will be liable in damages to them if he is negligent in performing those services. Before the House of Lords' decision in *Hedley, Byrne & Co Ltd* v. *Heller & Partners Ltd* [1964] AC 465, it was the law that he could only be held liable for negligence to those with whom he was in a contractual relationship, i.e. his client. The *Hedley Byrne* case (which did not concern a valuer) established that, unless there is an explicit disclaimer of responsibility to third parties, there exists an enforceable duty of care not just to the contracting party but to anyone who the valuer might reasonably expect would rely on his valuation.

---

[4] *Frank H Wright (Constructions) Ltd* v. *Frodoor Ltd* [1967] 1 WLR 506.

It has long been established as a matter of public policy that judges and arbitrators are immune from an action for negligence. This protection extends to those who, though not judges or arbitrators, nevertheless perform arbitral or judicial functions. The expert valuer or the architect certifying the value of work completed were regarded as 'quasi-arbitrators' and were accordingly believed to be not liable for negligence. The generally accepted doctrine at that time was succinctly expressed by Buckley LJ in *Arenson* v. *Arenson* [1973] Ch 346:

> . . . where a third party undertakes the role of deciding as between two other parties a question, the determination of which requires the third party to hold the scales fairly between the opposing interests of the two parties, the third party is immune from an action for negligence in respect of anything done in that role.

In the House of Lords' decision in *Sutcliffe* v. *Thackrah* [1974] AC 727 and *Arenson* v. *Casson, Beckman, Rutley & Co* [1977] AC 405, however, this doctrine was overturned. The former case concerned whether an action for damages could be brought against an architect in respect of the negligent over-certification of work done on a building contract. The latter case concerned the auditor of a company who had acted as an expert in valuing some shares in accordance with a shareholder's agreement. It was the sequel to the Court of Appeal decision in *Arenson* v. *Arenson*, supra. In both cases the certificates of value were binding on the parties. In *Sutcliffe* v. *Thackrah* the court held that the architect was not immune to an action for negligence. Although he was required to act fairly both to his own employer and the builder when certifying the value of work done, this did not of itself constitute him arbitrator. It was a fallacy to argue that as all persons carrying out judicial functions must act fairly, therefore all persons who must act fairly are carrying out judicial functions. In Lord Reid's words:

> There is nothing judicial about an architect's function in determining whether certain work is defective. There is no dispute. He is not jointly engaged by the parties. They do not submit evidence as contentious to him. He makes his own investigations and comes to a decision. It would be taking a very low view to suppose that without being put in a special position his employer would wish him to act unfairly or that a professional man would be willing to depart from the ordinary honourable standard of professional conduct.

Lord Morris of Borth-y-Gest put it this way:

> In summarising my conclusions I must preface them by the observation that each case will depend on its own facts and circumstances and on the particular provisions of the relevant contract. But in general any architect or surveyor or valuer will be liable to the person who employs him if he causes loss by reason of his negligence. There will be an exception to this and judicial immunity will be accorded if the architect or surveyor or valuer has by agreement been appointed to act as an arbitrator. There may be circumstances in which what is in effect an arbitrator is not one that is within the provisions of the Arbitration Act. The expression quasi-arbitrator should only be used in that connection. A person will only be an arbitrator or quasi-arbitrator if there is a submission to him either of a specific dispute or of present points of difference or of defined differences that may in future arise and if there is agreement that his decision will be binding.

The House of Lords in the *Arenson* case re-affirmed the new doctrine in *Sutcliffe* v. *Thackrah* that the mere fact that an expert valuer was required to hold the scales fairly between the opposing interests of the two parties did not of itself invest the expert with arbitral immunity from an action for negligence. In the *Arenson* case the shareholders' agreement under which the shares were valued was in the form of a letter from nephew to uncle in the following terms:

18 March 1964

Dear Mr and Mrs Arenson,

A. Arenson Limited

In consideration of your procuring the Company to continue to employ me, I hereby agree the following arrangements concerning the Shares of which you have made me a gift:

1 I will not sell the Shares other than to Mr Arenson or to Mrs Arenson should he predecease her.

2 Should I wish to dispose of my Shares, Mr Arenson will purchase them from me at the Fair Value, but I shall not require him to purchase from me for five years from the date hereof.

3 Should I wish to sell the Shares after the death of Mr Arenson I will first offer them for sale to Mrs Arenson, who shall have the right to

purchase them at the Fair Value but she shall not be under an obligation so to do.

4   Should Mr Arenson decide to dispose of his Shares in the Company, then I hereby agree to sell my Shares in the Company to Mr Arenson at the same price per share as Mr Arenson will be receiving in respect of his Shares.

5   In the event of my employment with the Company terminating for whatsoever reason, I will offer to sell my Shares to Mr Arenson and it is agreed that he will purchase them from me at a Fair Value. Should Mr Arenson be dead then Mrs Arenson shall have the option to purchase Shares from me at the Fair Value.

6   'Fair Value' shall mean in relation to the Shares in A. Arenson Limited, the value thereof as determined by the auditors for the time being of the Company whose valuation acting as experts and not as arbitrators shall be final and binding on all parties.

Please indicate your acceptance of the above conditions by signing the carbon copy sent herewith, and returning it to me.

Yours sincerely,

I. Arenson

The nephew's employment with Arenson Ltd was terminated on 4 April 1970 and the auditors were instructed to determine the fair value of the nephew's shares. This they did and duly issued a non-speaking valuation certificate. Some eight months later the company obtained a Stock Exchange listing. The prospectus price was over six times the value placed on the shares by the auditors and the nephew sought: (a) to have the valuation set aside as being fundamentally erroneous; or (b) to bring an action in negligence against the auditors.

The auditors had applied to the court to have the statement of claim against them struck out as disclosing no reasonable cause of action. In other words, even if negligence were proved no action could be brought against them because they enjoyed immunity. The High Court granted the application and this was upheld by the Court of Appeal, with Lord Denning MR dissenting. The House of Lords in *Arenson* v. *Casson Beckman Rutley & Co*, supra[5], overturned the High Court and Court of Appeal decision. Their Lordships' decision is of interest not only because it re-affirmed the doctrine enunciated in *Sutcliffe* v. *Thackrah* that an expert was not necessarily immune from a negligence action, but also because it pointed to a further significant evolution in judicial thinking on the question of arbitral immunity.

---

[5] Reported as *Arenson* v. *Arenson* in the lower courts.

Five Law Lords heard the case and although they reached a unanimous conclusion that the expert may be liable in negligence, the individual judgments showed a range of opinion as to the scope of arbitral immunity. Lord Wheatley and Lord Simon of Glaisdale were reluctant to go beyond the reasoning in *Sutcliffe* v. *Thackrah*. A valuer acting as an expert is not *per se* immune from an action for negligence. It all depends on the circumstances. If his role, by whatever name it is called, is similar to that of an arbitrator he would enjoy immunity. In Lord Wheatley's words:

> I therefore content myself with a number of observations.
> (1) It is clear from the speeches of Lord Reid, Lord Morris of Borth-y-Gest and my noble and learned friend, Lord Salmon, in *Sutcliffe* v. *Thackrah* that while a valuer may by the terms of his appointment be constituted an arbitrator (or quasi-arbitrator) and may be clothed with the immunity, a valuer simply as such does not enjoy that benefit.
> (2) It accordingly follows that when a valuer is claiming that immunity he must be able to establish from the circumstances and purpose of his appointment that he has been vested with the clothing which gives him that immunity.
> (3) In view of the difficult circumstances which can surround individual cases, and since each case has to be decided on its own facts, it is not possible to enunciate an all-embracing formula which is habile to decide every case. What can be done is to set out certain indicia which can serve as guidelines in deciding whether a person is clothed . . .
> . . . The indicia are as follows: (a) there is a dispute or a difference between the parties which has been formulated in some way or another: (b) the dispute or difference has been remitted by the parties to the person to resolve in such a manner that he is called on to exercise a judicial function: (c) where appropriate, the parties must have been provided with an opportunity to present evidence and/or submissions in support of their respective claims in the dispute: and (d) the parties have agreed to accept his decision.

Lord Kilbrandon went further than this. He too could see no reason why the expert valuer should be immune from an action for negligence, but nor could he see why the arbitrator should be so privileged. His point of view was as follows:

> The question which puzzled me as the arguments developed was: what was the essential difference between the typical

valuer, the auditor in the present case, and an arbitrator at common law or under the Arbitration Acts? It was conceded that an arbitrator is immune from suit, aside from fraud, but why? I find it impossible to put weight on such considerations as that in the case of an arbitrator (a) there is a dispute between the parties: (b) he hears evidence: (c) he hears submissions from the parties, and that therefore he, unlike the valuer, is acting in a judicial capacity. As regards (a), I cannot see any judicial distinction between a dispute which has actually arisen and a situation where persons have opposed interests, if in either case an impartial person has had to be called in to make a decision which the interested parties will accept. As regards (b) and (c), these are certainly not necessary activities of an arbiter. Once the nature and limits of the submission to him have been defined, it could well be that he would go down at his own convenience to a warehouse, inspect a sample of merchandise displayed to him by the foreman, and return his opinion on its quality or value. I have come to the opinion that it is a necessary conclusion to be drawn from *Sutcliffe* v. *Thackrah* and from the instant decision that an arbitrator at common law or under the Acts is indeed a person selected by the parties for his expertise, whether technical or intellectual, that he pledges skill in the exercise thereof, and that if he is negligent in that exercise he will be liable in damages.

Lord Fraser professed himself in the same difficulty as Lord Kilbrandon in seeing why arbitrators as a class should have immunity from suit if expert valuers do not. Lord Salmon's point of view seemed midway between these two positions. He suggested that an arbitrator who performed a judicial function would have immunity but one who, though appointed as an arbitrator, performed no judicial function would not. He said:

> . . . an expert may be formally appointed as an arbitrator under the Arbitration Acts, notwithstanding that he is required neither to hear nor read any submission by the parties or any evidence and in fact, has to rely on nothing but his examination of the goods and his own expertise. He, like the valuer in the present case, has a purely investigatory role: he is performing no function even remotely resembling the judicial function save that he finally decides a dispute or difference which has arisen between the parties. If such a

valuer who is appointed as arbitrator makes a decision without troubling to examine the goods, surely he is in breach of his duty to exercise reasonable care, so would he be if he made only a perfunctory and wholly careless examination.

I find it difficult to discern any sensible reason, on grounds of public policy or otherwise, why such an arbitrator with such a limited role, although formally appointed, should enjoy a judicial immunity which so called 'quasi-arbitrators' in the position of the respondents certainly do not.

In the *Arenson* case the auditors were found to be acting as mere valuers. There was no dispute between the parties beforehand; in fact they had agreed to have the valuation of the shares determined by the auditors in order to avoid a dispute. In this respect their terms of reference were like those often found in the articles of private companies, where on a transfer notice being given by the vendor, the auditors are required to determine the fair value. An expert valuer who is negligent in such circumstances will almost certainly be liable to be sued for damages. Where the articles provide that the auditors shall determine the fair value only in default of agreement between the parties, there is some ground for arguing that the valuer is required to settle a dispute. However, it would be highly inadvisable for the valuer to assume that he enjoys arbitral immunity in such a case, since: (a) the onus of proof that he is a 'quasi-arbitrator' is on him; and (b) the 'dicta' of three of the five Law Lords in the *Arenson* case question the continued immunity of the 'quasi-arbitrator' and indeed of the arbitrator appointed as such. Thus, even if the valuer is appointed under the Arbitration Acts but his real function is that of valuer, he may not enjoy immunity from damages in negligence.

Interpreting the terms of reference

The correct interpretation of the valuer's terms of reference is crucially important if for no other reason than that failure to do so may provide the grounds for upsetting the valuation. For example, a certificate based on market value when in fact the agreement stipulated fair value would almost certainly suffer from an error of principle rendering it liable to be set aside as being something the parties never contracted for. Unfortunately the valuer's terms of reference are not always clear, particularly where these appear in a company's articles of association, and identifying the value concept to be used may not be straightforward. Although fair value is the usual value concept adopted in private company articles, other value concepts, which have no accepted significance in valuation theory or practice, are sometimes encountered. Articles of association have been known to require the auditors to certify a 'proper value' of the company's shares. Sometimes it is 'current worth', other times it may be the 'fair selling value' or simply 'the value'. The variations are legion, and any one may have the confusing 'willing buyer/willing seller' appendage.

How should the valuer interpret these ambiguous formulae? He may seek legal advice particularly if the amounts at stake are considerable, but usually the problem can be solved with commonsense. It will be recalled from Chapter 2 that, apart from the concept of owner value which underlies all value concepts, there are two basic value concepts in share valuation: market value and fair value. Market value is a concept recognised everywhere, whereas the fair value concept is little known outside the realm of share valuation.

If the members of a company intended shares to be transferred at market value they would surely say so and would not need to cast around for synonyms. Furthermore, the market value concept is highly inappropriate for valuing minority shareholdings in private companies and very difficult to apply.[6] Only someone with little or no knowledge of the realities of the private company would prescribe it. There must be a strong presumption, therefore, that, unless market value is specifically stated as the required concept, the intention is to exclude it. On this reasoning all those other forms of words such as, the proper value, the current worth, the fair selling price, the true value, merely indicate to the valuer that something other than market value is required. The only other value concept which makes sense in these circumstances is fair value, and this is how the author at least would be inclined to interpret these other formulae.

Although valuations required under the articles or by virtue of a shareholders' side agreement account for most legal valuations, court orders, particularly under s.461 of the Companies Act 1985,[7] or orders of the Industrial Tribunal account for not a few. Here one usually encounters a formula such as 'net asset value, including goodwill'. This is not a value concept but a valuation basis. As has been demonstrated repeatedly in this book, the value of a business bears no necessary relation to the value of its separable assets, nor can goodwill be valued as a separable asset. As the only way goodwill can be valued (albeit not

[6] The market value concept is discussed in Chapter 2.
[7] Formerly, s.75 of the Companies Act 1980.

separately identified) is by valuing the business as a whole, and as the power to dispose of the firm's assets is the prerogative of the controlling shareholder, the author interprets this valuation formula as requiring a valuation of the entire business. In his view it does not mean that separate professional valuations of all the assets have to be obtained. The business should be valued as a going concern (if that is what it is), and the value of any surplus assets should be added to this going concern value. Depending on their nature, the surplus assets may need to be professionally valued. If the company is an asset-based investment intermediary, such as an investment trust or a property investment company, it may well be necessary to obtain professional valuations of most of the assets.

This conclusion that the formula 'net assets value including goodwill' does not necessarily entail a professional valuation of all the firm's assets can be justified by the usual meaning of the term 'goodwill'. As explained in Chapter 8, most accountants view goodwill as the excess of the value of a business as a whole over the aggregate value of its separable net assets. On this generally accepted but, in the author's opinion, misconceived view of goodwill, the application of the valuation formula 'net asset value including goodwill' would always produce a valuation of the business as a whole. This is because goodwill, as thus defined, is merely a balancing figure. A higher value for the assets, such as might be obtained by a professional valuation, will mean a correspondingly lower value for goodwill and vice versa. This will not apply, of course, when the assets, separately valued, are worth more than the business as a whole. But this would mean that there is no goodwill and that the business would be worth more if it were wound up. This state of affairs is the exception rather than the rule. On these grounds, therefore, one is justified in interpreting the formula 'net asset value, including goodwill' as indicating a valuation of the entire business to be arrived at in the normal way. For most trading, manufacturing or service businesses this will mean by reference to future profits. For investment intermediaries, such as investment trusts or property investment companies, it may well mean the assets basis in which case professional valuations would probably be required.

Another point the valuer should watch carefully is whether his instructions require him to value on a minority or a controlling interest basis. It is not uncommon for articles of association to provide that the auditor shall invariably value on one or the other basis. However articles of association, like most legal documents, are not necessarily intended to reveal their true meaning on a first reading. The auditor may not find an explicit statement, for example, that a minority basis is always required, but the wording of the articles on closer scrutiny may nevertheless contain an implicit requirement to that effect. Consider, for instance, the following clauses in a private company's articles:

> The person desiring to transfer *any share* (hereinafter called 'The Vendor') shall give notice in writing (hereinafter called 'a sale notice') to the Company of such desire stating the sum which he fixes as *the price for such share*. A sale notice shall constitute the Company the Vendor's Agent for the sale of *the share* to the person or persons specified in Article x hereof at the price so fixed or at the option of the Vendor or the Purchaser at the fair value to be fixed by the Auditors of the Company in accordance with these Articles. *A sale notice may include several shares and in each case shall operate as a separate notice in respect of each share.* A sale notice shall not be revocable without the sanction of the Board of Directors.
>
> If the Company shall within the period of 28 days after being served with a sale notice or the receipt of the auditors' certificate find a person or persons as provided by Article x hereof willing to purchase *the share* either at the price fixed by the Vendor or at the fair value and shall give notice thereof to the Vendor, the Vendor shall be bound to transfer *the share* to the Purchaser within 14 days after such last mentioned notice on payment of the purchase money.
>
> The Auditors for the time being of the Company shall on the application of either party certify in writing a sum which in their opinion is the fair value, and such sum shall be deemed to be the fair value: and in so certifying the Auditors shall be considered to be acting as experts and not arbitrators and accordingly the Arbitration Act 1950 shall not apply. [Emphasis added.]

The required value concept is quite clearly fair value, but it needs close reading to detect that these articles appear to stipulate that the auditor is to value a share in isolation. The fair value per share will therefore be that of the smallest possible minority shareholding — one share — and this will be so whatever the size of the shareholding being transferred. In cases such as this, particularly where the sums of money are substantial, the valuer may well have to seek legal advice as to the correct interpretation of the articles. The essential point here is not so much that the valuer should be able to interpret legal documents in a conclusive manner but that he should be aware when a problem of interpretation exists. Advice can then be sought in the appropriate quarter.

Where the articles or other contract provide that shares shall be valued on a control basis irrespective of the size of the holding the relevant wording is usually unambiguous. The articles might state that the value is to be such proportion of the value of the entire equity as the shares in question bear to the total number of equity shares. This would be the full *pro rata* control value. Sometimes, however, this intention is not expressed in the most precise manner, leaving some doubt as to what the requirement is. The following clause from the share transfer provisions of a company's articles will illustrate the point:

> Any valuation of shares in the Company to be carried out by the Company's auditors in accordance with the provisions of these Articles shall for all purposes ignore the fact that the shares to be so valued represent a minority holding in the Company's issued share capital.

The commonsense interpretation of these words is that they require the company to be valued as a whole and the resultant value per share applied to the number of shares being valued. It would not take a clever lawyer to point out, however, that this is not necessarily what the articles ask the valuer to do. It merely says that the shares shall not be valued as a minority holding. There are, of course, different levels of control: bare control at 51%, the ability to pass a special resolution at 75%, and compulsory acquisition powers at over 90%. Which level of control should the valuer assume? It could be quite important since in theory, if not always in practice, the value per share will reflect the degree of control and will be highest where 100% of the equity is involved, and lowest for a 51% holding. Where does a 50% shareholding fit into the picture?

The other difficulty is that, taken literally, it tells the valuer of a minority interest to assume that he is in fact valuing a controlling interest since this is presumably the only alternative to a minority interest. Does this mean that the minority shareholding is deemed to have a majority of the votes? Does it mean that the minority interest is deemed to be entitled to a majority share of profits and dividends? What size of majority holding should be assumed?

But this is merely playing with words and amply demonstrates the futility of going beyond the obvious ordinary meaning of the sentence taken as a whole in its context of the articles and customary provisions for valuing private company shares. Nevertheless, as the reader will appreciate, loose wording such as this gives considerable scope for mischief if either party seeks to upset the valuation, and the valuer ought to consider carefully whether he should seek legal advice as to the precise meaning of the words in law.

Fair value

The concept of fair value is important to the expert valuer as this is the value concept most commonly stipulated in the share transfer provisions of articles of association. The valuer should be thoroughly familiar with this concept and how it may be interpreted.

There is no legal definition of fair value. It is suggested here that what distinguishes fair value from market value is the desire to be equitable to both parties. The transaction is not in the open market; the buyer has not been able to shop around for the lowest price, nor has the seller been able to hold out for the highest price. In effect, the articles have restricted the market in the company's shares. In order to be fair, therefore, the value determined under the articles must recognise what the seller gives up in value and what the buyer acquires in value through the transaction. It should take into account all the circumstances. Chapter 2 examines in detail the fair value concept and gives a number of examples of how the author would interpret it in given circumstances. It is not proposed to repeat this material here as Chapter 2 is taken as read.

Although there is no legal definition of fair value the question as to whether an auditor's determination of fair value was correctly founded came before the court in *Dean* v. *Prince*, supra. There, it will be recalled, the auditors made the mistake of giving reasons for their valuation and the plaintiff was thereby put in a position to challenge the certificate. This case, which will now be discussed in detail, throws some interesting light not only on the interpretation of the fair value concept but also on the difficulty inherent in a judicial review of the technical competence of an expert.

The facts of the case, as far as they can be culled from the law reports, were as follows. The share capital of a small private company carrying on a light engineering business in Sheffield consisted of 200 shares of £1 each. The company had three shareholders all of whom were directors working in the business. The chief shareholder was Mr Dean who owned 140 shares, his two colleagues held 30 shares each. Mr Dean died on 6 November 1951. Article 9(g) of the company's articles of association provided as follows:

> In the event of the death of any member his shares shall be purchased and taken by the directors at such price as is certified in writing by the auditor to be in his opinion the fair

value thereof at the date of death and in so certifying the auditor shall be considered to act as an expert and not as an [arbitrator] and accordingly the Arbitration Act, 1889, shall not apply. Unless they otherwise agree the directors shall take such shares equally between them.

This article was unusual in that it imposed on the directors the obligation to take up the deceased's shares.

The company's circumstances at the date of death were not propitious. In the six previous years the profit before directors' remuneration averaged £1,300 per annum. After deducting the modest remuneration paid to each of the working directors there was a trading loss over the whole period of £2,500 or on average a loss of £424 per annum. The company was able to sustain these losses and to continue in business, as it did, because during the period in question it obtained from the Inland Revenue tax repayments totalling over £3,000. The company's balance sheet at 31 May 1950 was approximately as follows:

	£		£
Share capital	200	Fixed assets	4070
Retained profits	3960	Current assets	
	——	Stock	500
	4160	Debtors	1246
Current liabilities		Cash	1247	2993
Trade creditors	791		——
Loan — Mrs Dean	800		
Loan — Exors. of Mr Dean	1312	2903	
	——		——
	7063		7063

The fixed assets consisted of plant, machinery, fixtures and fittings at cost less depreciation. The depreciation was roughly half the original cost. The company had no saleable interest in its premises. One part of the factory premises was held on a monthly tenancy and the other part was held by Mrs Dean on an 800-year lease. The company had contracted to buy the lease for £5,000 payable by annual instalments of £200, a contract which Mrs Dean was entitled to terminate in the event of the company's suffering any process of execution, being wound up, or failing to observe the covenants contained in the contract. The company had no right to assign the contract. One floor of the company's four-storey factory premises was occupied by a Mr Goodyear as tenant or licensee of the company and he was in the same line of business as the company.

On 6 December 1951, the auditors delivered their valuation as at the date of death. This amounted to £7 per share. The basis of valuation was that of a break-up of the business. The justification for this basis was stated in the auditors' valuation notes as follows:

> In view of these trading results [i.e., the losses in recent years] and taking into account to some extent the difficult position in which the company would be placed if the amounts due to Mrs Dean had to be paid, it was clear that no value could be put on the shares on a normal going concern basis other than something purely nominal. It became necessary, therefore, to consider the only other basis which could apply: i.e. break-up value.

An independent professional valuation of the plant and machinery was obtained in the sum of £1,785 and this was substituted for the balance sheet fixed assets figure of £4,070. Enquiry revealed that work-in-progress of £400 related to a partly finished machine which was unlikely ever to be sold, and would probably have to be scrapped. The scrap value was £50. Finally a deduction of ten per cent was made from debtors to reflect the bad debts usually sustained when debts are called in all at once. The losses on realisation were therefore as follows:

	Balance sheet £	Proceeds of sale £	Loss £
Fixed assets	4,070	1,785	2,285
Stock	400	50	350
Debtors	1,246	1,121	125
			2,760

When deducted from balance sheet shareholders funds of £4,160 this produced a break-up value for the company of £1,400 or £7 per share. After proceedings had started the sum due to Mrs Dean was found to have been overstated by £200 and it was conceded that the valuation should be increased by £1 per share to £8 per share.

Harman J at first instance did not agree that an immediate break-up was the appropriate basis of valuation. He also concluded that the auditor had erred in not taking into account the fact that the shareholding in question was a controlling interest. The relevant extracts from his judgment are set out below:

In his evidence, Mr Jenkinson, partner in the firm of auditors, adhered to the view that, though the physical assets of the company, if sold at an auction in a most disadvantageous way, would possibly produce a value of £7 a share, the shares were of no value at all if looked at on what he called a 'going concern basis'. Although it was pointed out to him that this was nonsense, he adhered to his view. What he meant, I suppose, was that if he were advising a client who was going to buy a parcel of these shares, he would advise him to buy them only at a nominal price because, in his view, the company's prospects were very poor. If a person were buying an interest such as that of one of the defendant directors, i.e., thirty shares in a private company which was making a loss, as this company was doing, it would be right to assume that the buyer would be in an unhappy position as he would not get a dividend. But Mr Jenkinson did not look at the substance of the matter, viz., that what was for sale was not thirty shares of the company, or some small parcel of shares, but one hundred and forty shares, which carried with them the right to control the company. It never occurred to him that it made any difference whether he was valuing a minority or a majority interest, and he left that matter altogether out of his calculations. Being of the opinion that the company ought to be wound-up, he instructed a local valuer to value the machinery on the basis that the company had ceased business on the day of the deceased's death and that its physical assets were sold at the earliest auction sale to which they could be taken. The valuer said that he valued the machines as so many loose chattels to be sold at auctions, and some of the machines were old and, accordingly, had only scrap value. He went on to say: 'A valuation *in situ* would have been higher, but I was not asked to value on that basis.' In the circumstance, one is not surprised to find that he valued the machinery at a very low sum. His valuation was given on Nov. 23, and his report to Mr Jenkinson was in these terms:

'As requested, we have inspected the fast and loose plant and machinery, office furniture and motor vehicles owned by the above company, as per detailed inventory herewith, with a view to giving you our opinion of what these articles would be likely to realise if offered for sale by auction: i.e. their break-up value.'

The figure arrived at was £1,785 . . .

Counsel for the defendants contended that, even if the basis of valuation were wrong, it was merely an error of judgement on behalf of the auditors, and the parties, having agreed to be bound by the auditor's judgement, could not now complain if it proved to be bad. There is a good deal of force in that argument, but the answer, I think, is that the auditors did not merely make a valuation on a wrong basis — namely, break-up value, which I regard as the wrong basis — but they left out of account altogether the question of control. Mr Jenkinson said that he would have valued a minority parcel of shares on exactly the same lines as he valued the shares belonging to the deceased. The company had made a trading profit for a number of years. There was no urgency to put an end to its life, it had no creditors who were threatening to destroy it, it had a factory and machinery which was well maintained, and yet no enquiry was made whether the factory and machinery could be sold in its entirety. Evidence was given before me that at this time in Sheffield factory space was short, that trade in the light engineering world was good, and that it was likely that someone could have been found who could come forward and make a bid for the whole concern. If anyone purchased the deceased's shares, he would be in a position to turn out the defendants, re-organise the factory and put in his own business, or sell everything. None of those possibilities was considered. The auditors left out of account the control factor, and that, in my view, shows that their valuation was altogether wrong. I do not doubt that the company had no goodwill, but it does not seem to me that the alternative to that is to treat the company as being closed down and in urgent need of having its assets sold under a forced sale. It can be sold as a going concern. That does not necessarily mean that, when so sold, the machinery will fetch more than its value, but, of course, it all depends on how it is sold. A representative of one of the largest dealers in secondhand machinery in the country told me that he had examined the machinery and valued it at £4,800, which was more than the balance sheet figure by some considerable amount, and he said that, in his opinion, that was the value of the machinery to anyone entering the factory to take it over.

Even if one deals with the assets purely on the basis of their physical value, the price must be very different if the machinery is sold on the footing that it is ready to operate immediately, fixed in a factory, than if each piece is removed and sold at an auction.

. . . . In this case the auditors made their valuation on the basis that the company was to be wound-up immediately and that the buyer of the deceased's shares would have no control over the fortunes of the business. In both those matters they were wrong, and, in my judgment, the valuation cannot stand. I propose, therefore, to declare that the valuation is not binding on the plaintiff.

This decision was reversed by the Court of Appeal and it is illuminating to see what the three Appeal Court judges, Sir Raymond Evershed MR, Denning LJ and Wynn-Parry J thought of Harman J's judgment.

Sir Raymond would have agreed with the trial judge's conclusion but for one important circumstance: the terms on which the company held its premises. He felt that but for this circumstance the auditor had erred in valuing the company on a break-up value basis. The Master of the Rolls agreed, nonetheless, that the auditor was right to reject the going concern valuation based on the expectation of future profits, since this would have necessarily produced a negative figure. He disagreed with the auditor that the only other basis was that of an immediate forced sale of the company's assets. In his opinion the auditor ought to have enquired whether the factory with the plant *in situ* could have been sold to anybody. The Master of the Rolls attached great significance to the fact that Mr Goodyear, who carried on a similar business in the same factory building, said in evidence that he was interested in the company's plant and its business in the event of sale. According to the expert evidence of the professional valuer a valuation of the fixed assets *in situ* would have produced a higher figure than on a sale by auction although what the increase would have been was not stated. '. . . still', said Sir Raymond, 'it must be remembered that even ten per cent on the figure of £1,785 would mean an extra 17s 6d [87½p] per share.'

The Master of the Rolls clearly thought that the auditor was wrong to exclude, 'on accountancy principles', the possibility of a sale of the factory and plant *in situ*. He also stated that the majority holding, even though not a three-fourths majority, would enable a buyer to control the method and speed of disposal. It was this point (the fact that the shares in question constituted a majority holding) that, in his view, was relevant. The implication here is that with more time to dispose of the company's assets a better price would have been obtained for them.

The unusual terms on which the company held its premises, however, put an entirely different complexion on matters. Sir Raymond concluded his judgment in the following terms:

> In the result, therefore, Mrs Dean would, in my judgment, *prima facie* be entitled to the relief she claimed and if the matter ended there I should for myself agree with Harman J, in his conclusion, but there remains the special circumstance which I have mentioned above. We were informed that some part, unspecified but, I suppose small, of the company's property was held by it on the terms of a monthly tenancy. But the greater part (or so I assume) of the company's business premises was the subject of a business agreement dated Nov. 27, 1950, an agreement of a most unusual, and, from the company's point of view as things have turned out, a most unattractive character. By this agreement Mrs Dean contracted to sell and the company contracted to buy for £5,000 the premises in question which appear to have been vested in Mrs Dean for a term of eight hundred years from Mar. 25, 1837, at a ground rent of £10 10s. per annum. The company thereupon became entitled in equity to the long term of years. It was, however, provided that the purchase price should be payable by yearly instalments of not less than £200 in any one year and at the material date one only of such instalments had been paid; and it may be added that, on the evidence, it is at least doubtful if the premises are worth as much as the unpaid balance of the purchase money. It is, however, further provided (by clause 8) that if the company should:

> 'suffer any process of execution or distraint . . . or be wound-up either compulsorily or voluntarily, or fail to observe any of the covenants [earlier mentioned] or fail in any one year to pay to the vendor a minimum of £200 on account of the purchase money, the vendor may give three months' notice in writing to the purchaser . . . and if before the expiration of the notice the purchaser shall not comply with' . . .

> . . . the requirement in the notice (which the company would not appear to be able to do in the case of a winding-up) the vendor is entitled to terminate the contract and

re-enter and re-sell the premises. Finally, by the succeeding clauses the company is prohibited from assigning or charging the benefit of the contract without the vendor's written consent. It is unfortunate that the nature and effect of this contract were little referred to or considered at the trial. As a practical matter the company might well, no doubt, be able to grant licences to others to occupy all or part of the factory and such persons might then be willing to pay the company a price for the plant *in situ*. But the tenure of such persons of the premises would appear to me to be of a somewhat precarious nature unless arrangements were made for the completion of the purchase or at least for payment of a substantial part of the outstanding purchase price — considerations obviously highly significant to the sale of a company's plant *in situ* which was the only alternative basis suggested by counsel for the plaintiff. In the event of a winding-up the company might, moreover, be in some difficulty in removing certain of the plant for any purpose.

I have had the advantage of reading in advance the judgments prepared by my two brethren who are of the opinion that the appeal should be allowed — in the case of Wynn-Parry J, 'with some reluctance'. I share the reluctance of Wynn-Parry J, for I cannot help feeling that the amended price of £8 per share was and is appreciably less than the true worth of the shares. I repeat again the fact that an increase of £200 in the valuation of the assets represents an addition of £1 per share to the valuation. But having regard to the clear opinion of my brethren and bearing in mind that as in other actions the plaintiff must make good a case, I have felt compelled to the conclusion that though, as I think, Mr Jenkinson erred in principle in treating himself as bound on accountancy principles to regard only the break-up value, Mrs Dean has, nevertheless, failed sufficiently to establish that a consideration of the values of the plant *in situ* or otherwise would produce, in all the circumstances, a figure of value materially different from that at which Mr Jenkinson arrived.

Wynn-Parry J also reviewed the matter on these two counts, namely, should the auditor have specifically taken into account the fact that the shares in question were a controlling interest, and should he have obtained a valuation of the fixed assets *in situ* on the basis that a purchaser could reasonably be envisaged, who would take over the assets or the shares in the company with a view to carrying on some other business for which the plant and machinery were suitable?

In Wynn-Parry J's opinion, the wording of the articles, i.e., 'the fair value shall be the auditor's valuation of the current worth of the company's shares' precluded the auditor from placing any extra value on a block of shares because it constituted a controlling interest. Furthermore, as the shares in question would in all probability be taken up equally by the remaining shareholders it could not be assumed that the shares would remain as a block. Wynn-Parry J concluded therefore that Harman J was wrong in criticising the auditor for not valuing the shares as a controlling interest.

As regards the second point, Wynn-Parry J expressed no objection to the auditor's conclusion, based on accountancy principles, that the company should be valued on a break-up and that there would be no buyer for the assets *in situ* at a price in excess of the auction price. On the other hand, he seemed to think it important that the auditor had not apparently considered whether a buyer could have been found for the shares as opposed to the assets or business undertaking. His judgment was concluded as follows:

> Now those two answers show, to my mind, that the auditor was still thinking of the whole undertaking of the company, and was not envisaging a purchaser who designed to buy the shares in order to carry on a different business on the premises. I conclude, therefore, that he never had that consideration in mind.

> The question, however, remains, should he have had this consideration in mind? In the course of his argument, counsel for the plaintiff first proceeded on the basis of envisaging a purchaser who would take over, not the shares, but the factory and the plant and machinery with a view to carrying on in the factory a business of his own, but in view of the very unusual terms of the agreement of Nov. 27, 1950, under which the company held the premises, he was constrained to rest his case on the basis of a buyer who would purchase the shares, and then, through the medium of the existing company, carry on his existing or proposed business. I am bound to say that such a proposition, namely, the purchase of the shares of a private company in order to carry on a different business on its premises with its plant, made necessary because of the very unusual provisions on which it

holds its premises, is such an unusual proposition that I cannot conclude that in not taking it into consideration the auditor was making such a substantial mistake or proceeding on such an erroneous principle as to entitle the court to interfere, and in coming to this conclusion I do not forget that there was a tenant, Mr Goodyear, who, according to his evidence, would have been willing to take over the rest of the premises. The evidence, however, does not show that he was conversant with the provisions on which the company held the premises. I would therefore, though with some reluctance, allow the appeal.

Denning LJ came to the same conclusion as his fellow judges but his reasoning was altogether different. He said:

In this case the judge has upset the valuation on the ground that the auditor failed to take into account some factors and proceeded on wrong principles. I will take the points in order.

(a) The right to control the company
The judge said that the auditor should have taken into account the fact that the one hundred and forty shares were a majority holding and would give a purchaser the right to control the company. I do not think that the auditor was bound to take that factor into account. Test it this way. Suppose it had been Mr Prince who had died, leaving only thirty shares. Those thirty shares, being a minority holding, would fetch nothing in the open market. But does this mean that the other directors would be entitled to take his share for nothing? Surely not. No matter which director it was who happened to die, his widow should be entitled to the same price per share, irrespective of whether her husband's holding was large or small. It seems to me that the fair thing to do would be to take the whole two hundred shares of the company and see what they were worth, and then pay the widow a sum appropriate to her husband's holding. At any rate, if the auditor was of the opinion that that was a fair method, no one can say that he was wrong. The right way to see what the whole two hundred shares were worth, would be to see what the business itself was worth, and that is what the auditor proceeded to do.

(b) Valuation of the business 'as a going concern'

The judge seems to have thought that the auditor should have valued the business as a going concern. I do not think the auditor was bound to do any such thing. The business was a losing concern which had no goodwill, and it is fairly obvious that, as soon as Mrs Dean had sold the one hundred and forty shares to the other two directors — as she was bound to do — she would in all probability call in the moneys owing to herself and to her husband amounting to £2,000. The judge said that she was not likely to press for the moneys because that would be 'killing the goose that laid the eggs', but he was wrong about this, because as soon as she sold her shares, she would have got rid of the goose and there was no reason why she should not press for the moneys. She was an executrix and the company's position was none too good. It had only £1,200 in the bank to meet a demand for £2,200. In these circumstances, the auditor was of the opinion that there was a strong probability of the company having to be wound-up, and he rejected the going concern basis. For myself, I should have thought he was clearly right, but, at any rate, no one can say that his opinion was wrong.

(c) Valuation of the assets of the business

Once the going-concern basis is rejected, the only possible way of valuing the business is to find out the value of the tangible assets. The judge thought that the assets should have been valued as a whole *in situ*. It was quite likely, he said, that 'some one could have been found who would make a bid for the whole thing, lock, stock and barrel'. But the judge seems to have forgotten that no one would buy the assets *in situ* in this way unless he could also buy the premises, and the company had no saleable interest in the premises. In respect of part of the premises the company had only a monthly tenancy. In respect of the rest, the company had only a contract for the purchase of the premises on paying £200 a year for twenty-five years. It had no right to assign this contract, and its interest was liable to be forfeited if it went into liquidation, either compulsory or voluntary: and the probability was, of course, that, if it sold all the assets, it would go into liquidation, and hence lose the premises. The company could, therefore, only sell the assets without the premises. That is how the auditor valued them and no one can say that he was wrong in so doing.

(d) Valuation on a 'break-up' basis

The auditor instructed the valuer, Colonel Riddle, to value the plant and machinery at the break-up value as loose chattels on a sale by auction. The judge thought that was a wrong basis because it was equivalent to a forced sale. I would have agreed with the judge if the business had been a profitable concern. The value of the tangible assets would then have been somewhere in the region of £4,000 or £5,000, being either the balance sheet figure of £4,070 or Mr Pressley's figure of £4,835. But the business was not a profitable concern. It was a losing concern, and it is a well known fact that a losing concern cannot realise the book value of its assets. There is an element to be taken into account which is sometimes spoken of as 'negative goodwill'. It comes about in this way: if a business is making a loss, that shows that its assets, regarded as an entity, are not a good investment. A purchaser will decline, therefore, to buy on that basis. He will only buy on a piecemeal basis, according to what the various assets, taken individually are worth, and it is obvious that on a sale of assets piecemeal, the vendor will suffer heavy losses as compared with the book figures. The auditor was, therefore, quite justified in asking the valuer to value the assets as loose chattels sold at an auction. At any rate, if he honestly formed that opinion, no one can say he was wrong.

(e) The special purchaser

The judge thought that someone could have been found to buy the one hundred and forty shares who would use his majority holding to turn out the two directors, and reorganise the factory and put in his own business. In other words, that the shares would have a special attraction for some persons (namely, the next-door neighbour) who wanted to put his own business into these premises. I am prepared to concede that the shares might realise an enhanced value on that account, but I do not think it would be a fair price to ask the directors to pay. They were buying these shares — under a compulsory sale and purchase — on the assumption that they would continue in the business as working directors. It would be unfair to make them pay a price based on the assumption that they would be turned out. If the auditor never took that possibility into account, he cannot be blamed, for he was only asked to certify the fair value of the shares. The only fair value would be to take a hypothetical purchaser who was prepared to carry on the business if it was worthwhile so to do, or otherwise to put it into liquidation. At any rate, if that was the auditor's opinion, no one can say he was wrong.

I have covered, I think, all the grounds on which the judge upset the valuation. I do not think that they were good grounds. I would, therefore, allow the appeal and uphold the valuation.

A fascinating aspect of this case is the markedly different reasoning by which the three Appeal Court judges came to their unanimous conclusion. It is clear that Sir Raymond Evershed MR and Wynn-Parry J shared Harman J's view that the auditor's valuation was appreciably less than the true worth of the shares. They allowed the appeal 'with reluctance' because of the company's unusual tenure of its factory premises — an aspect of the valuation which was not adequately considered at the trial. Denning LJ, on the other hand, completely vindicated the auditor. He examined each of the trial judge's criticisms of the valuation and proceeded to rebut each one of them convincingly. Who was right?

Judges are not expert valuers. Words not figures are their stock in trade. In a case such as this they have to be guided largely by the expert witnesses. If these witnesses fail to explain the reality of the situation adequately a judge, unless he has some experience of these matters or has a natural affinity with the subject, is at a decided disadvantage. What Sir Raymond Evershed MR, Wynn-Parry J and the trial judge clearly found difficult to grasp — indeed never clearly understood — was why a business which was manifestly solvent at the valuation date should have to be valued on a break-up basis. Yet to a share valuer it is obvious. The company had by all account no prospects of making any profit in the future and, most importantly, it was financed to a considerable extent by loans of over £2,000 from Mr and Mrs Dean. These loans were, repayable on demand. Once Mrs Dean had sold her shares it was to be expected that she would press for repayment immediately. She knew the company was making losses and had no prospect of profit. Delay on her part could only prejudice the recoverability of her loan. On the face of it, repayment of these loans would cripple the company and bring it to its knees.

Sir Raymond Evershed MR said, 'The question for Mr Jenkinson (the auditor) was: What in truth were these one hundred and forty shares worth? In other words, if Messrs Prince and Cowen paid £x for the shares, would they get that much value for their money?' He then went on to talk about the generally good prospects, not for this company in particular, but for Sheffield light engineering businesses generally, and also about the fact that Mr Goodyear had expressed an interest in buying the company's plant and business in the event of a sale. But was that a realistic way of looking at the value of these shares to the two other directors? They worked in the company and could only benefit from any enhanced value the company may have had on that account by giving up their source of livelihood. As the company barely made enough to pay their remuneration any sum paid for the shares would yield no return on a continuing annual basis. This was presumably what the auditor had in mind in paragraph 7 of his valuation notes, which were cited by Sir Raymond:

> The foregoing showed that to a third party the shares were unlikely to be worth more than £1,400 and that it was by no means certain that that amount could be realised. To the parties who are under an obligation to buy the shares it left out of account altogether one important factor, viz., that they could realise the break-up value only at the expense of losing their employment. To retain their employment, i.e., considering the transaction on a going concern basis, they would be paying £7 for shares on which we could place no value. In view of this position it could be regarded as a matter of grave doubt whether a valuation of £7 a share did not substantially favour the seller.

Furthermore as Mrs Dean was almost certain to demand repayment of the loans once she had sold her shares, the directors would have to inject a substantial sum of money into the company to keep it afloat. These sums would also be regarded, for valuation purposes, as a cost incidental to the acquisition of the shares. On this analysis, the auditor's grave doubt that his valuation did not favour the seller seems well founded.

Sir Raymond felt the auditor erred in overlooking the fact that the plant could be sold *in situ*. Yet for this to be a serious error the value of the plant sold *in situ* would have had to be materially higher than if sold by auction. But, it seems from the Master of the Rolls' judgment that the fixed asset valuer was never asked to state by how much extra he would have valued the plant if sold *in situ*. There was no way of knowing, therefore, whether this was a material error or not. Certainly Sir Raymond's preference for looking at this in terms of the effect on the value per share was illogical. The number of shares into which a company's share capital is divided is purely an accident of circumstance. To insist, as Sir Raymond did, that having regard to the small number of shares 'an increase of even ten per cent on the figure of £1,785 would mean an extra 17s 6d per share' gives the impression that an error of ten per cent is all the more serious because it produces such a large effect on the value per share.

Wynn-Parry J devoted a significant part of his judgment to proving from the transcripts of the evidence that although the auditor had considered the possibility of a buyer for the whole undertaking (at break-up value), he had not considered a person who designed to buy the shares, as distinct from the assets, in order to carry on a different business on the premises. However, such a business would have to be markedly different from that then being carried on by the company, otherwise the conclusion would have been that the company had a prospect of profitable manufacture — something everyone agreed it lacked. The profit earning potential of this different business — whatever it may have been — could not, therefore, have stemmed from the company's existing undertaking. The buyer would then be bringing into the company the wherewithal to make profits. But, unless he were a simpleton, he would not countenance paying an inflated price on that account. The auditor made exactly this point in cross examination:

> [Counsel for the plaintiff]: On that point, which is an important point, you did not consider, did you, whether the factory with the plant could be disposed of to anybody? You assumed that that was quite impossible, did you not?' [A.]: I assumed that it would be unlikely that you would find a willing buyer at more than the price I put on it to take over this factory and the plant as it was, as it stood, with a view to carrying it on. The reason I came to that conclusion was because the evidence was all to the effect that unless he, the buyer, was going to put into it something which it had not already got — and that was no concern of mine — what he was buying would only continue to lose money for him and, therefore, a willing buyer of the whole thing was in my mind regarded as unlikely at a figure above my valuation, £1,400.

However, this eminently reasonable conclusion was not allowed to stand. Both Harman J and Counsel for the plaintiff pecked away at it:

> [Harman J]: You did not ask for it to be valued on the basis that there might be a buyer, did you? [A.]: No. [Harman J]: Did you ask the valuer whether he could find a buyer, or

whether he thought there might be a buyer? You see, you are not a valuer yourself? [A.]: I did not ask any particular valuer that question, no. [Harman J]: I do not expect that aspect of the matter ever entered your head? [A.]: I certainly considered the possibility, but I considered it most unlikely that anybody would want to take it over. [Harman J]: Were you qualified to have an opinion on that subject, being a chartered accountant and not a valuer? [A.]: Yes, I think so, because I came to that conclusion on accountancy principles. [Counsel for the plaintiff]: In other words, you assumed that if any buyer should come forward to buy the factory with the plant and machinery *in situ* then he would not pay any more than £1,400.[A.]: Yes. My job was to value shares, and that was the value. [Counsel for the plaintiff]: I know your job was to value shares, but I want to put that question again. You came to the conclusion that if any buyer did come forward and take the factory and the plant and machinery there *in situ* he would not pay more than £1,400? [A.]: That is right. Not just for the plant, but for the whole thing.

It was a pity that the auditor used the expression 'accountancy principles', since this confused rather than clarified the issue. His conclusion was merely a reasonable supposition from the facts, a deduction which anyone with his experience of the economics of business was qualified to make. There appears to be scant grounds indeed, not only for Harman J's original decision, but also for the 'reluctance' of Evershed MR and Wynn-Parry J in allowing the appeal.

All this goes to show that it is as easy to find fault with a legal judgment as it is to pick holes in a valuation. Both are so much a matter of opinion on which experts may, and do, legitimately differ. The case is, however, an excellent example of the importance of circumstances in the valuation of private company shares. Denning LJ's judgment is a model of perception as well as clarity in this regard. The effect of the shareholders' loan, the relationship of the other directors to the deceased and to the company, the current terms on which the company occupied its premises, the special purchaser next door are all identified and their significance considered.

To the experienced valuer these circumstances will not appear all that unusual. Shareholder loans are fairly common. Their treatment for valuation purposes is discussed in Chapter 2 under 'going concern value'. Enquiry into the company's tenure of its premises is vital. Shareholders sometimes own the premises directly, letting it either at will or on some stated basis which may or may not be satisfactory from the company's viewpoint. In the realm of private company shares the special purchaser is more the rule than the exception.

What, then, can the 'dicta' in *Dean* v. *Prince* tell us about the legal interpretation of the fair value concept? First it must be said that there was no specific consideration given to the distinction between fair value and market value. Indeed, it is possible that it never occurred to Harman J, Sir Raymond Evershed MR, and Wynn-Parry J that there was any difference between market value and fair value. Harman J took it to mean current worth since the articles provided that 'the fair value shall be the current worth of the company's shares'. It seems that Sir Raymond Evershed MR and Wynn-Parry J concurred in this view, although both Appeal Court judges emphasised that the valuation should recognise the fact that the directors were bound to take up the shares and that Mrs Dean was bound to sell them. The word 'fair', however, was not seen as imposing any particular criterion by which current worth had to be judged. According to Sir Raymond the question for the auditor was simply: what in truth were the shares worth?

Denning LJ did not discuss the meaning of the fair value requirement in the articles but, in dealing with the trial judge's grounds for setting aside the valuation, his view as to what was fair played an important part. Two points are worthy of note in this connection. First, Denning LJ thought that, no matter which director it was who happened to die, his widow should be entitled to the same price per share, irrespective of whether her husband's holding was large or small. The fair thing to do, in his view, would be to take the whole 200 shares of the company and see what they were worth, and then pay the widow a sum appropriate to her husband's holding. The second point concerned the effect of the special purchaser — the next door neighbour who wanted to put his own business into the company's premises. Denning LJ thought it unfair to make the two defendants, who intended to continue in the business as working directors, pay a price based on the assumption that they would be turned out.

Denning LJ's views of fair value, like the views on value of the other judges, are in no way binding. It illustrates, however, a legitimately tenable interpretation of the concept, one with which the author is in entire agreement, as will be evident from the discussion of fair value in Chapter 2.

Further support for this free interpretation of the fair value concept can be found in *In re Bird Precision Bellows Ltd* [1984] 2 WLR 869. This case did not concern the determination of fair value under a company's articles of association, but whether the minority basis of valuation ought to apply when an oppressed minority's shares were being purchased by the majority shareholders under a court order. Two shareholders holding in total 26% of the equity presented a petition under s.75 of the Companies Act 1980 (now ss.459 to 461 of the Companies Act 1985) that their shares should be purchased by the respondents at their fair value. At the first hearing of the petition in November 1981 it was ordered by consent that the respondents should purchase the petitioners' shares at a fair price to be determined by the court. In 1983 the court duly considered the fair value of the petitioners' shares. Counsel for the petitioners argued that whenever a minority holding of shares is ordered to be purchased pursuant to s.75, their price should be fixed *pro rata* according to the value of the shares as a whole. Counsel for the respondents argued that the price should always be discounted. He also argued that the question of any discount was a matter of valuation to be decided on the evidence of valuers.

Nourse J held that there was no rule of universal application as to whether the fair price should be fixed on a *pro rata* basis or on a discount basis. As to whether or not there should be a discount was a question of law for the court. The size of any discount was a matter of valuation. There was a general rule, however, that where the purchase order was made in respect of the shares of a quasi-partnership company the fair price should be determined on a *pro rata* basis provided, of course, that the petitioners are quasi-partners.[8] Nourse J's reasoning was as follows:

> I would expect that in a majority of cases where the purchase orders are made under s.75 in relation to quasi-partnerships the vendor is unwilling in the sense that the sale has been forced upon him. Usually he will be a minority shareholder whose interests have been unfairly prejudiced by the manner in which the affairs of the company have been conducted by the majority. On the assumption that the unfair prejudice has made it no longer tolerable for him to retain his interest in the company, a sale of his shares will invariably be his only practical way out short of a winding up. In that kind of case it seems to me that it would not merely not be fair, but most unfair, that he should be bought out on the fictional basis applicable to a free election to sell his shares in accordance with the company's articles of association, or indeed on any other basis which involved a discounted price. In my judgment the correct course would be to fix the price *pro rata* according to the value of the shares as a whole and without any discount, as being the only fair method of compensating

[8] As to when a company might be a 'quasi-partnership' see Lord Wilberforce's judgment in *In re Westbourne Galleries Ltd* [1973] AC 360. This is discussed in Chapter 4 pp. 82–84.

an unwilling vendor of the equivalent of a partnership share. Equally, if the order provided, as it did in *In re Jermyn Street Turkish Baths Ltd* [1970] 1 WLR 1194, for the purchase of the shares of the delinquent majority, it would not merely not be fair, but most unfair, that they should receive a price which involved an element of premium.

In *Dean* v. *Prince*, too, one party was bound to sell and the other bound to buy, and the company was almost certainly what would today be regarded as a quasi-partnership. From a valuation standpoint, there are thus important similarities between the two cases, and the fact that Nourse J's interpretation of fair value is very much in line with that of Denning LJ's some 30 years earlier is significant.

When the fair value of shares falls to be determined under a company's articles it is usually as a direct result of a free election on the part of the member concerned to sell his shares. There exists an element of compulsion, nevertheless, in that a member is not free to sell to anyone but only to fellow shareholders or persons of whom the directors approve. This may be why Nourse J thought that ' . . . even without such [unfairly prejudicial] conduct, that [the undiscounted *pro rata* basis] is, in general, the fair basis of valuation in a quasi-partnership case . . .'.[9]

Procedure

The procedures to be followed in carrying out a binding or legal valuation are in many respects little different from recommended practice in all types of valuation. However, what for the run-of-the-mill valuation would be regarded as best practice should be considered as obligatory for binding valuations. It is convenient to discuss procedures under the following headings: (a) accepting the engagement; (b) obtaining information; (c) the valuation summary; (d) the form of certificate; and (e) conduct during and after the valuation.

Accepting the engagement

Before accepting instructions to act as an expert, the valuer should take the precaution of checking that the formalities or prerequisites atten-

[9] Nourse J also said that if the petitioner had deserved his exclusion from the affairs of the company he had, as it were, made a constructive election to sever his connection with the company and thus to sell his shares. In such a case he would not be entitled to the full *pro rata* value but merely that which he would have got on the fictional basis applicable to a free election to sell his shares in accordance with the company's articles of association. There seems to be an inconsistency here since, according to the learned judge, the *pro rata* basis is the fair basis of valuation in quasi-partnerships anyway, i.e., it is the fictional basis.

dent on his appointment have been duly complied with. If, for example, a company's articles of association provide that a seller shall give the company a transfer notice and that there shall be a reference to the auditors only if the parties are unable to agree on the price, the valuer should confirm that the transfer notice has been given and that the parties have tried to agree the price. This is only commonsense but it sometimes gets overlooked, particularly in the smaller private company where the directors may not be familiar with the detailed share transfer provisions.

The general rule that an engagement letter be sent to the client setting out the terms on which the engagement is accepted is particularly important in legal valuations. The purpose of the engagement letter is to avoid misunderstandings at a later stage about the way the valuer intends to proceed, the hourly rate he will charge, the costs he is likely to incur, and so on. If property or fixed asset valuations are necessary he should mention this fact in the engagement letter, or at least alert the parties to the possible requirement.

If the valuer is appointed under a court order or an order of the Industrial Tribunal both parties to the valuation will probably be strangers to him. In this type of assignment, where there is an underlying dispute, it usually happens that at least one of the parties has a prickly personality. It is essential, therefore, that the valuer spells out precisely in the engagement letter the level of access to information he requires and the cooperation he expects.

He should state that his certificate will be final and binding, that it will not disclose the reasoning behind the valuation and that he will not entertain any enquiries as to how he arrived at his valuation. As one or perhaps both of the parties may well be dissatisfied with his value determination, it is advisable to insist on the payment of fees before issuing the certificate. A valuer has a lien on the certificate for the payment of his fees and this is a perfectly acceptable procedure. If the valuer intends to insist on the payment of fees beforehand, it should be stated in the engagement letter.

The auditor acting as an expert under articles of association will not generally need to take these precautions. His fee will probably be paid by the company and he will most likely be well acquainted with all concerned.

Obtaining information

This is not generally a problem for the auditor-valuer. He has the audit files and his personal knowledge of the company. Nonetheless, the audit approach is different from the valuation approach and certain information will have to be obtained from the company. When enquiring about current trading and future prospects the auditor should not accept answers uncritically and he should seek independent corroboration of statements which may be questionable. It is advisable to obtain confirmation that: (a) the company has no intention to seek a listing for its shares; and (b) that a sale of the entire company is not in prospect. Either of these two possibilities could lead to a materially different valuation of the shares.

The valuer under a court order may be fortunate enough to receive the full cooperation of both parties and adequate access to information. But it will not always be so. The statutory information such as audited annual accounts and the articles of association will be available in any event, although the accounts may not be up to date. For the interpretation of this information and for an assessment of current performance and prospects the valuer has to depend largely on one or both of the parties. By the time a valuer is appointed the parties will in all probability have reached the last stages of a long process of litigation, itself preceded by the circumstances of the dispute. Much emotional as well as financial capital will have been invested in the dispute, and in all likelihood the parties will not be on speaking terms with each other. Obtaining information in such a situation may be difficult. There will rarely be anything as crude as a flat refusal to supply information but delaying tactics may be employed. Each side to the dispute will have his own interest to defend and will be highly partial. It may be that the only way to make any progress is to compare the answers of both sides to the same questions — a technique which in experienced hands can be a great help in getting to the truth of the matter.

Two further sources of information should be considered. First, the valuer should conduct his own enquiries into the industry background and the trading performance of competitor firms. It may be necessary to obtain the financial statements of the firm's competitors and compare their performance with that of the company. Any marked differences between the performance of the firm and that of its competitors and of the industry as a whole should be thoroughly investigated. Second, the valuer should obtain, if possible, copies of the pleadings, the judge's summing up or of the law report if the case has been reported. Solicitors for each side, who usually arrange for the appointment of the valuer, can be asked to supply copies of the statement of claim, affidavits etc., presented to the court. These trial documents may contain valuable background information. It is to be expected in cases of unfair dimissal or conduct unfairly prejudicial to shareholders that in the tribunal or court hearing much information on the company's history, the nature of its activity, its financial and trading performance and perhaps its assets, will come to light. This can save the valuer much time and effort. It also provides another independent source of information against which the veracity of statements by the parties on related matters may be tested.

Much of the information obtained by the valuer will be in the form of explanations obtained during interviews with the parties. It is essential that the valuer maintains a full written record of these interviews and of any telephone conversations. These memoranda should give an accurate flavour of the discussion and not merely a list of the main points or facts agreed.

The valuation summary

Once the valuer has concluded his enquiries he should proceed to the preparation of his valuation summary or conclusions. This should be based on information and explanations contained on the file, enabling every fact or assertion to be appropriately referenced.

The format of the valuation summary is a matter for individual taste and will, to some extent, vary with the circumstances. Whatever format is used, however, it is vital that the summary shows as far as possible every aspect of the valuer's reasoning. If, for example, a certain approach or factor is considered but rejected, that fact should be stated together with the relevant discussion. No one can gainsay the valuer's judgement of the facts, but the valuer can be criticised if he fails to consider all relevant factors. Great care should be taken over this summary even though it is purely a file document not intended for disclosure. Formalising one's thoughts is an invaluable discipline. It is in the interests of the parties involved and it stands as evidence of the work done in any future enquiry.

The form of certificate

The certificate should be formal in tone. It should recite the valuer's terms of reference or instructions and then proceed to state the valuation, keeping as close as possible to the wording of the terms of reference. If the articles, for example, require the auditor to 'certify' the fair value then words such as 'I hereby certify' should be used; if 'determine', then 'I hereby determine'. No explanation or reasoning must be given. If the valuer is also giving his opinion on other related matters where he does not act in the capacity of expert these matters should be communicated to the parties under separate cover.

Conduct during and after the valuation

The essential qualities of conduct for an expert valuer are independence and impartiality. Where there is an underlying dispute one or other of the parties may be difficult to deal with, even obnoxious. The legal proceedings, with which the valuer will become familiar, may put the character of one or both parties in a bad light. There will be an understandable temptation, particularly if the assignment drags on, to lose patience. The valuer must not allow the personalities of the parties or the frustrations of the job to colour his judgement.

In some ways, independence and impartiality can be in greater danger where personal relationships are amicable and there is no formalised dispute. Take, for example, the auditor acting as an expert under the articles of association. Reference has already been made to the borderline case between collusion, which would be a ground for setting aside the valuation, and the lack of a proper degree of professional independence. The auditor must tread a particularly careful path. He must be careful not to give any prior indication of his likely valuation, especially where the articles provide for his appointment only in default of agreement between the parties. In such a case, the valuer who gives a prior indication of the likely fair value to one party confers an unfair advantage on that party and jeopardises his own independence as a valuer. A simple example will illustrate the point.

The articles of XYZ Ltd provide that shares shall be freely transferable among members but that if vendor and purchaser fail to agree a price the fair value shall be determined by the auditor whose decision shall be final and binding. Mr A, the chairman and managing director, has entered into negotiations to purchase some shares from another shareholder. He asks the auditor informally what the fair value is likely to be, mentioning the negotiations which are in progress. In the author's opinion, it would be wrong for the auditor to disclose the likely fair value in such circumstances. There are two good reasons for this. First, by giving the figure to Mr A and not to the other shareholder the auditor confers a negotiating advantage on Mr A, who now knows the highest price he need bid for the shares. Second, informal valuations are not researched as thoroughly as formal ones and it is quite possible that on mature reflection the auditor might wish to alter his valuation. But, having given an indication of the likely fair value to Mr A, it will be difficult and extremely embarrassing for the auditor, on an official reference to him under the articles, subsequently to determine the fair value at a figure very different from the one given informally. He has, thus, forfeited his independence and frustrated the intention of the articles.

Even if Mr A, the chairman, undertook to disclose the auditor's informal assessment of fair value to the vendor, or if the vendor and purchaser both informally requested a fair value, the auditor would be well advised to decline. His role under the articles is to settle a dispute as to price. If no dispute has arisen, he should remain silent. This professional standard of behaviour may be inconvenient and entail loss of valuable work.

Consider the example, this time of a mining venture between two substantial corporations, Company A and Company B. The joint venture company is owned 50/50 by the two parties and is audited by Company A's auditors. There is a side agreement between the two shareholders conferring pre-emption rights on each other and providing for a fair value to be determined by the joint venture auditors if the shareholders fail to agree on price. For various reasons, Company B wishes to withdraw from the venture and opens negotiations with Company A for the sale of the 50% shareholding. Whereupon Company A asks its auditors, who also audit the joint venture, for advice on the price to pay. As shown in the preceding example, the audit firm would be conferring an unfair advantage on its client, Company A, and could be jeopardising its own independence in any subsequent fair value determination if it provides Company A with advice on value. The auditors ought therefore to decline to advise Company A on the price it should pay, nor should they give any indication of the likely fair value. Company A will, therefore, have to seek its professional advice from another quarter.

Once his certificate has been issued the golden rule for the expert valuer is silence. He must not enter into any discussion, whether orally or in writing, as to how he has arrived at his valuation. This can only serve to thwart the intentions of the parties that his certificate be final and binding.

Conclusion

The certificate of an expert valuer binds the parties. They have to accept his figure whether they agree with it or not. Because of the responsibility this imposes on the expert, legal or binding valuations are the most difficult and challenging of all. They should not be undertaken lightly, and there can be no question of tailoring the work to suit the fee. Much of this work is uneconomic on its own.

As the intention of the contract, court order or agreement is to bind the parties, the valuer must strive to ensure that nothing he does should jeopardise the binding force of the valuation. The grounds on which the court may set aside a valuation were considered. These fall under three headings, viz., fraud or collusion, mistake (but only where a 'speaking' certificate has been issued), and error of principle, such as a valuation of the wrong thing. The expert valuer should be familiar with the position in law of his certificate.

The law as regards the expert valuer's liability for negligence has undergone a fundamental change in recent years. Prior to the House of Lords' decisions in *Sutcliffe* v. *Thackrah* and *Arenson* v. *Casson Beckman, Rutley & Co*, it was generally believed to be the law that an expert enjoyed immunity from an action for negligence. He was considered to be performing an arbitral function in holding the scales fairly between parties with opposing interests. Arbitrators have always enjoyed the same immunity from an action for negligence as have judges on grounds of public policy, and this immunity was extended to the expert who was considered as a quasi-arbitrator.

As a result of these two decisions in the House of Lords the expert can no longer rely with certainty on arbitral immunity. The mutual valuer, the court decided, does not perform an arbitral role and will be liable in damages for negligence. A mutual valuer is an expert to whom two parties (or more), who are not in dispute, refer a matter of valuation. In the *Arenson* case, the agreement between uncle and nephew stipulated that the shares would be valued by the auditors whose valuation was to be binding. There was no prior dispute as to value, and the auditors were thus mutual valuers.

Where parties who have been unable to agree a value between themselves refer the matter to an expert, there exists, arguably at least, a dispute. This situation did not arise in the *Arenson* case, but it was considered by the five Law Lords as part of their general review of the liability of experts for negligence and the question of arbitral immunity. Two of the Law Lords in the *Arenson* case were of the opinion that if an expert could show that in his role of valuer he was performing an arbitral function he may enjoy immunity. This would depend on the facts and Lord Wheatley set out certain 'indicia'. The onus would lie on the expert to prove that he was in fact an arbitrator. This view, however, was not shared by the other Law Lords. Lord Fraser and Lord Kilbrandon questioned the whole concept of arbitral immunity. They saw no valid distinction between the expert and the arbitrator. Both pledge skill in the exercise of their expertise and if they are negligent in that exercise they should be liable in damages. Lord Salmon's point of view lay between these two positions. The prudent course for the expert valuer, therefore, is to assume that, dispute or no, he will be liable in damages for negligence. The existence of a remedy against the valuer means that in future the courts will probably be even more reluctant to set a valuation aside.

Interpreting the terms of reference or instructions correctly is vital. These are usually contained in a company's articles, a legal agreement or an order of the court. The required value concept may be unclear and it is not always apparent when a minority basis of valuation is to be used. Ambiguity can arise when a controlling interest basis is specified. Orders of the court or the Industrial Tribunal usually specify 'net asset value (including goodwill)' as the required valuation basis. The text discusses how this basis might be interpreted.

Fair value is perhaps the most commonly used value concept in legal valuations. Chapter 2 examines this basis in detail and gives many examples of how the author would interpret it in practice. In this chapter we examine how this basis has been interpreted by the courts. This is done by a detailed review of the judgments in *Dean* v. *Prince* and the decision in *In re Bird Precision Bellows Ltd*. Thee are no hard and fast rules for the determination of fair value: it is at the discretion of the valuer. The analysis shows, however, that the interpretation given in Chapter 2 is consistent with recent judicial thinking.

The chapter ended with a brief discussion of points of procedure. Perhaps the most important point here is for the valuer to maintain his independence and to act impartially.

16

Fiscal share valuations

Fiscal share valuations are required in order to assess the tax liability of individuals and companies arising from the transfer of shares by way of gift (including sales at non-arms-length prices), and from the transmission of shares through the operation of a will, settlement, trust deed or other legal disposition. The main taxes are capital transfer tax (to be renamed inheritance tax), capital gains tax and stamp duty. Share valuations may also be required for income tax purposes where an employee is given shares in his company or where share options are granted to him. Companies are not liable to capital gains tax as such but they pay a similar sum in the form of corporation tax.

It is interesting to see the contribution of capital taxes to total tax revenue and the changes in relative importance of the individual capital taxes since 1973/74, just before estate duty was withdrawn and replaced by capital transfer tax.

	1973/74		1979/80		1984/85	
	£m	%	£m	%	£m	%
Capital transfer tax	—	—	401	27	674	29
Estate duty	412	44	32	2	6	—
	412	44	433	29	680	29
Capital gains tax	324	35	431	29	720	31
Stamp duty	190	21	620	42	910	40
(a) Total capital taxes	926	100	1,484	100	2,310	100
(b) Total tax revenue	17,408		50,477		88,910	
(a) as % of (b)	5.3%		2.9%		2.6%	

Source: Board of Inland Revenue: Report for the year ended 31 December 1984.

Although the yield from each tax has risen sharply over the 10-year period (taking estate duty and capital transfer tax together), the percentage contribution of capital taxes to total tax revenue has halved from 5.3% to 2.6%. Interestingly, capital transfer tax, despite the grim warnings accompanying its introduction, seems to have been a lighter burden than estate duty. Stamp duty, doubtless because of the limited reliefs available and its mainly *ad valorem* basis, has changed places with estate duty/capital transfer tax as the main revenue raiser. Capital gains tax has proved more reliable as a source of revenue than capital transfer tax but it has, nevertheless, lost some ground over the period.

The purpose of this chapter is to examine the basis of valuation required for fiscal valuations and to consider its practical implications. In order to do this, however, it is first necessary to provide a brief description of the way these taxes give rise to a valuation requirement. This résumé, which is not meant to be a tax guide, is followed by an examination of the statutory valuation hypothesis and the rules of interpretation laid down by the courts over the years. There then follows a discussion of various points of interest relative to fiscal share valuation work. These comprise the relevance of case law, the influence of the Stock Exchange, non-dividend paying minority shareholdings, the shareholder with other roles in the company, and the valuation of goodwill.

The requirement for fiscal valuations

Capital transfer tax

Capital transfer tax (CTT) was introduced in 1975 to replace estate duty. It differs from estate duty in two important respects. First, it applies not only to property passing on death but also to gifts during the taxpayer's lifetime. Second, as regards lifetime transfers, tax is chargeable not on the value of the property transferred but on the loss to the donor occasioned by the transfer. In calculating the loss to the donor, related property must be brought into account. Related property is property held by the taxpayer's spouse or property transferred to a charity and exempt from CTT.

The related property rule can make a significant difference to the value of the transfer. For example, A owns 35 of the 100 ordinary shares in X Ltd. His wife also owns 35 ordinary shares in the company. Valued as separate shareholdings they are each worth £50,000 but valued as a combined shareholding of 70 shares they are worth £150,000. The value of A's shareholding for CTT purposes is not its value on its own but 35/70ths of £150,000, i.e., £75,000.

The requirement that the transfer of value be set at the diminution in the value of the transferor's estate can also have an appreciable effect on the value transferred. Assume, for example, that A owned 55 of the 100 ordinary shares in B Ltd and made a gift of ten shares to his son. A's holding of 55 shares was worth £150,000 and the value of his holding after the transfer, i.e., 45 shares, was £100,000. The value of a holding of ten ordinary shares was £8,000. A's transfer of value is not £8,000 but £50,000, as set out below:

	£
Value of estate before the transfer — 55 shares in B Ltd	150,000
Value of estate after the transfer — 45 shares in B Ltd	100,000
Loss to donor	50,000

Furthermore, if A pays the tax on the gift, the value of the transfer has to be grossed up accordingly.

The rate of tax on any transfer, whether made in the taxpayer's lifetime or on death, depends on the cumulative total of non-exempt transfers in the previous ten years. There are two scales of rates: one for transfers on death or within three years of death; and another for lifetime transfers.

The main occasions on which CTT is charged are gifts (including gifts into settlement) made during a person's lifetime, and transfers on death. There are also special rules charging property comprised in a settlement. Apart from these rules and special provisions for close companies, CTT applies only to transfers by individuals.

Capital gains tax

Capital gains tax (CGT) is chargeable on gains on the disposal of assets. The tax applies to any disposal — not just a sale. A disposal takes place for this purpose when the ownership of the asset is transferred, whether in whole or in part, but it does not include assets passing on death. CGT may, therefore, be chargeable when assets are given away or exchanged or sold at under-value.

CGT is chargeable on the gain accruing. In a sale at arms-length the gain will normally be the profit on sale. Valuations are required when assets are disposed of by way of gift or sale at under-value. In both these instances the legislation requires that the gain be measured by the difference between base cost and the market value at the date of disposal. A gift may therefore trigger off a charge both to CGT and CTT.

Assets owned on 6 April 1965, the date of introduction of CGT, may also need to be valued as at that date. This is because the CGT legislation is not retrospective in its effect and any gain attributable to the period of ownership prior to the introduction of CGT is exempt from the tax. For unquoted shares the gain attributable to the period prior to 6 April 1965 is determined by a process of time apportionment unless the taxpayer elects for it to be determined by reference to the market value of the shares on 6 April 1965. A valuation may be required to establish whether it is worthwhile making such an election.

The very high rates of inflation in the UK during the 1970s and early 1980s altered the fiscal character of this tax. From being a tax on capital gains — the taxpayer being obliged to contribute a proportion of this profit on sale to the Revenue — it was increasingly perceived as a levy on capital. This was because most of the gains being realised on disposal were not real gains; when adjusted for the change in the purchasing power of money they were often losses. An attempt to mitigate this injustice was made by the Finance Act 1982 which provided an indexation allowance in respect of inflation since March 1982. The allowance was calculated on base cost. By virtue of the Finance Act 1985 this allowance can now be calculated on the market value of the shares as at March 1982, if the taxpayer so elects. This concession, too, may give rise to a valuation.

The rate of CGT is 30% and is charged on the total gains less losses in the year and less any unallowed losses of earlier years. Where gains accrue to companies they are in general charged to corporation tax.

Stamp duty

Stamp duties are duties chargeable on various instruments, such as agreements, bills of sale, bonds, covenants, conveyances, stocks, shares and the like. Sometimes these are fixed in amount; sometimes, as in the case of stocks and shares, they are *ad valorem*. Under s.6 of the Stamp Act 1891 *ad valorem* duty is calculated 'on the value, on the day of the date of the instrument . . . of the stock or security according to the average price thereof'. This is interpreted as meaning that stamp duty is payable on the value of shares transferred. Consequently, if shares are transferred at less than market value, stamp duty is payable on the market value. This is so even where the transferor had no intention of making a gift. Share valuations are therefore required for stamp duty purposes whenever shares are transferred as a gift or by way of sale at under value.

Income tax

If an employee is given shares by his employer he is normally assessable to income tax under Schedule E on the value of the shares in the same way as he would be liable to tax on a cash bonus. If he receives shares as of right, as for instance, under a share incentive scheme, he may also be liable to income tax on any increase in the market value of the shares over a period starting at the date of acquisition and ending at the earliest of the following dates:

(a) seven years from the date of acquisition;
(b) the date he ceased to have a beneficial interest in the shares;
(c) the date when the shares become free from any restrictions.

Thus two valuations may be required: one when the shares are issued and another when they are deemed to be disposed of.

The Finance Act 1978 introduced a scheme under which shares issued to employees would escape the two income tax charges above, i.e., the charge when the shares are issued and the 'growth in value' charge. Under such approved schemes, shares have to be issued at market value. This has to be agreed with the Inland Revenue beforehand.

Share options are another area which can give rise to an income tax liability. The general rule is that when an employee exercises a share option granted to him as an employee, income tax is chargeable on the difference between the market value of the shares when the option is exercised and the amount paid for them. Where unquoted companies are concerned a valuation of the shares on exercise of the option will be required. If the option is itself granted at under market value the shortfall is assessed to income tax. The savings-related share option scheme introduced by the Finance Act 1980 and, in particular, approved share option schemes under the Finance Act 1984, provide an effective means of by-passing this income tax liability.

From this brief review it will be seen that there are many occasions on which a taxpayer's liability to tax hinges on a share valuation. Although the valuer is not a tax expert it will obviously be helpful if he has a basic knowledge of the underlying transactions and the tax laws.

Statutory open market value

Market value is the value concept required for fiscal valuations. Section 150(1) of the Capital Gains Tax Act 1979 defines market value as 'the price which those assets might reasonably be expected to fetch on a sale in the open market'. This definition is the same as that found in s.160 of the Capital Transfer Tax Act 1984 and is regarded as applying to share valuations for stamp duty and income tax purposes. There are two statutory qualifications to this definition as it applies to unquoted securities, viz.:

(a) it shall be assumed that in that market there is available to any prospective purchaser of the shares or securities all the information which a prudent prospective purchaser might reasonably require if he were proposing to purchase them from a willing vendor by private treaty and at arm's length; and

(b) the price shall not be assumed to be reduced on the ground that the whole property is to be placed on the market at one and the same time.

These two qualifications can be found in ss.150(2) and 152(3) of the Capital Gains Tax Act 1979 and ss.160 and 168(1) of the Capital Transfer Tax Act 1984.

Qualification (a) was introduced to counter the effect of the House of Lord's decision in *Lynall* v. *IRC* [1972] AC 680. A holding of 28% of the shares in a large private company fell to be valued for estate duty purposes. The taxpayer's executors were unable to reach agreement with the Revenue on the value of the shares and the matter went to the High Court. In the process of discovery, documents came to light showing that at the valuation date the Board of Directors were seriously discussing the prospects or likelihood of the company going public. Interim monthly financial statements were also revealed. The Revenue claimed that this information would have been available to the purchaser of a significant minority interest. When large blocks of shares in private companies change hands, contended the Revenue, the seller engages an expert who selects the person or group whom he thinks most likely to be prepared to pay a good price and to be acceptable to the directors. If the purchaser is willing and the directors agree to co-operate, a highly reputable firm of accountants are engaged to whom all relevant information is made available in strictest confidence. The sale is then made at a fair price fixed by the accountants.

Lord Reid rejected this argument:

> In my view this evidence is irrelevant because this kind of sale is not a sale in the open market. It is a sale by private treaty made without competition to a selected purchaser at a price fixed by an expert valuer. The 1894 [Finance] Act could have provided — but it did not — that the value should be the highest price that could reasonably have been expected to be realised on sale of the property at the time of death. If that had been the test then the Respondents would succeed, subject to one matter which I need not stop to consider. But the framers of the Act limited the enquiry to one type of sale — sale in the open market — and we are not entitled to rewrite the Act. It is quite easily workable as it stands.

Section 152(3) of the Capital Gains Tax Act 1979 and s.168(1) of the Capital Transfer Tax Act 1984 have overriden this decision, but these enactments do not apply to stamp duty.

When valuing shares for the purposes of stamp duty, therefore, the decision in the *Lynall* case remains good law. When valuing shares for income tax purposes the capital gains and capital transfer tax rules apply in most cases.

Qualification (b) to the statutory open market value has been on the statute book since the Finance (1909–10) Act 1910. It seems intended to preserve equality of treatment between the taxpayer of modest means and the very wealthy one. It often happens, for example, that a large block of quoted shares can only be sold at a discount to the market price. If this discounted price were taken to be market value for tax purposes it would result in the small shareholder having a higher value per share for tax purposes than the big shareholder. With unquoted shares, however, the value per share generally rises with the size of the shareholding. There is no parallel to the discount found in the stock market when large lines of stock change hands. Placing the whole of a shareholding on the market at one and the same time does not, therefore, reduce the value but increase it.

Section 171 of the Capital Transfer Tax Act 1984 provides that the value of a person's estate immediately before death shall fully reflect any changes in the value of his estate by reason of his death. This is not intended to be a qualification to the statutory valuation hypothesis; its purpose is to ensure that assets such as life assurance policies would be included in the value of the estate. Any relevance it has for share valuation purposes is subsumed under the discussion headed 'The shareholder with other roles in the company'.

Interpreting the valuation hypothesis

The statutory open market basis of valuation first appeared in the Finance Act 1894. This Act introduced estate duty. Section 7(5) provided that 'the principle value of any property shall be the price which, in the opinion of the commissioners, such property would fetch if sold in the open market at the time of the death of the deceased'. Although the wording is slightly different the valuation requirement is the same as that for capital gains tax and capital transfer tax.

As evident from Chapters 1 and 2, the market value concept is not generally appropriate for unquoted shares. It is not surprising, therefore, that disputes have arisen in applying this concept to the valuation of unquoted shares for tax purposes. A number of these disputes have come before the courts with the result that there now exists a body of case law on the detailed interpretation of the statutory valuation hypothesis. The fact that much of it predates the introduction of capital gains tax and capital transfer tax is irrelevant since the statutory basis of valuation has remained virtually unchanged. The fiscal share valuer must be familiar with this case law. The purpose of this section is to present the rules of interpretation in an accessible way and to indicate the relevant cases.

Before going any further the reader should familiarise himself with Chapter 2, particularly the section on market value. This will give him a better understanding of the problem faced by the judiciary in formulating workable rules for applying the statutory valuation hypothesis.

Share transfer restrictions

An obvious and fundamental difficulty in applying the market value concept is the existence of share transfer restrictions and pre-emption rights. If the holder is not free to sell the shares on the open market how can a market value be postulated for them? Some companies' articles also impose a fixed price for share transfer purposes. Is this not the price they would fetch in the open market? These questions first arose in the Irish Court of Appeal case of *Attorney-General* v. *Jameson* [1905] 2 IR 218, where Fitzgibbon LJ said:

> In my opinion s. 7(5) turns 'value' into 'price' for the purpose of estimating its amount; that price is to be ascertained upon a sale assumed to take place in the open market and that means the price which would be obtainable upon a sale where it was open to everyone, who had the will and the money, to offer the price which the property of Henry Jameson in the shares was worth as he held them. The price was to be that which a purchaser would pay for the right 'to stand in Henry Jameson's shoes', with good title to get into them, and to remain in them, and to receive all the profits, subject to all the liabilities of the position.

This construction of the valuation requirement has been accepted in all subsequent cases and is now a settled principle of law. The share valuer ignores the fact that the articles preclude a transfer to a non-member, or whatever the transfer restrictions are, and asks himself the question: what would someone pay to be registered as the holder of these shares, bearing in mind that he will be subject to the articles? Thus, if he subsequently wishes to sell his shares he may face difficulties; he may have to accept a low fair value under the articles. On the other hand, he may be entitled to pick up shares cheaply because of the pre-emption rights of existing shareholders.

Purchaser orientation of the valuation hypothesis

In assessing what someone would be prepared to pay for the shares the valuer must envisage the generality of purchasers. He must not assume that the shares are sold to a particular person, nor must the valuation hinge on the identity of the seller. In the words of Lord Morris in the *Lynall* case: 'It became common ground that the price to be decided on was that which would have been paid (a) by a hypothetical willing purchaser (b) to a hypothetical willing vendor (c) in the open market . . . '.

The hypothetical willing purchaser is a person of reasonable prudence who informs himself with regard to all the relevant facts and fixes the return he ought to receive after considering the risks involved in carrying on the business.[1] The willing seller is not a forced seller willing to take any price he can get, however low.[2] However, the words 'if sold in the open market' impose the assumption of a sale in the open market[3] and in this sense the seller must be assumed to be under compulsion to sell at the best price he can get. He is by hypothesis a willing seller at that best price. No matter how low that price may turn out to be, he is willing to accept it in the absense of anything better.

In the author's opinion, therefore, the statutory open market value concept, like the real world open market value concept, is purchaser orientated. It is not so much a question of what the vendor is willing to accept but what the purchaser is prepared to pay. This statement can be confirmed by reference to almost any of the valuation cases. Fitzgibbon LJ's definition of statutory open market valuation in the *Jameson* case, quoted above, bears this out as do the following extracts from various notable cases:

Per Rowlatt J in *re: Courthope* (1928) 7 ATC 538:

> I have, of course, to consider those questions but I have to consider them through the supposed purchaser in the market. I have to look for a man who after he has considered those things and has considered everything else and what

---

[1] Per Lord Fleming in *Findlay's Trustee* v. *CIR* (1938) 22 ATC 437.
[2] *IRC* v. *Clay* [1914] 1 KB 339.
[3] *Attorney-General* v. *Jameson*, supra; *IRC* v. *Crossman* [1937] AC 26; and *Duke of Buccleuch* v. *IRC* [1967] 1 AC 506.

else he could do with his money and all the rest of it finally makes up his mind to give a certain price. That is the sort of way in which I have to look at it.

Per Lord Fleming in *Salvesen's Trustees* v. *CIR* (1930) 9 ATC 43:

The problem can only be dealt with by considering all the relevant facts so far as known at the date of the testator's death and by determining what a prudent investor, who knew these facts, might be expected to be willing to pay for the shares.

Per Lord Fleming in *Findlay's Trustees* v. *CIR* (1938) 22 ATC 437:

In estimating the price which might be fetched in the open market for the goodwill of the business it must be assumed that the transaction takes place between a willing seller and a willing purchaser; and that the purchaser is a person of reasonable prudence, who has informed himself with regard to all the relevant facts such as the history of the business, its present condition, its future prospects and the general conditions of the industry; and also that he has access to the accounts of the business for a number of years. (Lord Fleming made no reference to the attributes of the willing seller.)

Per Maguire J in *McNamee* v. *Revenue Commissioners* [1954] 1R 214 where he affirmed Lord Ashbourne's formulation in the *Jameson* case:

I have to imagine a sale in the open market at which this small lot of shares would be offered, the number of prospective purchasers, prudent and cautious, these shares would attract, the exhaustive enquiries in the history of the company they would make, their examination of the balance sheets, the dividends, the dividend earning capacity of the company . . . .

Per Danckwerts J in *Holt* v. *IRC* [1953] 1 WLR 1488:

By the terms of the section I have to imagine the price which the property would fetch if sold in the open market. This does not mean that a sale by auction (which would be improbable in the case of a company) is to be assumed, but simply that a market is to be assumed from which no buyer is excluded . . . at the same time, the court must assume a prudent buyer who would make full enquiries and have access to accounts and other information which would be likely to be available to him . . . .

Per Lord Reid in *Attorney-General of Ceylon* v. *Mackie* [1952] 2 All ER 775:

> So the shares must be valued on the footing that the highest
> bidder in the open market would have been registered as a
> shareholder, but that he would then have become subject to
> the restrictions in the articles.

Per Lord Morris in *Duke of Buccleuch* v. *IRC* [1967] 1 AC 506:

> The value of a property is to be estimated to be the price
> which it would 'fetch' if sold in the open market at the time of
> the death of the deceased. This points to the price which a
> purchaser would pay. The net amount that a vendor would
> receive would be less. There would be costs of and incidental
> to a sale.

Per Lord Reid in the *Lynall* case:

> We must decide what the highest bidder would have offered
> in the hypothetical sale in the open market, which the Act
> requires us to imagine took place at the time of Mrs Lynall's
> death.

There are only two cases where the attributes of the hypothetical
willing vendor came up for review. These are *IRC* v. *Clay,* supra, and
Glass v. *IRC* [1915] SC 449. Both these cases concerned the effect of a
special purchaser.[4] When Scrutton J said in the *Clay* case, 'the seller is
not to be assumed to be making a forced sale at any price he can get,
however low. He must be willing to sell, not demanding compensation
for a forced sale, but he is not required to exclude the principal bidder
from his market, because that principal bidder wants the house more
than any one else and will therefore give more for it', he was merely
reaffirming the fact that the vendor is by hypothesis a willing vendor
only at the best price obtainable. Similarly Lord Johnston was doing
the same thing in *Glass* v. *IRC* when he declared:

> . . . the statute in using the term 'sold at the time in the
> open market by a willing seller in its then condition', does
> not confine the attention of the valuer to sale by auction only,

---

[4] It should also be noted that the *Clay* and *Glass* cases both concerned not shares but the value of
land for incremental land value duty introduced by the Finance (1909–10) Act 1910. Under
s.25(1) of that Act the land was to be valued at 'the amount which the fee simple of the land, if sold
at the time in the open market by a willing seller in its then condition, free from encumbrances . . .
might be expected to realise'. This statutory valuation formula, unlike the estate duty one, makes
explicit reference to a willing seller. These cases are considered in greater detail under 'the special
purchaser'.

and does not mean by 'willing seller' a person willing to sell without reserve for any price that he can obtain, but one who is willing to sell making the most, in the circumstances, of his property; and that the most, in the circumstances, he can make of his property cannot be determined without consideration of the circumstances, and in particular, cannot be ascertained without excluding the consideration of the known wants of the purchaser?

In view of this, the valuer need not concern himself with the acceptability or otherwise of the notional best price to the hypothetical seller. His efforts should be directed solely to an assessment of what the shares in question would be worth to prospective purchasers in the open market.

This point needs emphasising since it marks a fundamental difference between the statutory open market valuation hypothesis and the way in which shares in private companies are normally valued in arms-length commercial transactions. When such shares come up for sale the price is usually agreed by private treaty on a one-to-one basis and will be a function of both sides owner values, as illustrated in Chapter 1. There must be mutuality of interest, i.e., something in it for each party, for a transaction to take place. If the shares are worth more to the seller than the purchaser is prepared to pay, the seller will withdraw. The market value of his shares, however, is the best price he can get for them — whether he likes that price or not.

The open market

Although the statutory valuation hypothesis requires one to envisage a hypothetical purchaser and a hypothetical vendor it does not require the assumption of a hypothetical open market. The property is assumed to be sold in *the* open market. What is this open market? Fitzgibbon LJ's definition in the *Jameson* case, already cited, is as good as any: 'that [i.e. a sale in the open market] means the price which would be obtainable upon a sale where it was open to everyone, who had the will and the money, to offer the price which the property . . . in the shares was worth as he [the deceased] held them'. There is no suggestion here of any assumed open market in unquoted shares. The world is taken as it is, the sole exception being that the share transfer restrictions of the company are assumed to be lifted allowing any person so inclined to bid for the shares in question and be entitled to registration as the holder. This implies that the shares should be valued as just one investment opportunity amongst a host of others. The other competing attractions for the investor's funds would include equity investment on the Stock Exchange, the market in British Government and local authority securities, bank and building society deposits. In theory, the market would embrace all forms of real property investment, the commodity markets, traded options, Eurobonds and even the more esoteric investment outlets such as fine art, racehorses, vintage and veteran cars and the like.

The special purchaser

In the discussion so far the effect of the special purchaser has been ignored. As far as portfolio investors are concerned, of course, there are no special purchasers. All portfolio investors have the same angle. If they arrive at different evaluations of the same equity investment this is because they hold different views about the same outcome — future dividends or the dividend-paying potential. There is nothing special in this, however, and these differing views are transformed by the market mechanism into a ruling market price. What would happen, however, if a purchaser appeared in the market to whom the shares have a special value over and above their portfolio investment value? What would happen, too, if a special purchaser appeared in that corner of the open market reserved for controlling shareholdings and entire companies?

Perhaps the two most frequently cited cases in this regard are *IRC* v. *Clay*, supra, and *Glass* v. *IRC*, supra. These two cases concerned the value of land for incremental land value duty. This short-lived impost was introduced by the Finance (1909–10) Act 1910, and imposed a duty on the increase in site values. The intention was to measure the increase against a datum level (at 30 April 1909) so as not to tax any appreciation in site values occurring before the introduction of the tax. It was therefore in the taxpayer's interest to have as high a datum land value as possible.

The circumstances in the *Clay* case were as follows. A dwelling house and garden at No. 83 Durnford Street, Portsmouth, was sold to a nursing home which owned the neighbouring house and needed further accommodation. The value of No. 83 as a domestic residence was agreed to be £750 but the nursing home paid £1,000 for it in September 1910 because of its special value to them. As the value of the site was calculated by deducting notional building costs from the gross value of the property, the higher the value of the property the greater the value of the site. The taxpayer claimed that the special purchaser influence was also present on 30 April 1909 and that the site value at that date should be determined not by the 'normal' market value but by what the special purchaser would have paid for the property. The Court upheld his contention.

It is clear from Scrutton J's judgment that it would have paid the nursing home to offer up to £1,200 rather than build elsewhere. The price of £1,000 was therefore a compromise between the 'normal' market value of £750 available from any buyer and the full value in use of £1,200 or over to the special purchaser. Scrutton J ruled out the possibility of the vendor holding out for the maximum price obtainable from the special purchaser since that would then make the vendor not a 'willing seller at the time'. The learned judge's comments on the vendor not being a forced seller at any price he can obtain, however low, have been quoted on page 381.

In *Glass* v. *IRC*, supra, the facts were different but the principle was much the same. The taxpayer argued that the datum site value at 30 April 1909 of two farms in Kinross should be fixed not by the agricultural land value but by the value of the land to a special purchaser, the local Water Board, who required to buy the land in order to protect the purity of the water supply. In 1911 the taxpayer in fact sold the farms for £5,000 to the Water Board, thus triggering off a potential charge to incremental land value duty. The measure of the increase in site value was the difference between the site value on 30 April 1909 and on the date of sale. The Revenue contended that the datum site value should have been computed from the agricultural value of the farm at the time, i.e., £3,379, this being the market value and not a special purchaser value. The court rejected this and held that the market value of the site at 30 April 1909 should take into account the probability of a sale to the Water Board there being adequate evidence at that time that the Water Board would have paid a price of around £5,000 for the farms at that time. Lord Johnston's remarks about the willing seller being a person who makes the most of his property in the circumstances and not someone who sells without reserve for any price he can obtain have already been quoted on page 381.

Lord Cullen gave a dissenting judgment. He argued that in the supposed open market sale envisaged by the statute no one apart from the Water Board was interested in the property other than for agricultural purposes. Hence the Water Board would not need to offer a price more than one point higher in the bidding than the normal or general value of the lands to the general public. This line of reasoning was countered by both Lord Johnston and Lord Salvesen with the arbitrage argument. It was known that the Water Board was in the market and would pay an inflated price if necessary. If the price failed to rise to this inflated level speculators would enter the market as buyers with a view to selling the property to the Water Board at a profit. This would drive up the price close to the special purchaser value.

These two judgments indicate that where a special purchaser is known to be in the market, the price the property in question will fetch on a notional sale is not the normal market price or one point in the bidding over that price. The price will be a substantial increase over the ruling market price but not the full value to the special purchaser. It is the price the vendor could expect to get without much difficulty and without taking an intransigent stand on price. That much, at least, would seem clear from the *Clay* case and probably, too, from the judgment in *Glass* v. *IRC* although in that case how far the actual sale price fell below the value to the Water Board was not disclosed.

Other cases often discussed in this context concern compulsory purchase[5] and rating assessments.[6] Some of the material in these judgments supports the view taken in the *Glass* and *Clay* cases; some of it is against, notably in the compulsory purchase cases. But since the basis of valuation in these cases is not identical to that required by the taxing statutes and the circumstances differ markedly from those of the shareholder in a private company, it is doubtful whether a detailed and necessarily lengthy analysis of these cases would throw any more light on the subject than the analysis of *Clay* v. *IRC* and *Glass* v. *IRC*.

The *Glass* and the *Clay* decisions were about land values and incremental land value duty. The first time the courts were asked to consider the effect of a special purchaser on the statutory valuation of shares in a private company seems to be the *Crossman* case. That case was primarily concerned with the effect of share transfer restrictions on the determination of market value for tax purposes. However, the court was also asked to decide a subsidiary point concerning the effect of a special purchaser. Evidence called for the Crown indicated that a particular trust company would have been willing to give a good deal more than the ordinary market price because of a special value the shares had to the company. Finlay J at first instance fixed the value of the shares at £355 based on the evidence of an expert witness, Lord Plender, who 'did not exclude anybody or include anybody in particular; he considered the matter generally'.

Viscount Hailsham LC in the House of Lords approved of this way of arriving at the open market value. The trust company had to be brought into the market as one of the prospective purchasers. 'On the

[5] *Raja Vyricherla Narayana Gajapatiraju* v. *Revenue Divisional Officer, Vizagapatam* [1939] AC 302; *In re Lucas and Chesterfield Gas and Water Board* [1909] 1 KB 16; and *In re Gough and Aspatria, Silloth and District Joint Water Board* [1904] 1 KB 417.

[6] *Robinson Bros (Brewers) Ltd* v. *Houghton and Chester-le-Street Assessment Committee* [1937] 2 KB 445.

other hand', he said, 'I think it a fair construction to put on the learned judge's judgment that the extra sum which could be obtained from trust companies was not an element of the value in the open market, but rather a particular price beyond the ordinary market price which a trust company would give for special reasons of its own. I do not think that it would be right to appreciate the value of the shares because of this special demand for a special purpose from a particular buyer.' None of their Lordships dissented from this view. Interestingly, neither the *Clay* nor *Glass* decisions were referred to.

In the *Lynall* case, which was primarily concerned with the extent of information available, the question of the special purchaser also came up for review. Harman LJ's comments in the Court of Appeal affirmed the view taken in the *Crossman* case:

> It was the taxpayer's argument that directors must be excluded from amongst possible purchasers because they would be special purchasers. I do not accept this and am of opinion that this is not an ingredient in the *Crossman* decision. In Crossman's case it was decided that the fact that a 'special' purchaser, namely a trust company, would have offered a special price must be ignored, but this was because that particular purchaser had a reason special to him for so doing. So here a director who would give an enhanced price because he would thus obtain control of the company would be left out of account. But that is not to say that directors as such are to be ignored. All likely purchasers are deemed to be in the market.

This point was briefly mentioned by Lord Pearson in the subsequent appeal to the House of Lords. His judgment includes an interesting reference to the *Clay* case:

> It is, however, suggested that it [information] would have been available in two ways. First, it is said that the likely purchasers might have included a director of the company, and he would have had the information *ex officio*. But unless others also knew it, his possession of the information would not materially affect the market price which he or any other purchaser would have to pay. The situation differs from that in *Inland Revenue Commrs* v. *Clay* where the special fact enhancing the price of the property was assumed to be a matter of local knowledge.

Try as one might it is almost impossible to identify a general principle running through all four cases. The decisions in *Glass* v. *IRC* and *IRC* v. *Clay* indicate unequivocally that the known existence of a special purchaser in the market will drive up the market price by an appreciable amount and not just one point up in the bidding. The *Crossman* case, on the other hand, quite clearly states that, although the special purchaser cannot be excluded from the market, it would be incorrect to appreciate the price on that account. There was no suggestion in the *Crossman* case that this conclusion was in any way affected by the presumed knowledge or ignorance of the existence of the special purchaser on the part of the investing public generally. In the *Lynall* case Harman LJ affirmed the *Crossman* position. Thus, the special value of the shares to a director who would thereby gain control of the company would be left out of account. It is noteworthy however that Lord Pearson's remarks in the House of Lords put a slightly different emphasis on the point. He felt that the directors as special purchasers armed with confidential information would not have materially affected the price unless others were aware of the information.[7] This harks back to the concept in the *Clay* case where all depends on whether or not the existence of a special purchaser is general knowledge.

Although the decisions in *Glass* v. *IRC* and *IRC* v. *Clay* accurately reflect the commercial reality of what the property in question would have fetched if sold at the relevant time, it is questionable whether they accurately reflect market value. The basis of market value, as shown in Chapter 2, is the assumption that if comparable property fetches a certain price then the subject property will realise the same price, or something near to it. There can be little doubt that an estate agent specialising in residential property in the area around Durnford Street, Portsmouth at the time Mrs Buchanan sold her house to Clay's Nursing Home would not have taken the sale price as indicative of the market value for houses in that area. An estate agent in Kinross would similarly have discounted the inflated price Glass received from the Water Board when advising clients what to offer or demand for comparable farms.

[7] Under the Company Securities (Insider Dealing) Act 1985 it is a criminal offence for the director of a quoted company in possession of unpublished price sensitive information to deal in the company's securities. The Act is aimed at dealings on anonymous securities markets and not private treaty deals such as occur in the sale of shares in private companies and occasionally in quoted shares. In the *Lynall* case the directors were clearly in possession of unpublished price sensitive information. It is interesting to speculate on the attitude the court would now take if a case with similar circumstances came before it. In the statutory open market, which is presumably also an anonymous one, would insider trading be permissible? Would directors in possession of unpublished price sensitive information be admitted as special purchasers, or even ordinary purchasers?

In *Glass* v. *IRC* and to a lesser extent in *IRC* v. *Clay* the suggestion was made that speculators, knowing that the property had a special value to a particular purchaser, would pay more than the 'normal' market value so as to sell it to the special purchaser at a profit. This would drive the price up well above the normal market value and up to the price which the special purchaser would be likely to pay. However, this sort of speculation is highly risky since the speculator never knows with certainty how far the special purchaser can be pushed nor for how long he, the speculator, will have to wait. He will expect a handsome profit on his trade. This means that he will stop bidding at a price well below the one he estimates the special purchaser will be prepared to pay. In neither case was this point thought through.

More importantly, however, it is not clear how this arbitrage mechanism could function in the hypothetical sale of unquoted shares. Assume, for example, that a small minority shareholding in a private company has to be valued for fiscal purposes. The normal market value is £5 per share, but there is a special purchaser, an existing shareholder, who by acquiring these shares would gain control of the company. This is public knowledge. According to the arbitrage theory, a speculator would step in and offer a higher price in the hope or expectation of selling the shares on to the special purchaser. Let us say that he pays £15 per share in the belief that the special purchaser will ultimately be prepared to pay £20 each for them. The statutory valuation hypothesis assumes one sale only of the shares. The speculator, therefore, becomes registered as a member of the company. How does he then set about selling his shares to the special purchaser if, as may well be the case, the articles of association provide that shares must first be offered to other members *pro rata* to their existing holdings at an auditor-determined fair value? Evidently he is not free to negotiate the price. In fact he could well lose heavily since the auditor-determined fair value is likely to be nearer the normal market value of £5 per share than his cost price of £15 per share. No one would speculate against a special purchaser in such circumstances.

It may also be relevant to place the decisions in *Glass* and *Clay* in the context of the unusual and unfamiliar land value duty imposed by the Finance (1909–1910) Act 1910. As mentioned earlier, this duty was levied on the increase in land or site values arising after 30 April 1909. The charge to tax occurred on specified 'occasions', notably on a sale and on death. When a property was sold, the value of the site was compared with its value at 30 April 1909 and any increase was taxed. Under s.2 of the Act the value of the site on a sale was the consideration actually received. Thus, the site value for disposal purposes was always based on the price the property actually fetched, irrespective of whether it was sold at market value or at a special purchaser price. However, in estimating the datum value of the site (i.e., at 30 April 1909) the market value criterion set out in footnote 4 was stipulated. If the special purchaser influence existed at 30 April 1909 as well as at the date of sale, it would clearly be a gross injustice to the taxpayer to have it counted in a sale or disposal but excluded from the base or datum site value. It could be argued, therefore, that in order to achieve the intention of the legislation the court was disposed to 'bend' the interpretation of market value so as to include special purchaser value.

Market value in the technical sense of the term excludes any special purchaser value. However, the popular meaning of market value is the price property will fetch if sold, and one would normally expect some reference to the price which a known special purchaser would pay. Scrutton J in *IRC* v. *Clay* put his finger on the point precisely:

> If the owner of No. 83 had said to an expert, 'I wish to sell, but am not forced to, and can wait and negotiate; my house is worth £750 to private owners to live in, but my next-door neighbour desires to extend his premises, and my house is so convenient and well built that it will pay him to go up to £1,200 rather than build elsewhere; what do you think I can realise by a sale?' I think such an expert would have answered, 'Well, I think it depends on diplomacy in bargaining, but I should think you could be sure of selling for at least £1,000, and if you refuse to sell except at your price you can very likely get more'. I exclude the last hypothesis of refusal, as I do not think the vendor would then be a 'willing seller at the time', but I see nothing in the Act to require me to exclude the first hypothesis, which seems to me the obvious business way to look at the transaction.

In the author's opinion, too, this is the obvious business way to look at the transaction — a way which is advocated in Chapter 2. However, this does not alter the true nature of the transaction which is that of a sale by private treaty where one party, the vendor, has the advantage of knowing he is guaranteed at least the normal market price for his house which he can get by selling to someone else. The arbitrage argument has some force in theory at least, but for the reasons already stated it would not drive the price up to £1,000 since this would leave the arbitrageur with no recompense for the risk and trouble involved. The notional market value would be substantially below £1,000. More importantly, because of share transfer restrictions and pre-emption rights it is highly questionable whether the arbitrage argument can be sustained as far as private company shares are concerned.

In the personal opinion of the author, therefore, the special purchaser should not have a significant effect on statutory open market value. This view is consistent with the *Crossman* and *Lynall* cases, both of which concerned share valuations. The decisions in *Glass* v. *IRC* and *IRC* v. *Clay* run counter to this argument but in view of the age of those cases, the unusual circumstances of the land value duty, the inapplicability of the arbitrage argument to private company shares and the, perhaps intentional, failure to distinguish between exchange value and market value, there are very good grounds for ignoring them.

The interpretation suggested here applies where there is a single special purchaser. Where there are two or more special purchasers, however, the effect on price may be significant since special purchasers can be expected to bid against each other. There is no suggestion here of arbitrage, merely the normal mechanism of competitive bids. In theory, the best price obtainable will be one point in the bidding over the next to highest special purchaser value. An example will illustrate the point. Suppose again that a small minority shareholding in a private company has to be valued for fiscal purposes. It has a value for portfolio investment purposes of £5 per share, but three individuals, existing shareholders, would particularly like to acquire these shares because of the way it would improve their voting strength. A would be prepared to pay £8 per share, B, £10 per share and C, £15 per share. For C to buy the shares he need bid only fractionally more than £10 since this is the lowest price which excludes all competition.

Would such a price be market value? It probable would, the reason being that there would then be a special purchaser market superimposed on the portfolio investment market. It would not be a 'flash-in-the-pan' price, valid once only. These special purchasers would remain in the market and continue to have an effect on price. The more special purchasers there are, of course, or the greater the weight of money behind them, the less 'special' they become until their influence determines market price every time.

As to whether a special purchaser market exists is not a matter of hypothesis but of fact. Consider for example, a private company with three shareholders, A, B, and C each holding one-third of the equity. C transfers his shares into a settlement and a valuation is required for capital gains tax and capital transfer tax purposes. If A and B do not get on well together each can be expected to bid strongly for C's shares, since these constitute the balance of power. On the other hand, if A and B are on friendly terms and trust each other they would merely agree between themselves to bid just one point above the general portfolio investment value, each buying an equal number of shares. The point made here is that a special purchaser market is not deemed to exist merely because the shares in question could be worth a special amount to certain individuals. It is a question of fact, decided upon by the evidence available, such as the attitude of the shareholders, their financial resources, personal relationships and so on. In practice, one suspects that it is extremely difficult to prove that such a market exists. In the absence of reliable evidence to the contrary it is safer to proceed on the assumption that no special purchaser market exists.

Hindsight inadmissible

Fiscal share valuations mostly take place at some time in the past. The information on which such valuations are based must have been in existence at or before the date of the valuation; hindsight is inadmissible. In the words of Danckwerts J in *Holt* v. *IRC*, supra: 'It is necessary to assume the prophetic vision of a prospective purchaser at the moment of the death of the deceased, and firmly to reject the wisdom which might be provided by the knowledge of subsequent events'. This rule was also applied in *IRC* v. *Marr's Trustees* [1906] 44 Sc. LR 647 and in the *Lynall* case.

Although hindsight is inadmissible, there is no reason why subsequent events should not be reviewed to see whether they throw any light on information which was available at the valuation date but of which there is now no trace. If, for example, the valuation is dependent on whether or not draft trading results were available at the time, it may be possible to infer whether or not they existed at the relevant time from the date the final audited accounts were published, even though these may not have been issued until after the valuation date.

Combined holdings

If a person transfers two or more types of security in the same company, he is assumed to take the course which gets the largest price for the combined holding.[8] Take as an example a company with voting and non-voting ordinary shares as follows:

	£
100 'A' voting ordinary shares of £1 each	100
10,000 'B' non-voting ordinary shares of £1 each	10,000
	10,100

Apart from votes, 'A' shares and 'B' shares rank *pari passu*. A share-

[8] *Attorney-General of Ceylon* v. *Mackie* [1952] 2 All ER 775.

holder transfers his entire holding of 60 'A' voting shares and 6,000 'B' non-voting shares. If these holdings were valued separately they would not realise as much as they would if sold together. The voting 'A' shares have a tiny equity entitlement — less than one per cent of the total. However, they carry a majority of the votes. As explained in Chapter 10, control *per se* without the accompanying equity entitlement has no substantial value since it produces no return. The equity holders derive all the benefits of efficient management. In reality, a majority interest in the 'A' voting shares would never be sold on its own; it would always be sold with a large block of the non-voting equity. This is also the requirement in fiscal share valuations. The two shareholdings would be valued together.

Expenses of sale not deductible

The wording of the statutory valuation hypothesis, 'the price which those assets might reasonably be expected to fetch on a sale in the open market', points to the price which a purchaser would pay and not the amount which the vendor would receive after the deduction of expenses.[9] It will be recalled from Chapter 2 that this is the generally accepted convention in the commercial world. The purchaser will, nonetheless, take into account his costs when making a bid.

Time of hypothetical sale

The hypothetical sale takes place at the very moment of transfer of the shares, whether by death, gift or sale. Any necessary preparations for the sale, such as, advertisement, are deemed to have taken place beforehand.[10]

Consideration in cash

The price property is estimated to fetch on the statutory open market is a cash price. Deferred payment terms may never be hypothesised unless they are used as the basis for calculating a valuation date cash equivalent. The real relevance of this point, however, lies in the use of Stock Exchange comparisons. If, for example, a controlling interest is being valued, the price at which takeover bids on the Stock Exchange have been successfully concluded may be used to justify or derive the

---

[9] *Duke of Buccleuch* v. *IRC*, supra. However, for capital gains tax purposes expenses of sale are deductible in computing the gain on disposal (s.32 Capital Gains Tax Act 1979).
[10] *Duke of Buccleuch* v. *IRC*, supra.

valuation. Most takeovers on the Stock Exchange are by way of a share-for-share exchange with a cash alternative. It is the cash alternative which should be used to derive rates of return or other investment data. If no cash alternative is offered in a particular bid, a rule of thumb is to deduct ten per cent from the paper value of the offer. If the point is significant, this should be confirmed by reference to recent bids where a cash alternative is provided.

Other topics of interest

Although knowledge of the statutory valuation hypothesis and of how it has been interpreted by the courts is fundamental to the fiscal share valuer, problems arise in practice which do not fit into the neat categories of the preceding analysis. Some of the difficulties are of general application; others concern specific types of valuation.

The relevance of case law

Anyone who casually picks up a book on share valuation to obtain some idea of the subject would doubtless be intrigued by the way in which the 'dicta' of learned judges are cited as the authority for almost every statement made. It is as if the art of valuation is to be learnt by a careful reading of legal judgments. Yet the role of the judge is to apply the law in the settlement of a dispute, not to value shares. The judgments themselves show clearly that the judge does not regard himself as a valuer, but as a person appointed to settle a dispute as to value in the light of the expert witnesses' evidence. This is abundantly clear from the *Holt* case where the Crown claimed a value of 125p per share and the taxpayer, 86p. Danckwerts J in determining the value said, 'I am entitled, therefore, to assume that the principal value of the shares is one or other of these figures . . . or some other value somewhere in between'.

As the reader of this book will have hopefully realised by now, if he was not aware of it before, value concepts and valuation techniques do not have their origin in the courtroom but in the market place. It follows, therefore, that anything a judge may say on a technical matter of valuation has no binding force on the share valuer nor should it set a precedent binding future cases. This needs constantly to be borne in mind when Revenue officials base their arguments on the fact that judge so-and-so approved a discount for non-marketability of x per cent, or how in such-and-such a case the dividend yield basis was rejected, and so on. None of this has any necessary relevance, particularly as there have been no recent share valuation cases where up-to-date expert evidence has been given.

The relevance of case law therefore does not lie in the techniques of valuation which may or may not have been adopted in the various cases. The fundamental relevance of case law lies in the judicial interpretation of the statutory valuation formula. The statutory valuation hypothesis on its own cannot be applied with consistency and certainty to private company shares. It needs interpreting. This the courts have done in a series of cases starting with the *Jameson* case in 1904. This is the framework within which Revenue and taxpayer have to reach agreement on value, and the valuer must be thoroughly conversant with it.

The influence of the Stock Exchange

In commercial share valuation work the Stock Exchange is not usually a directly relevant factor. This is because the motives for holding private company shares are rarely those of portfolio investment. The transaction will be by private treaty and one side at least will have an owner value based on control. Considerations such as family ties, employment, and business or personal relationships often enter into the equation. The statutory valuation hypothesis is not concerned with this little world but with the open market, where the shares must offer a reasonable rate of return when compared with the alternatives.

In highly developed capital markets such as those of the UK and the US, the various investment opportunities are priced in terms of their relative riskiness. Although the link between investments at both ends of the risk spectrum is tenuous, the relationship between investments with comparable risk characteristics is strong and direct. Thus, the treasury bill rate affects the short end of the gilt-edged market. Building society deposit rates must be competitive with bank deposit rates and the rate of return on government stocks. Exactly where equity investment fits into this picture is a matter of debate, but it seems hardly in doubt that an individual contemplating the purchase of unquoted shares as a portfolio investment would regard quoted shares as the nearest alternative. In the author's view, therefore, it is, generally speaking, legitimate to derive the required rate of return by analogy with quoted companies. The reader is referred to Chapter 5 where this point is discussed under the heading 'extent and nature of comparability'. Chapter 5 provides a description of security markets in the UK, published share price information and the various share price indices.

It requires little imagination (merely a question of putting oneself in the shoes of the hypothetical purchaser weighing the merits of a Stock Exchange investment against one in a private company, with no ready means of selling his shares and a dividend policy at the whim of the directors or controlling shareholders) to see that the 'open market' price of the unquoted share will be substantially lower than that of any Stock Exchange analogue. The difference in price will reflect two basic factors: risk and marketability. There is no reason why risk should be higher (or lower) for the private company. It all depends on the circumstances. As a general rule, however, a smaller business will tend to be riskier than a larger one since it is less able to withstand shocks. As private companies are usually much smaller than quoted companies they will tend to be riskier on size grounds. The relationship between risk and the rate of return is discussed in Chapter 7. Marketability discounts are considered in Chapter 9.

Where a controlling interest has to be valued a different class of hypothetical purchaser has to be envisaged. Institutional investors such as unit trusts, investment trusts, pension funds, life assurance companies and the like are usually banned as a matter of policy from purchasing controlling shareholdings. The individual Stock Exchange investor will not usually have the funds to buy a controlling interest or the expertise to manage one. For all practical purposes, therefore, the market for controlling shareholdings is very thin and confined generally to other companies, chiefly competitor ones. Stock Exchange prices are applicable solely to small parcels of shares and are not a reliable guide to the value of a controlling interest.

As explained in Chapter 3 under 'the legal nature of a share' the controlling shareholder, for valuation purposes if not for legal purposes, is a part owner of the company's business undertaking. Earnings are the return on his investment and not dividends. The purchaser of a controlling interest evaluates his investment on a different basis to that of the portfolio investor. When takeover bids are launched on the Stock Exchange the effect of this difference becomes apparent, a substantial premium over the current share price generally being offered. This premium is sometimes referred to as premium for control. As a bidder's perception of earnings prospects may well differ from the market's and as there are also likely to be substantial gains from rationalisation or 'synergy', it is not surprising to find that this premium varies considerably. It would be a mistake, therefore, to conceive of there being a going rate for this premium which, when applied to Stock Exchange prices, could be used to value controlling interests.

In the real world, prospective buyers for controlling shareholdings are few and far between, and each purchaser will have his own evaluation of, and hence price for, the business. It is never very satisfactory, therefore, to give an unqualified opinion as to market value for a controlling interest. Indeed, it is debatable whether in reality the conditions of exchange for controlling shareholdings constitute a market. As explained in Chapter 10, there are two approaches to the selection of a required rate of return for controlling shareholdings, viz., the comparable company method and the investment approach. In commercial valuation work the investment approach is preferred by the author, for the reasons stated in Chapter 10. However, for fiscal purposes the comparable company approach may be more suitable since it is easier to negotiate values based on publicly available information.

Non-dividend paying minority shareholdings

Many private companies do not pay dividends even though they make good profits. As dividends are the return to the minority shareholder, they are the obvious valuation basis for minority shareholdings. How then should minority shareholdings in non-dividend paying companies be valued? This topic has already been discussed in detail in Chapter 9, and the reader should familiarise himself with that discussion before proceeding farther. The discussion in Chapter 9 concerned commercial and not fiscal share valuations. It drew a distinction between transactions motivated by portfolio investment and those motivated by other considerations, such as, employment, family relationships, control and so on. The latter category accounts for most of the transactions in private company shares. Prices in such transactions are a function of the owner values of each party, their bargaining strengths and weaknesses and negotiating skills. At least one side will have an owner value based on control. Even where dividends are paid, as likely as not they will be only a subsidiary factor. In the overwhelming majority of such cases, price will be determined on some discounted control value.

Different considerations apply in transactions motivated by portfolio investment. Here the institutional investor is better placed than the private individual. Institutional investment in unquoted companies has become very popular in recent years and includes the provision of finance for management buy-outs, development capital for established businesses, and venture capital for business 'start-ups'. Finance may be provided by a package of loans and equity or simply by equity. Some institutions insist on a running yield, particularly those who are themselves financed by borrowings and under the obligation to meet substantial interest charges. Others, perhaps most, are not bothered about dividends. All institutions, however, expect ultimately to make a substantial capital profit on their investment.

There are three distinguishing features of this type of portfolio investor. Firstly, by and large the money invested represents fresh capital for the company as opposed to the purchase of existing shares. Secondly, the company or its major shareholders usually solicits the funds from the institution, possibly via an intermediary or contact. A proposal or request has to be submitted to the institution; a representative of the institution will visit the company, tour its premises and have detailed discussions with management; probing questions are asked and answered. The information an institutional investor is likely to be given will be much greater than that available to the shareholders generally. Thirdly, the arrangements will make provision for the institution's ultimate 'exit route'. This will be by a public flotation of the company either on the official market or on the USM, the sale of the entire company or perhaps the company agreeing to buy in the institution's shareholding. The price the institution is prepared to pay will be based on its estimate of this eventual 'exit' price, unless of course a running yield is provided and this, too, will come into the reckoning.

The private individual as a portfolio investor is a very rare creature indeed. It is not difficult to see why. The typical private company board of directors does not welcome outside minority shareholders. It would be most unusual for a complete outsider to be allowed to buy shares in the company. Even if the directors had no objection to the admission of an outsider, he would have to surmount the pre-emption rights of existing shareholders who may well have the opportunity of acquiring the shares at a low prescribed price or auditor-determined fair value.

From the portfolio investor's viewpoint, an investment in a private company presents severe drawbacks, notably the lack of marketability and the absence of any pressure on the company to pay dividends. Admittedly minority rights have been strengthened considerably by recent legislation, but legal action, with its costs and uncertainty, does not appeal as a means of ensuring that an investment pays. Those individuals whose status in a private company is that of the outside portfolio investor have rarely opted for the position as a matter of investment choice. They probably inherited the shares or perhaps they were insiders but, having left the company's employment or resigned from the board, they no longer have any working involvement with their erstwhile colleagues. Even if there were no restrictions on transfer, the price which the typical portfolio investor would offer for the shares in the smaller private companies would almost certainly be too low to interest an insider.

This then is how shares in non-dividend paying companies come to be valued in practice. But how should the task be approached when the fiscal open market concept is applied? First, it seems that the valuer cannot proceed as though he were dealing with a typical transaction between stated parties where each side's owner values would be assessed. This is because the statutory valuation hypothesis requires the valuer to imagine a hypothetical willing vendor and a hypothetical willing purchaser. No particular purchaser or vendor is to be envisaged. Private deals such as these are not open market transactions. The institutional investor approach is likewise difficult to reconcile with the statutory valuation hypothesis, since at a minimum it requires the directors or existing shareholders to enter into undertakings which ensure an ultimate 'exit route' for the institution. No such assumptions may be made under the statutory valuation hypothesis. Furthermore, the circumstances of these deals are reminiscent of the private treaty sales which the House of Lords in the *Lynall* case were firmly of the opinion did not constitute the open market. This leaves the private investor and any institutions prepared to invest in unquoted companies without being given assurances about their 'exit route'. The question which each of these eligible market participants must be presumed to ask himself is: Given the alternative forms of investment open to me, what is it worth my paying to step into the vendor's shoes?

One way to set about answering this question is to split it into two parts: what is the cash return I can reasonably expect as a shareholder, and what rate of return should I apply to that cash return in order to calculate its present day worth to me? The cash return consists of dividends received during the period of ownership and the amount realised on eventual sale of the shares. Obviously, if the company does not pay any dividends the only way a profit can be made on the investment is on ultimate sale. The value of minority interest in non-dividend paying companies must therefore be based on the expected ultimate resale value.

It is necessary to qualify this generalisation slightly. First, if there are good reasons for believing that substantial dividends will be paid in the future even though the company currently pays no dividend then clearly future dividends would provide a basis for valuation. Second, it might be possible to put pressure on directors to pay a dividend by threatening to present a petition under s.459 of the Companies Act 1985. Any dividends the hypothetical purchaser might expect to be paid as a result of this course of action or any order the court might make would have to be taken into account. But in the vast majority of cases there will be no grounds for a successful petition and the hypothetical purchaser would have to look solely to the likely value on resale.

From this point on, the fiscal valuation approach may be very much like the commercial one where the valuer has to envisage a particular buyer or buyers. They way the shares are held will, therefore, be of the utmost importance. Some shareholders may stand to benefit considerably by acquiring the shares. Others may have no particular reason for purchasing them. The company's articles of association usually have an important bearing on the matter. If there is a prescribed price for share transfers, this determines the ultimate sale value. The existence of fair value pre-emption clauses may thwart the hypothetical purchaser's attempt to make the most of his shareholding's value to particular parties. Other possibilities which would have to be considered include a Stock Exchange or USM listing, a bid for the entire company or the company purchasing the shares.

In some cases this assessment of the likely eventual sale price may be no more than intelligent guesswork entailing a high degree of speculation, even hope. In other cases, the probable outcomes will be fairly obvious and assessable with some confidence. In the author's view the larger the minority holding, the more confident the valuer will be about the expected outcomes. This is because a substantial minority interest can be a major irritant for the controlling shareholders. A large minority shareholder would have a much greater incentive to avail himself of the minority protection afforded by the Companies Act 1985 than would the owner of a one per cent holding. More would be at stake. Similarly, the controlling shareholders would feel their freedom of action circumscribed much more by the existence of a large minority interest than they would by a tiny one. Controlling shareholders in private companies are often working proprietors. Their incentive for building up the business is considerably weakened by the existence of a significant minority interest. They would probably see it as a levy on their industry and effort.[11] Paradoxically, because the hypothetical purchaser would be an outsider there would be an even greater incentive for the controlling shareholders to buy him out.

Where small minority interests are concerned, however, these considerations hardly come into play. The dilution effect may be negligible, particulary where directors' remuneration is generous. In addition, the cost/benefit ratio of legal action is unattractive for someone with only a small investment. This points to very low, even derisory values for small minority interests in companies where the policy is not to pay dividends. As the size of the minority shareholding rises the

---

[11] This attitude is much less likely to exist in a property investment or 'money box' company. Such companies are investment intermediaries. They do not generate wealth but merely tap it. The sweat and toil takes place at one remove from the 'money box'. On the other hand, the hypothetical purchaser locked into an investment he has no control over might well be seen by the controlling shareholder as the opportunity for buying shares on very advantageous terms. The owner value for the controlling shareholder would be full asset value, but in view of the weak position of the minority the shares could probably be acquired at a substantial discount.

value per share should increase steeply. It is vital in this type of valuation to form a view of the holding period. Can the hypothetical purchaser expect to find a buyer within months or must he wait years? Money has a time value, a point which will not be lost on the hypothetical purchaser faced with a long holding period without any annual return.

Having thus formed an opinion on the likely return on the shares — in effect what he could reasonably expect to sell them for and when — the hypothetical purchaser has to select a required rate of return with which to express that future return in present day terms. The required rate of return is a function of the risk-free rate, as typified by the rate of return on gilts, and a premium varying with the riskiness of the investment. It must also reflect the poor marketability of the unquoted share. In the type of investment being considered here there is, in addition to the business risk of the company's operations, the inherent uncertainty surrounding both the timing of the eventual disposal and its amount. Given this, the required rate of return will normally be much higher than that expected for Stock Exchange investment.[12] In many cases the investment will be every bit as risky and speculative as venture capital, for which expected rates of return of 50% a year are common.[13] In the author's opinion, the rate of return in current conditions would be not less than 30% a year.

Let us illustrate with a simple example how this approach might be carried out in practice.[14] Assume that a private company's shares are held as follows:

	%
A	37
B	33
C	30
	100

C dies and you have to value his 30% shareholding for probate purposes. The company does not pay any dividends. The return to the hypothetical purchaser could arise in the following ways:

(a) a sale of his shares to A or B;

[12] The way to assess expected rates of return on quoted companies is set out in Chapter 9. The long-term risk premium on UK quoted equities is discussed in Chapter 7.
[13] See Chapter 9, page 204.
[14] A similar example, but showing the commercial approach, is given in Chapter 1, page 13.

(b) a sale to A or B *pro rata* to their existing shareholdings, or alternatively, the company buying his shares;
(c) a bid for the entire company;
(d) an eventual listing.

On enquiry you rule out the possibility of a bid or of a listing. As A or B could get control of the company by acquiring the hypothetical purchaser's shares you feel it realistic to assume that the 30% shareholding would fetch its *pro rata* control value if sold to either of these two but not to both. In view of all the circumstances, including the share transfer provisions of the company's articles, you conclude that the most likely outcome is a sale of the shares to A. This sale should take place within the next five years.

The next step is to estimate the likely price on eventual sale. In practice this would probably be done in two stages — first, an estimate would be made of the price the shares would fetch based on today's values. This would then be increased by the expected growth rate over the holding period and the terminal value would then be discounted by the required rate of return. In fact, one would simply discount the current price by the required rate of return net of the growth rate. If a reasonable rate of return to expect is 30% and growth of 10% a year compound is likely, C's shareholding might be valued as follows:

Assumed value of C's shares today in a sale to A		£100,000
Required rate of return	30%	
Less growth rate	10	
Net discount rate	20%	
PV factor — 20% for 5 years		0.4019
Present value		£40,190
Say		£40,000

However, in view of all the imponderables it would be more realistic to calculate a range of present values using different growth rates and different resale dates. This might take the following form:

Present value matrix — D's shareholding
(rate of return, 30%)

Year of sale	Growth rate		
	5%	10%	15%
4	40,960	48,225	57,175
5	32,768	40,190	49,718
6	26,214	33,490	43,233

The matrix shows the sensitivity of the valuation to changes in the variables. The required rate of return, 30%, has been held constant, but the effect of changing this variable could also be calculated.[15] The valuation would still be based on a 15% growth rate and a disposal in year 5, since this is considered the most likely possibility. However, the range of possible values indicates the scope for negotiation.

Two further points need emphasising in this type of valuation. The fact that the valuation is based on the price. A is expected ultimately to pay for the shareholding does not make it a special purchaser value even though A is almost certainly a special purchaser. This is because the value arrived at is not the price A would be prepared to pay for the shares in the hypothetical open market sale envisaged by the statutes. The value arrived at is the estimated price the generality of purchasers would be prepared to pay for stepping into C's shoes where the only conceivable way of ultimately disposing of the shares would be to a special purchaser.

Second, it is not so much the declared intentions of A, or any other possible buyer which should be the determining factor but what they might reasonably be expected to do.[16] If it is a reasonable supposition that sooner or later A would buy C's shares, this would be acted upon by the generality of purchasers. In the Stock Exchange, admittedly a different form of market, investors continually seek out potential bid targets. These are companies which it is reasonable to suppose some other company or companies would have an interest in acquiring. Disavowals of interest, where they lack commercial logic, fail to carry much weight and are often ignored. People are prepared to back their own judgement.

Lastly, before leaving this topic, we should perhaps turn to the hypothetical dividend yield basis of valuation described in Chapter 9. This technique is sometimes used to value minority shareholdings in non-dividend paying companies. For the reasons given in Chapter 9 this method should never be used in commercial or legal valuation work. It has no realistic basis to it. It seemes to be used in the valuation of shares for fiscal purposes (not by the author), and if it enables agreement to be reached on the correct values it may serve a useful purpose. However, it should only be used to justify a valuation arrived at by correct principles; it should never be used to arrive at a value in the first place.

---

[15] In this example we have opted for one outcome, i.e., the eventual sale of the shares to A. If other outcomes were also considered likely they, too, would have to be assessed. As each outcome has a number of variables, i.e., the growth rate, the rate of return and date of sale, the number of possible values may become difficult to handle. In practice, however, the likely outcomes are usually very limited.

[16] This is a point of interpretation of the valuation hypothesis. Ultimately it would be for the court to decide.

The shareholder with other roles in the company

The law draws a clear distinction between a person as a shareholder and the same person acting in another capacity, such as an officer or employee of the company, a supplier or a loan creditor.[17] This distinction, which must always be observed, can have very significant implications for the valuation of a company's shares if the shareholder in his other capacity is in a position to determine the fortunes of the business.

This point has already been considered in Chapter 2 under 'going concern value'. The example is given there of a small, civil engineering business heavily dependent on one customer and on the expertise and flair of one person. Other examples can easily be cited: the small, highly profitable insurance broking business set up by two experienced individuals and entirely dependent on them; the flourishing wine importer over-reliant on the contacts and flair of its founder; the profitable subsidiary of a pharmaceutical company whose sales consist entirely of products manufactured by its parent. In all such cases one vital characteristic of value is lacking — independent profit-earning potential. If the key man were to leave immediately — or die — the business would be crippled and in all probability would not survive. If the parent company decided to market its products through another outlet, the subsidiary's business would wither away.

As explained in Chapter 2, the shares in such businesses cannot be given an unqualified going concern value. The valuation must always be qualified as to the assumed willingness of the vendor to give all the necessary undertakings which a purchaser would require. It is these undertakings which give the shares their going concern value — namely, the commitment on the part of the key man to stay on for as long as is necessary to ensure the transfer of goodwill, or a legally binding agreement on the part of the parent company to continue to supply the subsidiary with products on acceptable terms. These undertakings are given by the vendor but not in his capacity as shareholder. It is as an employee or officer of the company that the vendor enters into a service agreement and it is as a supplier that the parent company commits itself to continue supplying its former subsidiary.

The statutory valuation hypothesis only covers the vendor's behaviour as a shareholder. There are no assumptions to be made as regards his behaviour in his other roles in or out of the company. Therefore, when a controlling interest in such a company is being

---

[17] The distinction has been recognised by the courts on numerous occasions, e.g., in *Rayfield* v. *Hands* [1960] Ch 1; *London Sack and Bag Co* v. *Dixon & Lugton* [1943] 2 All ER 763; *Eley* v. *Positive Government Security Life Association* (1876) 1 Ex D 88.

valued the valuer must assume that no undertakings are given by the vendor in any of his other roles. He must approach the valuation in exactly the same way as he would if vendor and key man/sole supplier were separate persons. He must ask himself: given the change of ownership, on what terms, if any, would the key man be prepared to enter into a service agreement with the company, thus enabling goodwill to be transferred? On what terms, if any, would the pharmaceutical company be prepared to continue supplying its former subsidiary?

In business relationships a person will endeavour to obtain the maximum advantage for himself and will rarely settle for less than his fair reward where similar rewards are available elsewhere. The key man, if the business truly depends on him, will demand most of the profit; so too will the sole supplier. The purchaser of the shares has the title of proprietor and the ability to reach the assets, but he is in no position to resist the demands of the key man or sole supplier as this is where the economic viability of the business resides. In the absence of the necessary undertakings no purchaser would evaluate such a business on a going concern basis. He would pay no more than the shares would be worth on a liquidation.[18] To count on anything else would be imprudent.

This approach will produce a very low value. It may entail valuing a business on a break-up basis when in fact it is a highly successful going concern. This should not discourage the valuer although it may be stoutly resisted by the Revenue. What matters is that the valuation approach and assumptions are consistent with the statutory valuation hypothesis. It is then a matter of fact, which can be decided by an appeal to the evidence, as to whether or not Mr X is the very lifeblood of the enterprise or whether the business could survive without its source of supply. Obviously anyone who adopts this approach must be sure of his facts. Even if the facts would not justify the assumption of a liquidation basis, due allowance should be made for the remuneration which a key individual would reasonably demand were he not also a shareholder in the company.

Many of the smaller private companies, particularly those in service industries, could not be sold without some form of undertaking or warranty being given by the vendors. When advising on the value of

---

[18] If the controlling interest is less than 75% of the equity the purchaser cannot force a liquidation. He would, nevertheless, still value on this basis because he would have to make the prudent assumption that the key man would not cooperate other than on terms which gave him substantially all the profit. If the key man left, the business would collapse and a liquidation would inevitably ensue. Similarly, if a sole supplier set up an alternative outlet or a major customer, say, one accounting for over three-quarters of total sales, withdrew its custom the business would fold up and a liquidation ensue.

shares for fiscal purposes the valuer should always consider what the effect on value would be if these undertakings were not given.

This rule will not necessarily affect the value of a small minority shareholding as much as it may affect the value of a controlling interest. This could conceivably result in the paradox of a small minority interest having a higher value per share than a controlling one. Suppose, for example, that X, a theatre impresario, owns 80% of ABC Ltd, the remaining 20% being held by various members of his family. ABC Ltd makes good profits from the productions which X mounts. It is entirely a creature of X who could equally as well use another company to operate through. For the reasons already given, this complete dependence on X would deprive the company of any going concern value for fiscal purposes. If a small minority interest, say a five per cent holding, were being valued this 'key man' characteristic would certainly be a depreciatory factor but it would not produce the same degree of conflict between the role of X as controlling shareholder and key man. If dividends are paid and X can be seen to get what he wants out of the company, the valuer might be justified in valuing the shares on a dividend yield basis. Unless the company is asset rich, the resultant value per share could well be higher than a liquidation-based value. The smaller the minority shareholding the less the 'key man' effect.

Besides being a key man or a vital source of supply, the vendor shareholder may fill another role: that of creditor to the company. Here, too, the statutory valuation hypothesis makes no distinction between a loan from a shareholder and one from a third party. If the shareholder loan is repayable on demand it must be deemed to be so for valuation purposes even though the shareholder would not in reality call it in. This point has also been discussed in Chapter 2, under 'going concern value', where an example is given of a private company financed largely by a loan from its major shareholder. The capital structure is summarised below:

	£000's
Share capital	1
Reserves	124
	125
Shareholder's loan	400
Net capital employed	525

No interest is charged on the loan and for all practical purposes it is *de facto* equity. The value of the business is assessed at £600,000. However, no one would pay that much for the shares since after the shares had changed hands the loan would probably be called in. In practice, therefore, the vendor would either accept £200,000 for his shares and be repaid the loan of £400,000 (the purchaser providing the company with the necessary finance), or he would waive the loan and take £600,000 for the shares. When valuing shares for fiscal purposes this latter course must be ruled out since no distinction is to be made between a third party creditor and a shareholder creditor. Thus, for fiscal purposes the entire equity in this company would be valued at £200,000. This would also be the approach in legal or binding valuations; Lord Denning's judgment in *Dean* v. *Prince* is a good example of this.[19] Obviously, the bigger the shareholder's loan the lower the value of the equity. In extreme cases where virtually all the finance is provided by way of shareholder loans the equity will be almost worthless. As with the 'key man' company the valuer must be sure of his facts before putting forward a valuation on this basis. In many cases the company may well be able to repay the loan from its own resources or by borrowing. If so, the value of the equity would be derived from the likely future stream of profits after taking into account the effect of repaying the loan.

Goodwill

Goodwill is a form of property for the purpose of capital transfer tax, capital gains tax and stamp duty. However, it does not need to be separately valued for capital transfer tax purposes, since the measure of a transfer of value is the diminution in the value of the transferor's estate, and there is no requirement to apportion a transfer of a value to individual assets comprised in it. But, for capital gains tax and stamp duty purposes, goodwill may need to be separately valued. For example, in the the transfer of a sole trader/partnership business to a company or the incorporation of a business previously carried on as part of the Division of a group, the Capital Gains Tax Act 1979 provides that all the chargeable assets transferred must be valued at market value. *Ad valorem* stamp duty on the instrument conveying the business to the new company will be payable on the market value of the property transferred and this, too, will entail a separate valuation of goodwill.

In Chapter 8, goodwill was defined as that intangible quality which distinguishes a firm or enterprise from the assortment of unrelated economic agents it would otherwise be. This echoes Lord Eldon's definition; 'nothing more than the probability that the old customers will resort to the old place even though the old trader or shopkeeper has

---

[19] See Chapter 15 under 'fair value' for the relevant extracts from his judgment.

gone', and also Lord McNaghten's: 'the benefits of the good name, reputation and connection of a business. It is the attractive force which brings in custom'. As shown in Chapter 8, these definitions have no necessary connection with profit, super-profits or the firm's tangible assets. What is termed goodwill in financial statements is not goodwill, nor is there any such thing as negative goodwill. Goodwill cannot be sold separately from the business nor can it be bought. It cannot be separately valued. So-called purchased goodwill is merely the excess of the purchase price of a business over its net tangible asset value and would be more accurately described as acquisition premium, or in the case of negative goodwill, acquisition discount.

How can this position be reconciled with the fact that goodwill may have to be separately valued for tax purposes? The need to value goodwill for tax purposes arises from the fact that in law the unincorporated business is not a separate legal entity but merely a collection of assets personally owned by the entrepreneur and various liabilities due by him. When an incorporated business is sold, however, much more than a collection of assets changes hands. Goodwill, as the term is used for tax purposes, bridges the gap between the aggregate net value of those assets and the value of the business as a whole. It is a convenient concept which enables the price paid for a business to be allocated entirely to individual assets. The whole of the gain on the sale of the business will, therefore, be brought into charge to capital gains tax, the gain manifesting itself not as the gain on sale of the business — this could not happen for tax purposes since the business is not a separate legal entity — but as a gain on the sale of specific assets.

It seems clear, therefore, that goodwill for capital gains tax and stamp duty purposes is no more than the excess of the value of the business as a whole over the aggregate value of the separable net assets. It is, of course, not goodwill. But here the criticism is simply of the label chosen. There is clearly a need, as far as unincorporated businesses are concerned, for the creation of a property concept to ensure that on a sale the whole value of the business is brought into charge to tax. It follows, however, that this type of goodwill, which might well have been termed acquisition premium, should always be valued as the difference between the value of the entire business and the aggregate value of the separable net assets. Techniques such as the super profits method should never be used since these are based on the erroneous view that goodwill, properly understood, is an asset capable of being valued. It is conceivable, too, that the value of goodwill, as thus calculated, when added to the value of the net assets, could exceed the value of the business as a whole.

When an unincorporated business is sold to a company not all the assets and liabilities are necessarily transferred. In some cases the proprietor may retain certain assets, and sometimes it is more convenient for him to pay off some of the liabilities himself. Where this happens it is important to remember that 'tax' goodwill is the excess of the value of the firm over the aggregate net value of all its assets, whether transferred or not. It is not the difference between the value of the firm and the value of the assets transferred.

Conclusion

The fiscal basis of valuation, 'the price which those assets might reasonably be expected to fetch on a sale in the open market', is in essence a commercial basis of valuation. The whole of this book is, therefore, relevant to fiscal share valuations. The purpose of this chapter is not to give the reader a brief summary of the way to do fiscal share valuations but rather to examine the way in which the statutory valuation formula, as interpreted by case law over the years, departs from the principles and procedures outlined elsewhere in this work.

The capital transfer tax and capital gains tax legislation contains two important qualifications to the statutory valuation hypothesis. The first one is intended to prevent flooding of the market. Thus, the price shall not be assumed to be reduced on the ground that the whole property is to be placed on the market at one and the same time. The second one concerns the degree of information assumed available. It shall be assumed that all the information is available which a prudent prospective purchaser might reasonably require from a willing seller in an arm's length private treaty transaction. Additionally, for capital transfer tax purposes the value of a person's estate immediately before death shall fully reflect any changes in the value of his estate by reason of his death.

The text then examined how the statutory valuation hypothesis has been interpreted by the courts over the years. The principles laid down by the courts may be summarised briefly as follows:

(a) The existence of share transfer restrictions, pre-emption rights, or even a prescribed price for the shares in a company's articles of association does not invalidate the market value hypothesis. These restrictions and requirements are temporarily lifted so as to allow the hypothetical sale to go through.

(b) The open market envisaged by the statutes is not an imaginary market. It is interpreted to mean 'the price which would be obtainable upon a sale where it was open to everyone, who had the will and the money, to offer the price which the property . . . . in the shares was worth as he [the taxpayer] held them'.

(c) The statutory valuation hypothesis, like the market value concept in the real world, is purchaser oriented. The seller is not a forced or anxious seller in the normal meaning of those words but he is compelled to sell at the best price obtainable even if he does not like it. In this restricted sense he is a forced seller. Thus, the essence of the fiscal valuation approach is the assessment of what the generality of purchasers would be prepared to pay.

(d) The hypothetical sale is between a hypothetical vendor and a hypothetical purchaser. No particular vendor or purchaser is to be assumed.

(e) The *Crossman* and *Lynall* cases indicate that all prospective purchasers, including the special purchaser, must be included in the market, but that it would be wrong to inflate the price to reflect the high price a special purchaser might be prepared to pay. The earlier cases of *Glass* v. *IRC* and *IRC* v. *Clay* do not support this view. They indicate that where a special purchaser is known to be in the market the price obtained will reflect the special purchaser value. These two cases did not concern shares but the value of land for the purposes of increment value duty, a long defunct tax. There are good reasons, explained in the text, for disregarding the decisions in these two cases. In the author's view, the *Crossman* and *Lynall* decisions are to be preferred since they are more consistent with the concept of market value.

(f) Hindsight is inadmissible. Valuations as at a time in the past must be based exclusively on information existing at that time. Information coming to light after the valuation date must not be used in the valuation. However, subsequent events may be examined for information which, for one reason or another, must have been available at or before the valuation date.

(g) If a person transfers two or more types of security in the same company, he is assumed to take the course which gets the largest price for the combined holding.

(h) Expenses of sale are not deductible in arriving at statutory open market value. However, there is an exception for capital gains tax where expenses of sale are deductible in computing the gain.

(i) The hypothetical sale takes place at the very moment of transfer of the shares whether by gift, death or sale. The necessary preparations for the sale are deemed to have taken place beforehand.

(j) The price property is expected to fetch on the statutory open market is a cash price.

Various practical problems arise in fiscal share valuation work and these were discussed in some detail. The relevance of case law to technical matters of valuation can be a source of confusion. Revenue officials are prone to cite legal cases as the justification for certain valuation techniques. However, judges do not claim to be valuers and valuation techniques do not have their origin or obtain their sanction from the court but from the marketplace. Besides, most of the cases are old and probably out of date as regards valuation techniques.

The relevance of Stock Exchange prices to the valuation of unquoted shares for fiscal purposes is a good example of a point which is hardly a matter which can be established by case law precedent. It is essentially a matter of valuation, depending on the circumstances. In the open market for fiscal purposes, the Stock Exchange is an obvious alternative to the hypothetical purchaser of a minority holding of unquoted shares. Where controlling interests are being valued Stock Exchange prices may be used, but only those which evidence the price for controlling interests. This means examining the terms of successful takeover bids. However, the notion that there is a standard or 'going rate' premium for control when bids are launched on the Stock Exchange is highly suspect. It would be wrong to value a controlling interest in an unquoted company by applying some such premium to the minority price. For the reasons stated in the text, the comparable company approach to valuing controlling interests is not as reliable as the investment approach. The former may be easier to negotiate, however.

As a general rule, to which there are important exceptions, dividends are the appropriate basis for valuing minority shareholdings. This is because dividends constitute the return for the uninfluential minority shareholder. However, many private companies do not pay dividends even though they have the profits to do so. This creates problems in valuing minority interests in such companies. This problem was discussed in Chapter 9 as far as commercial transactions are concerned. In this chapter the problem was considered from the fiscal valuation standpoint. The discussion is detailed and does not lend itself to a brief summary. In essence, however, the approach is to estimate (or speculate on) the price the hypothetical purchaser might reasonably expect to obtain when he ultimately sells his shareholding, and to discount this for waiting time, risk and uncertainty.

In the smaller private companies, and some of the larger ones too, it is not uncommon for the shareholder to play more than one role in the affairs of the company. Thus, as well as being a member he might also be a director or officer of the company, an employee, a guarantor of its liabilities or undertakings, or he might have lent funds to the company.

Whenever a vendor in one of his other capacities, say, as key man or loan creditor, is in a position to determine the fortunes of the business the purchaser will insist on some form of undertaking or service contract being entered into by the vendor. As mentioned in Chapter 2, this point is easily taken care of in commercial share valuation by the insertion of an appropriately worded qualification. If, in the unlikely event that no such undertakings could be given, it may well be inappropriate to value the company on the going concern assumption.

The law also draws a distinction between an individual as a shareholder and the same person acting in another capacity. As the statutory valuation hypothesis is concerned solely with the assumed behaviour of the hypothetical vendor and not the actual shareholder, no other assumptions can be made as to the shareholder's behaviour in any of his other roles. This may have very significant implications for the value of the shares. Examples of circumstances where this point may be of relevance are given in the text.

The chapter concluded with a discussion of the valuation of goodwill for tax purposes. The need to value goodwill arises principally when an unincorporated business is sold. It was argued that what has to be valued is not goodwill since, as explained in Chapter 8, goodwill, properly understood, cannot be valued as a separate asset. The notion of goodwill for tax purposes is merely a method of ensuring that on a disposal the full value of a business is brought into charge to tax. Goodwill for tax purposes, therefore, should always be calculated as the excess of the value of the entire business over the aggregate value of separable net assets. The super-profits method, or any other similar technique, should be avoided.

As the discussion in this chapter has shown, the market value concept used for fiscal valuations is necessarily artificial, and values agreed for tax purposes cannot be expected to approximate the price which might be obtained in the typical privately negotiated transaction. Fiscal valuations and the negotiations around them often have an abstract, almost academic quality. Values in such circumstances will be what they can be argued to be; rarely will they be testable in the real world. The valuer must, therefore, bring to the task all his practical and theoretical knowledge, deploying his arguments skilfully and realistically.

17

Analysis of the company and other preliminaries

It is impossible to produce an accurate valuation based on an inaccurate perception of the company. The ability to analyse financial statements and to visualise the reality behind the figures is the single most important element in the art of valuation; it is also the most time-consuming. The assessment of the company typically takes up well over 50% of the total time spent on a valuation assignment. Bearing in mind the need to investigate comparable companies, the work of financial analysis can easily account for 75% or more of total time required. Financial analysis and the assessment of the company's past, its strengths and weaknesses, and its prospects, is for valuation like the submerged part of an iceberg — it accounts for the bulk of the structure, is often not visible or appreciated, and if ignored can have disastrous consequences.

Company analysis

Financial reporting in this country is mainly shareholder oriented, and this can make the physical reality difficult to grasp. The shareholders' main concern is profits and dividends, and financial statements are primarily intended to show a true and fair view of the profit for the year. This presentation gives the impression that profit is a fairly precise, easily identifiable figure whereas, in fact, it is an extremely elusive concept, impossible to measure accurately. In particular, the published profit and loss account gives little idea of how profit is arrived at, and of all the many varied factors which determine it.

The money measurement concept underlying financial statements imposes severe limitations on their scope. The accounts record only those facts and events which can be expressed in monetary terms. They do not reveal, for example, that the firm has just made a technological breakthrough in the design of a new product, or that industrial unrest has been simmering in the works for some time, or that new legislative controls on waste disposal are likely to impose severe strains on profits and liquidity.

Because of inflation, the currency itself has a different value from year to year. With rates of inflation like those experienced in this country in recent years, unadjusted historical cost accounts can give a completely erroneous impression of trading performance. Sales and profits may show modest but respectable growth rates in historical cost terms, but when adjusted for inflation, the picture could well be one of steady and continual decline in real terms. Furthermore, even though statements of standard accounting practice have considerably reduced the choice of accounting bases available to a company, there still remains an element of judgement which gives scope for legitimate differences of opinion as to the profit arising in given circumstances. Whilst the financial statements are useful, they are insufficient on their own. They must be supplemented by other enquiries. A short chapter such as this cannot possibly cover all the techniques of financial analysis, nor is it intended to do so.[1] The aim is rather to give the reader some idea of the approach favoured by the author. The factual content of the report under this approach is not dissimilar to that found in a typical offer for sale document or prospectus.

The extent and depth of analysis required varies from assignment to assignment. Sometimes the valuer will have access to the subject company's internal records and will be able to discuss matters with company management. Detailed budgets and medium-term projections may be available. This is likely when a substantial stake in a company is being acquired. In these situations, the valuer must probe as deeply as he feels necessary, placing particular emphasis on the assumptions underlying the projected results. These must be tested in the light of the company's past performance and the industry background. Often, however, as when a small minority shareholding is changing hands, the valuer may only have the subject company's published financial statements to work on. He must then make all reasonable enquiries from other sources to try to put the company's performance in an industry perspective.

Whatever the extent of the analysis required, the valuer must commit it to writing. In large assignments the client will often request a written report which will include a review of the company and of any comparable businesses. Even when this is not required, an internal memorandum setting out the analysis undertaken should always be prepared. This is both of practical help in formulating one's thinking, and a useful reference should the valuation ever be questioned or challenged.

Although the nature of these enquiries will vary with each assignment, certain features are common to most valuations. The valuer's report might well have the following headings:

---

[1] Textbooks on financial analysis are legion. For a highly readable, practical treatment of the subject see Stewart Y. McMullen, *Financial Statements: Form, Analysis and Interpretation*, 7th ed. (Homewood, Ill.: Irwin, 1979).

(a) history of the company;
(b) activity;
(c) management and personnel;
(d) accounting policies;
(e) trading record;
(f) source and use of funds;
(g) balance sheet review;
(h) prospects.

Each of these headings is now considered in turn.

History

This is not the most important area of enquiry, but it is an appropriate starting point and should not be overlooked. In some cases, knowledge of a company's history can put an entirely different complexion on its financial record. The history should start from the origins of the business and include any acquisitions or divestitures, any changes in basic form of organisation, any major changes in line of business or major changes in geographical areas served. Details of major changes in ownership should also be supplied. Emphasis should be placed on the recent history as this is likely to be more relevant to the valuation.

Activities

There are numerous aspects of a company's activities such as its products, markets served, its manufacturing or production process, key raw materials, energy, plant and equipment, labour, and the regulatory climate. These will depend to some extent on whether the company is engaged in manufacturing or the provision of services, or whether it is a trading company.

The description of activities should start with a general overview of the company's position. This will contain a brief reference to the size of the company measured in a number of ways, such as annual turnover, number of employees, market share of its products. Its physical characteristics should also be mentioned: the size and location of its factories; whether the company operates its own warehousing and distribution system; its sales force; perhaps the name of a major customer (e.g., the Government, if the company is a defence contractor). This introductory overview should indicate the main divisions or product groupings which can then be described in greater depth under their own sub-headings.

What the valuer puts into this description of the company's activities will only be a fraction of the information obtained. He should enquire of the company's management how it sees the company's role in its industry or market; what its objectives are; what developments or trends are expected in the industry in the future and how these are likely to affect the company; how the company perceives its own strengths and weaknesses; and if there are any key factors (e.g., quasi-monopoly) which enable the company to operate profitably.

The valuer should enquire about future major capital expenditures, any planned diversification, acquisitions or disposals. He will want to know whether the company has a programme of corporate development, including further development of existing products or the launching of new ones. How much is being spent on research and development and how is it being financed? These enquiries are so broad and will vary so much from one company to another, that only a very general indication can be given here. The aim of these preliminary enquiries is to give the valuer an understanding of, or a feel for, the company . . . What are the key determinants of its sales? What are the main factors affecting costs? How vulnerable are profits?

From these fairly general enquiries the valuer should move to a more detailed examination of the company's operations. The sales are the most important element in a firm's success and the valuer should devote as much time as possible to this area. The company's products and the markets they serve will have been identified already. If possible, the valuer should obtain a list of competitors and an estimate of market share held by the company for each of its products. The list of competitors may be useful in identifying comparable companies for valuation purposes.

It is important to know the characteristics of each of the company's markets. Who uses the company's products and why? What is the economic outlook for those markets? Are there seasonal or cyclical influences at work? What are the forces that determine the demand for the company's products? Are there technological changes in progress or in prospect that will alter the shape of the market? Are other companies likely to enter the market as competitors?

This level of information will not always be available, either because the company does not have it, or because the size of the shareholding being valued is small and would not warrant any negotiations or discussions with the directors. The valuer then has to consult the industry sources available and reconstruct the picture as best he can. This is not an impossible task. There is a wealth of statistics published in the United Kingdom covering every aspect of the country's economic activity. Government sources are particularly useful and, as a rule, easily accessible. The Department of Trade's Business Monitor service provides monthly and quarterly statistics on sales volume and value by industry and numerous sub-sectors of industry. These can often give a good indication of market size and can be used to estimate the subject company's market share.

Most industries have their own trade association or organisation whose job it is to represent the interests of their members in negotiations with government, employees or generally. Trade associations can be a useful source of information, statistical and otherwise. Most of them publish an annual report as well as a trade or industry journal. Trade directories can also be of use. Various private and semi-public organisations specialise in the production of industry reports or surveys, and much valuable information can be obtained from them. All the information referred to here, and much more, can be obtained at any good reference library.

The valuer should undertake some independent researches, whether or not he has access to the company. Talking to company management will give him the company's view of itself, its markets and its position. The analyst must judge for himself the validity of these views. This can best be done by briefing himself from publicly available sources. There are advantages in doing this before consulting the company.

Having obtained a good grasp of the company's markets and the competition the valuer's attention should focus on the company's operations. The line of enquiry will depend on the nature of the company's business. The operations of a trading company will be quite different from those of a manufacturing company or a service company. In a manufacturing or trading company supplies or purchases are an important factor in operations. The following questions need to be asked: Is the company heavily dependent on one source of supply for any of its key raw materials? Are there any question marks over the continuity of supply? Are raw material prices particularly volatile? It would be rare to find a manufacturing company, or perhaps even a trading company, whose inputs were not subject to some constraints of price or supply.

The valuer's enquiries should cover the company's plant and equipment. A tour of the company's facilities gives a good idea of the company's operations from a physical viewpoint and enables the valuer to form an opinion of the plant's adequacy. Questions that might typically be asked are: How much spare capacity exists? What are the opportunities to extend capacity? Is the plant and machinery modern? Are the facilities cramped? Are they well maintained? What is the scope for future cost savings? Some reference to the state of plant and machinery, capacity utilisation and potential should be made in the report.

The review of activities might well be rounded off by a discussion of the regulatory climate. Government intervention in industry has increased considerably over the years. It takes many forms — price and dividend controls, pay restraint, quality standards, monopoly or fair trading legislation, environmental protection. Some of these restrictions can markedly affect a company's value. The valuer will ascertain how much the company is subject to regulation, either by industry or Government, and enquire whether these regulations are likely to have an adverse effect on the company's earning capacity.

Management and personnel

Looked at from the economist's viewpoint, a company is merely the legal umbrella under which the factors of production, i.e., land, labour and capital, combine. Viewed in this way, the paramount importance of labour is obvious. Labour is a business's greatest asset even though it does not feature in the balance sheet. Without labour, the assets are useless. As mentioned in Chapter 1, when a company has a low return on capital employed, people often talk about the need to make the assets work. But assets do not work on their own, and the only way that the return on capital employed can be improved is by the efforts and cooperation of management and labour. Labour is the active element and capital the passive one. The ability of management and the skills, diligence and industry of the workforce are the most critical factors in a company's success. As most investors in unquoted shares must take a long-term view, the quality of management is all the more important.

Assessing the quality of management is extremely subjective. The most significant and objective indicator of management calibre is the company's operating record. An efficient management team will normally be reflected in high growth rates in profits and sales and in a financially sound balance sheet. However, when the trading background is difficult, and other less well managed businesses are making losses or even going into liquidation, static sales and falling prices can indicate superior management performance.

Some businesses rely heavily on the talents of key individuals and have no management succession. This happens sometimes in the smaller private companies and is particularly common in certain types of 'people' business, such as advertising agencies and insurance brokers. Businesses dependent on a few individuals are highly risky and have low ratings. The management structure of a company will be evident from an organisation chart. A simple rational structure with clear lines of authority and responsibility is a good sign. The company's annual reports in recent years will show whether there have been many changes in the board of directors. Frequent changes in the board indicate policy or personality clashes; these do not augur well for efficient management. The valuer should make a list of key personnel, their age, qualifications, experience and background. Remuneration levels should be noted. Underpaid employees are liable to be poached by other employers whilst excessive remuneration may indicate scope for economies. When control of a company is being acquired, excessive directors' remuneration should be treated as profit distribution. Where a company has a workforce, the valuer should assess its efficiency and effectiveness. As with management, the greatest testimony to the efficiency and effectiveness of the workforce is the trading performance of the company. Does the company have a reputation for quality, service and timely delivery or completion? What is the strike record? Are labour relations happy? Is labour turnover high? How do pay levels compare with industry norms? Is the workforce unionised? The continued availability of labour is also highly important. A company may have to shelve its expansion plans if local labour becomes scarce. The labour market in an area can be transformed almost overnight by the entry of a large employer offering pay at attractive rates. This might oblige companies to raise their pay rates to retain their employees or, as sometimes happens, pay levels do not rise sufficiently and the quality of the workforce deteriorates as the best workers go to the highest bidder.

Accounting policies

The six major accountancy bodies, acting on the proposals of the Accounting Standards Committee, have established accounting standards in the United Kingdom and Ireland. These standards are promulgated in the form of Statements of Standard Accounting Practice (SSAPs). These are the definitive standards of financial accounting and reporting. If a company does not observe standard accounting practice, a note to this effect must be made in the accounts and the effect, if material, disclosed. If the auditor disagrees with the company's non-observance, he must refer to the matter in the audit report.

Accounting policies are defined as the specific accounting bases followed by a business. They must be disclosed by way of note to the accounts.[2] Different bases (policies) can, therefore, be used to report the same transactions. The choice of accounting policy or basis is up to the company. Management should select the most appropriate policies for the circumstances of the company and those best suited to present fairly its results and financial position.[3]

[2] SSAP 2.
[3] Ibid.

It is a well known fact that different accounting policies when applied to the same transactions can result in widely divergent reported profits. Certain areas of financial reporting are particularly sensitive to different accounting policies. These include the valuation of stocks and work-in-progress, depreciation rates and policy, the treatment of research and development, income recognition, the treatment of extraordinary and exceptional items, foreign currency translation procedures and accounting for the results of associated companies.

It is not possible to examine here all the varied effects which different alternative accounting policies may have. Some of these are relatively easy to identify. For example, the effect of different depreciation rates is usually obvious, if difficult to quantify precisely; the degree of conservatism in the treatment of resesearch and development costs should be apparent from the disclosure in the accounts, and the effect of the treatment of intangibles should be clear. But the effect of the different accounting policies for stock and work-in-progress can be extremely difficult to fathom.

Stocks should be stated at the lower of cost or net realisable value.[4] However, the concepts of cost and net realisable value may be extremely difficult to apply in practice. There are, for instance, various definitions of cost. These include unit cost, average cost, FIFO (first in, first out), LIFO (last in, first out), replacement cost and standard cost. Each of these definitions of cost could produce a different valuation of stock and, therefore, a different cost of sales and trading profit. Income recognition and the valuation of work-in-progress, particularly in a contracting company, can vary substantially according to the accounting policy in use. It is one of the most difficult areas for the outsider to evaluate. The valuer must have a sound grasp of the effect of different stock valuation policies.

The valuer must review the accounting policies of the company, decide whether they are normal or unusual and consider the effect they are likely to have on the financial reporting of the company's operations.

Trading record

The review of the company's trading results should cover at least three years, and preferably the last five years. A longer period may be necessary, especially if the company has a long manufacturing or trade cycle. An unrepresentative year, e.g., one of abnormal profits or sales, should be avoided when selecting a base year.

[4] SSAP 9.

The presentation of the trading record is a matter of individual preference in the light of the particular circumstances of the company. The format suggested below should cover most circumstances:

	£
Turnover	_____
Trading/operating profit	
Interest received	
Interest paid	
Exceptional items	_____
Profit before tax	
Tax	_____
Profit after tax	
Extraordinary items	_____
Profit after extraordinary items	
Minority interest/preference shares	_____
Earnings	==========
Dividends	==========

Audited consolidated accounts should be used whenever possible. Figures extracted from unaudited, draft or management accounts should be appropriately identified.

From his enquiries into the history and activities of the firm, the industry background and the competition, the valuer will be aware of the operating environment during the period covered by the review. He must appraise the company's trading performance against this background. It is normally convenient, as a first step, to express this performance in absolute terms. The compound annual growth rates in sales, trading/operating profit and earnings are useful for this purpose. The valuer might describe the change, if any, in trading profit margins over the period and comment on the level of interest payable or on the income gearing. The vagaries of the tax charge should also be explained. A concise statement of the company's overall performance in absolute terms can then be made.

The next step is to relate this level of achievement to that of the industry as a whole or that of competitors. This comparison is essential if any meaningful judgement of the company is to be made. How does sales growth compare with the industry average? It is important when looking at sales to isolate volume from price effects if possible. Has the company increased or lost market share? Perhaps the company has been raising prices, taking profits, but losing market share. If the firm has introduced new products or withdrawn from some markets, these facts should be woven into the valuer's interpretation of the trading results.

The depth of analysis possible is dependent on access to the company's records. In important valuations where the valuer has more or less unlimited access to information, the analysis will be as thorough as necessary. At the other extreme, the valuer may only have financial statements with the minimum of legal disclosure. But it should be possible, nevertheless, to put company performance in some context or other, even if only that of the rate of inflation experienced during the period and some crude macro-economic statistics for company profits.

Exceptional items should be investigated. The analyst should be wary of companies which show exceptional items every year, almost as a rule. A continual stream of exceptional losses reflects badly on management. But the concept itself is helpful as the analyst is looking for underlying trends which can be projected into the future. Those trends will not be apparent if trading results in any year are affected by material non-recurring items. Care is also necessary with extraordinary profits and losses, and the analyst should ascertain the nature of all material items.

The level of interest charges is a reflection of financial management and should be related to the balance sheet review. A high level of income gearing indicates a risky investment, with earnings vulnerable to small changes in operating results.

The abolition of stock appreciation relief and the phasing out of generous first year allowances means that the effective rate of tax (i.e., the actual tax charge as a percentage of pre-tax profits) should be much closer to the nominal rate than it has been in the past. However, companies still have considerable discretion in setting their deferred tax provision and this will continue to be a source of irregularity. Sometimes, no corporation tax is payable because of tax losses brought forward. Unrelieved tax losses should be disclosed in the notes to the accounts and the duration of any tax holiday can be estimated.

The minorities item can be a source of information to the valuer who has limited access to information. The movement in the minority item over the period is an indication of the fortunes of that subsidiary. It may be possible to infer from this how other parts of the group have fared.

It will be difficult to draw much significance from the bottom line earnings figure if the tax charge has been abnormal or irregular.

Source and use of funds' statement

This statement, which almost invariably forms part of the audited accounts, can provide useful insights into major transactions not immediately apparent from the profit and loss account or balance sheet. It is especially useful in highlighting the company's liquidity characteristics. The source and use of funds statement should show separately: new capital raised, whether by issuing new shares or by medium-or long-term borrowing; and acquisitions and disposals of fixed and other, non-current, assets.[5] The statement should reveal the extent to which the company's operations are self-financing. In addition, heavy capital expenditures or major property disposals will probably indicate important developments within the company.

Balance sheet review

The main purpose of the balance sheet review is to ascertain the financial position of the company. The latest audited balance sheet should be sufficient for this purpose if it is recent. The previous year's figures should be included in the presentation. A company's financial position is a function of its gearing (i.e., the level of borrowing in relation to equity funds) and of its liquidity. There are different ways of measuring gearing: some include bank overdrafts, some take into account bank balances in hand. The most suitable measure will depend on the circumstances. For instance, if the bank overdraft is large and a semi-permanent feature of the balance sheet, it should be included in the calculation of the gearing ratio. If the bank balance is swollen by the proceeds of sale of a major asset (e.g., a ship), shortly to be replaced, it would be misleading to deduct the whole of the cash balance from borrowings. Intangibles are customarily deducted from the equity funds, but there is no reason why they should be unless their value is known to be overstated.[6]

The calculation of a company's gearing ratio might well be based on the following analysis of capital employed:

	£	£	%
Equity funds			
Share capital			
Reserves (including retained earnings)	———		
Borrowings			
Long-term loans			
Medium-term loans			
Bank overdraft	———	———	———
Capital employed			100

[5] SSAP 10.
[6] See Chapter 8.

Borrowings may be expressed as a percentage of capital employed, or as a ratio to the equity, or sometimes as a percentage of the equity. It is a matter of individual preference. If large amounts of borrowing are due for repayment shortly, the valuer should ascertain how this is to be financed. Is the company heavily dependent on short-term borrowing? Does it have unused lines of bank credit? It is advisable to compare the balance sheet gearing with the income gearing. The latter is a measure of the extent to which borrowing charges (i.e., interest payable) are covered by operating profits. It takes account of the rate of interest payable and is arguably the more relevant measure of gearing.

There are two popular measures of liquidity: the current ratio and the quick ratio or acid test. The current ratio is calculated by dividing current assets by current liabilities. It is a measure of the extent to which short-term assets of varying degrees of liquidity are available to cover fairly imminent liabilities. The quick ratio is calculated in the same way as the current ratio but with stock and work-in-progress excluded. Stock is generally the least liquid of a firm's current assets and also the one most subjectively valued. The quick ratio is an important measure of the firm's ability to meet its current liabilities without relying on the realisation of stocks.

The liquidity and gearing ratios mean little on their own; they must be related to some norm, such as the industry average or the equivalent ratios for comparable companies or competitors. If the company's ratios deviate far from the appropriate norms, the valuer must enquire further. Ideally, the valuer should have access to the company's cash flow forecasts from which he will be able to obtain a more reliable view of the liquidity position. But these forecasts are not usually available.

Having appraised the balance sheet from the viewpoint of gearing and liquidity, the valuer's next job is to examine each balance sheet item in conjunction with the relevant notes to the accounts. The object of this scrutiny is to ascertain any peculiarities in arriving at the balance sheet amount of the company's assets.

Fixed assets are normally shown at historical cost less accumulated depreciation. The existence of freehold or leasehold property should be noted and the market value ascertained. Freehold property is generally worth more than cost and it can have a substantial value independent of the business. Any significant difference between the aggregate balance sheet figure for land and buildings and its market value must be mentioned in the Directors' Report,[7] though it is rare to find this difference precisely quantified. Heavily depreciated assets suggest old

---

[7] Section 235 of the Companies Act 1985.

plant and equipment and an unduly low depreciation charge in the profit and loss account.

The most common forms of intangible assets encountered in company balance sheets are goodwill, patents and trademarks. Patents and trademarks are often written down to a nominal sum. This may or may not be what they are worth. Some patents and trademarks are highly valuable and the valuer must enquire about the nature of all such assets. Goodwill, where it features at all, is often stated in the balance sheet as a substantial amount. The valuer should find out how this amount has been arrived at and whether it is being written off. As shown in Chapter 8, goodwill cannot be valued as a separate asset and what appears under this label in a company's balance sheet is not goodwill at all. It is nothing more than a book-keeping fiction. Sometimes research and development costs are carried in the balance sheet as deferred revenue expenditure. This is not a marketable asset and has no value independent of the earning power of the company.

Enquiry should be made about the nature of any trade investments. These are often stated at cost but may have a very different value. As a general rule, the valuer should pay particular attention to all non-current assets. They can sometimes have a material bearing on the valuation.

Current assets are held for realisation and should be stated in the balance sheet at their net realisable value, or cost if this is lower. The valuer should look closely at the valuation of stock. From his knowledge of the company's relevant accounting policy, he can judge whether stocks are undervalued as they might be, for example, if the LIFO method is in use. The stock turnover ratio is sometimes a useful efficiency indicator. It is calculated by dividing stock into sales. To mean anything, it must be compared with some industry average or norm. A low turnover ratio indicates that the company holds excessive stocks, and capital tied up in this way does not earn a return. A high stock turnover ratio suggests efficient stock control but it might also indicate hand-to-mouth buying, with sales missed due to inadequate stock.

Trade debtors can be appraised through the debtors to sales ratio. This shows the average collection period and should be compared with the company's advertised credit sales terms. It should also be compared with the industry average or norm. The debtor to sales ratio is found by dividing debtors into sales. The resultant figure when divided into 365, or more commonly 360, gives the number of days' sales tied up in debtors. Care must be taken in drawing too much signficance from this ratio if the company has substantial, but undisclosed, cash sales.

Contingent liabilities are disclosed by way of note to the accounts. These should be examined closely. They often relate to guarantees given by the company, legal actions outstanding or disputed claims. The valuer should also try to ascertain the amount of any off-balance sheet liabilities, such as unfunded pension requirements.

Balance sheet net assets are often used for calculating the rate of return on capital employed. The ability to earn a satisfactory rate of return on equity shareholders' investment is an important characteristic of the successful business. The return on equity is the product of the profit margin on sales and the net asset (i.e., equity funds) turnover ratio, as shown below:

$$\frac{\text{Earnings}}{\text{Equity funds}} = \frac{\text{Earnings}}{\text{Sales}} \times \frac{\text{Sales}}{\text{Equity funds}}$$

The earnings/sales ratio can be analysed into its constituent elements (of which one is the trading profit margin) and the same process can be applied to the sales/equity funds ratio. This produces a pyramid of ratios sometimes referred to as a *du Pont* chart. These ratios fall into five groups: liquidity ratios; asset management ratios; debt management ratios; profitability ratios; and market value ratios. John Sizer gives some useful advice on the interpretation of these ratios[8] and, for the valuer with the time, the necessary information, and the inclination, this task should be rewarding.

Prospects

The accurate evaluation of prospects is vital to an assessment of the future benefits of owning the shares and, accordingly, to their valuation. The valuer's researches into the company's activities and its markets, his review of the trading record and his examination of the balance sheet are all directed towards a realistic assessment of prospects.

If interim or management accounts are available, these can be used by the valuer as the basis of his estimate of prospective results for the current year. The valuer must test the assumptions in these budgets or forecasts against independent evidence and check whether they look reasonable in the light of performance to date, as shown by management accounts. In his survey of the company's activities, the valuer will have identified sources of information on the relevant industries and, hopefully, will have located independent surveys of trends in, and

[8] John Sizer, *An Insight into Management Accounting*, 2nd ed. (Penguin Books, 1979), p. 177.

prospects for, those industries. These may assist the valuer in arriving at his own estimates or may help him to gauge the realism of the management's forecasts. The outlook for the national economy should be referred to briefly.

Prospects beyond the current year are more difficult to quantify. This does not mean, however, that the quality of the analysis must deteriorate. On the contrary, the accurate assessment of longer term prospects is more important than that of short-term prospects as the purchase of unquoted shares is a long-term investment. If the valuer has access to the company, as would normally happen in the acquisition or disposal of a controlling interest, the assessment of longer term prospects becomes much easier.

Most companies undertake some degree of corporate planning and many will have a plan covering the following five years. The valuer must examine the plan carefully and form his own opinion as to its realism and reliability. He should list the critical assumptions and test them against independent evidence. For example, sales figures in the five year plan may be based on the assumption that sales volume will rise by two per cent a year over the five years and that the growth in demand will enable the company to raise its prices by five per cent a year in real terms over the period. The analyst would then ask why sales volume growth of two per cent a year is expected. Is it because the company is aiming for increased market share or is it because the market is expected to grow by two per cent or some combination of these and the other factors? If the company expects the market to grow by two per cent a year, what are the grounds for this expectation? Are they reasonable? If the company is looking for increased market share, how is this going to be achieved? Have the necessary expenditures, such as advertising or sales promotion, been taken into account? As regards the price rises, what has been the company's recent experience? How elastic is demand for the company's products?

In his report the valuer should provide a critique of the five year plan, indicating the sensitivity of the projected results to changes in key assumptions and the extent to which he accepts the figures as a reliable assessment of prospects. If the company does not have a corporate plan, the valuer should try to persuade his client to undertake one, if need be with the valuer's assistance.

Where a minority shareholding is being valued, the valuer may be unable to approach the directors and talk to company management. His assessment of prospects must then be based on his ability as a financial sleuth, seeking clues in telltale pieces of information found in the financial statements and elsewhere. He will have to rely heavily on industry or trade sources and use these to build up a thorough survey of industry prospects. He then has to guage how the company will meet the challenges, or grasp the opportunities, which the industry environment is likely to provide. A key factor in this assessment will be the valuer's interpretation of the company's trading record. This shows how the company had fared against the industry background in the past and it is the best indication the valuer has as to how management will perform in the future.

Finally, if the valuation assignment is a big one, the company assessment will be lengthy. In such cases, a synopsis should be made and included in the valuation proper. Carrying out the synopsis is itself a useful discipline as it forces the valuer to identify the key characteristics of the firm. The synopsis would typically consist of one, or possibly two, sentences for each major heading in the assessment.

Other valuation preliminaries

Private company shares are subject to restrictions on transfer. These restrictions are set out in the articles of association, and are legally binding on all the members. However, the nature and severity of these restrictions vary from company to company, and this clearly affects the value. The valuer must, therefore, read the articles carefully and ascertain precisely the extent of the restrictions. The clauses covering the restrictions on share transfer are usually grouped together and are thus easily identifiable. Legal terminology and style make heavy reading, and it will probably be necessary to read the relevant clauses twice or possibly three times to extract the precise meaning. If there is any doubt about the interpretation of the wording, legal advice should be sought. The articles often lay down, as part of the restrictions, a procedure for the transfer of shares. The valuer should satisfy himself that this procedure is being observed as far as his involvement in the transfer is concerned.

If the company's share capital consists of more than one class of share, the valuer should ascertain from the articles the rights of the other shares. Different classes of shares generally enjoy different rights as to dividend, votes and return of capital in a winding up. These different rights affect the relative values of the different classes of shares. It is important, therefore, to appreciate the different attributes of each class of share. The rights attaching to the various classes of shares are usually set out in a specific group of clauses, as with the share transfer clauses, but private company articles can be notoriously unpredictable. Strange clauses with devastating effects are sometimes tucked away in unlikely places. It is advisable, therefore, to at least scan the articles in their entirety.

As well as listing the different classes of shares in issue, the valuer should call for an analysis of the shareholdings. This will reveal the existence of any controlling interests and possibly connected parties. The distribution of the shares among the other members can be highly significant for the valuation, since those shareholders are the most likely buyers for the shares. If one or more of the shareholders has an obvious interest in acquiring the shares in question because, combined with his present holding, they would give him a strategic or controlling stake in the company, the valuer must reflect this in his valuation.

Appendices: Case studies

Introduction

Valuation is an individual art and it would be wrong to suggest that there is a single correct way of carrying out a valuation. The case studies in the appendices which follow are not therefore presented as the one true way of valuing shares. In fact, the case studies reveal subtle differences in approach and exhibit varying levels of analysis, investigation and reasoning. Nevertheless, they have certain features in common such as a description of the business, a review of its performance and prospects, an examination of the members' rights and duties under the articles, a discussion of the way the shares are held and so on. The case studies have been adapted from actual valuations although the names and places are entirely fictional. These valuations show the way the approach advocated in this book can be put into practice and also the compromise that sometimes has to be made between strict theory and valuation practice.

Four case studies are presented here. Appendix 1 shows a formal valuation carried out with full access to information within the company. It was intended to act as a catalyst in breaking a deadlock between the controlling shareholders and a dissident minority, which it did. It had no binding force. To gain the acceptance of the parties concerned it was essential to demonstrate that every effort had been made to present all the facts fairly and to weigh their significance objectively. In this respect, the valuation reasoning could well serve as an example of the approach required for a binding fair value determination under a company's articles of association.

Appendix 2 sets out the valuation of a non-dividend paying minority shareholding in a private company. Like many valuations, this one had to be done at speed with inadequate, second-hand information and without the opportunity of physically inspecting the business or of discussing the valuation with company management. As with the case study in Appendix 1, this valuation was required for a transaction between stated parties.

Appendix 3 shows the valuation of a small key-man business. The proposed transaction involved the purchase by a trustee of trust property. As the transaction was not at arms-length the trustees sought an independent valuation. As the market value concept was used, this valuation could equally well have applied for fiscal purposes.

Finally, Appendix 4 presents a fiscal valuation of a substantial non-dividend paying minority shareholding. As advocated in Chapter 16, this is a special purchaser valuation at one remove. The questions the valuation attempts to answer are: What would the generality of prudent prospective purchasers be prepared to pay for the opportunity of stepping into the transferor's shoes? What would be perceived as the likely outcome of such an investment? As can be imagined, this is a highly subjective exercise, and no doubt some readers will disagree with the likely outcome assumed in this valuation. This does not matter since in circumstances such as these there is no single, correct value. The value is what it can be argued to be. He who has the most convincing story wins.

Appendix 1

A Scott Esq,   13 April 1984
Company Secretary,
B J Black Limited,
424 Paul Street,
London.

Dear Mr Scott,

B J Black Limited

In accordance with your instructions dated 10 February 1984 I have valued the 1667 ordinary shares and the 13,333 preference shares held by Messrs M White, D White and A White for the purposes of a sale of these shares to the other shareholders.

As requested, I have assumed that the vendors' shares constitute a single block and that the other shareholders act in concert and collectively constitute a controlling block. However, none of the other shareholders has a controlling interest nor will anyone have a controlling interest as a result of any sale of the White family's shares pursuant to this valuation.

On these assumptions and solely for the purpose stated, I value the White family's holdings of ordinary shares and preference shares at, in total, £37,500 (paragraph 10.22). In my opinion, the open market value of the entire ordinary and preference share capital of the Company is in the region of £200,000 (paragraph 10.17).

The information on which this valuation is based consists of the audited accounts for each of the four years ended 31 December 1982, the draft unaudited accounts for the year ended 31 December 1983, my own researches into the industry background and the information and explanations given to me by the directors. I have visited the Company's showrooms at Paul Street and the freehold factory at Hackney, the latter having been professionally valued for the purposes of this report (paragraph 7.2).

Finally, I would like to record my appreciation of the help given to me by you and your colleagues in the preparation of this report.

Yours sincerely,

C G Glover

Valuation report

B J Black Limited

Contents

Valuation report

B J Black Limited

1 History

1.1 In 1901 the firm of James Black was established in Bishopsgate producing office furniture and fittings for customers in the City and elsewhere. With the exception of a brief and unprofitable interlude in the West End the firm has remained in the City ever since that date.

1.2 In 1936 Mr Brown acquired control of the firm, which was by then known as B J Black Limited ('the Company'), from Mr B J Black on the latter's retirement. Mr Brown remained a director of the Company until his retirement in 1956. Three new directors were then appointed, namely Mr H White, Mr W Jones and Miss M Cullen. Mr Brown continued to exert an influence over the Company's affairs after his retirement through his ownership of the Company's premises and his holding of preference shares.

1.3 In 1962 Miss Cullen retired and was replaced in May of the following year by Mr A Scott who acquired her shareholding. In February 1968 the three directors, Messrs Jones, White and Scott, bought out Mr Brown's preference shareholding.

1.4 In 1970 a compulsory purchase order was placed on the Company's Moorgate showrooms (which were rented from Mr Brown) and six months' notice to quit was given. The Company succeeded in disposing of the leasehold interest in the premises to a property speculator for £50,000. This provided the Company with the funds to purchase the freehold of the Hackney factory from Mr Brown. The price eventually agreed was £28,000. In 1971 the Company moved its office and showroom to their present premises in Paul Street.

1.5 Mr H White died in 1975 and was replaced by Mr P Hooper. Mr White's 33% shareholding is now split equally between his three sons, none of whom has a working interest in the Company. This independent valuation has been commissioned to provide the basis of a possible sale of the White family shareholdings to the other shareholders.

2 Industry background

2.1 The office furniture market contains three main product groups, namely, seating, desking and tables, and storage. Seating can be of the adjustable type, that is, with swivel action and variable seat and back rest height; non-adjustable, used for occasional seating; and unholstered, used in reception areas and board rooms. Wood and metal are the most widely used materials. Metal based chairs with upholstered seats and backrests, usually adjustable, are very popular.

2.2 The conventional desk design, consisting of the flat top with a leg in each corner or fitted onto pedestals with or without drawers, has remained virtually unchanged for decades. Product quality and price is determined primarily by the status of the user, ranging from the secretary or clerk at one end to the company executive or director at the other. The expensive executive desk is almost a bespoke product and most manufacturers, no matter how small, offer one. They are reckoned to account for 20% in value of total traditional desk sales.

2.3 Storage comprises filing cabinets of steel or wood distinguished by size, method of closure (i.e., folding or sliding doors, doors which open out, etc.) and filing systems inside.

2.4 A significant feature of the office furniture market is its split between conventional unit furniture and systems or contract furniture. With conventional unit furniture the customer can buy single items, replacing a chair, desk or filing cabinet as required. With systems furniture the supplier offers the customer a furniture package designed to fit within a defined space, often on an open plan basis with screening a common feature. The work entails consulting and design in view of the need to tailor the system to the customer's needs. According to a recent *Key Note* survey the relative importance of these two categories is as follows:

	Sales value 1982[1]
	%
Conventional unit furniture	78
Systems furniture	22
	100

[1]At manufacturer's selling prices.

2.5 Systems or contract furniture is increasingly linked with the developing use of modern office technology in the form of computers, VDUs, word processors and the like, all of which require a mass of cables. These cables have to be accommodated in the office furniture either by trunking or open channels, and wire management, as this has come to be known, is an important part of systems furniture.

2.6 There are an estimated 200 firms supplying the office furniture market. Vickers and Aaronson are the two market leaders with between eight and nine per cent of the total market.

The following companies have a market share in excess of four per cent:

Company	Parent/ultimate holding company
Antocks Lairn	Wagon Industrial Holdings
Carsons Office Furniture	Twinlock
The Shannon	Twinlock
William Vere	—
G A Harvey Office Furniture	Butterfield Harvey
Caplan Furniture	Pentos
Evertaut	—
Tan-Sad	GEC (Avery's)

In the systems furniture sector the UK manufacturers face stiff competition from leading US manufacturers such as Westinghouse and Herman Miller.

2.7 An estimated 43% of office furniture sales by volume are distributed directly to the end user. Such sales, which include system or contract sales, are to large organisations, such as Government departments and big financial and commercial concerns. The remaining 57% is distributed through office furniture specialists, discount and cash and carry warehouses, mail order firms and other retail outlets. The proportion supplied through wholesalers is small.

2.8 The size of the office furniture market is a matter of debate within the industry. The Government statistics are incomplete as regards both the coverage of firms and the type of products. *Key Note*, in their recent survey, estimated the size of the market in new office furniture at £180 million at manufacturers' selling prices. This was somewhat in excess of other industry estimates, making it unlikely that the market's size is much greater than this figure. Second-hand sales account for at least ten per cent, if not nearer 15%, of the total market. This suggests a total market size, including both new and second-hand furniture, of about £200 million.

2.9　Although Government statistics understate the size of the market they nevertheless provide a useful indicator of trends in recent years. The *Business Monitor* series, for example, gives the following picture of UK manufacturers' sales from 1978 to 1982:

	1978 £m	1979 £m	1980 £m	1981 £m	1982 £m
Seating	27.0	29.0	24.4	20.9	20.6
Desking	35.1	40.8	36.9	32.9	40.6
Storage	28.3	35.1	32.9	28.6	29.8
	90.4	104.9	94.2	82.4	91.0
Index (1979 = 100)	86	100	90	79	87

The year 1979 was apparently a peak period for sales of office furniture. This was followed by two years of steeply falling demand with a modest upturn occurring in 1982.

2.10　Price rises, of course, conceal the full effect of the fall in demand. This can be gauged properly only by the trend in sales volume. The following indices are based on manufacturers' volume sales as disclosed by *Business Monitor:*

Manufacturers' sales of office furniture Volume index (1979=100)				
	1978	1979	1980	1981	1982
Seating	103	100	75	69	56
Desking	109	100	79	63	73
Storage	91	100	85	73	60

The volume index suggests that the upturn in sales value apparent in 1982 (paragraph 2.9) was attributable mainly to price rises; desking was the only sector to show any volume growth. It is interesting to note that other industry statistics, although they show significant differences from the Government ones, reveal the same overall trend.

2.11　Government statistics for 1983 as a whole are not yet available. However, figures for the first three quarters of the year indicate that sales value has risen at the rate of 6.5% per annum. This compares with the *Key Note* estimate of four per cent growth in total industry sales for 1983. Interestingly, the *Key Note* survey concluded that whilst the total market had been contracting in volume terms the system furniture sector had been growing slowly but steadily.

3 Activity

3.1 The Company is an old established City-based firm engaged in the manufacture and supply of office furniture and furnishings. With a small factory in Hackney and showrooms in Paul Street, the Company offers a varied selection of modern and traditional office furniture, some of which it makes itself but most of which it obtains from outside suppliers. Its excellent contacts in the trade enable the Company to obtain timely delivery of most makes of office furniture and it is a stockist for Twinlock, Harvey and William Vere & Co, as well as other suppliers. The Company's own range of furniture, manufactured in the Hackney factory, includes desks (modern and reproduction), work stations, storage units and seating suits. These are provided in a variety of sizes and finishes. Because of the low volumes and high quality standards at the Hackney factory, the Company's own manufactured furniture tends to be more expensive than the mass produced equivalent. The directors estimate that the ratio of bought out furniture to furniture produced at Shoreditch is approximately 5:1.

3.2 The Company also undertakes office refurbishment and redecoration contracts, and in recent years this has become the most important part of the business. Employing its own carpenters and decorators and sub-contracting out electrical work, plumbing, carpet laying, plastering etc, the Company can offer a comprehensive service, carrying out an entire office redecoration, alteration or replanning contract, including structural work such as the installation of staircases and suspended ceilings. The Company has close links with its sub-contractors, most of whom it engages on a regular basis. The Company is thus able to coordinate the various trades effectively and to ensure a high standard of work.

3.3 Many customers have specialised furniture requirements, such as dealing desks for stockbrokers, and the Company is able to manufacture such custom built furniture from its Hackney factory. The Company's success in this field is evidenced by the relatively large contracts secured in recent years. For example, an interior refurbishing and alterations contract worth £150,000 was carried out for a firm of stockbrokers in 1982/83 and the Company has just completed a £250,000 staged contract for a well-known fund management company.

3.4 In this connection the directors estimate that approximately 75% of the factory's output is accounted for by custom built fitments and supplies for site works (i.e., contracts), with the remainder being production of standard line furniture. The factory also renovates furniture, such as, antique tables and chairs from City board rooms.

3.5 Most of the Company's customers are drawn from the City and include merchant banks, finance houses, stockbrokers, City livery companies, accountants, solicitors and other professional firms. The Company's policy is to provide flexible, tailor-made solutions to customers' requirements, to supply only quality furniture and furnishings and to give good after sales service. Because of this policy the Company has many long standing customers and benefits considerably from customer recommendation.

4 Directors and personnel

4.1 W G Jones (aged 64) is chairman. He has 48 years' service with the Company and became a director in 1957. Due to retire in June 1984, his executive duties consist of customer liaison and public relations.

4.2 A Scott (aged 61) is the Company Secretary. He joined the Company on leaving school in 1936, and is responsible for the financial and management accounting system. He has been a director since 1962 and is due to retire in June 1987.

4.3 P Hooper (aged 49) is in charge of the Hackney factory. He has 33 years' service with the Company and became a director in May 1978.

4.4 M Corbett (aged 43) has been with the Company for 27 years, becoming a director in January 1984. He is responsible for bought-out sales and their administration.

4.5 D Jones (aged 34) is the Site Works manager responsible for the supervision of contracts. He joined the Company in 1967 and was made a director in January 1984.

4.6   Mr Corbett and Mr D Jones were appointed Directors in order to provide the succession to Mr W Jones and Mr A Scott both of whom are due to retire fairly soon.

4.7   Directors' remuneration comprises a basic salary plus a commission dependent on profits.

4.8   There are 20 employees excluding the directors. Apart from two transport drivers the work force is more or less equally divided between the factory at Hackney and City-based contract work. The Company's employees, like the directors, have long service records and are accustomed to flexible working.

4.9   Staff are remunerated by way of a basic salary supplemented by an annual bonus. By long standing agreement the amount allocated for the payment of bonus has been no less than 20% of profits before tax and the bonus. Whatever the strict legal position may be, the payment of staff bonus has come to be regarded by the employees as part of their total contracted salary.

5 Premises

5.1   The Company premises consist of a showroom and offices in Paul Street and a freehold factory in Hackney. The freehold factory in Hackney is on a site zoned for general industrial use. It is a three-storey building constructed mainly in the 1930s which provides 617 sq metres of floor space. It is equipped with somewhat dated, but perfectly serviceable, machinery which meets the Company's needs adequately. No major capital outlays are envisaged.

5.2   The lease on the showrooms in Paul Street expired in December 1983. Negotiations for renewal of the lease at a higher rental are in progress. The new lease will be for a 14-year period with five yearly rent reviews.

6 Trading results

6.1   The Company's trading results for the five years ended 31 December 1983 are summarised below. The results for 1979 to 1982 are taken from the audited accounts for those years. The 1983 figures are based on the draft unaudited accounts.

	1979 £	1980 £	1981 £	1982 £	1983 £
Sales	520,188	516,252	715,124	912,046	984,265
Gross profit	144,556	134,353	184,360	252,282	288,531
Overheads	75,939	75,342	99,169	134,426	166,885
Trading profit	68,617	59,011	85,191	117,856	121,646
Directors' remuneration	(37,775)	(35,540)	(49,265)	(82,884)	(85,459)
Investment income	1,570	2,809	1,395	2,529	4,162
Profit before tax	32,412	26,280	37,321	37,501	40,349
Taxation	13,139	9,333	12,856	15,381	15,150
Profit after tax	19,273	16,947	24,465	22,120	25,199
Dividends	7,360	5,360	7,360	7,360	7,360

6.2 Over the four year review period sales have nearly doubled in marked contrast to the downward industry trend. The gross profit margin has risen from 27.8% in 1979 to 29.3% in 1983. This together with the rising turnover has produced a compound annual growth rate in gross profit of approximately 19%. The equivalent inflation rate over the period has been approximately 10.5% per annum. Higher overheads, particularly the sharply rising costs of pensions, have absorbed most of this increase, leaving pre-tax profit growth over the period at 5.6% per annum compound. The elements in this general picture are now examined in more detail.

6.3 The Company's management information analyses sales into three categories, namely, bought-out sales, site works and factory sales. Bought-out sales refer to sales of office furniture purchased from outside suppliers and also to sub-contract work not associated with site works; site works refer to the office refurbishment contract work; and factory sales comprise custom-made furniture and fittings supplied for contract work, sales of own-manufactured office furniture, i.e. the Company's standard range of office furniture, and furniture renovation work. The following table shows the analysis of total sales over these categories for each of the years under review:

	1979 £	1980 £	1981 £	1982 £	1983 £
Bought-out sales	264,940	261,269	325,694	245,088	253,468
Site works (contracts)	128,884	136,419	238,301	416,326	531,076
Factory	126,364	118,564	151,129	250,632	200,421
	520,188	516,252	715,124	912,046	984,965

6.4 The most striking feature of the above analysis is the growth of site works, which accounts for almost all the increase in total sales over the period. Furthermore, these figures understate the true significance of site works since factory sales include custom-built furniture and fitments ordered for site works. Although the Company's records do not provide an analysis of factory sales, the directors have indicated that as a rule of thumb 75% of factory sales are for site works. Applying this approximate and variable percentage, sales for 1982 and 1983 can be re-analysed as follows:

	1982 £	%	1983 £	%
Bought-out sales	245,088	27	253,468	26
Site works	604,300	66	681,392	69
Own manufacture standard furniture (including renovation)	62,658	7	50,105	5
	912,046	100	984,965	100

Although these figures must be interpreted with caution, they suggest that the business is heavily dependent on site works.

6.5 With the notable exception of 1981 when turnover rose by 25%, bought-out sales have declined marginally over the review period. However, when the effect of price rises is taken into account, the reduction in the volume of goods sold appears to have been significant. For example, the producer price index for wooden furniture and upholstery rose by 30% between 1979 and 1982 and the wholesale price index for all manufactured goods rose by 40% over the same period. Making an estimated allowance for five per cent for price rises in 1983 — the producer price index for that year is not yet available — it would seem that office furniture prices probably rose by 35 to 40% over the review period. As bought-out sales were 4.3% lower in 1983 than in 1979 the implication is that the volume of sales in 1983 was over 40% lower than in 1979. This experience is broadly similar to that of the industry as a whole (paragraph 2.10).

6.6 Factory sales have risen much in line with total sales although it would be interesting to know how much of this was attributable to site works and how much to the Company's standard range of office furniture.

6.7 The movement of the gross profit percentage and its breakdown by section is shown below:

	1979 %	1980 %	1981 %	1982 %	1983 %
Bought-out sales	25.9	21.4	22.9	21.5	30.4
Site works	38.1	29.1	31.3	29.0	31.7
Factory	21.1	32.7	23.3	31.5	21.3
Total	27.8	26.0	25.8	27.7	29.3

Site works is clearly the most profitable section of the business. Little significance can be drawn from the fluctuating gross profit margin of the factory since factory personnel are often assigned on an irregular basis to site works. The gross margin on bought-out sales improved considerably in 1983, rising by 8.9 percentage points. The accounting explanation for this is that the cost of purchases was much lower in 1983 than in 1982, i.e., £165,000 compared with £184,000, sales remaining at much the same level. However, there has been no change in policy or obvious improvement in the terms of trade for bought-out sales, and the reasons for this increase in margins are at present unclear.

6.8 The major factor in the rise in overheads has been the escalating cost of pension provision. The Company has two schemes. The main one is a non-contributory pension scheme for all the employees including the directors. This was started as recently as 1974, becoming contracted out in 1979. As this fund would provide an inadequate pension for those directors approaching retirement, a top-up scheme was started. Because of the initial inadequacy of pension provision, the cost of pension contributions has risen steeply, from £14,000 in 1979 to £51,000 by 1983.

6.9 Directors' remuneration consists of a basic salary plus profit related commission. This accounts for the slight dip in directors' remuneration in 1980 when profits fell somewhat, and for the strongly upward trend in subsequent years.

6.10 The Company's records do not show the breakdown of pre-tax profits by sector of the business. However, this split is available in respect of profits before the staff bonus and directors' commission. The contribution to profit as thus defined has been as follows:

	1979 %	1980 %	1981 %	1982 %	1983 %
Bought-out sales	63	64	53	7	18
Site works (contracts)	40	23	51	64	76
Factory	(3)	13	(4)	29	6
	100	100	100	100	100

6.11 Although the factory appears to make a loss in some years and only a modest contribution to profits in other years, it would be wrong to conclude that it has a purely marginal signficance for the business as a whole. The factory employees are a valuable reservoir of skilled labour to meet temporary peaks in contract work. Furthermore the factory's ability to produce custom-built furniture and fitments to tight deadlines is an essential ingredient in the successful outcome of contract work.

6.12 Apart from 1980, which witnessed a fall in profits, site works has increased its share of pre-tax profits considerably over the period. By 1983 its share of profits had risen to over three-quarters. However, as with the analysis of total sales, the true significance of site works is understated. On the assumption that profit margins are the same on site work done by the factory as on the factory's other manufacture, the profit contributions for 1982 and 1983 can be re-analysed in the same way as were the sales figures (paragraph 6.4).

	1982 %	1983 %
Bought out sales	7	18
Site works	86	78
Own manufactured standard furniture (including renovation work)	7	4
	100	100

Again, the crucial significance of site work is apparent.

6.13 Tax has been provided for at the small companies' rate of 40% up to April 1982 and at 38% thereafter.

6.14 The dividends declared have been as follows:

	1979 £	1980 £	1981 £	1982 £	1983 £
Preference dividend	3,360	3,360	3,360	3,360	3,360
Ordinary dividend	4,000	2,000	4,000	4,000	4,000
	7,360	5,360	7,360	7,360	7,360

The ordinary dividend was temporarily reduced in 1980 in view of the lower profits in that year. Apart from this it has remained unchanged throughout the review period. With the exception of 1979 when the pay-out ratio was 38%, the preference and ordinary dividends have constituted, in total, between 29% and 33% of distributable profits in each year.

7 Balance sheet

7.1 The Company's draft unaudited balance sheet as at 31 December 1983 is summarised below. The audited balance sheet as at 31 December 1982 is shown for comparison purposes.

		As at 31 December 1983 (draft) £	1982 (audited) £
Fixed assets		46,197	33,731
Investments		21,056	20,986
Current assets			
Stock	59,759		59,083
Debtors	271,739		200,612
Cash	16,419		38,772
	347,917		298,467
Current liabilities			
Creditors	220,890		180,650
Taxation	15,150		10,743
Dividends	7,360		7,360
	243,400		198,753
Net current assets		104,517	99,714
		171,770	154,431

APPENDIX 1: VALUATION REPORT

	As at 31 December	
	1983 (draft) £	1982 (audited) £
Share capital	45,000	45,000
Profit and loss account	110,493	93,154
General reserve	10,000	10,000
	165,493	148,154
Pension and sickness fund reserve	6,277	6,277
	171,770	154,431

Both balance sheets indicate a strong financial position with current assets comfortably in excess of current liabilities and no bank overdraft or other borrowings. The more important balance sheet items are discussed below.

7.2   Fixed assets are analysed as follows:

	Cost £	Depn £	Net £
Land and buildings			
— Freehold	28,454	—	28,454
— Leasehold	338	338	—
Goodwill	150	—	150
Plant, fixtures and fittings	10,798	5,842	4,956
Motor vehicles	16,849	4,212	12,637
	56,589	10,392	46,197

The freehold land and buildings consist of the Hackney factory. Adamsons, chartered surveyors, have valued these premises at £67,000 on an open market basis. Because of the property's uneconomic layout, its poor situation in a 'twilight' industrial zone beyond the City office fringe and the likely class of tenant if the building were let, the property apparently merits a very low yield, in the range of 15 to 20%.

7.3   The investments are made up as follows:

	£
Average Unit Trust	19,842
Safe Building Society	1,214
	21,056

Cash includes the sum of £2,292 on bank deposit account.

7.4   Debtors at the year end represented almost 14 weeks' sales com-
      pared with 11 weeks as at end-1982. This reflects heavy invoicing
      in December 1983 rather than an extension of the normal period
      of credit. Creditors consist mainly of expense items the most
      important of which is the year-end allocation of profit for the staff
      bonus and directors' commission.

7.5   The pension and sickness fund reserve of £6,277 is the residue of a
      capital profit which was realised on the sale of the Moorgate lease
      in 1971. It has been earmarked for the benefit of employees and
      directors with limited pension fund rights.

8 Prospects

Short-term

8.1   Economic growth is likely to continue throughout 1984. The
      OECD's latest survey for the UK economy predicts a growth rate
      of 2½% compared with the Treasury's forecast of three per cent.
      With the climate for investment better and business confidence
      improving, the OECD expects investment in services and dis-
      tribution to rise by three per cent in 1984. Although unem-
      ployment is not expected to fall appreciably it should not rise
      and the phenomenon of a shrinking office population, which
      has been a feature of earlier years, should be absent from 1984.
      The economic and industry background, therefore, is broadly
      favourable — certainly no worse than in 1983. With its strength in
      contract work and a reasonable outlook for office furniture sales,
      the Company should be able to achieve real growth of the order of
      five per cent in 1984. Given a likely inflation rate of five per cent
      for 1984, the results should in money terms show an increase of
      about ten per cent.

8.2   The outlook for 1985 depends much on the durability of the
      economic recovery which by then will be entering its fourth year.
      Although the OECD expects a falling-off in the growth rate to two
      per cent in the first half of 1985, the situation is highly fluid and
      there is much uncertainty. On present knowledge, however, some
      deterioration in growth prospects seems likely. This will probably
      be reflected in weak demand for office furniture and strong com-
      petition for the contract work. There is no reason to believe,
      however, that the Company cannot maintain its results in real
      terms against this background.

Longer term

8.3 There are several disquieting features about the present economic recovery which suggest that the macro-economic background is unlikely to revert to the conventional postwar pattern of alternate boom and recession in an underlying upward trend. Firstly, the present recovery has been fuelled by a boom in consumer spending resulting from earnings rises in excess of the rate of inflation. The effect of this rise in earnings on manufacturing output and on investment has been slight, much of the increased consumer spending being reflected in higher imports. Secondly, interest rates remain at high levels both at home and abroad. The huge US budget deficit is likely to keep interest rates in that country at a high level and, given the interest rate sensitivity of international currency flows, it is unlikely that the UK Government could hold interest rates in this country at a much lower level than in the US for any appreciable period. Thirdly, unemployment is expected to remain high everywhere.

8.4 Whilst the general economic background holds little prospect of an 'Eldorado' in the medium- to long-term, there are certain trends within the overall picture which are bullish for the Company's prospects. The continuing trend in the UK economy out of manufacturing and into services should underpin in some measure the demand for office accommodation and, hence, for office furniture. Furthermore, the sharp contraction in demand for office furniture in recent years represents to some extent postponed replacement of furniture. Whilst most office furniture has a relatively long life, replacement cannot be put off indefinitely. It should also be borne in mind that the City, which accounts for most of the Company's custom, is by no means dependent on the national economy. Its international orientation often enables it to prosper despite a poor domestic economic environment. In addition, the financial services revolution which seems to be in prospect following the withdrawal of the Restrictive Practices Court's investigation into the Stock Exchange Rule Book could bring a wave of mergers and amalgamations as well as an influx of overseas businesses wishing to take advantage of the new regulations. This type of activity often generates demand for new offices. In fact, recent moves by City institutions suggest that the practical effects of this 'revolution' may even be felt in 1985 if not 1984.

8.5 Finally, the demand for system or contract furniture should remain strong and may well show considerable growth. As noted in Section 2, this sector is increasingly linked with the development of modern office technology. The rate of development in electronic office equipment in recent years has been staggering and the possibilities of the new technology are being appreciated by an ever increasing number of firms. A survey carried out by *Which Office System?* revealed that only 16% of companies use a portable personal computer. However, this is expected to rise to 27% within 12 months and to 41% in five years' time. The same survey also suggested that nearly two-thirds of executives will be doing their own personal word processing within five years.

8.6 It seems therefore that the future holds considerable potential for the Company. Whether this potential can become a prospect as opposed to merely a possibility depends on a number of factors. The size of the contracts won by the Company has increased in recent years and it would be reasonable to assume that even bigger contracts may be open to the Company as its abilities and reputation in this area become more widely appreciated. However, it is unlikely that the existing workforce could cope with a much higher level of work and a significant jump in the size of the workforce would be necessary. The problem of recruitment is made more acute by the age structure of the Company's employees. A number of them will be due for retirement within the next five years and in the past it has not proved easy to attract skilled workers with the required degree of commitment and flexibility.

8.7 Second, with the present size of the Company, administration costs are very low. If the Company expanded, a more formal administrative structure would be required with its attendant costs, and the directors themselves would have to become more involved in management. In addition, a successful move into the larger contracts would bring the Company more directly into competition with major firms in the industry.

8.8 The Company therefore faces some difficult decisions. In essence the choice is between the opportunities presented by the likely development of the market with all the change, costs, risk and potential rewards that they offer, or to adopt a more passive role, keeping the business at its present size and eschewing any risk. There seems little doubt that even on the latter course the Company should be able to earn reasonable profits for some years. Eventually, however, it may find itself being bypassed by the changes in the market and in long term decline.

9 Share capital and articles

9.1 The Company's authorised and issued share capital consists of 5,000 ordinary shares of £1 each and 40,000 cumulative preference shares of £1 each, held as follows:

	Ordinary shares	%	Preference shares	%
Mr A Scott	1,111	22.3	13,333	33.3
Mr P Hooper	911	18.2	—	—
Mrs V Hooper	200	4.0	—	—
Mr M Corbett	556	11.1	—	—
Mr D Jones	555	11.1	—	—
Mrs E Jones	—	—	13,334	33.4
Mr M White	556	11.1	4,444	11.1
Mr D White	556	11.1	4,444	11.1
Mr A White	555	11.1	4,445	11.1
	5,000	100.0	40,000	100.0

9.2 The preference shares are entitled to a fixed cumulative preferential dividend at the rate of 8.4% net per annum (12% gross) payable quarterly, and in a winding up to the return of the amount paid up plus any arrears of cumulative preference dividend. They have no further right to participate in the profits or assets of the Company. The preference shares do not carry the right to attend and vote at general meetings of the Company except in the following circumstances:

(a) if the preferential dividend is more than 12 months in arrears;
(b) if there is a resolution to wind up the Company, reduce the share capital, increase the voting share capital, vary the rights of the preference shares or alter any borrowing restrictions in the Articles;
(c) if an offer is made to purchase all the ordinary shares without an offer being made to buy the preference shares.

In these circumstances, and in these circumstances only, every preference shareholder shall have one vote for every eight preference shares held.

9.3 Article 8 provides that a member can transfer his shares, whether ordinary or preference, to his or her spouse, child or other issue. Apart from this, there are no other provisions regarding the transfer of preference shares. However, any other transfer of ordinary shares must be made in accordance with the provisions of Articles 9 to 15. These clauses provide that a member intending to transfer his shares must give notice in writing to the Company stating the number of shares and the price per share. This sale notice operates as a separate notice in respect of each share and cannot be withdrawn without the directors' permission. The directors may offer the shares to a non-member if they think fit. Otherwise the shares must be offered to the other ordinary shareholders *pro rata* to their existing shareholdings. Upon the application of either vendor or purchaser the transfer price shall be the fair value as certified by the auditors acting as experts. If no buyer has been found within 28 days of submission of the sale notice or receipt of the auditors' certificate, the vendor shall be at liberty within the following three months to sell or transfer the shares to any person at any price. However, the directors have the overriding right 'in their absolute discretion and without assigning any reason therefor' to refuse to register any transfer of shares, whether preference or ordinary, except, of course, where ordinary or preference shares are transferred to the spouse, child or other issue under Article 8, as mentioned above. On the death or bankruptcy of a member the directors may require the personal representative or trustee to serve a sale notice for that member's ordinary shares, provided that no spouse, child or other issue is entitled to them.

10 Valuation

10.1 A valuation is required of a block of 1,667 ordinary shares and 13,333 preference shares, representing one-third of the shares in each class, as between the White family as vendors and the remaining, controlling shareholders as purchasers. In such a valuation the concept of market value has little or no relevance since no market exists in the Company's shares in the commonly accepted meaning of that word. The role of the valuer in these circumstances is to assess the value of the shares in question to both purchaser and vendor and to recommend an exchange value which gives full recognition to these different owner values and the bargaining strengths and weaknesses of both sides. The value of these shares to the vendors is considered first.

10.2 From the vendors' point of view, their shareholdings are not a particularly attractive investment given the fact that the remaining shareholders act in concert and control the Company. The vendors are an isolated minority interest dependent on the directors for the continued payment of dividends. Even if the dividends on the preference shares were passed and these thereupon became entitled to vote, the relative voting strength of vendors and purchasers would remain unchanged. The Company's articles impose severe restrictions on the transfer of ordinary shares. A vendor has first to offer the shares to the existing shareholders or even a non-member nominated by the directors. Furthermore, the purchaser (or vendor for that matter) can elect to have the fair value of the shares certified by the auditors. It would certainly be in his interests to do so since the Articles apparently require the auditors to certify the value of a single share, giving no recognition to the size of a shareholding. (This is the implication of Article 9 which stipulates that a sale notice operates as a separate notice in respect of each share.) In addition to these difficulties or disadvantages, the directors may in their absolute discretion refuse to register a transfer of shares.

10.3   In view of these severe disabilities and the resultant lack of marketability, I am of the opinion that the vendors' shares should be valued as an income stream. The preference dividend has been paid throughout the review period and there is no reason to assume that it will not be paid in the future. Although no immediate increase in the ordinary dividend is proposed, the dividend should rise when the directors are confident that profits have moved to a higher maintainable level. Thus dividend increases are likely to lag somewhat behind profit increases, but the two should nevertheless move broadly in line with each other over a long period if a consistent dividend policy is maintained. The long-term growth rate in profits is unknown and any estimates are by their nature quite subjective. However, on present evidence it is reasonable to expect the growth in profits at least to keep pace with inflation. Inflationary expectations are much lower these days and the general consensus amongst forecasters seems to be that the rate of inflation is unlikely to rise above five to six per cent per annum in the foreseeable future. If the Company's real rate of profits' growth in the long term is of the order of two to three per cent per annum the nominal growth rate (i.e., the growth rate in money terms) would be seven to eight per cent. Allowing directors' commission or profit share of, say, 35% of profits, distributable profits ought to grow at five per cent per annum i.e., seven to eight per cent less 35%. The ordinary dividend ought therefore to grow at approximately this rate in the long-term.

10.4　The rate of return appropriate for discounting the future dividends is a function of the rate of return available on other types of investment with due allowance being made for degree of risk and poor marketability. In choosing an appropriate rate of return the following market rates are relevant:

	Rates of return *4 April 1984* *%*
Sterling certificates of deposit	
— one year	9.25
Local authority deposits	
— two years	10.00
High coupon gilts[1]	
— 5 years	10.79
— 15 years	10.77
— 25 years	10.16
Debentures and loans — 15 years	11.36
Preference shares	12.79

[1]Gross yield to redemption

Source: Financial Times of 5 April 1984

10.5　The above rates of return, certainly as regards the gilts, are the nearest equivalent to a risk-free rate of return. The rate of return demanded for investment in equities is considerably higher than these rates to compensate for the risk assumed. Individual equities have different degrees of risk and their rates of return vary accordingly. This, together with the difficulty in estimating the dividend growth rate — the perceived rate of return depending very much on one's estimate of the growth rate — makes it difficult to generalise about the size of the risk premium at the present time. It is interesting to note, however, that the risk premium over a long period of time — in fact from 1919 to 1977 — has averaged nine per cent for UK quoted equities in general.

10.6　In any particular year the equity risk premium could well be more or less than this amount. At the present time when equity investment is very popular and share price indexes are at record high levels, the risk premium is probably below its long-term average. Even on the unlikely assumption that the risk premium has fallen to five per cent, the implied rate of return for equity investment would be of the order of 15–16%. Relating this to the

Company, with its unmarketable equity, its private company status and the risk inherent in its size, I am of the opinion that a rate of return of between 20 and 25%, say 22½%, would be required for an investment in the ordinary shares. As for the preference shares, their cumulative preferential dividend and protective voting rights would in my opinion justify a lower rate of return, say, 17½%.

10.7   On this basis the investment value of the vendors' holding of preference and ordinary shares works out as follows:

	Ordinary shares	Preference shares
Required rate of return	22½%	17½%
Estimated growth rate	5%	—
Initial yield (i.e., capitalisation rate)	17½%	17½%
Prospective dividend per share		
—gross	£1.14	12p
Value per share	£6.51	68.6p
Say	£6.50	69p

Barring a listing or takeover of the Company, neither of which is remotely in prospect, the 1,667 ordinary shares and 13,333 preference shares in question have an investment value to the vendors of approximately £20,000 made up as follows:

Ordinary shares	
1,667 of £6.50 each	£10,836
Preference shares	
13,333 at 69p each	£9,200
	£20,036
Say	£20,000

10.8   In addition to their investment value, the vendors' block of shares has a nuisance value. It constitutes one third of the Company's voting capital and can block a special resolution. Although the minority cannot interfere with the day-to-day management of the business, there are occasions when the inability to pass a special resolution can be both a nuisance and an embarrassment. Without the minority shareholders' consent, for example, the Company cannot buy in its own shares, alter its

name, issue any further shares or change its articles of association. These negative powers cannot be evaluated in an investment sense. They nevertheless have an influence on price and
this is discussed later.

10.9   The value of the vendors' block of ordinary and preference
shares to the controlling shareholders is now considered. As a
first step, it is necessary to place a value on the Company's
equity as a whole. This is the price the equity might reasonably
be expected to fetch if sold to a bidder — probably a competitor.
In my view, it is highly unlikely that the Company could be sold
without the directors entering into long-term service contracts.
This would be seen by the prospective purchaser as essential in
preserving the custom and goodwill of the firm. Furthermore,
the loyalty and commitment of the employees to the Company
would be seriously impaired if the directors resigned. However,
the directors are under no obligation to enter into service contracts with the Company, and it would not be in their interests to
do so on terms which did not provide them with a remuneration
package at least as attractive as their existing one.

10.10 In my opinion, the value of the Company to a bidder would be a
function of the perceived future profit potential. The assets of the
Company, discussed later on, are unlikely to be a dominating
influence. As indicated in section 8 (prospects), the growth
prospects for the business in its present size are limited, and
whilst considerable potential exists, it can be transformed into a
prospect only by a major re-orientation of the Company. The
extra profits arising from this potential are of a speculative
nature and are contingent on so many unknown factors that
their influence on the present value of the Company is slight. In
my view, the attractions of the Company to a prospective
purchaser consist essentially of its enviable reputation and the
skills, flexibility and degree of commitment of its employees and
directors.

10.11 The future prospects for the Company have been discussed in
section 8 of this report where it was concluded that pre-tax
profits should rise by ten per cent in 1984 in view of the general
economic and industry background (paragraph 8.1). The longer
term growth rate on existing policies was estimated at five per
cent per annum after allowing for directors' commission (paragraph 10.3). These projections, however, take no account of any
savings or additional costs that are at present foreseeable. Of

particular concern to a prospective purchaser would be the impact on profits of the retirement of Mr W Jones and subsequently of Mr A Scott, as well as the likely increase in rent following the renegotiation of the lease of the Paul Street showrooms. As regards the latter, it seems from discussions so far that the rent is likely to increase by £6,000 per annum.

10.12 When Mr W Jones and Mr A Scott retire, savings in pension contributions and directors' salaries are expected. However, the salaries of the two directors appointed in 1984 will rise to reflect their promotion and two extra junior staff will be recruited. On present indications, the effect on profits is likely to be as follows:

	On the retirement of:	
	Mr W Jones	Mr A Scott
	£	£
Savings		
— Pension contributions	5,000	5,000
— Salary	12,250	14,000
— Gross savings	17,250	19,000
Additional costs		
— Extra staff salaries	(8,000)	(5,000)
— Directors' salary and pension increases	(6,000)	
	3,250	14,000

Given the imminent increase in rent of £6,000 there appears to be no net savings on Mr W Jones' retirement. When Mr Scott retires in 1987 there should be savings of the order of £14,000 per annum at 1983 prices.

10.13 In my opinion, based on my experience of valuing smaller businesses, a rate of return of the order of 30% per annum would be sought by a purchaser of the Company's entire share capital. To achieve this rate of return, given a long-term growth rate of five per cent per annum, an initial yield or capitalisation rate of 25% is required. Independent evidence as to the appropriateness of this yield can be found in the terms of two recent acquisitions by Bullough plc. One of these acquisitions was an office equipment manufacturer (Westwood Holdings Limited) and the other was a Marks & Spencer supplier of refrigerated display equipment (George Barker and Company (Leeds) Limited).

10.14 The relevant particulars of these acquisitions are set out below:

	Westwood Holdings £000	George Barker £000
Acquisition cost	4,800	6,500
Profit before tax and exceptional items for 1983	1,162	1,654
Net tangible assets	2,682	2,841
Pre-tax profits yield	24.2%	25.4%
Premium to net assets	79%	129%

Without an inside knowledge of the negotiations which took place when these two companies were acquired there is no way of ascertaining the future profits growth, and therefore the rate of return, which the purchaser had in mind when agreeing the acquisition cost. Consequently, the inferences which can be drawn from the above statistics are limited. Nevertheless, the pre-tax profits yield of 24/25% is the same as that now proposed for the Company.

10.15 On this basis, therefore, the value of the whole of the Company's issued share capital works out as follows:

	£
Prospective pre-tax profits for 1984 (£40,000 for 1983×110%)	44,000
Savings on Mr Scott's retirement	14,000
Longer term prospective profit	58,000
Capitalisation rate/yield	25%
Prospective value of the Company	232,000
Deduct present value of an annuity of £14,000 for 3 years at 5 per cent (factor 2.7232)	38,000
Present value of the Company	194,000

The annuity deduction reflects the fact that the saving on Mr Scott's retirement will not be realised for another three years.

10.16 Although the company's asset backing does not determine its value, it would nevertheless be of interest to the purchaser. The calculation of asset backing, based on the draft balance sheet as at 31 December 1983, is set out below:

	£	£
Shareholders' funds (para 7.1)		165,493
Property surplus		
Market value	67,000	
Less book amount	28,454	38,546
		204,039

The earnings-based valuation of £194,000 is five per cent below this figure. As a general rule profitable, well managed businesses have an earnings-based value considerably in excess of their revalued net assets. It is noteworthy in this connecton that the two acquisitions cited in paragraph 10.13 showed premiums to net assets of 79% and 129%. The comparision with the net asset backing suggests, therefore, that the Company's earnings-based valuation of £194,000 is, if anything, conservative.

10.17 Assets surplus to the requirements of the business are generally valued separately. The only surplus assets appear to be the Company's investments. These had a balance sheet amount of £21,056 at end of 1983 and this is probably equivalent to their value. The income from these investments amounted to £4,000 in 1983 and this has been included in capitalised profits. Had these assets been valued separately and their income excluded from capitalised profits the valuation of the Company would have been approximately £6,000 higher. Thus the value of the Company should be raised to £200,000.

10.18 Where a bid is made for the whole of a company's share capital it is customary to offer par for the preference shares. The split of the total value of £200,000 between ordinary shares and preference shares would then be as follows:

	£
Preference shares	
40,000 @ £1 each	40,000
Ordinary shares	
5,000 @ £32 each	160,000
	200,000

10.19 One of the reasons why the earnings-based valuation shows such a small premium to the asset backing lies in the effect of directors' profit commission on prospective profits. It would, of course, be open to the directors to accept a lower level of remuneration and a higher value for the shares. For example, the directors could agree to freeze their profit participation at the 1983 level of £54,000, leaving their basic salaries to rise in line with inflation. This would increase the prospective growth rate from five to eight per cent (see paragraph 10.3) and lower the initial yield from 25 to 22%. The effect on the valuation would be as follows:

	£
Prospective profits (paragraph 10.15)	58,000
Capitalised at 22%	264,000
Capitalised at 25%	232,000
Increase	£32,000

The annuity adjustment and the addition of £6,000 for surplus assets are not affected by the capitalisation rate and have therefore been excluded from the calculation.

10.20 However, the ability to increase the value of the shares in this way does not arise from any attribute of the shares but from the crucial importance of the directors to the Company's operations. It is a value personal to the directors and does not pass with the transfer of the shares. Nevertheless, the shares are essential to the directors if they wish to convert earned income into capital in this way. In particular, any rise in the value of the shares resulting from such a move would be spread over the whole equity including the one-third minority interest. It could be argued, therefore, that the prospective owner value of the minority shareholding to the controlling shareholders exceeds the proportionate part of the £200,000 sale value of the Company. One cannot quantify this higher value since it depends very much on the personal attitudes of the directors. In the example given in paragraph 10.19 the value of the Company would rise to £232,000 (i.e., the existing value of £200,000 plus the increase of £32,000).

10.21 Having examined in some detail the value of the shares to the vendors and to the prospective purchasers, it is now necessary to put into the balance the bargaining strengths and weaknesses of the two sides and to suggest a price or exchange value which reasonably reflects that balance. In my opinion the ordinary and preference shares in question have a minimum investment value to the vendors of approximately £20,000 (paragraph 10.7). Their maximum value to the purchasers is unlikely to be less than £67,000, i.e., one-third of £200,000 (paragraph 10.18) and could well be as high as £77,000, i.e., one-third of £232,000 (paragraph 10.20). The considerations to be borne in mind in determining a fair balance between these opposing positions are in my opinion as follows:

(a) Although the directors collectively own a controlling interest, no director has a controlling shareholding nor will any director have one as a result of any sale of the vendors' shareholdings.

(b) In December 1983 and January 1984 Mr W Jones sold 1,567 ordinary shares and Mr A Scott sold 455 ordinary shares to fellow directors. These were arms-length transactions, the price of £4 per share being fixed by the auditors. This price is below even the minimum investment value of £6.50 per ordinary share (paragraph 10.7).

(c) From the vendors' point of view the alternatives to a sale to the directors are not attractive. Given the directors' power of veto over any share transfer (paragraph 9.3) it could well prove impossible for the vendors to dispose of their shares at other than an auditor-determined value under the articles. Any attempts to bring legal pressure to bear on the Company would be costly, time-consuming and risky.

(d) From the controlling shareholders' point of view, the minority interest has a considerable nuisance value. As mentioned earlier (paragraph 10.8) the inability to pass a special resolution can be both an embarrassment and a nuisance. The Company, for instance, cannot buy in its own shares without the minority's consent. Furthermore, as all the authorised share capital has been issued and a special resolution is required to raise the authorised capital, the Company is powerless to issue any new shares.

(e) The minority has a claim, albeit an indirect one, of one-third of all the future increase in value of the Company. This increased value is created by the controlling shareholders. It is in their interests therefore to secure it all for themselves by buying out the minority.

(f) Failure to agree a price could result in a more aggressive attitude on the part of the minority. The scope for litigation has been greatly increased since the passing of the Companies Act 1980. Section 75 of that Act (now s.459 of the Companies Act 1985) has considerably increased the protection afforded to disaffected minority shareholders. Litigation, even if it has little hope of success, can have a damaging effect on the business.

10.22 Weighing the balance of these factors, I am of the opinion that the minority interest has a value of £37,500 as between the White family as vendors and the controlling shareholders as purchasers. This is, of course, a quite subjective judgement. However, from the vendors' angle, it represents a substantial premium (88%) on the investment value, which itself is much higher than the likely fair value under the Articles (paragraph 10.21). From the controlling shareholders' standpoint, they acquire for £37,500 shares which could have a value to them of £67,000, if not more. The price is pitched so as to confer one-third of the value gap on the minority and two-thirds on the majority shareholders, as set out below:

	From £	To £	Mid-point £
Value to the majority	67,000	77,000	72,000
Value to the minority	20,000	20,000	20,000
Value gap	47,000	57,000	52,000
One third thereof to vendors			17,333
Add investment value			20,000
Exchange value			37,333
Say			37,500

The balance of advantage is expressed arithmetically in the same proportion as the shareholdings, i.e. two to one in favour of the controlling shareholders.

10.23 The allocation of the value of £37,500 between ordinary shares and preference shares has been left open so that the tax position of the parties can be taken into account. However, it would be unusual to ascribe a value to the preference shares in excess of par. This suggests a value of at least £14.50 each for the ordinary shares, as follows:

	£
Preference shares	
13,333 @ £1 each	13,333
Ordinary shares	
1,667 @ £14.50 each	24,167
	37,500

Appendix 2

J B Scholes,
Fizzy Drinks Limited,
Pop Street,
Bristol.

Dear Mr Scholes,

Stonnington Limited

I enclose a valuation memorandum about your company's proposed purchase of a 20% shareholding in Stonnington Ltd from Mr Francis Harding. It is not a straightforward valuation as everything depends on the view one takes of Stonnington's ability to continue its remarkable progress and on the benefits which the proposed association of the two companies will produce for each party.

Apart from some independent enquiries I have made about the industry background, all the information on which the valuation is based has been supplied by Mr Harding through you. I have not met Mr Harding nor have I visited Stonnington's premises or had any contact with its employees. The information is sparse and in parts inconsistent. I must therefore reserve the right to amend the valuation substantially if better information becomes available.

This valuation is intended to help you and your colleagues in negotiations with Mr Harding. It is not valid for any other purpose.

I shall be pleased to elaborate on any of the points raised in the valuation memorandum should you so wish.

Yours sincerely,

C G Glover

Valuation memorandum

Stonnington Limited

1 Introduction

1.1 Fizzy Drinks Limited ('FDL'), a subsidiary of The Drinkwater Brewery Co Limited wishes to enter into a trading relationship with Stonnington Limited, a privately owned company manufacturing soft drinks for bulk dispensing. This trading relationship is to be established by FDL acquiring a 20% shareholding in Stonnington from its proprietor, Mr Francis Harding. A valuation of the shares in Stonnington is required for this purpose.

2 Activity and trading record

2.1 Stonnington was set up in 1970 by the present managing director, Mr Francis Harding. It manufactures and sells soft drinks for bulk dispensing. Stonnington has a freehold factory and distribution centre in Stafford which also houses Stonnington's administrative offices. There are three other distribution depots, all leasehold. These are situated in Rotherham, Lancaster and Stevenage. There are 72 employees.

2.2 The trading record, based on figures supplied by Mr Harding, is summarised below:

	1976 *£*	*1977* *£*	*1978* *£*	*1979* *£*	*1980* *£*
Turnover	250,537	332,474	457,145	794,642	1,309,281
Gross profit margin	51.3%	62.3%	69.5%	74.5%	75.5%
Profit before tax	49,571	80,438	112,499	183,079	310,712
Net profit margin	19.8%	24.2%	24.6%	23.0%	23.7%

Year ended 30 September

2.3 Over the period under review the soft drinks market as measured by manufacturers' sales has probably grown at 16.5% a year compound and carbonated soft drinks, by 13.5% a year compound. (Source: *Econsult*). Measured against this background Stonnington's trading performance looks outstandingly good. Its turnover and pre-tax profits have risen by, respectively, 51% and

58% a year compound over the period. An interesting feature of the record is the improvement in the gross margin from 51.3% to 75.5%. The net margin, however, has been fairly stable since 1977.

2.4   No dividends have been paid since the business was established.

3 Net assets

3.1   Stonnington's audited balance sheet as at 30 September 1980 is summarised below:

	30 September 1980		*Memo 1979*
	£	£	£
Fixed assets		864,156	475,239
Current assets			
Stock	42,405		51,496
Debtors	272,599		233,292
Cash	—		459
	315,004		285,247
Current liabilities			
Creditors	340,861		212,826
Bank overdraft (secured)	30,488		50,202
	371,349		263,028
Net current assets (liabilities)		(56,345)	22,219
		807,811	497,458
Shareholders' funds			
Share capital		10,000	10,000
Reserves		357,903	208,906
		367,903	218,906
Loans		52,133	56,070
Deferred Tax		387,775	222,482
		807,811	497,458

3.2   Stonnington's financial position appears sound, the bank overdraft and loans representing a very small percentage of capital employed. Liquidity, however, looks finely balanced with current liabilities exceeding current assets and no cash in hand.

3.3   The loans of £52,133 are made up as follows:

	1980 £	1979 £
Bank (secured)	64,090	67,859
Hire purchase	19,719	9,294
	83,809	77,153
Less: Repayments due within 12 months	31,676	21,083
	52,133	56,070

As interest charges rose in 1980, the fall in borrowings apparent at the year end may not be typical of experience during the year.

3.4 Fixed assets are shown at cost less depreciation, as follows:

	Cost £	Depreciation £	Net £
Leasehold property	114,630	3,814	110,816
Plant, equipment, fixtures and fittings	1,094,877	464,741	630,136
Motor vehicles	182,862	59,658	123,204
	1,392,369	528,213	864,156

According to Mr Harding's memorandum the Stafford factory is freehold, but there is no mention of freehold properties in Canvermoor's accounts. Additions to fixed assets in 1980 totalled approximately £667,000 (1979, £379,500) and capital expenditure authorised but not contracted for amounted to £750,000 as at 30 September 1980. This may be in connection with the extension of the factory premises at Stafford referred to by Mr Harding.

3.5 Stonnington's operations seem to require a very modest investment in stocks. Dividing year-end stocks of £42,405 into Stonnington's cost of sales of £356,257 indicates a turnover ratio of 8.4, equivalent to 1.4 months' stock. Total debtors on the other hand represented approximately 2½ months' sales.

3.6 Deferred tax, which is provided for using the liability method, is a material constituent of total capital employed. It is represented almost entirely by accelerated capital allowances. Stock appreciation relief accounts for only £11,003.

4 Prospects

4.1 Unaudited accounts for the nine months ended 30 June 1981, as supplied by Mr Harding, are summarised below:

	9 months ended 30 June 1981 £
Sales	1,246,307
Gross profit	986,902
Percentage margin	79.2%
Profit before tax	281,072
Percentage net margin	22.6%

Mr Harding estimates that sales for the year to 30 September 1981 will total approximately £2 million and pre-tax profits, £500,000. This implies that sales and pre-tax profits in the final quarter, which takes in the summer months, will be £754,000 and £219,000 respectively.

4.2 The longer term prospects, as seen by Mr Harding, are of continued growth at levels similar to those already achieved 'for at least the next five years'.

5 Share capital and articles

5.1 Stonnington's issued share capital consists of 10,000 ordinary shares of £1 each held as follows:

	Ordinary shares
Francis Harding	9,000
David Beale	1,000
	10,000

Stonnington's articles of association provide that a shareholder who wishes to sell his shares must go through the directors, who may then dispose of the shares to other members at a price agreed between the selling member and the directors, or failing agreement at a price to be fixed by the auditors as the fair value. If the directors cannot dispose of any or all of the shares within 28 days, the seller may dispose of any unsold shares 'in any manner he thinks fit' within a further two months. The directors may, in any event, refuse to register a transfer of shares to a person of whom they do not approve.

5.2   Article 13 provides that a director may contract with the company as if he were not a director.

6 Valuation

6.1   In a transaction between specific parties the price paid is normally a function of, on the one hand, the value the seller parts with in selling his shares and, on the other, the value the purchaser acquires in buying those shares.

6.2   Mr Harding owns 90% of the shares in Stonnington and therefore enjoys almost unfettered control over Stonnington's business. His position is analogous to that of a proprietor, and the profits Stonnington earns are the return on his investment. The fact that no dividends are paid is all but irrelevant. The value of Mr Harding's shares is therefore the capitalised value of the attributable earnings.

6.3   The capitalisation rate should take into account the likely future growth rate in profits and the degree of risk in Canvermoor's business. The future growth rate in profits is particularly difficult to assess as Stonnington seems to be unaffected by the conditions in the soft drinks industry generally. (For example, Stonnington's sales rose by 65% in 1980 compared with seven per cent growth in sales of carbonated soft drinks for the UK as a whole). Stonnington reckons that there is plenty of growth potential in the present 17 sales areas, only four of which can be considered at anywhere near saturation point. This takes no account of growth potential in South London and the South West which would be one of the benefits of an association with FDL.

6.4   If Stonnington's predictions prove accurate and turnover and pre-tax profits grow by, say, 50% a year compound over the next five years, the trading profile will look as follows:

Year to 30 September	Turnover £000	Pre-tax profits £000	No of employees	Shareholders' funds £000
1982	3,000	750	108	868
1983	4,500	1,125	162	1,408
1984	6,750	1,687	243	2,218
1985	10,125	2,531	364	3,433
1986	15,187	3,797	546	5,255

These projections assume that the number of employees rises proportionately to turnover, that pre-tax profits will be taxed at

52%, leaving 48% to be added to shareholders' funds, and that the business will be able to generate the cash flow required to finance its expansion.

6.5 These projections strain credulity to breaking point, as no doubt a profit projection of £500,000 for 1981 would have done in 1976 when pre-tax profits were £50,000. However, there must be a limit to the potential for growth at the rate of 50% a year compound and a limit also to the size of a business which one man can run largely on his own. In Mr Harding's view, Stonnington has reached this limit. The fact that Stonnington is heavily dependent on Mr Harding's entrepreneurial flair and that it probably has no management structure are significant depreciatory factors in the valuation.

6.6 The pre-tax profits set out in the projections above represent the most optimistic outcome. If these profits are discounted at 25% a year they have a present value of around £4.5 million and, discounted at 35%, of £3.5 million. I suggest that on the most optimistic assumptions Stonnington might be worth £4 million. But in my experience buyers are extremely sceptical about numerical profit forecasts more than two to three years hence. I doubt whether any investor would accept the profit projection in paragraph 6.4 at face value and most people would expect a falling off in Stonnington's growth rate as the management structure is developed and the benefit of Mr Harding's personal skills is diluted. I have not met Mr Harding and have only a superficial knowledge of his business and of the soft drinks industry. It is extremely difficult therefore to assess Stonnington's likely growth rate in the future, although I believe it will be well below 50% a year compound over the next five years. In these circumstances any valuation is a matter of highly subjective judgement — even of intuition. Subject to this, I feel that Mr Harding would find it difficult to sell Stonnington for more than £3 million.

6.7 Mr Harding holds 90% of the shares in Stonnington and would probably regard a disposal of 20% of the shares as reducing the value of his shareholding by a proportionate amount, i.e., 2/9ths. Assuming a 90% shareholding is worth £2.7 million the proposed sale would entail a reduction in the value of his shareholding of £600,000 or thereabouts. However, Mr Harding knows he cannot expect to receive a price as high as this if he wants the sale to go ahead. He can justify accepting a lower price on at least three grounds:

(a) The link-up with FDL should lead to increased sales and profits and therefore increase the value of his remaining 70% shareholding.

(b) He is apparently keen to become a member of FDL's board and probably sees an association with a large, prestigious brewery company as an accolade for his achievements.

(c) I understand that Mr Harding intends to use part of the proceeds of sale of these shares to buy out the other shareholder, Mr Beale. The price Mr Harding gets from FDL may influence the price Mr Beale feels he ought to get.

6.8   I now turn to the value to FDL of acquiring a 20% shareholding in Stonnington.

6.9   I suggest that the value to FDL of a 20% shareholding in Stonnington should be a function of the return which FDL is likely to obtain on its investment. It seems to me that there are three ways in which FDL might obtain a return. These are:

(a) dividends received on its shareholdings;

(b) any capital gain on ultimate sale of its shareholding;

(c) profits made by FDL through its trading relationship with Stonnington.

Factors (a) and (b) determine the independent investment value of the proposed shareholding. Consideration of factor (c) indicates the premium FDL can afford to pay over the ordinary investment value. In my view the earnings attributable to a 20% shareholding cannot properly be considered as the return on the investment since FDL would be powerless to reach those earnings as a minority shareholder.

6.10 If FDL continues to grow, as seems likely, it will doubtless reach a size and maturity when it becomes an extremely attractive acquisition prospect or when it may wish to seek a listing for its shares. Either of these two events, which would come under (b) above, would 'unlock' the earnings value of the 20% shareholding and produce the prospect of a substantial capital gain. Dividends, I understand, are unlikely to be declared for some years and can therefore be ignored as a source of return and an influence on the valuation.

6.11 The likely capital gain on ultimate diposal of the 20% shareholding cannot be estimated with any accuracy. It makes sense therefore to put forward a number of possible outcomes to obtain some idea of the sensitivity of the valuation to the underlying assumptions. In the table below I set out suggested values for the 20% shareholding based on a notional bid for Stonnington five years hence, assuming three different growth rates in pre-tax profits — 20%, 30% and 40%. The discount factor used is 35%.

| | Assumed growth rate | | |
| | 20% | 30% | 40% |
	£000	£000	£000
Estimated pre-tax profits in 1981	500	500	500
Compound growth rate factor (5 years)	2.4883	3.7129	5.3782
Projected pre-tax profits in 1986	1,244	1,856	2,689
Capitalised at 25% to obtain value for			
100% of the equity	4,976	7,424	10,756
Attributable to 20% shareholding	995	1,485	2,151
Present value discounted at 35% a year			
for 5 years (PV factor 0.2230)	222	331	480

6.12 In considering whether the discount rate of 35% is appropriate the following factors should be borne in mind:

(a) FDL's own required rate of return.

(b) The nature of the investment. Once FDL becomes a shareholder in Stonnington it is bound by the articles of association. If for any reason things do not work out as planned, FDL is not in a strong position. It has no independent influence on the management of Stonnington — FDL's nominated director could easily be removed — and, if FDL wanted to sell its shares, it would be extremely difficult to find a buyer. Its investment is illiquid and virtually unmarketable.

(c) The value of the shares depends on events in the fairly distant future which might never come about. The outcomes of these events are themselves almost impossible to estimate with any accuracy.

7 Conclusions

7.1 The open market or independent investment value of a 20% shareholding in Stonnington is extremely difficult to assess because the return on the shares — both its timing and amount — is unknown and can only be guessed. In paragraph 6.11, I set out the possible bid value of Stonnington five years hence under three different growth rates. When discounted at 35% a year to the present they produce values for a 20% shareholding of £222,000

(20% growth), £331,000 (30% growth) and £480,000 (40% growth).

7.2 A bid for Stonnington five years hence is, of course, only one of many possibilities, and if FDL believes that a different outcome is more likely, then that outcome should be evaluated and used for determining the value. My tentative conclusion is that 20% shareholding in Stonnington has an independent investment value of at least £250,000 and possibly substantially more, depending on the assumptions used. This ignores any premium value FDL could justify paying because of any trading advantages the association with Stonnington might bring.

7.3 This memorandum has also examined the value of the 20% shareholding in Stonnington to Mr Harding. This is based on a valuation of 100% of the equity at the present time — also a subjective exercise but much less uncertain than the value of a 20% shareholding to FDL. In my opinion, the whole of the issued share capital of Stonnington is unlikely to have a value greater than £3 million (paragraph 6.6). The maximum price Mr Harding could rationally demand is therefore around £600,000 (i.e. 20% of £3 million). I believe, however, that there are good grounds for persuading Mr Harding to accept a substantially lower price than this (paragraph 6.7), and I feel that there should be scope for a transaction in the range of £250,000 to £500,000.

7.4 Stonnington is a private company with restrictions on the transfer of its shares (paragraph 5.1). It is possible to enter into a legal agreement with the other shareholders to bypass the share transfer provisions of the articles as regards any future transfer of FDL's proposed shareholding, and FDL may wish to consider this possibility. It is also possible to so arrange things that FDL receives dividends on its shareholding although no dividends are paid on the other shares. Such a device could be used to offset the effect of a higher price.

Appendix 3

Valuation report

E B Caldwell Limited

1 Introduction

1.1 James Fennell, the owner of 99% of the ordinary shares in E B Caldwell Limited, insurance brokers, died intestate in January 1977, leaving a widow and two children. The widow, Mrs Ida Fennell, is co-administrator of the estate together with a Mr Smith. In accordance with intestacy law, Mrs Fennell, as the widow, has a life interest in one half of the residue of the estate, with remainder to the children. The other half of the residue is held on trust for the children until they attain the age of 18 years or marry earlier.

1.2 As shares in E B Caldwell Limited ('the Company') are not authorised trustee investments, the trustees must sell these shares and replace them with authorised investments. Mrs Fennell has expressed an interest in buying these shares and, as this involves a trustee purchasing trust property, the permission of the Court has to be obtained. As part of this process, I have been instructed to value the estate's holding of 6,930 ordinary shares. The required basis of valuation is that of a willing buyer and a willing seller in the open market.

2 Activity

2.1 The Company's activity is that of insurance brokers. The business comprises some 7,000–8,000 clients, with premiums split as follows:

	%
Private individual	85
Companies and groups	10
Sole traders and partnerships	5
	100

Client turnover is low — approximately ten per cent a year — and major clients have been with the Company for some years.

2.2 Commissions received are analysed below:

	%
Motor insurance	85
Commercial risks	5
Householders	8
Life	2
	100

2.3   The Company has two offices, one in Gateshead and the other in Sunderland. The Gateshead premises are freehold and consist of a ground floor and first floor of 450 sq.ft each. The Sunderland premises are leased from the Electricity Board on a quarterly tenancy at a rent of £90 per quarter, unchanged since 1965. Most of the business is conducted through the Sunderland office.

2.4   There are three directors, namely Mr A E Fennell, Mr G Cotton and Mrs Ida Fennell. Mr A E Fennell is aged 69 years and is the father of James Fennell, deceased, the former owner. Mr Cotton is Mr A E Fennell's son-in-law. Both Mr A E Fennell and Mr Cotton have been running the business since the death of James Fennell in January 1977. Neither of these gentlemen has a service contract with the company. Mrs Ida Fennell, the widow, keeps the books and records of the Company and helps in an administrative capacity. Two female clerks operate the Gateshead branch, and at the Sunderland branch Messrs Fennell and Cotton are assisted by five female clerks.

3 Trading record

3.1   The Company's trading record, based on the audited accounts for the last five years, is summarised as follows:

| | Year ended 31 December | | | | |
	1977 £	1978 £	1979 £	1980 £	1981 £
Premium income	384,498	443,896	508,161	653,775	684,153
Gross profit	72,747	88,292	87,839	113,059	104,235
Expenses	(31,838)	(32,632)	(39,918)	(48,801)	(52,755)
Interest receivable	10,090	9,870	16,884	21,925	17,617
Operating profit	50,999	65,530	64,805	86,183	69,097
Directors' remuneration	(24,623)	(28,000)	(34,700)	(50,675)	(56,000)
Interest payable	—	—	—	—	(5,500)
Profit before tax	26,376	37,530	30,105	35,508	7,597
Taxation	12,615	14,431	13,150	13,994	2,740
Profit after tax	13,761	23,099	16,995	21,514	4,857
Dividends	—	—	—	26,500	14,000

3.2 It appears that 1980 was an exceptional year in terms of growth in premium income, gross profit and operating profit. In 1981, with only a 4.6% rise in premium income and the gross profit margin falling from 17.3% to 15.2%, operating profit fell almost 20%.

3.3 In the nature of the Company's business substantial cash balances arise, and their temporary investment produces significant amounts of interest receivable. Treating this as operating income, it is apparent that the profit available for the payment of directors' remuneration and dividends has risen from £50,999 in 1977 to £69,097 in 1981, having reached £86,183 in the previous year.

3.4 Directors remuneration is analysed below:

	1977 £	1978 £	1979 £	1980 £	1981 £
Mrs Ida Fennell	12,623	10,450	13,850	12,775	15,000
Mr A E Fennell	12,000	10,500	11,000	21,000	25,000
Mr G Cotton	—	7,050	9,850	16,900	16,000
	24,623	28,000	34,700	50,675	56,000

Mr A E Fennell became a director in January 1977 on the death of his son, and took over control. Prior to that, he had helped out in the office part-time, on a self-employed basis. Mr Cotton also worked on a self-employed basis with the Company, but was appointed director in April 1978. The salaries of Mr A E Fennell and Mr Cotton were increased in 1980 to bring them into line with market rates.

3.5 The interest payable in 1981 relates to the loan account with the estate of James Fennell, deceased. This loan account bears interest at the prevailing building society rate.

3.6 Substantial amounts were distributed by way of dividends in 1980 and 1981. These payments were made both to avoid shortfall assessments on the Company and to provide an income on the shares in view of the fact that they had become trust investments. These dividends, which were all interim ones, are analysed below:

	Per share £	Amount £
1978	1.00	7,000
1979	1.00	7,000
1980	1.78	12,500
Total		26,500
1981	2.00	14,000

No final dividends were proposed for 1978 to 1980 inclusive and none was recommended for 1981.

4 Balance sheet

4.1 The Company's audited balance sheet as at 31 December 1981 is summarised below:

	£	£
Fixed assets		17,651
Goodwill		10,000
Current assets		
Debtors	17,741	
Advance corporation tax	11,357	
Cash	184,707	
	213,805	
Current liabilities		
Creditors	69,081	
Directors' bonuses	21,000	
Directors' current accounts	35,667	
Proposed dividend	14,000	
Estate loan account	30,350	
	170,098	
Net current assets		43,707
		71,358
Share capital		7,000
Reserves		64,358
		71,358

4.2 The Company's financial position appears sound, with cash in hand sufficient to pay off all the current liabilities. Although there were no bank borrowings, there was a substantial amount of external financing in the form of directors' bonuses and current accounts and the estate loan account. These monies are repayable on demand, and, with the exception of the estate loan account, do not bear interest.

4.3 Fixed assets are made up as follows:

	Cost £	Depreciation £	Net £
Freehold land and buildings	8,255	—	8,255
Motor vehicles	20,600	13,370	7,230
Fixtures and fittings	4,412	2,246	2,166
	33,267	15,616	17,651

The company owns the freehold of its premises at Gateshead. These are some fifty years old and are in a good state of repair and decoration. Planning consent has been given for current use. The directors think the property could be rented out at about £1,500 per annum which suggests to them a top value of £12,000.

4.4 The motor vehicles consist of the following:

	Date of purchase	Cost £	Written down value (approx) £
Daimler	1968	10,600	3,000
Volkswagen	1968	4,000	1,200
Volvo	1981	4,000	3,000
			7,200

The market value of these cars is not in excess of the written down values.

4.5 Goodwill of £10,000 was inserted in the account of the Company in January 1973. The basis of calculation is not known.

4.6 The debtors are made up as follows:

	£
Debtors	14,492
Trust Holdings	1,239
W Jones & Co	2,010
	17,741

The largest single debtor is for approximately £5,500. The average of other debtor balances is around £200. All debts are considered good. The balance with Trust Holdings, which has been unchanged for some time, earns interest at market rates. W Jones & Co was an estate agency business owned by Mr James Fennell and Mrs Ida Fennell. It is now defunct, and the balance of £2,010 is owed by Mrs Ida Fennell as the surviving partner. There has been no movement on the account since 1979.

4.7 The ACT of £11,357 represents tax at 30% on the grossed up equivalent of the net dividends in respect of 1980 and 1981.

4.8 Creditors consist of insurance creditors (£44,347), expense creditors (£21,534) and tax payable of £3,200. The directors' current accounts are unsecured, non-interest bearing balances of undrawn remuneration. They are not regarded as long-term loans and in fact £20,000 has been withdrawn since December 1981.

4.9 The estate loan account represents the unpaid dividends due in respect of the shares held by the estate of James Fennell, deceased. These dividends have been left in the Company where they earn interest at the prevailing building society rate. The loan account is made up as follows:

	£
Dividends declared in 1980	26,500
Net loan interest	3,850
	30,350

4.10 Apart from a share premium account of £600, the reserves consist entirely of revenue reserves.

5 Prospects

5.1 The economic recession continues to have an adverse effect on the Company's business. Intense competition among insurance companies has checked the growth in premium income, and hence in commission. In addition, the rate of commission itself has come under downward pressure, the rate for motor insurance now averaging as little as 12% compared with some 16% only a couple of years ago.

5.2 This poor outlook is reflected in the Company's results so far this year. I understand from Mr A E Fennell that premium income for the ten months to end-October 1982 amounted to approximately £512,000, equivalent to an annual rate of £614,000. This suggests a ten per cent fall in premium income. Wages and office expenses have continued to rise and, although actual costs have not been supplied to me, I understand that the rate of increase is of the order of ten per cent. Interest rates have fallen signficantly this year, which is likely to produce a further fall in interest receivable. All the indications therefore point to lower profits in 1982 and perhaps even a pre-tax loss, assuming the level of directors' remuneration is unchanged.

5.3 The sharp fall in interest rates and the Chancellor's recent indication of possible tax cuts next year reinforce the view that a cyclical recovery, albeit in a longer term recessionary trend, will probably occur next year. As the main feature of this recovery is expected to be a modest rise in consumer spending, there could well be some improvement in the Company's trading results in 1983 and perhaps in 1984.

5.4 The outlook beyond 1983–84 will depend on the performance of the economy, and in particular, on the level of unemployment. On present Government policies there is little likelihood of a significant fiscal stimulus to the economy or much prospect of an end to the secular recessionary trend. Although Mr A E Fennell is confident of the Company's ability to hold on to its customer base, and is therefore confident of its longer term viability, it seems there is little prospect of sustained long-term growth in profits.

6 Share capital and articles

6.1 The Company's issued share capital consists of 7,000 ordinary shares of £1 each, held as follows:

	£1 ordinary shares	%
The administrators of the estate of James Fennell, deceased	6,930	99
Mrs Ida Fennell	70	1
	7,000	100

6.2 The Company's articles provide that shares may be freely transferred between members (article 14) and shares may be transferred by a member (or his executors or administrators in the case of a deceased member) to non-members within specified degrees of kinship to the member concerned (article 15). Subject to these exceptions, a proposing transferor must give the Company notice in writing of his intention to sell. This notice constitutes the Company his agent for the sale of the shares to any person — whether member or non-member — selected by the directors. Shares can only be transferred at the fair value to be fixed by the auditors.

7 Valuation

7.1 The shares being valued represent 99% of the equity and vest virtually unfettered control of the Company in the hands of the holder. The share transfer restrictions in the Company's articles can therefore be disregarded for valuation purposes since the vendors could pass the resolutions necessary to change the articles and to remove the directors.

7.2 The Company's business was originally built up by James Fennell. On his death in 1977 Mr A E Fennell assumed control and succeeded in holding the business together in the difficult transitional period when strenuous efforts were made by rival broking firms to poach the business from the Company. As the trading record shows, the business has prospered under Mr A E Fennell's and Mr Cotton's direction. Such I understand is the strength of the personal relationship between these two directors and the clientele of the Company, that, if they were to leave the Company, most of the custom would follow them.

7.3 Small insurance broking businesses usually change hands at a price between one and one-and-half year's purchase of gross commissions. The buyer invariably insists on the vendor entering into an agreement not to compete or on his entering into a service contract with the business under its new ownership. This practice recognises the fact that insurance broking is a highly personalised business and that the goodwill lies with the individual and not with the business itself. This is certainly true of the Company's business and it is unthinkable that the Company would be sold without the appropriate undertakings or agreements on the part of Mr A E Fennell and Mr Cotton.

7.4 Neither Mr A E Fennell nor Mr Cotton has a service contract with the Company and both are free to set up in competition to the Company. In these circumstances the shares being valued have no independent revenue or profit earning potential. In my opinion their open market value derives solely from the shareholders' funds which the buyer would be able to realise by putting the Company into liquidation.

7.5 The most recent audited balance sheet available is that as at 31 December 1981. In my opinion the prospective buyer would make the following adjustments to shareholders' funds in order to arrive at a price which would give him a reasonable profit on his outlay:

(a) The value of the Company's property at Gateshead is estimated at £12,000. This compares with the book amount of £8,255 and indicates a surplus of £3,745. After corporation tax at the effective rate of 30% on the chargeable gain, the net accretion to shareholders' funds would be £2,622. The value of other fixed assets is unlikely to be materially different from their book values.

(b) Goodwill of £10,000 has no realisable value and must be deducted.

(c) As the Company is unlikely to pay much mainstream corporation tax in respect of 1982 — it could well make a loss in that year (paragraph 5.2) — and as an imminent liquidation is being postulated for valuation purposes, the ACT of £11,357 must be treated as irrecoverable.

(d) If the Company's business ceased, redundancies would occur, the estimated net costs of which would be £3,280. If notice could not be worked out on a cessation, the staff would be entitled to an estimated £2,500 wages in lieu of notice. If the directors insisted on their full entitlement the total wages in lieu of notice would be an estimated £5,800.

(e) Although there are few fixed assets there are many involved and detailed debtor and creditor accounts to be resolved, and this, together with taxation, would take up the greater part of time spent on liquidation. On this basis the costs of liquidation have been estimated at between £3,000 and £4,000.

(f) The purchaser would obviously not pay the full liquidation value of these shares since this would leave him with no interest in the transaction. He would therefore apply a discount to the net realisable value of the assets to reflect waiting time (approximately one year), the risk that the liquidation may not go as planned, and his profit. In my opinion this discount is unlikely to be less than one third.

7.6 I set out below my calculation of the liquidation value of the Company's shares based on the audited balance sheet as at 31 December 1981 as adjusted for the items detailed in paragraph 7.5.

APPENDIX 3: VALUATION REPORT

	£	Paragraph 7.5
Shareholders' funds as at 31 December 1981 (as paragraph 4.1)	71,358	
Property surplus, less tax	2,622	(a)
Goodwill eliminated	(10,000)	(b)
ACT irrecoverable	(11,357)	(c)
Redundancy costs	(3,280)	(d)
Wages in lieu of notice (say 50% of £5,800)	(2,900)	(d)
Liquidation costs — say	(3,500)	(e)
Net realisable value of assets	42,943	
Discount for waiting time, risk and profit — one third	(14,314)	(f)
Liquidation value of share captial	28,629	
Number of shares in issue	7,000	
Value per share	£4.09	
Say	£4.00	

No account has been taken of any movement in shareholders' funds since 31 December 1981 as results for 1982 are unlikely to show much, if any, profit.

7.7 I conclude therefore that the open market value of the 6,930 shares in the Company held by the administrators of the estate of James Fennell, deceased, is £27,720 (i.e. 6,930 shares of £4 each).

7.8 This valuation is based on the information and explanations given to me by Messrs Trusted & Co, the Company's auditors, and on my discussions with Mr A E Fennell at the Company's Sunderland office. Messrs Trusted & Co have confirmed the factual accuracy of the information on which the valuation is based.

Appendix 4

A Ledger Esq,
Trusted & Co,
Chartered Accountants,
High Street,
Marlow,
Bucks.

Dear Mr Ledger,

A A Butcher Limited

I enclose a valuation memorandum which suggests a value of £200,000 for Mr F B Butcher's proposed transfer of 1,000 ordinary shares to his son, S J Butcher. This valuation is solely for capital transfer tax purposes.

In a tax planning exercise it is essential to use values which the Revenue are likely to accept. The tax consequences of the transfer can then be assessed with some confidence. For this reason I have not suggested the lowest arguable value but one which I believe is fair and reasonable. I should add, however, that the Revenue will in no way be bound by this valuation. They will treat it on its merits. The fact that you have been to a professional valuer obviously helps, but they will not necessarily see it as an independent valuation. Valuations of minority interests in non-dividend-paying family companies are notoriously subjective and I cannot guarantee that this valuation will have an easy passage.

Yours sincerely,

C G Glover

Valuation memorandum

A A Butcher Limited

1 Introduction

1.1 The issued share capital of A A Butcher Limited ('the Company') consists of 10,000 ordinary shares of £1 each, held as follows:

Mr F B Butcher	3,000
Mrs G Butcher	1,000
Mr C G Andrews	2,000
Mr J P Butcher	2,000
Mrs P Smith	2,000
	10,000

Mr J P Butcher and Mrs P Smith are the children of Mr F B Butcher and Mrs G Butcher. Mr C G Andrews is their son-in-law. Mr F B Butcher, who is aged 64 years, wishes to transfer 1,000 shares to a fourth child, S J Butcher. My opinion is required as to the value of such a transfer for capital transfer tax purposes.

2 Activity and trading record

2.1 The Company is engaged in plant hire contracting and has an extensive range of hire equipment operated by its own workforce, many of whom are employed by Raton Ltd, a Butcher company which hires them to the Company at no profit or loss to itself. The Company serves the construction industry where it has established expertise in main drainage, reinforced concrete, sea defence works, road construction, canal restoration work and bulk earth works. The head office, which is in Marlow, Bucks, is owned by Raton Ltd. There is no tenancy agreement with the Company and no rent is payable. The current market rental is around £35,000 a year. Much of the Company's equipment is owned by Butcher Leasing Co Ltd, whose hire charges are within ten per cent of market rates. Butcher Leasing Co Ltd is owned by the Butcher family.

2.2 The trading record in recent years is summarised below:

	Year ended 30 September				
	1980 £000	1981 £000	1982 £000	1983 £000	1984 £000
Turnover	1,776	2,804	2,692	3,946	4,731
Operating profit	66	530	207	223	261
Interest payable	29	59	57	49	72
Profit before tax	37	471	150	174	189
Taxation	—	—	22	2	8
Profit after tax	37	471	128	172	181
Directors' remuneration	31	35	42	48	63

Source: audited annual accounts.

2.3   In 1982/83 the Company embarked on a policy of turnover growth and began to bid for work on the basis of marginal cost. This policy explains the 47% increase in turnover in 1982/83 and the 20% increase in the following year — a period of unrelieved depression for the construction industry. It also accounts for the marked deterioration in the percentage profit margin. On the other hand it has enabled the Company to retain its workforce, and has produced a modest improvement in pre-tax profits.

2.4   The exceptionally high turnover and profit in 1980/81 were due to a large profitable sea defence contract in the Channel Islands.

2.5   The tax charge has been insignificant due to the high level of capital expenditure and the availability of generous first year capital allowances.

2.6   No dividends have been paid.

3 Balance sheet

3.1   The Company's audited balance sheet as at 30 September 1984 is summarised below:

	£000	£000
Fixed assets		1,728
Current assets		
Work in progress	133	
Debtors	1,252	
Cash	—	
	1,385	
Current liabilities		
Creditors	1,168	
Bank overdraft	330	
	1,498	
Net current liabilities		(113)
		1,615
Share capital		10
Revenue reserves		1,605
		1,615

3.2 Interest payable in 1982/83 totalled £72,000. This implies an average overdraft during the year of about £500,000. This points to a level of borrowing somewhat higher than that evident from the balance sheet.

3.3 Debtors include loans totalling £453,000 to other Butcher companies, notably Raton Ltd and Butcher Leasing Co Ltd. Creditors include hire purchase liabilities due after more than one year. The main constituent of fixed assets is plant (net book amount £1.5 million). The Company does not own any freehold or leasehold properties.

3.4 The Company has guaranteed £1 million of bank loans made to Butcher Leasing Co Ltd.

4 Prospects

4.1 The outlook for the construction industry has improved hardly at all in recent times. As far as the public sector is concerned, continuing cuts in Government spending and renewed pressure on local authorities in the form of rate-capping suggest that no end to the present recession in civil engineering is in sight.

4.2 In the private sector, which accounts for around 40% of the Company's turnover, it is estimated that about half the Company's customers are vulnerable to liquidation and are particularly susceptible to the effect of high interest rates.

4.3   The phasing out of initial and first-year capital allowances and the abolition of stock relief are likely to lead to a substantial corporation tax charge from April 1986 onwards, if not before.

5 Valuation

5.1   Mr F B Butcher and his wife together hold 4,000 ordinary shares, being 40% of the total. After the proposed transfer Mr and Mrs Butcher will hold 30%. The value transferred for capital transfer tax purposes, therefore, is the difference between the value of a 40% shareholding and a 30% one. As there is a negligible difference in the value per share of these two sizes of shareholding, I suggest that the diminution in value as a result of the transfer be taken as 25% of a 40% shareholding.

5.2   The Company is a private company and its articles impose the usual restrictions on the transfer of shares.

5.3   I understand that the Company has grown to its present size largely through the efforts of Mr C Andrews, the son-in-law, who is the driving force behind the business. Relationships between the various members of the Butcher family are harmonious and a purchaser of 40% of the equity would be an outsider both as regards his shareholding and the management of the business. He could not expect a seat on the board nor any dividends. Whatever the reasons may have been for not paying a dividend in the past, the dire state of the industry and the need to conserve cash make the continuance of that policy a matter of corporate survival.

5.4   The investment attractions of a 40% stake in the Company are therefore very limited. It would be a highly speculative investment which could only be countenanced by those with substantial surplus funds who could afford to bide their time until the opportunity of selling out presented itself. As there is no question of the Company obtaining a Stock Exchange quotation, there are only two possibilities of ultimately getting out at a profit. The first would be the appearance of an approved bidder for the entire share capital of the company. The second would be the Butcher family's desire to buy out the minority.

5.5   In my opinion, the prospective purchaser would not place much reliance on the emergence of an acceptable buyer for the Company. First, the industry outlook is so depressed that it is difficult to envisage a buyer at a realistic price. More importantly, perhaps, it is unlikely that the Butcher family would want to sell.

Mr F B Butcher is nearing retirement and management of the business has devolved to the next generation, in particular, to Mr C Andrews, who now plays the dominant role and is keen to build up the firm. Furthermore, a sale of the company to a third party would almost certainly mean that the firm would no longer be a source of employment for members of the Butcher family and this would be unacceptable.

5.6 It seems to me, therefore, that the most likely outcome would be seen to be a sale of the 40% shareholding to the Butcher family. There are persuasive reasons why the Butcher family should want to acquire the outside minority interest. Although the family commands 60% of the votes, it would see the existence of such a large minority stake as a serious restriction on its freedom of movement. Members of the family would have to be careful not to lay themselves open to a petition under s.75 of the Companies Act 1980 (now s.459 of the Companies Act 1985). This could entail significant changes in the way the firm is run and in its dividend policy. A more powerful reason, however, would be the fact that as the value of the Company increases through the efforts of the working shareholders, a large part of that increase will ultimately redound to the benefit of outsiders who have contributed nothing. With most of their working lives ahead of them this is likely to be keenly resented by the younger members of the family. As anyone entering into an investment on these grounds would expect ultimately to obtain a price based on control, it is appropriate to start by assessing the present value of the Company's entire equity.

5.7 In the last three years the Company's pre-tax profits have shown a modest upward trend. In view of the vagaries of the construction industry and the uncertain outlook it would be unwise to count on annual pre-tax profits of more than £175,000, which is slightly more than the the straight average of the past three years. For valuation purposes, two adjustments to this figure are required. First, a deduction must be made for the notional rent of £35,000 a year for the head office premises owned by Raton Ltd but occupied rent-free by the Company. Second, the Company charges no interest on loans to associated companies. These loans stood at £435,000 at 30 September, 1984 and notional interest of, say, £60,000 (i.e., £435,000 @ 13.5%) ought to be added to profits before tax. These then become:

	£000
Current pre-tax profit potential	175
Adjustments	
Interest receivable on loans to associated companies	60
Notional rent charge for head office	(35)
Adjusted pre-tax profits	200

5.8 In my opinion, bearing in mind the risks of civil engineering at the present time, a rate of return of 30% or thereabouts would be expected on the purchase of the Company's business. With inflation at five per cent a year and real growth in the national economy running at around three per cent, the longer term growth rate in profits is unlikely to average more than ten per cent a year. This suggests an initial earnings yield of no less than 20%, i.e., the rate of return, 30%, less the growth rate, ten per cent. When related to profits before tax of £200,000 this produces a value of £1 million for the entire equity.

5.9 This earnings-based value of £1 million compares with shareholders' funds of £1,615,000 at 30 September 1984. However, the Company's assets consist for the most part of plant and equipment (£1.5 million) and debtors (£1.25 million). The plant is highly specialised and has no use outside the industry. If it were sold off the Company would have to cease operations. This would mean heavy book losses as well as redundancy and closure costs. Once it became known the business was closing, big losses would be incurred on the debtors, many of whom are in a precarious financial position. There would be little if any return to the shareholders in a winding up. The low value of the business reflects the near-impossibility of making a worthwhile rate of return on the assets.

5.10 A value of £1 million for the Company's entire equity indicates a maximum value of £400,000 for a 40% shareholding. The hypothetical purchaser of this shareholding could not expect to sell it on to the Butcher family immediately. It would take time and he would have to be patient. In my view he would probably allow at least two years in which to sell it. The required rate of return for evaluating this opportunity would take into account amongst other things the following considerations:

(a) On a sale to the other shareholders the prospective purchaser may well not be able to obtain the full control value of his holding.

(b) It may be necessary to wait considerably longer than two years before the opportunity of getting out presents itself. As there is no likelihood of dividends during this time the opportunity cost, with real interest rates at record levels, is very high.

(c) The head office with its three acre site plus much of the plant and equipment the Company uses is owned by Butcher family companies. One of these, Raton Ltd, employs the workforce and hires it to the Company. The Butcher family shareholders could, therefore, 'walk-away' from the Company and, by terminating the informal tenancy of the Head Office and refusing to hire plant, equipment and labour to the Company, they could bring the business to its knees and set it up in their own companies, using the same facilities and labour. This would be a drastic step but an entirely feasible one. It would be a powerful threat in the hands of the Butcher family and would considerably weaken the minority shareholders' bargaining position.

5.11 In my judgement, an investment of this nature is as risky as any venture capital project and a rate of return of at least 50% would be required. As the Company's profits, and hence its value, is estimated to grow at ten per cent a year, the net discount rate to be applied to notional sale proceeds of £40,000 two years hence is approximately 40% a year. The present value of a 40% shareholding therefore becomes £200,000, as set out below:

	£
Notional sale price two years hence at today's values	400,000
Present value factor — 40% for two years	0.5102
Present value	204,080
Say	200,000

The value of the chargeable transfer then works out at £50,000, being 25% of £200,000.

5.12 The Company has given guarantees of £1 million in respect of bank loans to Butcher Leasing Co Ltd (paragraph 3.4). This valuation assumes that no liability will arise under these guarantees.

Table of cases

IRC v. *Muller* [1901] AC 217

Jermyn Street Turkish Baths Ltd, In Re [1970] 1 WLR 1194; [1970] 3 All ER 57; revsd [1971] 1 WLR 1042; [1971] 3 All ER 184

Johnston v. *Chestergate Hat Manufacturing Co Ltd* [1915] 2 Ch 338

Jones (M) v. *Jones (RR)* [1971] 1 WLR 840; [1971] 2 All ER 676

Lock v. *John Blackwood Ltd* [1924] AC 783

London Sack and Bag Co v. *Dixon & Lugton* [1943] 2 All ER 763

Lucas and Chesterfield Gas and Water Board, In Re [1909] 1 KB 16

Lynall v. *IRC* [1972] AC 680; [1971] 3 All ER 914

McDougall v. *Gardiner* (1875) 1 Ch D 13

McNamee v. *Revenue Commissioners* [1954] IR 214

Menier v. *Hooper's Telegraph Works* (1874) LR 9 Ch App 350

National Drive-in Theatres, In Re [1954] 2 DLR 55

Nurcombe v. *Nurcombe* [1984] BCLC 557

Pavlides v. *Jensen* [1956] Ch 565; [1956] 2 All ER 518

Pender v. *Lushington* (1877) 6 Ch D 70

Prudential v. *Newman Industries (No 2)* [1981] Ch 257; [1980] 2 All ER 841; [1982] Ch 204; [1982] 1 All ER 354

Raja v Vyricherla Narayana Gajapatiraju v. *Revenue Divisional Officer, Vizagapatam* [1939] AC 302

Rayfield v. *Hands* [1960] Ch 1; [1958] 2 All ER 194

Robinson Bros (Brewers) Ltd v. *Houghton and Chester-le-Street Assessment Committee* [1937] 2 KB 445; [1938] 2 All ER 79

Russell v. *Wakefield Waterworks Co* (1875) LR 20 Eq 474

Salomon v. *Salomon & Co Ltd* [1897] AC 22

Salvesen's Trustees v. *IRC* (1930) 9 ATC 43

Scottish Co-operative Wholesale Society Ltd v. *Meyer* [1959] AC 324; [1958] 3 All ER 56

Shaw & Sons (Salford) Ltd v. *Shaw* [1935] 2 KB 113

Short v. *Treasury Commissioners* [1948] 1 KB 116; [1947] 2 All ER 298

Shuttleworth v. *Cox Brothers & Co* [1927] 2 KB 9

Sidebottom v. *Kershaw Leese & Co* [1920] 1 Ch 154

Sutcliffe v. *Thachrah* [1974] AC 727; [1974] 1 All ER 859

Towers v. *African Tug* [1904] 1 Ch 558

Trevor v. *Whitworth* (1887) 12 App Cas 409

Wallersteiner v. *Moir (No 2)* [1975] QB 373; [1975] 1 All ER 849

Welton v. *Saffrey* [1897] AC 299

Westbourne Galleries Ltd, In Re [1973] AC 360; [1972] 2 All ER 492

Wood v. *Odessa Waterworks Co* (1889) 43 Ch D 636

Wright (Frank H) (Constructions) Ltd v. *Frodoor Ltd* [1967] 1 WLR 506; [1967] 1 All ER 433

Index